Doing Diaspora Missiology
Toward "Diaspora Mission Church"

Doing Diaspora Missiology Toward "Diaspora Mission Church"

The Rediscovery of Diaspora for the Renewal of Church and Mission in a Secular Era

LUTHER JEOM O. KIM

WIPF & STOCK · Eugene, Oregon

DOING DIASPORA MISSIOLOGY TOWARD "DIASPORA MISSION CHURCH"
The Rediscovery of Diaspora for the Renewal of Church and Mission in a Secular Era

Copyright © 2016 Luther Jeom O. Kim. All rights reserved. Except for brief quotations in critical publications or reviews, no part of this book may be reproduced in any manner without prior written permission from the publisher. Write: Permissions, Wipf and Stock Publishers, 199 W. 8th Ave., Suite 3, Eugene, OR 97401.

Wipf & Stock
An Imprint of Wipf and Stock Publishers
199 W. 8th Ave., Suite 3
Eugene, OR 97401

www.wipfandstock.com

ISBN 13: 978-1-4982-3194-7

Manufactured in the U.S.A.   01/04/2016

Contents

Preface | vii

Introduction: Demographic Shifts in a Global Era | 1

1 Globalization, Demographic Trends, and the Phenomenon of Diaspora | 13

2 Theorizing Diaspora and its Christian Mission Awakening toward Diaspora Missiology | 31

3 Interdisciplinary Understandings of Diaspora | 60

4 Biblical Understandings of Diaspora | 83

5 The Theological Foundations and Implications of Diaspora | 125

6 Discoveries of the Missiological Problems and Issues in a Global Era toward the Formulation of Diaspora Missiology | 150

7 Contextual Theologizing for Diaspora Missiology | 185

8 The Transcendent Nature of the Church, the Missional Frameworks of 'Diaspora Mission Church', and its Three Ministry Areas | 225

9 Healing Empowerment of 'Diaspora Mission Church' | 275

Bibliography | 297
Index | 319

Preface

Under the colony of Rome, God's people had longed for the promised Messiah; Jesus Christ, our Lord, came to this world to save us about two thousand years ago. A multitude of people followed him as their Master and Savior. According to his promise, Jesus who was crucified in our place rose again and ascended into heaven, commanding his disciples, the community of the church, to preach the gospel. In his life, Jesus promised his disciples, "If I go and prepare a place for you, I will come back and take you to be with me, that you also may be where I am" (John 14:3).

As Charles Taylor points out in his book *A Secular Age*, however, today, immanent deism—reason centered life without God—has become more and more popular in the Christian mindset and life. It is fortunate that Diaspora missiology appear in this situation. First of all, I studied the biblical meaning of diaspora for doing Diaspora missiology and, surprisingly, I found its deep meaning, and I made sure that this concept could contribute to overcoming a secularized mind and life, hovering around Christian faith, church, and mission.

In this age, all churches around world, the Western and the Southern, worry about the church itself rather than overseas missions; the missional church movement is one of the trends representing this concern. This book also is intended to incorporate church ministry and mission through contextualizing Diaspora missiology into the local church setting. Finally, I suggest the model of "Diaspora mission church," in which sent churches do mission through all Diaspora Christians.

According to the Bible, all human beings are theologically and spiritually diaspora, irrespective of ethnicity and geography, because they were banished from the Garden of Eden, scattered around the world in God's judgment, and walk toward the encounter with Jesus Christ. They encounter with Jesus, scatter around the world, risk their life to preach the gospel as they see themselves as the seed of the kingdom, and finally, move toward heaven. This biblical concept of diaspora contributes to building a Diaspora mission church, moving toward doing faith, church, and mission of the renewal in a secular and immanent society.

I hope that we come back to the original Jesus Christ, written in the Bible. The concept of diaspora as "pilgrim" will help us to be back to the place where we were; for it is the starting point of doing faith, church, and mission of the renewal. The transcendent Diaspora gospel will guide all Christians beyond an immanent secular era to rediscover biblical perspectives of faith, church, and mission in the early church, which put fire on the renewal of Christianity in crisis.

—Luther
For his Kingdom.

Introduction
Demographic Shifts in a Global Era

"With so many people from so many origins moving in so many directions and landing in so many destinations, planned or unplanned, it could be concluded that we are fast becoming a "borderless world."[1] This is a typical expression of the Lausanne movement for demographic shifts in the recent global era; in addition, in "Faith on the Move: The Religious Affiliation of International Migrants," there are some report highlights regarding the flow of Christianity across the globe: nearly half of the world's migrants are Christians (49 percent)[2]. Jehu J. Hanciles, a professor at Candler School of Theology, Emory University, said, "All the so-called world religions achieved their status by virtue of migration and dispersion, none more so than Christianity."[3] This indicates the significance of migration in global Christianity and mission. All Christians believe that, in his sovereign will, God is moving people so that they may know and preach him; "Reaching the People on the Move is both an urgent necessity and an amazing opportunity for Christians and Churches. This certainly is a new paradigm in the mission of the contemporary Church."[4] Tetsunao Yamamori, Senior Advisor of the Lausanne Committee for World Evangelization, argued, "The People on the Move have serious implications toward world evangelization. They are not only subjects of evangelism and church growth, but have become powerful agents for the extension of the gospel."[5] The People on the Move, the phenomenon of Diaspora, are a demographic trend of the twenty-first century, and Diaspora missiology is becoming the new twenty-first century

---

1. Tira, "Ministering to the Scattered People," lines *14–15*.
2. Pew Research Center, "Faith on the Move," line 9.
3. Hanciles, "Mission and Migration Megatrends," 6–8.
4. LCWE, *Scattered to Gather*, 32.
5. Ibid., 3.

paradigm for Christian mission. That is, in response to global demographic shifts, Diaspora missiology is to rethink missiological ways, and refine its concept by understanding Diaspora in a global network. In 2002, Andrew Walls dealt with the relations of mission and Diaspora, suggesting the concept of "Mobile Faith" in his article "Mission and Migration: The Diaspora Factor in Christian History,"[6] and argued that "it is important to recognize that the missionary is a form of immigrant . . . The great new fact of our time—and it has momentous consequences for mission—is that the great migration has now gone into reverse. There has been a massive movement, which all indications suggest will continue, from the non-Western to the Western world."[7]

In regard to Walls's article, Jehu Hanciles comments: "in the last three to four decades, few scholars have done more than Andrew Walls to expatriate the challenge contours of global Christianity and highlight the dynamics of cross-cultural transmission intrinsic to its global spread."[8] According to Wan, the first attempt of doing Diaspora missiology by the Lausanne Movement was the Filipino Diaspora and Mission consultation on April 2–15, 2004 at Torch Trinity Graduate School (TTGS), Seoul, South Korea, which was mainly led by the Lausanne Movement. After three months, the Lausanne Committee for World Evangelization, Issue Group No. 26 A and B: Diasporas and International Students, made "The Lausanne Occasional Paper No. 55: The New People Next Door," which was produced by the Issue Group on this topic at the 2004 forum hosted by the Lausanne Committee for World Evangelization in Pattaya, Thailand.[9] However it was noted that Diaspora missiology needs more biblical theology studies and systematization.

In 2008, there was a great contribution to the systematic theologizing framework of Diaspora missiology. The book *Promised Land, A Perilous Journey*, co-edited by Daniel G. Groody and Gioacchino Campese, explored migration through four lenses: 1) foundations of a theology of migration; 2) mission, ministry, and migration; 3) the politics of sovereign rights, cultural rights, and human rights; and 4) constructive theologies of immigration.[10] Also in 2008, there were essays published regarding mission and migration by the British and Irish association of Mission Studies (BIAMS). In particular, in his article "Mission, Migration and the Stranger in our Midst," Tim

6. Walls, "Mission and Migration," 3–11.
7. Ibid., 5–6
8. Hanciles, "Migration and the Globalization of Christianity," 227–42.
9. LCWE Issue Group No. 26 A and B, "Lausanne Occasional Paper No. 55."
10. Groody and Campese, *Promised Land*.

Naish viewed the OT in the terms of Diaspora[11] and divided it as four main events—expulsion, evocation, exodus, and exile. In 2009, in *Beyond Christendom: Globalization, African Migration and the Transformation of the West,* suggesting the concept of "mobile faith," Jehu Hanciles argued a case for the migration of Christians as carrying within it the seeds of renewal for the whole church, which has the potential to reshape church, state, religion, and cultural relations globally.[12]

Finally, in the Cape Town 2010 Global Conversations of the Lausanne Movement, Diaspora missiology accomplished its peak in the booklet *Scattered to Gather: Embracing the Global Trend of Diaspora.* The Lausanne Movement proclaims, "a missiological paradigm different from traditional missiology is needed to cope with the new demographic reality of a large scale and intensified Diaspora movement of people in the 21st century."[13] After that, there have been two major representative books on Diaspora missiology, such as Wan's (2011) *Diaspora Missiology: Theory, Methodology and Practice,*[14] and S. Hun Kim and Wonsuk Ma's (2011) *Korean Diaspora and Christian Mission.*[15] In 2013, The International Society for Frontier Missiology 2013 Conference was held with the slogan "Global Peoples: Gates, Bridges and Connections across the Frontiers." This conference dealt with the Diaspora issue: The global diaspora of unreached peoples is a strategic mechanism for mission in our day. It is God who determines the boundaries and places of peoples across the remaining frontiers (Acts 17:26), and he opens opportunities for fresh new access, deployment, and method. The ISFM 2013 Conference also explored "the actual and potential connections across these global ethnoscapes, the bridges between homeland and diaspora populations, and the strategic gateways in our own American context."[16] These books and conferences show that the Diaspora issue is the theme of frontier missiology, confirming how important and essential the Diaspora is in current issues of global Christianity, and how the emergent North American church needs to dialogue with global Diaspora.

---

11. Naish, "Mission, Migration and the Stranger in our Midst."
12. Hanciles, *Beyond Christendom, Globalization.*
13. LCWE, "Seoul Declaration on Diaspora Missiology."
14. Wan, *Diaspora Missiology.*
15. Kim and Ma, *Korean Diaspora and Christian Mission.*
16. International Society for Frontier Missiology, "Global Peoples: Gates, Bridges and Connections."

MISSIOLOGICAL EXPECTATIONS FOR DIASPORA MISSIOLOGY REGARDING RECENT MISSIOLOGICAL ISSUES

In reality, twenty-first century Christianity was challenged by the rapid change of global shifts; traditional missiology has been challenged, and there have been emerging agendas in missiological circles. Recently, in global theologizing, sixteen scholars have proposed missiological issues that were summarized as fifteen emerging agendas, as they contribute to formulating a globalized theology. I pick up eight missiological and ecclesiological issues. These lists show what kinds of issues contemporary missiology has faced.

Missiological:

1. What are the nature and implications of the *Missio Dei* in our times?

2. How should a sequel to David Bosch's *Transforming Mission* (1991) be written, defining a biblical mission paradigm for the twenty-first century?

3. What are the implications of the current state of World Christianity for our mandate to *fulfill the great commission and make disciples of all nations*?

4. What can we as a global church learn from one another regarding the encounter of Christianity and non-Christian religions and various worldviews?

Ecclesiological:

1. What are the ecclesiological constants amid the diversity of forms and expressions of the church? How should the reality of a truly global Christianity affect our understanding and experience of the diversity and beauty in the body of the Christ?

2. How might an understanding of the Trinity provide insight into questions of unity and diversity in the church?

3. In what ways should the vision of a new humanity in Christ according to Ephesians 2 and other biblical texts be realized in the local and global church today?

4. How can the experience of the persecuted or suffering church enrich and fill gap ecclesiology?[17]

---

17. Ott, "Conclusion," 327.

As mentioned above, contemporary missiological circles seek to answer these questions, and Diaspora missiology also is called to answer these questions missiologically, ecclesiologically, historically, and ethically, and it participates in "creating a round table" and suggests some solutions. Diaspora missiology should challenge these questions and propose some solutions through applying the concept of Diaspora to the church and mission.

THE BIBLICAL SIGNIFICANCE OF THE CONCEPT OF DIASPORA HIDDEN BEHIND DIASPORA MISSIOLOGY

In its biblical significance rather than its missiological circle, Diaspora missiology is the rediscovery of one of the main biblical themes, flowing from Genesis to Revelation: because of sin, the human beings were banished from the Garden of Eden by God; they were existentially and spiritually scattered; they were scattered by God's judgment into various places around the world, longing for the gathering salvation by the Messiah, Jesus Christ. After the coming of Messiah Jesus Christ, Christians who believe in Jesus Christ as Savior also have been scattered for preaching the good news of the gospel. The whole story of the Bible is geared toward diaspora, which is composed of the main theme regarding God's salvation.

Several scholars have studied the theology of exile as diaspora. One example is John Howard Yoder, whose essay is "Prologue and Prototype: *Galuth* as Calling."[18] For Yoder, "To be scattered is not a hiatus, after which normalcy will resume. From Jeremiah's time on, rather, according to the message of the play, dispersion shall be the calling of the Jewish faith community."[19] With regard to the emergence of Diaspora theology, Smith-Christopher states, "to be specific, I agree with recent suggestions, especially by John Howard Yoder, Walter Brueggemann, and Stanly Hauerwas, that an exile theology promises to be the most provocative, creative, and helpful set of ideas that modern Christians can derive from the ancient Hebrew's religious reflections on their experience."[20] For these authors, diaspora, mainly represented in exile, is a key to understanding God's plan of salvation.

Raitt, a scholar called an exile theologian, invites, "let us be quite specific as to why exile is good, necessary for believers"; the exile experience offers these things for Christians:

---

18. Smith-Christopher, *Biblical Theology of Exile*, 7.
19. Yoder, "See How They Go," lines 12–5.
20. Smith-Christopher, *Biblical Theology of Exile*, 6.

1. Adversity is accepted. We learn not to expect winds of change always to blow in our favor.
2. An exile has to learn that God's love is not absent when events speak judgment. One learns to see God as present as much in judgment as in times when things go favorably.
3. Everything that is tragic and a source of self-pity in exile from a human point view is source of freedom and celebration from God's point of view. The dominant note in Second Isaiah is hymnic, and that is very appropriate.
4. We learn that God's love stands as much outside what we consider rational—what falls within our conception of religious logic—as his judgment . . . God's love is a kind of judgment.
5. Judgment (justice) gives deliverance (love) its integrity . . . He may turn around our minds with a new self-revelation, may inaugurate a new era and plan, and may buy freedom for an open-ended future for himself and for us.[21]

Exile experience has strong spiritual implications of God's salvation and God's kingdom; these explanations indicate that the concept of Diaspora permeates one of the core themes of biblical theology. These characteristics of Diaspora as exile oppose the misleading nature and functions of the church under the influence and attack of humanistic secularism and a distorted prosperity theology, prevailing among the contemporary church today.

More importantly, the story of Diaspora as scattered is represented in Pilgrim John Bunyan's work, *The Pilgrim's Progress from this World to that which is to Come*, which was published in February of 1678. Originally, diaspora has an image of "pilgrim," as is expressed in 1 Peter 1:1 and 2:11, in which Christians were called as sojourner, exile, and pilgrim.[22] In particular, Pilgrim is the one who is moving toward heaven beyond the earth. Pilgrim is an essential image of biblical Christianity. In history, Protestant missionaries translate Bunyan's *Pilgrim* secondly to the Bible. This shows how important John's *Pilgrim* is to explaining the meaning of the gospel to believers. It is noted that John Bunyan sees the nature of being Christian as being a pilgrim, and that of Christian life as the pilgrim's progress from this

---

21. Raitt, *Theology of Exile*, 299–30.

22. First Peter 1:1 states "strangers in the world, scattered . . ." In the Greek it is παρεπιδήμοις Διασπορᾶς. Here Διασπορᾶς (scattered) described and qualifies παρεπιδήμοις (strangers). This scattered is understood in terms of pilgrim (cf. American King James Version, 1 Peter 2:11: "strangers and pilgrims," and American Standard Version: "sojourners and pilgrims").

world to that which is to come. This shows how pilgrim theology becomes a powerful antidote to earthly secularism tending toward greedy prosperity, mommonism, and hedonism and so on.

What would happen if the lifestyle of diaspora as pilgrim were applied to contemporary Christians, church, and mission? Why is it surprising for Christians to hear the secret strategy of God to use Diaspora laypeople like Philip and Stephan in Acts 6? Why are we amazed to realize that the key of biblical Christian mission is diaspora—the secret seed of God for his redemptive plan[23]—and realize that the church was started along with diasporas "from every nation under heaven" (Acts 2)? This means that the biblical church is diasporic; the church as the community of Diaspora will serve God and God's kingdom as pilgrims, and call, empower, build up Diaspora as Philip and Stephan, and let them preach the gospel (Acts 6–8). The concept of Diaspora is the key for doing missiology globally, and more importantly, it is useful to reform the nature and functions of the church and Christians as pilgrims. Peter Phan understands diaspora immigrants as "the eternal mark of the church" by viewing Christians as "*paroikoi*—sojourners, displaced people without a home and nation, migration."[24] However, more than Peter Phan's argument, all human beings are theologically and spiritually diaspora irrespective of ethnicity, because they were banished from the Garden of Eden, scattered around the world, and walk toward the other world.

THE PURPOSE OF THE BOOK

Several books regarding Diaspora missiology were already published by authoritative and professional scholars. Why, then, do I try to write and publish one more book again? I agreed to write one more book on Diaspora missiology for the following ten reasons:

1. For doing Diaspora missiology, above all, it needs to fully describe and understand the nature of diaspora in terms of biblical, theological, and interdisciplinary perspectives. In particular, diaspora in itself has a hurt and suffering in scattered life; unfortunately, however, lots of researchers did not fully and deeply pay attention to the suffering of diaspora. Without understanding and having compassion for the suffering of diaspora, there is no deep understanding of Diaspora missiology, but only of its superficial theological formations. Hurt and suffering are one of the major identities of diaspora as exiles.

23. Jung, *Korea Diaspora and Christian Mission*, 65.
24. Phan, "Migration in the Patristic Era," 49.

2. Diaspora missiology needs to further develop its systematic interdisciplinary perspectives of diaspora, pivoting on biblical and theological descriptions for mission theologizing. In particular, for studying Diaspora missiology, the interdisciplinary descriptions of globalization are absolutely necessary because diaspora, by nature, is intertwined with global phenomena. Understanding the identity of globalization culturally, theologically, and biblically precedes the formation of Diaspora missiology.

3. To my understanding, a recent Diaspora missiology does not include how Diaspora missiology heals, trains, and empowers hurt Diaspora. Diaspora missiology necessarily calls for healing and training the hurt diaspora. If not, it is just emptiness of theological thinking. We all know that diaspora without being healed are just troublemakers, the "bitter root" (Heb 12:15) in the church community and social community. Automatically, a diaspora itself does not become a missionary, but needs healing and training. Thus far, there has been little research on dealing with problems of diaspora spirituality and on healing hurt diaspora.

4. In doing current Diaspora missiology, there has not been much discussion on contextual theology; generally speaking, global theologizing should be adapted to doing Diaspora missiology. We need to formulate the contextual process of doing Diaspora missiology. In particular, "double hermeneutics"[25] of the Bible and the context, proposed in this book, will examine praxis and challenge problems of traditional contextualization. We admit that non-biblical contextualization created multiplex secular gods in circles of Christian faith and the church; so it is time to check whether the context is for the text or not. If it is not, there would be no other way back to God witht repentance.

5. A recent Diaspora missiology needs to deal with the role and partnership of the host church in doing Diaspora ministry. Essentially, Diaspora missiology calls for the awaking of the host churches, which is the secret plan of God for revival and mission of the host church, as written in Acts 2. That is, Diaspora give the host church a new opportunity to rethink themselves and the concept of mission.[26] We all hope

---

25. The term *Double hermeneutic* is the theory expounded by sociologist Anthony Giddens, but this term was adapted to indicating the dialogue between the text and the context, pivoting on praxis in missiology. See Giddens, *Social Theory and Modern Sociology*.

26. J. D. Payne sees Diaspora as strangers next door in terms of North American mission. He asked, how should the host church respond to this diaspora as sojourners

for the second revival of world evangelization by global Christianity through partnership of the host and Diaspora church—the West and non-Western Christianity.

6. Contemporary churches and believers have fallen into the temptation of secularism, pluralism, and prosperity theology focusing on wealth and happiness, and have experienced spiritual fear, stagnation, and depression. At the same time, believers questioned the situation of churches trying to become mega-churches, confused with a worldly greed and neglecting the nature of the church, which guides believers to live the gospel and preach it in a secular word. I am sure that Diaspora theology can be helpful to seek the nature of the church as scattering diaspora, heal chronic diseases and problems of a misled Christian faith and church in the world, and challenge to transform the ministry frameworks of the Diaspora church moving toward a pilgrimage.

7. Many missional scholars and leaders think that the missiological role of the USA is becoming lessened and lessened, but my thought is contrary to this opinion; instead the USA will become a more important country in an age of Diaspora missiology than ever. The world will move toward the USA, the nation of immigration, especially from poor Southern countries, including unreached people. This means that the USA will have more chance to gain the souls and an authority over world mission. In a global era, in God's providence, the spiritual passion of the Southern will migrate to the Northern, and both hemispheres will get together to be partners. The real issue is whether the Northern will realize it and accept the Southern as patterns that God sends for global mission.

8. *Missio Dei* is one of the hot issues in current missiology, but its problematic theology—soteriology and ecclesiology[27]—have been questioned among evangelical circles. However, the major reason evangelical missiologists did not totally discard it is the powerful dynamic of God's initiative mission. To carry out the dynamics of God's initiative in *Missio Dei*, and correct its soteriological and ecclesiastical errors, the concept of diaspora as the seed of the kingdom is very useful because it represents the dynamic of God's initiative in mission and is

among us? In *Strangers Next Door*, J.D. Payne, professor of evangelism and church planting, introduces the phenomenon of migrations of peoples to Western nations and explores how the church should respond in light of the mission of God. See Payne, *Strangers Next Door*.

27. Bosch, *Transforming Mission*, 390.

focused on God's salvation and mission. In the concept of Diaspora, the *Missio Dei* and the institutional church can be reconciled.

9. Doing Diaspora missiology can be applied to build up the frameworks of the church as mission though planting the concept of Diaspora into all activities of the church; for successful Diaspora missiology, the church should be diasporic because the diaspora are essentially missionaries. This is called "Diaspora Mission Church." This means that the church and mission cannot be separated from each other; as Lesslie Newbigin puts it, mission should be ecclesial.[28]

10. Finally, this book will examine the future of global Christianity; some scholars argued for "the Global South";[29] others, "the shifting of Christianity's center of gravity from the West to the rest and from the Northern Hemisphere to the south."[30] However, the north and the South need to move beyond the center debate, toward global partnership; we help one another for world evangelization. Global Christianity should pay attention to the USA and the EU, which have immigrants—in particular, unreached people—flowing in from the south; the South should rethink why God providentially guides many unreached souls to the USA and the EU—the West. Diaspora missiology, in which the homeland and foreign land is transnationally and globally connected to each other, will open a new window to reach unreached people.

Through doing this whole process, I will suggest systematic theories and practices of doing Diaspora missiology imbedded in the life of the church—Diaspora church—mission. The aim of this book is to revive the Diaspora church, focusing mission beyond secularization and preach the gospel in the Holy Spirit locally and globally.

THE ORGANIZATION OF THE BOOK

The book is composed of nine chapters. Chapter 1 will introduce globalization, demographic trends, and the phenomenon of Diaspora. This chapter will explain demographic trends in a global era from the perspective of socio-cultural and political standpoints, and explore how globalization affects the mobility of diaspora. Chapter 2 will deal with the emergence of diaspora and various academic interests in diaspora, and explain the work of the Lausanne Movement to catch the core value of diaspora in globalization

---

28. Goheen, "Significance of Lesslie Newbigin," 88–99.
29. Jenkins, *Next Christendom*.
30. Wan, *Diaspora Missiology*, 4.

for world evangelization, and the theorizing of Diaspora by BIAM, CLSC, Andrew Walls, and Jehu Hanciles for Christian mission.

From chapter 3 on, the author will lay three foundations for formulating Diaspora missiology. First, it will provide interdisciplinary understandings of Diaspora (chapter 3). This is because Diaspora is in the vortex of interdisciplinary perspectives of globalization. Secondly, chapter 4 will describe biblical understandings of Diaspora, in which the concept will be studied in the two divisions of the OT and the NT: from Genesis to Revelation. Thirdly, in a final part of its foundation research, chapter 5 will investigate theological implications of Diaspora; from biblical, systematic, historical, and practical perspectives, the concept of Diaspora will be examined.

Chapter 6 will set the stage for the rediscovery of missiological issues toward the formulation of Diaspora missiology in a global era. This chapter will figure out what are the missiological problems and issues, and explain how Diaspora missiology reorients and solves these missiological issues. After that, chapter 7 will work contextual theologizing for Diaspora missiology. Contextual theologizing—part of globalizing theology—will be processed in the principles of double hermeneutics and critical contextualization, and focus on the text of the Bible itself and the work of the Holy Spirit with a heart of compassion for suffering diaspora.

Chapter 8 will apply Diaspora missiology to a local church, creating the model of Diaspora mission church. Diaspora mission church was based on the transcendent nature of the church as diaspora; in particular, it centers on the transcendent concept of diaspora as pilgrim, and moves against secularization. It also pivoted on the ten core values of Diaspora; it exists as mission and practices missional frameworks for the missionary church. Finally, chapter 9 will provide essential ministries to heal hurt diaspora, formulate a transcendent identity of diaspora for embracing others, empower them for effective evangelism, and finally train them to be global network builders.

In conclusion, the goal of this book is to do Diaspora missiology for effective world evangelism in an era of global mobility. The diaspora on the move stand in the middle of global flows; we are in an emergence of redefining a new concept of mission through studying diaspora biblically, theologically, and demographically. In particular, in "U.S. Population Projections: 2005–2050," Pew Research Center reported that "The nation's population will rise to 438 million in 2050, from 296 million in 2005, and fully 82% of the growth during this period will be due to immigrants arriving from 2005 to 2050 and their descendants. Of the 117 million people added to the population during this period due to the effect of new immigration, 67 million will be the immigrants themselves, 47 million will be their children, and 3 million will be their grandchildren."[31]

This shows that it is essential to study and understand how our mission, especially in the context of the USA, called the nation of immigrants, will respond to this huge mobility of immigrant diaspora. At the same time, more importantly, world Christianity has been under the attacking influence of secularism, pluralism, and relativism; Christian mission has been under high risk. Here, the most important question is how do we do faith and carry out Christian mission in a secular and anti-Christian society?

My conclusion is that if we cannot find ways to overcome the spirit of secularism in Christian faith, church, and mission, there will be little hope in the future of Christian mission; and that if the transcendent spirit and power of Diaspora is implanted in every area of a Christian faith and church and restores its nature as pilgrim, we can revitalize faith, church, and mission. We call it the "transcendent conversion" for future Christianity, which acts as a catalyst to overcome imminent secularism.

Now it is time for every diaspora in every nation to confess as Joseph did in Genesis 45: "7But God sent me ahead of you to preserve for you a remnant on earth and to save your lives by a great deliverance. 8So then, it was not you who sent me here, but God. He made me father to Pharaoh, lord of his entire household and ruler of all Egypt." This is the great awakening for God's providence in salvation and mission. Now every diaspora is invited to confess that "God sent me ahead of you to preserve for you a remnant on earth and to save your lives by a great deliverance"; "It was not you who sent me here, but God." This confession of "God's plan of saving life" and "God sent me" is the core of Diaspora missiology. Diaspora is a secret plan of God for his kingdom in his time and in his place that nobody knows; it is time to let every diaspora confess and live it. This is a core confession and vision of Diaspora missiology. Host churches also are the same; they are existent here as diaspora; they also are here as pilgrim. We all were diaspora as pilgrim existentially, biblically, and theologically, scattered by our God as a seed of his kingdom in the field of the world. That is why we are here! We believe that God will rebuild Christianity of the First World in the Anglo-American church through God's bringing in diaspora from the Third World. It is the time for partnership between the First and the Third. This book will show how it works through the model of Diaspora mission church.

—Luther Jeom Ok Kim, PhD
For his kingdom.

31. Pew Research Center, "U.S. Population Projections: 2005–2050," lines 7–10.

1

Globalization, Demographic Trends, and the Phenomenon of Diaspora

Many changes in missiology happened in an era of globalization, which is moving the people toward other countries; this demographical trend, the people on the move, is making the phenomenon of Diaspora global in scale. This creates multiple implications for world mission; at the same time, this is the great challenge to Christian faith, church, and mission, because it has accompanied secularism, religious pluralism, relativism and so on, which are attacking the absolute nature of Christianity. Recent missiology will consider these dramatic changes and challenges of globalization and the people on the move.

GLOBAL TRENDS: THE MOBILIZATION OF MIGRATION

Globalization and Migration

One of the undeniable realities in the twentieth and twenty-first centuries is the global phenomena of the peoples—people on the move. At the 2004 forum hosted by the "Lausanne Committee for World Evangelization, the New People Next Door: Lausanne Occasional Paper No. 55," international migration trends were analyzed. Based on their report, the total number of international migrants living around the world has grown substantially in the global age. The following is recent data of international migrants:[1]

- In 2004, there were an estimated 174 million migrants in the world (reliable statistics are very hard to obtain).
- In 2003, the fifteen countries making up the EU at that time had a net inflow of nearly one million migrants.
- In 2001, some twenty million non-European Union nationals were living in the EU, and this amounted to over 5 percent of the total population. Over 5 million people sought asylum in the EU between 1990 and 2000.
- By 2050, one in four people living in the USA are likely to be Hispanic.

In particular, "Faith on the Move," a new study focusing on the religious affiliation of international migrants, examined patterns of migration among seven major religious groups: Christians (49 percent), Muslims (27 percent), Hindus (5 percent), Buddhists (3 percent), and Jews (2 percent), adherents of other religions (4 percent), and the religiously unaffiliated (9 percent).[2] From the above picture, the biggest portion of religious international migrants are Christian; the second is Muslim; the third, Hindu; the fourth, Buddhist; and the fifth, Jewish. This shows how various religions meet in process of migration; this data also shows how important international migration is to a Christian mission toward other religions. That is, international migration is a mission field. As of 2012, "about 3% of the world's population has migrated across international borders. While that may seem like a small percentage, it represents a lot of people. If the world's 214 million international migrants were counted as one nation, they would constitute the fifth most populous country on the globe, just behind Indonesia and ahead of Brazil."[3] How many Christians are in immigrant populations? As of 2010, approximately 105,670,000 Christians—part of the number just behind Indonesia and ahead of Brazil—are moving toward other places around the world. We should pay attention to this movement. For this reason, we need to study demography; demographers are trained in social science and often cross disciplinary boundaries in search of theoretical explanations.[4] This indicates that interdisciplinary perspectives are needed in studying international migration for Christian mission.

---

1. LCWE Issue Group No. 26 A and B, "Lausanne Occasional Paper No. 55."
2. Pew Research Center, "Faith on the Move."
3. Ibid.
4. Kelly, "Demography and International Migration," 58.

The Theory of Migration

In regard to reasons for migration, Joe and Clairece Feagin propose four major types of migration; these can be seen as a continuum ranging from completely voluntary to involuntary migration:[5]

1. Movements of forced labor
2. Contract-labor
3. Movement of displaced persons and refugees
4. Voluntary migration

Historically, the movement of forced labor included the forcible movement of Africans to America; contract-labor movement included migration of Asians to North America; displaced persons included the streams of refugees produced by war. In particular, UNHCR [the United Nations High Commissioner for Refugees] counts twenty-nine different groups of 25,000 or more refugees in twenty-two nations who have been in exile for five years or longer; as of 2009, 42 million uprooted people are waiting to go home.[6] Finally, travelers or students compose a vast amount of migration.

Here, a crucial question arises: why is the number of international migrants increasingly growing in this age? It is reported that the following are factors that fuel this growth:

1. On-going economic inequalities
2. The quest for education and economic opportunity
3. Escape from political and social oppression
4. Demand for skilled workers
5. Aging populations in the developed world, in need of personal care and pension support
6. Religious persecution
7. Inter-tribal conflict
8. Students used to receive scholarships, but are now more likely to be funded by families
9. Urbanization
10. Population growth[7]

---

5. Feagin, *Racial and Ethnic Relations*, 33. See also Schmerhorn, *Comparative Ethnic Relation*, 98.

6. Guterres, "World Refugee Day," lines 1–5.

7. LCWE Issue Group No. 26 A and B, "Lausanne Occasional Paper No. 55," 8–9.

At times in history, religious persecution and strife have been major causes of migration. But many experts think that, on the whole, economic opportunities—better jobs and higher wages—have been the single biggest driver of international migration. At the same time, religion remains a factor in some people's decisions to leave their countries of birth and their choices of where to go. Also, regardless of motive, the movement of millions of people across oceans and continents can have significant effects on the religious makeup of nations. Regarding world refugees, UNHCR reported:

> Major refugee-hosting nations in 2008 included Pakistan (1.8 million); Syria (1.1 million); Iran (980,000); Germany (582,700); Jordan (500,400); Chad (330,500); Tanzania (321,900); and Kenya (320,600). Major countries of origin for refugees included Afghanistan (2.8 million) and Iraq (1.9 million), which together account for 45 percent of all UNHCR refugees. Others were Somalia (561,000); Sudan (419,000); Colombia (374,000), and the Democratic Republic of the Congo (368,000). Nearly all of these countries are in the developing world.[8]

Unfortunately, however, we cannot say that generosity and wealth are proportional to each other. As conflicts drag on with no political solutions, the pressure on many of these poor countries is nearing the breaking point. They need more international help now. Without it, UNHCR and other aid agencies will be forced to continue making heartbreaking decisions on which necessities must be denied to uprooted families. Of the global total of uprooted people in 2008, UNHCR cares for 25 million, including a record 14.4 million internally displaced people—up from 13.7 million in 2007—and 10.5 million refugees. The other 4.7 million refugees are Palestinians under the mandate of the UN Relief and Works Agency.

This migration of refugees seeks for "generosity and wealth"; "They need more international help now."[9] This is a mission field for gaining the souls who seek urgent help. This is a golden fishery—a new area of mission that global Christianity sends missionaries. The crucial issues of migration are ethnic ones. Regarding migration and ethnicity, a number of social science theories ask some basic questions:

1. How does one explain the origin and emergency of racial and ethnic diversity and stratification?

---

8. Guterres, "World Refugee Day," 37–43. Unfortunately, there was excluded the number of recent Syrian refugees from these data.

9. Ibid., 60.

Globalization, Demographic Trends, and the Phenomenon of Diaspora 17

2. How does one explain the continuation of racial and ethnic diversity and stratification?

3. How does one interpret internal adaptive changes within system of racial and ethnic diversity and stratification?

4. How does one explain major change in systems of racial and ethnic diversity and stratification?

Migration is not just movement of people, but an ethnic group contact, leading to cultural and ethnic conflict. That is, migration of ethnic groups causes confect, forming ethnic hierarchies.[10] In a similar way, Heisler describes migration issues in this way: "theory and research in international migration have centered on two basic sets of questions: why does migration occur and how is it sustained over time? Historically, sociologists have focused primarily on the second set of questions, leaving the first to economics and demographers. More recently, beginning roughly in the 1980s, however, sociologists have also paid increasing attention to the first set."[11] This question shows how immigration challenges and affects its social structure, called the sociology of immigration. More importantly, Joe and Clairece Feagin argued a phenomenon they called the "ladder of dominance," regarding the United State as of 1970. According to the authors, for that year, there were five social groupings in terms of such factors as overall economic or political power.[12]

Ethnic groups form a hierarchical structure; this indicates how migration causes ethnic hierarchical conflict. Missiology does not miss this point when doing missiology. This ethnic issue can be repeated in this contemporary time culturally or psychologically, even though not in a legal sense. Ethnic hierarchical structure is one of the missiological issues, as it is related to immigration.

GLOBALIZATION, ECONOMICS, AND SECULARIZATION

Globalization—Economics and Culture

In an initial stage of the study, we need to understand and describe globalization, because recent migration is intertwined with globalization. First of all, according to Deepak Nayyar, globalization is defined, simply, as the

---

10. Feagin, *Racial and Ethnic Relations*, 31.
11. Heisler, "Sociology of Immigration."
12. Ibid., 32.

expansion of economic activities across political boundaries of nation-states, referring to a process of deepening and increasing economic openness and growing economic interdependence between countries in the world economy.[13] Where globalization goes, economics go. A major issue of globalization is economics.

Secondly, globalization is the heart of culture. In his book *Globalization and Culture*, John Tomlinson argued that "Globalization lies at the heart of modern culture; cultural practices lie at the heart of globalization ... But it is to maintain that the huge transformative processes of our time that globalization describes cannot be properly understood until they are grasped through the conceptual vocabulary of culture; likewise that these transformations change the very fabric of cultural experience and, indeed, affect our sense of what culture actually is in the modern world. Both globalization and culture are concepts of the highest order of generality and are notoriously contested in their meanings."[14]

Jan Nederveen Pieterse's *Globalization and Culture* (2003) also conceived globalization as a human integration and hybridization, which is cultural mixing across continents and regions going back many centuries.[15] In the article, "Globalization of Culture," the Global Policy Forum, provided by ENESCO, describes globalization as the spread of global culture: "Technology has now created the possibility and even the likelihood of a global culture. The Internet, fax machines, satellites, and cable TV are sweeping away cultural boundaries. Global entertainment companies shape the perceptions and dreams of ordinary citizens, wherever they live. This spread of values, norms, and culture tends to promote Western ideals of capitalism."[16]

At the same time, there are some descriptions of the negative aspects of globalization. GPF asks several critical questions: "Will local cultures inevitably fall victim to this global 'consumer' culture? Will English eradicate all other languages? Will consumer values overwhelm peoples' sense of community and social solidarity? Or, on the contrary, will a common culture lead the way to greater shared values and political unity?"[17] These questions show that people in globalization, including diaspora, are in some negative effects of globalization. Main critics of globalization argue that because of free trade and investment, the gap between the rich and poor nations has gotten bigger and wider. Pritchett argues that if globalization

---

13. Nayyar, *Governing Globalization*.
14. Tomlinson, *Globalization and Culture*, 1.
15. Pieterse, *Globalization and Culture*.
16. Global Policy Forum, "Globalization of Culture," lines 1–7.
17. Ibid.

is a positive development, then the divergence between the rich and poor should not have occurred.[18]

Secularism

The crucial issue of globalization is a secular issue. It should be worthy of noting that a major spirit of globalization is secularism, removing religion from public life. In 2010, Linell E. Cady and Elizabeth Shakman Hurd edited *Comparative Secularisms in a Global Age*. This book explores the history and politics of secularism and the public role of religion in France, India, Turkey, and the United States, and they seek to interpret various kinds of secularism as a series of evolving and contested processes of defining and remaking religion.[19]

Regarding the relationship between globalization and secularization, the University of Missouri, St. Louis [UMSL] presented a PowerPoint entitled "Santa Claus—Secularization and Globalization: Cultural Geography." This tries to explain the secularization of Christian faith in globalization through the concept of Santa Claus. Its first sheet says, "Secularization can denote the transformation or broadening of a religious into a secular symbol. Santa, or Saint Nicholas, was originally associated with the Christian celebration of the birth of Christ. Today, around the world, Santa has been adopted by many people as a symbol of winter celebration with no reference to the birth of Christ;" in its second sheet, "Globalization is usually recognized as being driven by a combination of economic, technological, socio-cultural, political, and biological factors. The term can also refer to the transnational circulation of ideas, languages, or popular culture through acculturation."[20] Here, Santa Claus is used for secular purposes: to promote the commercial merchant's Santa, Santa in advertising, sponsorship events, Air Force Santa, sacrilegious Santa, naked Santa, and so on. This is an example of secularization; in the contemporary era, the meaning of secularization is not to remove religious names and forms but to distort or change religious nature.

Some scholars argued that there is a relationship between secularization and religious resurgence.[21] They say, "Experts once believed that as the world grew more modern, religions would be declined. Precisely, the opposite has proven true; religious movements are surging and driving 'alterna-

18. Pritchett, "Divergence, Big Time," 3–18.
19. Cady and Hurd, *Comparative Secularisms in a Global Age*.
20. UMSL, "Santa Claus—Secularization and Globalization," lines 2–3.
21. Volf, "Faith and Globalization: Secularization & Religious Resurgence."

tive globalization' across the world. Two leading thinkers offer a penetrating view of how and why religion of all kinds is shaping the global economy and political order."[22] The two thinkers here are: Peter Berger (Director of the Institute on Culture, Religion, and World Affairs at Boston University) and Moss Kanter (Ernest L. Arbuckle Professor of Business Administration at Harvard Business School). However, from the perspective of Christianity, we are still in secularization to remove religion from this society if we are in the resurgence of religions. It is because the teachings of contemporary Christianity in secularization are different from those described in the Bible and approved in history of the early church. This is why Christianity is still in secularization removing religion from the society.

In particular, the Berkley Center poses some crucial questions about globalization approaching a post-secular culture:

> How does globalization intersect with the resurgence of public religion? To what extent do we live in a post-secular world? The "Globalization, Religions, and the Secular" program brings together leading scholars across disciplines to explore different dimensions of these questions across states, regions, and religious communities.[23]

These questions seek to figure out the relationship between globalization, religion, and a post-secular world. They also ask what kind of a world globalization is being made, and ask how Christians approach the people on the move in migrations. These questions call for a deepened study of globalization socio-politically and theologically from the perspective of Diaspora mission.

THE PHENOMENON OF DIASPORA

Globalization and Diaspora

According to the *Oxford English Dictionary Online*, the word *Diaspora* in the English language was first used in 1876 referring "extensive *Diaspora* work (as it is termed) of evangelizing among the National Protestant Churches on the continent."[24] The dictionary defines the word Diaspora as "Jews living outside Israel"; it also suggests different kinds: (1) the dispersion of the Jews beyond Israel; (2) the dispersion of any people from their original home-

---

22. Ibid.
23. Casanova, "Globalization, Religions, and the Secular," lines 1–6.
24. *Oxford English Dictionary Online*, "Diaspora," lines 1–10.

land: "the diaspora of boat people from Asia"; (3) *the people so dispersed*: "the Ukrainian diaspora flocked back to Kiev." The dictionary added, "The main diaspora began in the 8th–6th centuries BC, and even before the sack of Jerusalem in AD 70, the number of Jews dispersed by the diaspora was greater than that living in Israel. Thereafter, Jews were dispersed even more widely throughout the Roman world and beyond."[25] The term became more widely assimilated into English by the mid-1950s, with long-term expatriates in significant numbers from other particular countries or regions also being referred to as a diaspora. The concept of Diaspora expanded beyond the Jewish Diaspora. In particular, as mentioned earlier, as of 2010, the 3 percent of the world population are on the move, which means that 214 million come to the category of diaspora. Globalization has propelled the phenomenon of Diaspora. How does globalization cause immigration and diaspora?

With the relations between globalization and diaspora, in *Global Diasporas: An Introduction*,[26] focusing analysis on the history and sociology of the world diasporas, Cohen, Professorial Fellow at Queen Elizabeth House, University of Oxford, suggests five aspects of globalization that have bearing on the study of Diaspora:

1. *A world economy* with quicker and denser transactions between its subsectors due to better communications, cheaper transport, a new international division of labor, the activities of transnational corporations, and the effects of liberal trade and capital flow polices.

2. *Forms of international migration* that emphasize contractual relationships, family visits, international stays abroad, and sojourning, as opposed to permanent settlement and the exclusive adoption of the citizenship of a destination country.

3. *The development of global cities* in response to intensification of transactions and interactions between the different segments of the world economy and their concentration in certain cities whose significance resides more in their global, rather in their national, role.

4. *The creation of cosmopolitan and local cultures* prompting or reacting to globalization.

25. Ibid.

26. In his book, Robin Cohen introduces his distinctive approach to the study of the world's diasporas, analyzing "the history and sociology of the world's diasporas." This book investigates the changing meanings of the concept and the contemporary diasporic condition. This book includes case studies of Jewish, Armenian, African, Chinese, British, Indian, Lebanese, and Caribbean people, serving as the foundational text in an emerging research and teaching field. See Robin Cohen, R., *Global Diasporas*, vii.

5. *A deterritorialization of social identity* challenging the hegemonizing nation-states' claim to make an exclusive citizenship a defining focus of allegiance and fidelity in favor of overlapping, permeable, and multiple forms of identifications.[27]

Each of these aspects of globalization show how they contribute to opening up the development for diaspora to thrive. The phenomenon of Diaspora is a complex, socio-cultural and political product of globalization. In particular, Cohen emphasizes the socio-political potential of global diaspora by saying "this has important implications for the conduct of commerce and industry and also changes the nature of certain cities, turning them into 'global cities' or cosmopolis."[28] This socio-political power of diaspora should be recognized by Christian mission.

Christian Migration and Diaspora

Since 2004, the Lausanne Diaspora Leadership Team (LDLT), belonging to the LCWE, also understands Diaspora movement of the global trend in terms of God's redemptive plan.[29] Here, the LDLT analyzed that "people on the move belong to God's global plan: Dispersion of persons and peoples is within God's redemptive plan in human history. From the perspective of the doctrine of 'the priesthood of all believers,' then, 'diaspora' and 'Diasporas' are the fulfillment of God's global plan and worldwide mission."[30] Furthermore, the LDLT noted that Diaspora is in the complex vortex of national interests:

> Every nation counts on the presence, participation, and power (either good or bad) of "diasporas" or "expatriates" (short-term, long-term, or those who have already acquired a citizenship status). This is why each nation is socio-politically interested in diaspora issues. Here it should be noted that the concept of diaspora is mixed with Christian as well as socio-political issues. This situation of diaspora calls for its classification and discretion so that it may not fall into the distortion and syncretism.[31]

In the case of Christian migrants, a major discovery is that among Christian migrants, the main destination regions have been North America

27. Ibid., 157.
28. Ibid., xii.
29. LCWE, *Scattered to Gather.*
30. Ibid., 22.
31. Ibid.

and Europe. European countries, as a whole, are also the leading source of Christian migrants, accounting for more than four out of ten worldwide (44 percent). About three out of ten Christian migrants originate from Latin America and the Caribbean (30 percent). The following figure depicts: 1) regional origins of Christian migration, and 2) regional destinations of Christian migration.

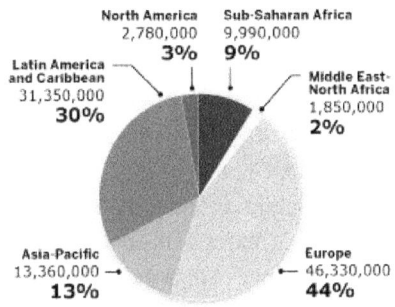
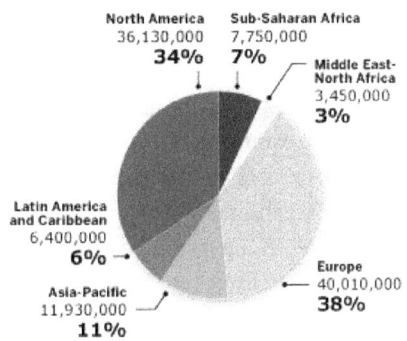

Figure 1: Regional Origins of Christian Migration and Regional Destination of Christian Migration

Figure 1 shows that international migration mainly moves from Southern (Latin America and the Caribbean, Asia-Pacific, and Sub-Saharan Africa) to Northern (North America and Europe). Here the point noted is Europe: European traditional Christians left that area and new Christians from the Third World—Latin America and the Caribbean, Sub-Saharan Africa and Asia-Pacific—arrived.

Interestingly, the USA is the world's number one destination for Christian immigrants. With its huge population of immigrants, the US is the world's number one destination for Christian migrants, who make up nearly three-quarters (74%) of all foreign-born people living in the United States. The United States is also the top destination for Buddhist migrants (including many from Vietnam) and for people with no particular religious affiliation (including many from China). It is the world's second-leading destination for Hindu migrants, after India, and for Jewish migrants, after Israel. Among Muslim migrants, however, the United States ranks just seventh as a destination—behind Saudi Arabia, Russia, Germany, France, Jordan, and Pakistan.

There is research on the relationship between globalization and evangelization. According to J. Steven O'Malley, about 400 million persons are living in a state of diaspora around the globe.[32] These dislocated persons are susceptible to receptivity of the Christian message and to finding their identity in the church, being scattered as diaspora outside homelands. According to Lundy, approximately "3% of the global population lives in countries in which they were not born."[33] Diaspora form three percent a global network for world evangelization; indeed, "the people on the move have serious implications toward world evangelization. They are not only subjects of evangelism and church growth, but have become powerful agents for the extension of the gospel."[34]

In "Diaspora Missiology and Mission in the Context of the 21st Century," Wan and Tira analyze the globalization trend in terms of Diaspora missiology. First of all, they see a new demographic reality of the twenty-first century in three perspectives: (1) Size and significance of diaspora increased globally; (2) Migrant population has increased globally; and (3) Center of gravity of Christianity—Southward shifting. After that, they described Diaspora missiology as: (1) a new paradigm for the twenty-first century, (2) supplementary to "traditional missiology," and (3) theological education.[35] In response to the demographic trends of the diasporas in the twenty-first century, Wan and Tira say, "We must recognize the immense potential in ministering to and through diaspora. People tend to be more receptive to the gospel while in transition. The phenomenon of a large scale of diasporas provides new opportunities and challenges in mission practice. There is now a new way of doing Christian mission; unhindered by geographical and cultural barriers, Christians can reach newcomers in their neighborhoods. In the West, ministries without borders for many of the "unreached people-groups" are rising.[36]

Here we found that the spiritual situation of diaspora is more open to the gospel while unsafe in transition; diaspora is a new way of Christian mission, and the provision of God for the redemptive plan. Based on biblical

---

32. O' Malley, *Revitalization amid Diaspora*.
33. Lundy, *Borderless Church*, xiv.
34. LCWE, *Scattered to Gather*, 1.
35. Wan and Tira, "Diaspora Missiology and Missions," 46.
36. Ibid., 50.

teachings, the LCWE sees diaspora as his provision: "The fact that God creates nations (Gen 25:23; Ps 86:9), his provision of languages/cultures (Gen 11:1, 6, 7, 9), and his determination over the place (spatial dimension) and the timing (temporal dimension) of our habitation (Acts 17:26, 29) imply that he not only had used "diasporas" as provision; but as missional means for his own glory, his edification of his people, and the salvation of the lost (Acts 17:21–22)."

This shows why the contemporary church and Christians should pay attention to the diaspora issue behind global flows. It is because diaspora is based on God's plan of spatial dimension and temporal dimension for practicing his salvation.

A New Perception of World Mission: Strangers Next Door

The concept of Diaspora is to challenge a traditional concept of global mission. In traditional missiology, mission was understood in terms of going abroad; in Diaspora missiology, mission can be understood in terms of strangers next door.[37] The concept of Diaspora mission is represented in the fields of the USA and the EU.

North America—The US

From a Christian Diaspora migrations perspective, the US, called the host country of diasporas in the global era, is a great mission field. First of all, *Missiologically Thinking* describes data that the US is the number one place for immigrant Christians and other religions:

A) Of the 43 million foreign-born people living in the United States as of 2010, an estimated 32 million (74%) are Christian. In addition, the U.S. also has been the top destination for Buddhist migrants (including many from Vietnam) and for people with no particular religion (including many from China).

B) The U.S. has been the world's second-leading destination for Hindu migrants, after India, and for Jewish migrants, after Israel. Among Muslim migrants, however, the U.S. ranks just seventh as a destination—behind Saudi Arabia, Russia, Germany, France, Jordan, and Pakistan. There were more than two million Muslim immigrants living in the U.S. as of 2010, representing about 5 percent of the U.S. immigrant population.

37. Payne, *Stranger Next Door*.

C) The U.S. leads all other countries as a destination for international migrants overall. One of every five international migrants alive today resides in the United States.

D) Mexico has been by far the largest country of origin for U.S. immigrants. In fact, the U.S. has received about as many migrants from Mexico alone (more than 12 million, including both legal immigrants and unauthorized ones) as any other nation has received from all sources combined. Among the other leading countries of origin for U.S. immigrants are the Philippines (1.8 million), India (1.7 million), China (1.4 million), and Germany (1.2 million).[38]

J. D. Payne announces the phenomenon of migrations of peoples to Western nations and explains how the Western church responds in light of the mission of God. He points out that the least reached people groups now live in and migrate to Western countries, and encourages that churches have unprecedented opportunities to share the gospel with them right next door. He continues to challenge American Christians in this way: "Why will we risk life and limb to go to some of the world's least reached peoples when we will not walk next door to share that gospel with those same people groups God has moved into our neighborhoods?"[39]

This question awakens Christians of the US to discover the people with whom they share the gospel. Now the US needs to rethink the meaning of the mission and what kind of strategy is needed to approach the people next door, which can be called a paradigm shift of Christian mission. This means that the church itself should be missional. Now this paradigm shift is realized in the name of missional church.[40]

Here is a remarkable book review of *Stranger Next Door* by Matthew Soerens, US church training specialist at World Relief and co-author of *Welcoming the Stranger: Justice, Compassion & Truth in the Immigration Debate*:

> Many in our society—and even within our churches—see immigration as a threat or an invasion, but J. D. Payne challenges us to see immigration as Scripture does: as a missional opportunity. Many immigrants bring a vibrant faith with them to their new country, breathing new life into local churches, but others do not yet know the hope of a transformational relationship with Jesus. If we have the eyes to see it, immigration presents

---

38. Payne, "Missions To, Through, and Beyond the Diasporas," lines 11–20. This source was originally taken from "Faith on the Move: The Religious Affiliation of International Migrants."

39. Payne, "Missions To, Through, and Beyond the Diasporas," lines 11–20.

40. Guder, *Missional Church*, 1–17.

an opportunity to 'make disciples of all nations' without even leaving our zip codes, and *Strangers Next Door* serves as an informative and practical guide.[41]

This review challenges American Christians see to immigrants not as a threat but as missional opportunity. Basically, we understand the concept of mission in terms of the stranger next door. By this it does not mean we do not go to abroad for mission, but that we first look around at our neighbors whom God already brought before us. Regarding the significance of Diaspora mission, the Lausanne movement proclaims: "The world has increasingly become "borderless" due to globalization, technological communication, and accelerated migration or diaspora (i.e. scattering or dispersion of people from their homeland), towards the end of the Second Millennium."[42]

These diasporas have created tremendous opportunities and challenges to evangelize and make disciples of millions of people who, just a century ago, were living in isolated countries and regions of the world described by missiologists as "closed" and "restricted" to Christian missions. Thus, the twenty-first century reality of mass movements of people requires the global church, here after referred to as the "whole church," to respond.[43] It is time to rethink and reorient Christian mission to a global diaspora perspective.

The European Union

On Friday, December 23, 2005, the BBC News reported, "Muslims in Europe: Country Guide." According to the BBC, "Islam is widely considered Europe's fastest growing religion, with immigration and above average birth rates leading to a rapid increase in the Muslim population."[44] Traditionally, the EU is Christian in majority; however, now the fastest growing religion in the EU is Muslim. On January 27, 2011, in a project on the future of the global Muslim population, regarding the European region, Pew Research reported about the number of Muslims in Europe. The following figure represents the shift of the Muslim population.

---

41. Soerens, Review of *Strangers Next Door*, lines 1–10.
42. Lausanne, "Consultations on Diaspora Missions," lines 1–3.
43. Ibid., lines 7–8.
44. BBC News, "Muslims in Europe: Country Guide."

EUROPE
Number of Muslims in Selected Countries

Countries	ESTIMATED MUSLIM POPULATION 2010	ESTIMATED PERCENTAGE OF POPULATION THAT IS MUSLIM 2010	PROJECTED MUSLIM POPULATION 2030	PROJECTED PERCENTAGE OF POPULATION THAT IS MUSLIM 2030
Austria	475,000	5.7%	799,000	9.3%
Belgium	638,000	6.0	1,149,000	10.2
Denmark	226,000	4.1	317,000	5.6
Finland	42,000	0.8	105,000	1.9
France	4,704,000	7.5	6,860,000	10.3
Germany	4,119,000	5.0	5,545,000	7.1
Greece	527,000	4.7	772,000	6.9
Ireland	43,000	0.9	125,000	2.2
Italy	1,583,000	2.6	3,199,000	5.4
Luxembourg	11,000	2.3	14,000	2.3
Netherlands	914,000	5.5	1,365,000	7.8
Norway	144,000	3.0	359,000	6.5
Portugal	65,000	0.6	65,000	0.6
Spain	1,021,000	2.3	1,859,000	3.7
Sweden	451,000	4.9	993,000	9.9
Switzerland	433,000	5.7	663,000	8.1
United Kingdom	2,869,000	4.6	5,567,000	8.2
Total for these countries	**18,267,000**	**4.5**	**29,759,000**	**7.1**

Population estimates are rounded to thousands. Percentages are calculated from unrounded numbers. Figures may not add exactly due to rounding. Table shows 17 of the 50 countries and territories in Europe.

Pew Research Center's Forum on Religion & Public Life • *The Future of the Global Muslim Population*, January 2011

Figure 2: The Future of the Global Muslim Population: Number of Muslim Population in Selected European Countries[45]

The project reports:

"The number of Muslims in Europe has grown from 29.6 million in 1990 to 44.1 million in 2010. Europe's Muslim population is projected to exceed 58 million by 2030. Muslims today account for about 6% of Europe's total population, up from 4.1% in 1990. By 2030, Muslims are expected to make up 8% of Europe's population. Although Europe's Muslim population is growing, Europe's share of the global Muslim population will remain quite small. Less than 3% of the world's Muslims are expected to be living in Europe in 2030, about the same portion as in 2010 (2.7%). Nevertheless, Europe's Muslim population will continue to grow at a faster pace than its non-Muslim population, which has been decreasing. As a result, Muslims are expected to make up a growing share of Europe's total population."

According to the above data, most European Muslims live in Eastern Europe, but some of the biggest increases in Europe's Muslim population are expected to occur mainly in the United Kingdom, France, Italy, and Germany. As of 2030, the big percent countries of the total population are France (10.3%), Belgium (10.2%), Sweden (9.9%), Austria (9.3%) ... As of 2010, 18,267,000 Muslim visited the EU; some of them live permanently in the EU. Is it accidental that this number of Muslim is moving to the EU?

45. Pew Research Center, "Future of the Global Muslim Population."

The Second Chance of Northern Christianity for World Evangelization: In Opposition to Jenkins's Prophecy

Philip Jenkins, the Edwin Erle Sparks Professor of the Humanities in history and religious studies at Penn State University, argued that Christianity is increasingly moving to the Southern Hemisphere toward its place of origin, and that the center of gravity of the Christian world has shifted from the US and Europe to the Southern Hemisphere.[46] However, the trend of current Christian migrants seems to be seemingly opposite to Jenkins's analysis: Christian migration is from the Southern to the Northern Hemisphere. My argument is that the revival of Christians in the Southern Hemisphere is moving to the Northern, known as secularized and stagnated Christianity. Christian migration toward the Northern Hemisphere has missiological implications for understanding a topographical map of the world Christianity. In other words, diaspora can be a catalyst to activate a balance between the Northern and Southern Christianity. Diaspora moving toward the Northern Hemisphere is missiologically approached by the Northern church, which requires a new concept of mission in an age of diaspora movement. It should be noted that it conveys God's secret plan for a global era.

In opposition to Jenkins's prophecy, Northern Christianity—in America and the EU—will have more change for world mission, than the Southern; the Southern turn their eyes to the Northern because unreached people are flowing into the Northern. Both Southern and Northern get together and do cooperative mission for unreached frontier people. The real issue is how Northern Christianity establishes forming Diaspora missiology, and how the Southern has partnership with the Northern. This can offer a chance to restart the second revival of Northern Christianity. Again this depends on how the Northern prepare for doing Diaspora mission.

In terms of the social-political, American history acknowledges the immigration of Southern diaspora transforming America. In *The Southern Diaspora: How the Great Migrations of Black and White Southerners Transformed America*, as James N. Gregory puts it, the changing technology of newspaper, radio, and music, alongside a change in popular literature in the twentieth century pushed the northern and western migration of increasing numbers of southerners.[47] In particular, he points out that southerner diasporas, particularly black migrants, took their evangelical, charismatic brand of religion into cities and joined churches that not only became social

---

46. Jenkins, *Next Christendom*, 14.
47. Gregory, *Southern Diaspora*.

networks but political and civic networks as well; he argues that Billy Graham or Oral Roberts affect this settlement of southern diaspora.

In his book *Beyond Christendom: Globalization, African Migration and the Transformation of the West* (2009), as already mentioned, Jehu Hanciles argues that the migration of Christians carries within it the seeds of renewal for the whole church. His main argument is that migration and mission are inextricably connected; challenging standard assumptions regarding "globalization." He argued that local cultures frequently reframe Western influences to suit their own purposes, and the massive migrations of people from South to North during the past few decades and the dynamic communities they have formed are reshaping the culture of the Western Europe and North America. In reality, immigrant communities from many locales have taken root in cities throughout the United States, and a growing number of churches in the global South are now planting immigrant churches and sending missionaries to Europe and North America. In a word, Hancile's argument is that through migration, the Southern transform and reshape the West and "every Christian migrant is a potential missionary."[48]

Thus Hancile's explanation affirms that the West has a potential to be revived. If Northern Christianity, along with the Southern, open their eyes and look at the fields. "They are ripe for harvest." Here is Jesus' saying:

> John 4: 34"My food," said Jesus "is to do the will of him who sent me and to finish his work.
> 35Don't you have a saying, 'It's still four months until harvest'? I tell you, open your eyes and look at the fields! They are ripe for harvest.
> 36Even now the one who reaps draws a wage and harvests a crop for eternal life, so that the sower and the reaper may be glad together.
> 37Thus the saying 'One sows and another reaps' is true.
> 38I sent you to reap what you have not worked for. Others have done the hard work, and you have reaped the benefits of their labor."

---

48. Hanciles, *Beyond Christendom*, 6

2

Theorizing Diaspora and its Christian Mission Awakening toward Diaspora Missiology

In social science, there have been discussions on diasporas for sociological purpose; literature—art and writing—has gained inspiration from diaspora life. Globalization with massive immigrants challenged a Christian mission to respond to these global demographical trends. Since 2004, Christian mission, centered on the Lausanne Movement, began to seek the meaning of diaspora for world mission. Wan and Tira, in partnership with the Lausanne movement, have focused on doing Diaspora missiology. In addition, BIAMS and CLSC proposed crucial issues in doing Diaspora missiology.

THEORIZING DIASPORA

Jewish Diaspora in the Hebrew Bible

The classical concept of Diaspora was initially founded in Jewish history; the word Diaspora was coined relating to Jewish people. The Jewish Diaspora, Hebrew *Galut* גלות, Yiddish *Golus,* was the historical exile and dispersion of Jews from the region of the kingdom of Judah. Historically, the Diaspora began with the 6th century BC conquest of the kingdom of Judah by Babylon, and following the destruction of Solomon's temple (c. 586 BC), the expulsion and dispersion of the Jews had occurred.

Around 66 AD the Jews began to revolt against the Roman Empire during the First Jewish-Roman War period, which culminated in the destruction of Jerusalem in 70 AD. During the siege, the Romans destroyed the second temple and the city of Jerusalem. This event caused an acute dispersion of many Jews. The discussion on when Roman anti-Judaism began is an issue of scholarly debate. However, historian Ben-Sasson has suggested that the "Crisis under Caligula" was the "first open break between Rome and the Jews."[1]

In particular, the name of the "ghetto" began to be applied to the isolated Jewish community; "Originally the street or quarter of a city in which the Jews were compelled to live, and which was closed every evening by gates; the term is now applied to that part of any city or locality chiefly or entirely inhabited by Jews."[2] The *Jewish Encyclopedia* introduces a sad story of the ghettos established in Vienna in 1570:

> They [ghettos] were chiefly an outcome of intolerance, and oppressive conditions were often added to compulsory residence within the ghetto. When a ghetto was about to be established in Vienna in 1570, the citizens objected to having a place outside the city assigned to the Jews for the following three curious reasons: (1) they feared that if the Jews lived alone outside the city they could the more easily engage in their "nefarious practices"; (2) the Jews would be liable to be surprised by enemies; (3) the Jews might escape! The citizens therefore proposed that all the Jews should live in one house having only one exit; that windows and doors should be well fastened, so that no one might go out at night; and that the possibility of entrance or exit by secret passages should also be guarded against. As the Jews objected to this scheme the project was soon dropped.[3]

This story explains the sadness of Jewish Diasporas; their lives were isolated into the ghetto from neighboring communities. . . . Today how is the Jewish Diaspora? This report is based on a 2010 world Jewish population study.[4] This data shows how the Jewish Diaspora has been processed

---

1. Ben-Sasson, *History of the Jewish People*, 37–41.
2. *Jewish Encyclopedia*, "Ghetto," 11–13.
3. Ibid.
4. DellaPergola, Sergio, et al., eds. "World Jewish Population, 2010." The following is a ranking of the twenty-one highest Jewish populations in the world. 1) Gush Dan (Tel Aviv and surroundings), Israel: 2,979,900. 2) New York City, New York: 2,007,850. 3) Jerusalem: 705,000. 4) Los Angeles, California: 684,950. 5) Haifa, Israel: 671,400. 6) Miami, Florida: 485,850. 7) Be'er Sheva, Israel: 367,600. 8) San Francisco, California: 345,700. 9) Paris, France: 284,000. 10) Chicago, Illinois: 270,500. 11) Philadelphia,

throughout long-term history; it also shows how it has affected world history.

This Jewish Diaspora offers a classical concept of Diaspora, relating to the Christian community. With the Jewish Diaspora's relations to the Christian community, Reimer, a faculty member at the University of Edinburgh, proposed:

> The sort of dual allegiance implied by the label 'residential alien' became part of early Christian self-identity. When the first generation of Christians thought of themselves as the new Israel, this sense of living in the diaspora came with it. New Testament writers pick up the language of exile and diaspora and developed with it a symbolic framework for talking about Christian life and hope.[5]

Therefore, the original concept of Diaspora has a root in the Jewish experience of exile, affecting Christians thought of themselves as "residential aliens." That is, exile and diaspora is a symbolic framework for talking about Christian life and hope—a Christian identity.

Anthropological Circles

In anthropology, it was Franz Boas who was first interested in immigrant issues regarding ethnic groups in the USA. Diaspora itself is the subject of anthropology, and a personal biography of the researcher, because many anthropologists were immigrants. At one time, anthropology approached diaspora in terms of ethnicity and racism. As time passed, anthropology moved from ethnic groups to diasporas and transnational mobility. In "An Anthropological Approach to Diaspora Missiology," Dr. Steven Ybarrola, Professor of Cultural Anthropology at Asbury Theological Seminary, quoting from Steven Vertovec, explains the development of diaspora study in anthology:

> When the anthropology of ethnicity was most thriving around the 1980s, the field was usually comprised of studies of identity and social organization among one or another distinct ethnic

---

Pennsylvania: 263,800. 12) Boston, Massachusetts: 229,100. 13) Washington, DC: 215,600. 14) London, United Kingdom: 195,000. 15) Toronto, Canada: 180,000. 16) Atlanta, Georgia: 119,800. 17) Moscow, Russia: 95,000. 18) San Diego, California: 89,000. 19) Cleveland, Ohio: 87,000. 20) Phoenix, Arizona: 82,900. 21) Montreal, Canada: 80,000.

5. Reimer, "Exile and Diaspora: Leaving and Living," 21.

group within a particular multi-ethnic (or post-migration, ethnic majority/minority) setting . . .[6]

According to Ybarrola, this started to change, however, in the late 1980s and early 1990s when anthropologists began to study not only the broader socio-cultural context in which members of ethnic groups interacted, but also the ties that many of these groups maintained with their home communities. During this period, a focus on diaspora and transnationalism developed within the anthropological study of ethnicity and migration that was largely based on the processes of globalization (e.g., more advanced and accessible communications; ease and affordability of travel; the flow of capital across borders; indeed, the efficacy of borders themselves in controlling the flow of migration and capital). Anthropology has contributed to the study of diaspora in terms of migration, ethnicity, identity, social relationship and transnationalism. These studies show who diaspora are socially, which is helpful towards understanding diaspora for doing Diaspora missiology.[7]

With regard to diaspora study in anthropology, here is a journal worthy of being noted, *Diaspora: A Journal of Transnational Studies*, published by the University of Toronto Press since 1991.[8] *Diaspora* is a journal of transnational studies, and is dedicated to the multidisciplinary study of the history, culture, social structure, politics, and economics of both the traditional diasporas and those transnational dispersions. These encompass groups including the African-American, the Ukrainian-Canadian, the Caribbean-British, and the new East and South Asian diasporas. This journal is helpful to understand the transnationalism of diaspora migration in context of globalization. Here the concept of transnationalism indicates multiple ties and interactions linking people, ideas, and institutions across the borders of nation-states.

> *Current Anthropology* also has contributed to diaspora study; especially Clifford, whom in its 1994 edition argued that, "we should be able to recognize the strong entailment of Jewish history on the language of diaspora without making the history a definitive model."[9]
>
> Consistent with Clifford, Kirshenblatt-Gimblett (1994) also argued that in discussing issues of homelessness, placelessness,

---

6. Ybarrola, *Anthropological Approach*, 4.
7. Ibid.
8. University of Toronto, "Diaspora: A Journal of Transnational Studies," line 1–5.
9. Cohen quotes originally from Clifford, "Diaspora," 302–38.

and statelessness, the Jew has served as the oncomouse of social theory.[10]

In particular, diaspora study in anthropology was more developed because of its acute transnational activities in a global era. According to UNESCO, transnational activities can be defined as:

> Those that take place on a recurrent basis across national borders and that require a regular and significant commitment of time by participants. Such activities may be conducted by relatively powerful actors, such as representatives of national governments and multinational corporations, or may be initiated by more modest individuals, such as immigrants and their home country kin and relations. These activities are not limited to economic enterprises, but include political, cultural and religious initiatives as well.[11]

Now the study of diaspora focuses on the transnational and mutational; this type of study has been intensified because of global flows and connectivity. This shows that diaspora study is one of the major themes in the study of human life and acute transnational activities in a global era.

Social Sciences and Humanities

It is social science that has a strong interest in diaspora study. With the emergence of theorizing diaspora, Brazil and Mannur explained:

> The theorizations of diaspora have emerged in area studies, ethnic studies, and cultural studies as major site of contestation. Since the journal *Diaspora: A Journal of Transnational Studies* was inaugurated in 1991, debate over the theoretical, cultural, and historical resonances of the term have proliferated in academic journals devoted to ethnic, national, and (trans) national concerns.[12]

Furthermore, theorizing Diaspora gives the room to think about discordant movement of modernity, massive migrations that have defined this century—from the late colonial periods through the de-colonialization era into the twenty-first century. This movement affected the ideas of nationalism,

---

10. Cohen quotes originally from Kirshenblatt-Gimblett, "Spaces of Dispersal," 339–44.
11. UNESCO, "Trans-nationalism," lines 5–11.
12. Brazil and Mannur, *Theorizing Diaspora*, 2.

transnationalism, or transmigrations, and linkage between nation and diaspora, explaining how and why the term is being deployed in critical scholarship.[13]

In *Diasporas in Modern Societies: Myths of Homeland and Return*, published in 1991, William Safran set out six rules to distinguish diasporas from migrant communities:

> I suggest that Connor's definition be extended and that the concept of diaspora be applied to expatriate minority communities whose members share several of the following characteristics: (1) they, or their ancestors, have been dispersed from a specific original "center" to two or more "peripheral," or foreign, regions; (2) they retain a collective memory, vision, or myth about their original homeland—its physical location, history, and achievements; (3) they believe that they are not—and perhaps cannot be—fully accepted by their host society and therefore feel partly alienated and insulated from it; (4) they regard their ancestral homeland as their true, ideal home and as the place to which they or their descendants would (or should) eventually return—when conditions are appropriate; (5) they believe that they should, collectively be committed to the maintenance or restoration of their original homeland and to its safety and prosperity; and (6) they continue to relate, personally or vicariously, to that homeland in one way or another, and their ethno communal consciousness and solidarity are importantly defined by the existence of such a relationship.[14]

Safran suggested crucial criteria that the group maintains a collective memory of their homeland, which means that diasporas regard their own ancestral homeland as their true home. Safran's definition of diaspora was influenced by the idea of the Jewish Diaspora; this implies that for him, diaspora is not applicable to other ethnic groups on the move. But later he expanded the use of the term.

In 2005, with the same issue, he wrote "The Jewish Diaspora in a Comparative and Theoretical Perspective," and developed a definition for the concept of diaspora in a broad sense.

> Diaspora [*galut*] connoted deracination, legal disabilities, oppression, and an often painful adjustment to a host land whose hospitality was unreliable and ephemeral. It also connoted the existence on foreign soil of an expatriate community that

---

13. Ibid., 3.
14. Safran, "Diasporas in Modern Societies" 83–84.

considered its presence to be transitory. Meanwhile, it developed a set of institutions, social patterns, and ethno-national and/or religious symbols that held it together. These included the language, religion, values, social norms, and narratives of the homeland. Gradually, this community adjusted to the host land environment and became itself a center of cultural creation. All the while, however, it continued to cultivate the idea of return to the homeland.[15]

In this article, he added that several of the above characteristics have applied to other expatriated communities, such as the Armenian, Chinese, Greek, Indian, Kurdish, Palestinian, Parsi, and Sikh, whose experiences of expatriation, institution building, cultural continuity, and refusal to relinquish their collective identities have demarcated them from mere immigrants. This means that his new concept of diaspora was even broader than his past concept.

However, there is another way that diaspora has been studied in relation to globalization. In 1997, Robin Cohen suggested for the value of diaspora study by arguing, "Globalization has enhanced the practical economic and affective roles of Diasporas, showing them to be particularly adaptive forms of social organizations."[16] In 2006, the study of diaspora was applied to politics; Gabriel Sheffer authored *Diaspora Politics: At Home Abroad*. This book used the term of diaspora politics, which is about an important cultural-political phenomenon: ethno-national diasporas. Generally, diaspora groups try to "feel at home" in their host countries, and at the same time maintain a close contact with their homelands to promote their culture and interests. The author tries to analyze the continuous struggle of diaspora to "maintain their identity, organize, and fight against all wishing to prevent permanent settlement and integration in the host countries.[17]

Furthermore, there is a new way that diaspora is studied in terms of ethnicity and its identity. Despina Lalaki's 2006 class, "Diaspora, Race, and Identity: Reimagining the Community," at Eugene Lang College shows how important the study of diaspora is to study race, as nationality, ethnicity, gender, and class. Lalaki introduces this class in this way:

> If we accept that questions of race and racism have been refashioned today in ways that emphasize cultural difference, then the study of Diasporas offers a key to the study not only of race, but also of other epistemological or historical categories of analysis

15. Safran, "Jewish Diaspora," 36–60.
16. Cohen, R., *Global Diasporas*, xii.
17. Sheffer, *Diaspora Politics*.

such as nationality, ethnicity, gender, class, as well as race. The objective of the course is to challenge the notion of the subject and the stability of identity, to expose racial notions of national identity, to examine the ways in which Diasporas threaten or reinforce existing social and cultural hierarchies and to appreciate the extent to which they shape culture and self-identity as well as social and political action. Diaspora has been studied from many diverse points of departure.[18]

In *Diasporas, Cultures, and Identities*, Martin Bulmer, emeritus Professor of Sociology at the University of Surrey, UK, and John Solomos, Professor of Sociology at City University London, UK analyzed the question of the role of diasporic ties and the social, cultural, and political processes that are engendered by the changing experiences of these communities.[19] According to the authors, for some time, the role of diasporic communities has been the subject of historical reflection; recently, it is in the social sciences and humanities that the concept of diaspora has become a core theme. There have been ongoing discussions about concepts such as transnationalism and cosmopolitanism and their appropriateness as conceptual frames of reference for analyzing the diverse experiences of diasporic communities across the globe. In particular, the concept of diaspora is related to the rethinking of race and identity in community.

Finally, it should be noted that it is in the socio-political arena that the concept of diaspora has been, in earnest, discussed; in particular, the issues—race, nationality, ethnicity, gender, and class—are discussed in the context of diaspora from many diverse points of departure, in which it is key to the studies of these issues. Diaspora, culture, and identity become main issues of citizenship and its meaning in immigrant policy because all nations become more and more multi-ethnic societies.

Literature—Arts and Writings—on Diaspora

In the late 1980s, at the African Literature Association Conference by Clark, Diaspora literacy was coined by literary scholar Veve Clark in her work "Developing Diaspora Literacy and Marasa Consciousness."[20] Diaspora literacy indicates the ability to understand and interpret the multi-layered meanings of stories, words, and symbols within any given diaspora community;

---

18. Lalaki, "Class Syllabus: Diaspora, Race, and Identity," lines 3–13.
19. Bulmer and Solomos, *Diasporas, Cultures and Identities*.
20. Spillers, *Comparative American Identities*, 40–60.

it moves beyond "Western or westernized signification."²¹ Readers interpret and understand literature by depending solely upon a knowledge and experience of historical and cultural climates of the various cultures of the diaspora, which serves as a foundation for interpreting literature.

In 2003, photographer Frédéric Brenner published *Diaspora: Homelands in Exile—Voices*. This work describes Jewish survivors in a gas chamber at the Museum of Tolerance, we find a highlighted nude. He seems to wait for death. This description shows how terrible the Holocaust was. This is a powerful warning of human pride and greed. The theme of diaspora in literature—art and writings—echoes a deep lesson on the human soul.²²

> Diaspora as a theme of literacy becomes a transnational journey of strangers. According to the book *Exiles, Diasporas & Strangers* by Kobena Mercer, migration has been a defining feature of twentieth century modernity including, in particular, much of twentieth century art. This book examines transnational and transformational journeys that have transplanted intellectuals from one cultural place to another, which made clear the creative role that migration, exile, and displacement have played in shaping the story of modern art. Finally, these connections or disconnections in traveling cultures signify artists' efforts to turn to terms with the postcolonialism.²³

The most recent addition to Diaspora literature appeared in Joyce E. King's 2006 article, "If Justice is Our Objective: Diasporic Literacy, Heritage Knowledge, and the Praxis of Critical Studyin' for Human Freedom." Here Joyce E. King holds the Benjamin E. Mays Endowed Chair for Urban Teaching, Learning, and Leadership at the Georgia State University College of Education. Her concept of heritage knowledge echoes diasporic heritage. She emphasizes the value of heritage knowledge for critical study.²⁴ GSU Foundation writer, Hiskey, says:

> Her current work stresses the value of "heritage knowledge" for prospective teachers and today's students, as an antidote to the "crisis of knowledge" throughout the educational system. Grasping a more complete history of diverse cultures gives all people freedom from bondage to stereotypes and bias. For instance, King said, African-American history curricula should begin with the African civilizations that built pyramids and formed

---

21. Ibid., 42.
22. Brenner, *Diaspora: Homelands in Exile—Voices*.
23. Mercer, *Exiles, Diasporas and Strangers*.
24. King, "If Justice is our Objective," 337–60.

complex written languages. She introduced "Songhay Exposition," a new gaming app that challenges players to use ancient African symbols to break a code.²⁵

For Joyce, diverse cultures give people freedom from intellectual bondage to bias. This shows how her heritage of African diaspora gives her intellectual freedom and critical thinking. She expresses the diaspora identity with heritage knowledge, leading to critical study and to human freedom; Diaspora literature is the field of the expression of diaspora heritage. This shows how her understanding of diaspora plays a key role in forming critical thought and study.

Finally, it is noted that there has been much interest in the concept of diaspora in a secular circles of academia for various purposes; the increasing interest of the socio-political arena in diaspora serves as a level on which diaspora builds up its global network for social involvement. Diaspora literacy brings sympathy for diaspora as scattered people among contemporary people, regretting human exploitations and oppression over the same, humans. However, Diaspora missiology does listen and refer to these stories of diaspora, but does not just follow the definition of social science or literature; it needs to seek for a distinctive biblical and theological definition of diaspora with our understanding of sufferings.

Debate on the Definition of Diaspora in Academic Circles

In 1991 and 2005, William Safran presented a list of characteristics of diaspora that can be used as a heuristic for categorization; the definition of diaspora is applied to expatriate minority communities whose members share several of the following characteristics. Here, Safran's definition of diaspora is to have a strong commitment to the homeland, which is too strict. However, in 2005, Rogers Brubaker suggests the criteria of diaspora in three criteria: The first is dispersion in space; the second, the orientation to a "homeland"; and the third, boundary for maintenance.²⁶

> [Firstly] This is today the most widely accepted criterion, and also the most straightforward. It can be interpreted strictly as forced or otherwise traumatic dispersion. The second constitutive criterion is the orientation to a real or imagined 'homeland' as an authoritative source of value, identity and loyalty.... . [Thirdly] Boundaries can be maintained by deliberate resistance

---

25. Hiskey, "Fighting Education Stereotypes," lines 13–19.
26. Brubaker, "'Diaspora' Diaspora," lines 1–19.

to assimilation through self-enforced endogamy or other forms of self-segregation.[27]

For Brubaker, suggesting the criteria of diaspora signifies how the definition of diaspora is difficult, which is expressed in his title "The 'Diaspora' Diaspora." This title teaches the reader to be careful about the usage of the term; he implies this objective of the article in the abstract: "[this article] assesses claims made by theorists of diaspora about a radical shift in perspective and a fundamental change in the social world; and proposes to treat diaspora not as a bounded entity but as an idiom, stance, and claim."[28]

Here we cannot fully understand what he means by his concept of diaspora, but it is sure that the term of diaspora will develop into an imaginable world idiom, stance, and claim. His final conclusion on the use of the term diaspora is:

> The point of this analysis has not been to deflate diaspora, but rather to de-substantialize it, by treating it as a category of practice, project, claim and stance, rather than as a bounded group. The "groupness" of putative diasporas, like that of putative "nations," is precisely what is at stake in [political, social and cultural] struggles. We should not, as analysts, prejudge the outcome of such struggles by imposing groupness through definitional fiat. We should seek, rather, to bring the struggles themselves into focus, without presupposing that they will eventuate in bounded groups.[29]

Brubaker's conclusion reminds us of the preciosity in how we define the term of diaspora. He proposes approaching diaspora not substantially, but practically. Sometimes, Diaspora missiology defines diaspora substantially and theoretically, and later finds that its definition is empty, failing to catch real diaspora practically. Diaspora experts may know diaspora theoretically but not know it practically, like knowing that fish live in water but not knowing water. He explains in this way:

> One of the virtues of "diaspora," scholars have suggested, is that it provides an alternative to teleological, nation-statist understandings of immigration and assimilation. But theories of "diaspora" have their own teleologies. Diaspora is often seen as destiny—a destiny to which previously dormant members (or previously dormant diasporas in their entirety) are now

27. Ibid., 5–6.
28. Ibid., 1.
29. Ibid., 19.

"awakening." Embedded in the teleological language of "awakening"—the language, not coincidentally, of many nationalist movements—are essentialist assumptions about "true" identities. Little is gained if we escape from one teleology only to fall into another.[30]

In 2008, the "1st Global Conference: Diasporas: Exploring Critical Issues," at Mansfield College, Oxford, July 5–8, 2008, provided a thinking space for those of us who are invariably interested in issues and concepts of the diaspora(s). The wide range of topics offered a broad scope of engagement with issues pertaining to what has become one of the most contestable concepts of our times: diaspora(s). The conference offered three sections– "Section I: *Diaspora*/Diaspora/Diasporas," "Section II: Home and Heimat," and "Section III: Diaspora—Performances and the Imaginary." This conference focused on the defining descriptions of diaspora and its characteristics.[31] This conference on diaspora made the range of the topic wider.

In 2013, the "6th Global Conference: Diasporas: Exploring Critical Issues," was held from Saturday, July 6 to Monday, July 8, 2013 at Mansfield College, Oxford. The scope of the conference was even broader than ever. The themes were the following: "Queering Diaspora," "Diaspora, Sex, and Gender," "Visible Diasporas, Invisible Diasporas," "e-Diasporas and Technology," "The Limits of Diaspora—Problematizing 'Diaspora,'" and "The Evolution of the Critical Language of Diaspora."[32] These topics show that diaspora studies have developed to explore critical issues in various contemporary social issues and technological applications.

Here, it deserves to be noted that in 2010 a new direction of diaspora study has been explored by Kim Knott and Sean McLoughlin in *Diasporas: Concepts, Intersections, and Identities*.[33] This book provides a comprehensive and authoritative overview of the political and cultural ideas and groups involved, and contains examinations of major concepts and theories, including postcolonialism, hybridity, migration, ethnicity, multiculturalism, cosmopolitanism, citizenship, and so on. Furthermore, Diaspora has the following intersections: diasporas and economies; diasporas and politics; diasporas, conflict, and security; diasporas and development; diasporas and cities; diasporas, race, and difference; diasporas and gender; diasporas and sexuality; diasporas and religion; diasporas and language; diasporas and material culture; diasporas, literature, and literary studies; diasporas and

30. Sheffer, *Diaspora Politics*, 19–21.
31. Fernandez, *Diasporas: Critical and Inter-Disciplinary Perspectives*.
32. Inter-Disciplinary, "6th Global Conference."
33. Knott and McLoughlin, *Diasporas; Concepts, Intersections, Identities*.

performance; diasporas, film, and cinema; diasporas and media; diasporas and cyberspace.

The study of diaspora developed a global profile and spanned a variety of disciplines, mapping new directions in research and testing the usefulness of diaspora for analyzing the complexity of transnational lives today. This means that the theme of diaspora is an aspiring story of suffered life, serving as a channel to communicate and bridge between human beings with similar experience.

So far, despite the gradually increasing importance of the concept of diaspora and its widespread use in academic case studies and in community networks, the subject has received relatively little general scholarly treatment. In Kim Knott and Sean McLoughlin's broad understanding of diaspora, this issue enlarges to be intersected with a variety of disciplines—diaspora has a crucial relationship with all area of a contemporary society. Through developing a global profile and spanning a variety of disciplines, this book provides an incisive account of the state of the art and emphasizes the evolution of theme and concept, enriched by an attention to specific historical events and cultural conditions, which make this book an indispensable companion to global studies. This broad study reminds us that Christianity should make haste to redeem the concept of diaspora for its missiological implications in the world.

THEORIZING DIASPORA FOR MISSION AND THE LAUSANNE MOVEMENT

The application of diaspora for mission has been mainly introduced and developed by the Lausanne Movement and its related consultations. In fact, two major representatives of Diaspora missiology are Enoch Wan and Sandra Joy Tira. These two scholars will be introduced in the middle of explaining doing Diaspora missiology according to the Lausanne Movement.

Occasional Paper 55 (2004)

"Lausanne Occasional Paper No. 55: The New People Next Door," was produced by the Issue Group on this topic at the 2004 forum hosted by the Lausanne Committee for World Evangelization in Pattaya, Thailand. The slogan of the paper was "A New Vision, a New Heart, and a Renewed Call." Lausanne Occasional Paper (LOP) #55 deals with "diasporas," including international students. It was said to be significant because, "Though its scope is limited and it lacks cohesive missiological implications for the Diasporas, LOP #55 managed to raise Diaspora awareness among the evangelical missions community."[34]

To our understanding of how Lausanne described diaspora, the content of the paper is introduced as follows:

> (1) We are all Migrants: The Scope of the Diasporas
>
> (2) Diaspora in the Bible: What is Behind the Diasporas?
>
> (3) Melting Pot or Salad Bowl: The Range of Changes
>
> (4) The Spiritual Opportunities: Where Christians Come In
>
> (5) Guiding Principles: Making a Difference
>
> (6) Options: Mobilizing Diaspora Communities
>
> (7) Appendices: Case Studies from the Diaspora.[35]

Here, the great benefit of the people next door is the spiritual opportunities where Christians come in; "Impacting the world without having to move; reaching unreached people groups; racial reconciliation; shaping future world leaders."[36] This new "next door" approach shifts missiological paradigm from overseas to neighboring communities in the twenty-first century global strategy.

In particular, it is noted that in discussion on Diaspora identity, it is understood as the *salad bowl* rather than the *melting pot*:

> There is no agreement on how diverse societies should live together. Different models are debated. The American ideal of society was the *Melting Pot* where everything is assimilated in the whole. For some that has been replaced by the Salad Bowl ideal in which each part contributes to the whole whilst maintaining its distinctive form and flavor. Some prioritize *Integration* while others emphasize *Multiculturalism*. Many want *Contact* but fear *Assimilation*, while others desire total *Separation*. Whatever forms the interaction may take, the result will still inevitably be change, and the changes have to be coped with.[37]

The core idea of the salad bowl is each having its own national identity and embracing others. In fact, the theory of the melting pot calls for the disappearance of his or her own self; in the theory of the salad bowl, "each part

---

34. LCWE Issue Group No. 26 A and B, "Lausanne Occasional Paper No. 55," 5.
35. Ibid., 5.
36. Ibid, 16.
37. Ibid., 13.

contributes to the whole." Here, there is no ethnocentrism moving toward discrimination.[38] Rather, each will be respected to redeem one other for the whole.

Lausanne Global Consultations for Doing Diaspora Missiology

According to Wan and Tira, its leading scholars, Diaspora missiology is a relatively new paradigm and it needs to be introduced to the global community of missiologists, mission scholars, and leaders. For this reason, the following consultations were organized in the past few years as listed below:

> (1) Filipino Diaspora and Missions Consultation held in April 2004 at Torch Trinity Graduate School of Theology in Seoul, South Korea
>
> (2) Filipino Theological Educators' Consultation held in January 2006 at Philippine Baptist Theological Seminary in Baguio City, Philippines
>
> (3) Global Diaspora Missiology Consultation held in November 2006 at Taylor University College and Seminary in Edmonton, Canada
>
> (4) The Institute of Diaspora Studies (IDS) launched in Asia and the United States. The IDS-Asia was established in April 2007 at Alliance Graduate School in Manila, Philippines
>
> (5) The IDS-USA established in May 2007 at Western Seminary in Portland, Oregon, USA.
>
> (6) Courses on Diaspora missions were offered in February 2010 at Ambrose University College in Calgary, Canada, and in April 2010 at Western Seminary.[39]

From the data, it follows that Wan and Tira are leading scholars of Diaspora missiology. The Philippines, Canada, the USA, and Korea are the pioneering countries that launched this project. In the near future, all nations will be globalized and a multitude of ethnic groups will move, leading to the emergence of multi-ethnic societies in the world.

---

38. Ethnocentrism or discrimination is rooted on ideological racism, which is defined as "an ideology that considers a group's unchangeable physical characteristics to be linked in a direct, causal way to psychological or intellectual characteristics, and that on this basis distinguish between super and inferior racial groups" (Feagin, *Racial and Ethnic Relations*, 7).

39. Wan and Tira, "Diaspora Missiology and Missions," 45–56.

Two Major Consultations

To prepare for upcoming discussion on Diasporas in Cape Town, two major consultations on Lausanne Diasporas were convened in 2009 as part of the "Road Map" to Cape Town in 2010. With this, Dr. Sadiri Joy Tira, Lausanne Senior Associate for Diasporas, said that the next step was to establish effective global evangelism strategies grounded in solid biblical and theological foundations, and moored in a strong missiological framework. To help accomplish this, the "Lausanne Diaspora Strategy Consultation" (hereafter referred to as the "Manila Consultation") was held in Manila, Philippines (May 2009); and the "Lausanne Diaspora Educators Consultation" (hereafter referred to as the "Seoul Consultation") was held in Seoul, South Korea (November 2009).[40]

Diaspora is a prominent demographic trend in a global era; global missiology is a new paradigm for twenty-first century world evangelization. However, a more important task of doing missiology is to lay its firm biblical and theological foundations. This is what the Lausanne consultations in Seoul and Manila were set to achieve.

Lausanne Diaspora Strategy Consultation: Manila Consultation

The consultation had three objectives: (A) To inform about the challenges and opportunities of ministries among diaspora groups; (B) to inspire a vision to explore new approaches to minister to these groups; and (C) to ignite a passion to mobilize the [whole] church to that end. Various professionals are involved in formulating Diaspora missiology—theologians, Bible scholars, ministry practitioners such as missionaries, evangelists, and pastors of international churches; anthropologists, sociologists, legal experts (i.e. migration lawyers), diplomats, demographers, and migration researchers. This shows how many various professionals are needed in doing Diaspora missiology. The major result of the consultation was the identification of diaspora peoples, various issues affecting diaspora peoples, and organizations, groups, and individuals who are ministering specifically with diaspora people.[41]

---

40. LCWE, "Consultations on Diaspora Missions," lines 34–40.
41. Ibid.

Lausanne Diaspora Educators Consultation: Seoul Consultation

The Torch Trinity Graduate School of Theology, a seminary in the heart of Seoul devoted to training Diaspora leaders for ministering to diaspora peoples hosted the consultation.

The objectives for this consultation were to: (A) Enhance our understanding of "Diaspora missiology" as an emerging field of study and ministry strategy; (B) engage in scholarly dialogue on "Diaspora missiology" and its educational implications; and (C) engender regional cooperation in anticipation of Cape Town 2010 where "Diaspora missiology" was to be a feature of the program. Finally, through the consultation, the LCWE decided to define Diaspora missiology: "Diaspora missiology" is defined as a "missiological framework for understanding and participating in God's redemptive mission among people living outside their place of origin."[42]

The Cape Town Lausanne (2010)

The Cape Town Declaration on "Care and Counsel as Mission" in the Cape Town 2010 documents represents the spirit of Cape Town 2010: "We live in a world of unprecedented suffering and brokenness. These human conditions include different types and levels of social and psychological suffering which are often minimized, neglected, or, because they are beyond what local people can cope with at a given time, left unattended or addressed from out-of-context perspectives."[43]

The theme of Cape Town 2010 was "care and counsel" for those who have suffering and brokenness. For this purpose, the Lausanne Movement commits itself to 10 confessions. Particularly, Part II, IIC, 5, "Living the Love of Christ among People of Other Faith of The Cape Town Commitment," proclaims, "Love reaches out to Scattered peoples," this deals the with diaspora issue:

> People are on the move as never before. Migration is one of the great global realities of our era. It is estimated that 200 million people are living outside their countries of origin, voluntarily or involuntarily. The term "Diaspora" is used here to mean people who have relocated from their lands of birth for whatever reason. Some relocate permanently, and others, like three million international students and scholars, temporarily. Vast numbers

---

42. LCWE, "Seoul Declaration on Diaspora Missiology," lines 10–13.

43. Third Lausanne Congress, "Content Library: The Cape Town Declaration," lines 7–9.

of people from many religious backgrounds, including Christians, live in Diaspora conditions: economic migrants seeking work; internally displaced peoples because of war or natural disaster; refugees and asylum seekers; victims of ethnic cleansing; people fleeing religious violence and persecution; famine sufferers—whether caused by drought, floods, or war; victims of rural poverty moving to cities. We are convinced that contemporary migrations are within the sovereign missional purpose of God, without ignoring the evil and suffering that can be involved.[44]

Here, the importance is that the Lausanne Movement recognized the existence of diaspora in global phenomena and migrations; more importantly, it confessed that "contemporary migrations are within the sovereign missional purpose of God, without ignoring the evil and suffering that can be involved." In addition, the most important recognition is that diaspora can involve "evil and suffering."

Following this, the Lausanne Movement urges three encouragements for diaspora and host Christians.

(1) Church and Christian Response to the Missional Opportunities Presented by Global Migration and Diaspora Communities

"We encourage church and mission leaders to recognize and respond to the missional opportunities presented by global migration and diaspora communities, in strategic planning, and in focused training and resourcing of those called to work among them."[45] The initial stage of church and Christians is "to recognize and respond to the missional opportunities presented by global migration and diaspora communities." We understand that diaspora *is* the missional opportunity for church and Christians.

(2) Christians in Host Nations to Bear Counter-cultural Witness to the Love of Christ in Deed and Word:

We encourage Christians in *host nations* which have immigrant communities and international students and scholars of other religious backgrounds to bear counter-cultural witness to the love of Christ in deed and word, by obeying the extensive biblical commands to love the stranger, defend the cause of the

---

44. Third Lausanne Congress, "Cape Town Commitment," lines 1–19.
45. Ibid., lines 10–12.

foreigner, visit the prisoner, practice hospitality, build friendships, invite into our homes, and provide help and services.[46] (Italics mine)

The responsibility of host churches for immigrants here is to obey "the extensive biblical commands to love the stranger, defend the cause of the foreigner, visit the prisoner, practice hospitality, build friendships, invite into our homes, and provide help and services." Here it is so important is that host churches show love, hospitality, and friendship by obeying the extensive biblical commands to love strangers and exiles. This is a critical factor of Diaspora missiology.

(3) Diaspora Christians for Bearing Witness to Christ in their Host Community and Seeking its Co-operative Efforts [Partnership] for the Gospel:

> We encourage Christians who are themselves part of *diaspora communities* to discern the hand of God, even in circumstances they may not have chosen, and to seek whatever opportunities God provides for bearing witness to Christ in their host community and seeking its welfare. Where that host country includes Christian churches, we urge *immigrant and indigenous churches* together to listen and learn from one another, and to initiate co-operative efforts to reach all sections of their nation with the gospel.[47] (Italics mine)

The encouragement here is for the diaspora community to believe in the hand of God; he or she has a mission to bear witness to Christ in their host community. Furthermore, for diaspora and host churches together to listen and learn from one another, and to work co-operative efforts to reach all areas of their nation with the gospel.

In sum, the discoveries of Diaspora missiology is summarized in the statement of the Lausanne: (1) The church and Christians should recognize and respond to the missiological opportunities given by global migration and diaspora communities; (2) Christians in host nations should bear counter-cultural witness to the love of Christ in deed and word; (3) immigrant and indigenous churches together should listen to and learn from one another, and initiate co-operative efforts with the gospel. Lausanne explained and prepared all core factors of Diaspora missiology; finally Lausanne's

46. Ibid., lines 13–17.
47. Ibid., 18–22.

endeavor of studying diaspora was produced as a small booklet, *Scattered to Gather: Embracing the Global Trend of Diaspora*. In the foreword of this book, Tetsunao Yamamori, PhD, Senior Advisor, Lausanne Committee for World Evangelization, states,

> I feel privileged to commend this booklet, *Scattered to Gather: Embracing the Global Trend of Diaspora*, as a tool for the churches and ministries represented by the participants of Cape Town 2010 (the Third Lausanne Congress on World Evangelization), to proclaim the gospel and, by the grace of God, engage in effective evangelism to gather the scattered into the fold of the redeemed.[48]

Finally, Diaspora theologizing for mission by the Lausanne has taken up an enterprising leadership toward a new paradigm for twenty-first century mission; it focuses on exploring implications of globalization theory. In his title, *The New Catholicity: Theology between the Global and the Local*, Schreiter argues, "we bring globalization theory itself into closer dialogue with theology by finding concepts in theology that globalization can inform but not determine. His assertion is that "theology must be able to interact with globalization theory out of its own internal history and resources and not be simply reactive to it";[49] for him, the theological response to the challenge of globalization is the concept of catholicity. He says:

> A renewed and expanded concept of catholicity may well serve as a theological response to the challenge of globalization. It can provide a theological framework out of which the church might understand itself and its mission under changed circumstances. Faced with the diversity of cultures and the implications of taking them seriously, and the challenge of maintaining the unity and integrity of the church worldwide, the eschatological sense of catholicity, so important to the orthodox and many Protestant churches, and reaffirmed by Roman Catholics at the Second Vatican council, takes on new salience at the interface of the global and the local. This is echoed in some reflections on catholicity: Avery Dulles speaks of catholicity as the ability to hold things together in tension with one another; Peter Schineller speaks of it as tentativeness, anticipating the whole.[50]

---

48. LCWE, *Scattered to Gather*, 3.
49. Schreiter, *New Catholicity*, 118.
50. Ibid., 127–28.

Schreiter defines catholicity as "wholeness and fullness through exchange and communication." First, "wholeness" refers to the physical extension of the church throughout the world; second, "fullness," to orthodoxy in faith. Third, "through exchange and communication" corresponds to the mode of universality in a globalization era.

Therefore, in a globalization era, there is exchange and communication between local churches, contributing to the rediscovery of truth scattered in the world. Schreiter's explanations of theological implications for globalization are applied to form Diaspora missiology. To put it in Schreiter's terms, it needs more "wholeness and fullness through exchange and communication." Thus, Diaspora missiology helps world Christianity to find the truth scattered in the world, contributing to the accomplishment of wholeness and fullness through exchange and communication.

THEORIZING DIASPORA, AND THE BIAM AND CLSC

Lausanne is a main subject in forming Diaspora missiology; yet two organizations—BIAM and CLSC—need to be introduced regarding theorizing diaspora in different situations and settings.

Mission and Migration: Papers Read at the Biennial Conference of British and Irish Association for Mission Studies (BIAMS) at Westminster College, Cambridge.

The BIAMS (British and Irish Association of Mission Studies) was formed in 1989 by a group of churches and agencies. The BIAMS explains its aim:

> It aims to promote the study of mission in its history, theory, and practice. BIAMS also provides a forum for dialogue for enrichment and collaboration in mission. To this end, BIAMS holds conferences, provides interest groups, and circulates a newsletter twice a year. Their website offers a free email discussion forum which facilitates the communication of news and information that may be of interest to scholars, students, and practitioners of mission.[51]

Also, on July 2–5, 2007, pivoting on mission and migration, the BIAMS at Westminster College, Cambridge, presented papers at the Biennial Conference. In its beginning, Spencer, editor of this volume, explains the

---

51. BIAMS, "Day Conference 2012: Marginalization," lines 1–5.

intent "not to resolve issues or provide answers but to establish territory, to raise questions, to lay out some items for the agenda," by addressing "the actual experience of migrants, strangers, aliens—their joys and pains, their trials and discoveries, the heart's aches and the heart's ease," and it states that these experiences "should not be forgotten."[52] The twelve contributors to the conference are Rebecca Cato, Timothy Gorringe, Gerrie ter Haar, Janice McLean, Philomena Mwaura, Tim Naish, Nicholas Sagocsky, Israel Selvanayagam, Susanna Snyder, Stephen Spencer, Thomas Whelan and Emma Wild-Wood.

This conference showed its aim: "in the last few decades, Christianity around the world has been given a new impulse by migration across continents and within continents. Many of these immigrants have founded new churches wherever they have settled, notably Christians from Sub-Saharan Africa. All of this reflects a new phase in church history. This volume of essays provides timely and penetrating analysis of this phenomenon."[53] This conference dealt mainly with Christians from Sub-Saharan Africa, Sub-Saharan Christian Diaspora; Diaspora mission "reflects a new phase in church history," leading to the significance of the global South.

More importantly, these papers contribute to studies on the root of biblical and missiological perspectives that seek to understand situations in the light of the migration . . . these papers contribute to forming Diaspora missiology by virtue of biblical and theological foundations of migration. On Tuesday, October 2, 2012, for example, the BIAMS offered a day conference at Redcliffe College; its topics were "Marginalisation and the Reign of God": issues and questions from the perspectives of biblical studies, mission studies, and theology. In addition, it is worthy of noting the theology of the mission, confessed by the BIAMS:

> The New Testament places the ministry and preaching of Jesus among those who are on the margins of both religious and civil society. It is here that the Reign of God seems to be located. Through his embrace of the marginalised, Jesus showed that they are at the heart of God's concern. The church, by doing the same, gives living expression to / incarnates what Jesus did. In following the example of Jesus, the church also bears witness to what the Reign of God, in its fullness, is all about . . . In serving the *Missio Dei*, should the church be known for its work with those on the margins, as well as for living in solidarity with them? This Conference will explore the many issues and

---

52. Spencer, *Mission and Migration*, 7–8.
53. BIAMS, "Day Conference 2012: Marginalization," lines 13–16.

questions that arise from perspectives of biblical studies, mission studies and theology.[54]

Both marginalization and the reign of God call for Diaspora mission; it challenges Christians to answer this question: "In serving the *Missio Dei*, should the church be known for its work with those on the margins, as well as for living in solidarity with them?"[55] This is a major conviction of Diaspora mission, connecting *Missio Dei*, the church, and the marginalized diasporas.

In sum, in Europe, the BIAMS has been in the process of doing Diaspora missiology. This represents the concept of *Missio Dei*, church, and diaspora as marginal; in a word, Diaspora mission in the BIAMS can be called the "embrace of the marginalized." Embracing the marginalized is the core value of Diaspora mission, which serves as a key concept for doing diaspora theologizing for mission.

CLSC: A Promised Land, a Perilous Journey

In 2008, Daniel Groody, Director of the Center for Latino Spirituality and Culture, explored the phenomenon of migration and its theological meanings and edited a book with seventeen contributors. The description on Amazon.com introduces the book: "A Christian theological interpretation of the border reality is a neglected area of immigration study. The foremost contribution of *A Promised Land, A Perilous Journey* is its focus on the theological dimension of migration, beginning with the humanity of the immigrant, a child of God and a bearer of his image."[56]

Daniel Groody is managing the Center for Latino Spirituality and Culture (CLSC), University of Norte Dame, established "to increase awareness of the growing importance of Latinos to the US Catholic Church, to engage Latino Catholic leaders in dialogue with the broader Catholic community, and to facilitate the development of the next generation of Latino religious leaders."[57]

Furthermore, the CLSC regularly opens international conferences to raise awareness of issues of Latino spirituality, including "The Option for the Poor" (2002), "Migration and Theology" (2004), and "Guadalupe,

---

54. Ibid.
55. Ott, "Conclusion," 327.
56. Amazon.com, "Book Description of *A Promised Land*," lines 1–3.
57. Institute for Latino Studies, "Center for Latino Spirituality and Culture," lines 1–5.

Madre de America" (2006). Diaspora issues in *A Promised Land, A Perilous Journey* are related to theological evaluations of migrations. In particular, he proposes four theological frameworks for immigrants: (1) every immigrant has *Imago Dei*, which should be restored, (2) the reconciliation of One Body, forgiveness should be applied to immigrants, (3) *Missio Dei*, the redemptive work of Jesus Christ should be applied to everyone without discrimination, and (4) *Visio Dei*, the vision of God's kingdom should be realized without borders.[58] It is valuable that Groody understands immigrant diaspora as a subject of theological dimensions.

In particular, Peter Phan's study of diaspora in terms of the biblical usages is helpful to understand who is diaspora. According to Peter Phan, Christian Diaspora of the early church were identified by three names: strangers (Greek, *kenos*), foreigners (Greek, *allotrios*), and sojourner (Greek, *paroikos*). Here, *paroikoi* is translated as exiles, meaning pilgrims, which was addressed in Peter 1:1.[59] They understand themselves as pilgrims, focusing on heaven and ignoring things of earth. Donald Senior argued that Christian evangelists belong to diaspora scattered around the world.[60]

Finally, the remarkable note here is a new awareness of the relationship between immigrant diasporas and the American church. The CLSC notes:

> The rapid growth of the Latino population over the past 30 years has created a fundamental shift in the makeup of the US Catholic Church. Studies show that while only 12 percent of US Catholics were Latino in 1970, today that number is estimated by US Catholic bishops at 40 percent. . . . These trends make it imperative for the Church and Catholic institutions like Notre Dame to understand and adapt to *their changing constituencies so that they may draw from the strengths and contributions of the Latino community*.[61] (Italics mine)

To consider the statement above, now host churches should pay attention to *"their changing constituencies."* Why? So that *"they may draw from the strengths and contributions of the [diaspora] community."* This phenomenon is the reality today; we cannot ignore or avoid it. That is, building the partnership between the host nations and the hosted diaspora is only the way to get through the future; there is not one in the world that can avoid this phenomenon.

---

58. Groody and Campese, *Promised Land*, 304–5.
59. Phan, "Migration in the Patristic Era," 48–49.
60. Senior, "Beloved Aliens and Exile," 24.
61. Ibid.

THEORIZING DIASPORA: ANDREW WALLS AND JEHU HANCILES

Andrew Walls

Andrew Walls is one of the pioneering experts of theorizing Diaspora. In 1991, Walls suggested and identified six historical phases regarding the development of Christianity:

1. The Jewish age, marked by *Jewish* practices and ideas.
2. The Hellenistic-Roman age, marked by the idea of *orthodox*.
3. The Barbarian age, marked by the idea of a *Christian nation*.
4. The Western European age, marked by the primacy of the *individual*.
5. The age of expanding Europe and Christian recession, marked by *cross-cultural transplantation* but also accompanied by massive recession from the faith among European peoples.
6. The Southern age, *featuring extensive penetration of new culture* in Africa, Latin America, the Pacific, and parts of Asia.[62]

Here the importance is that the final phase of Christianity is the Southern age, including Africa, Latin America, the Pacific, and parts of Asia. According to Jehu's analysis, "Walls's theory of Christianity's serial expansion implicitly points to the central role of human migration in the faith's global spread."[63] For Walls, migration and mission is a key concept for global spread of the gospel. First, through the Western missionary agents, the gospel was spread around non-Western world; in return, since 1960, in the global era, there was non-Western migration to Western America and the EU. His strong argument is that "the process of transmission no longer takes place necessarily from the Western intellectual's discourse. It is multicultural in its personnel; it will be increasing in multicultural expression and application."[64]

Faith and Leadership, an offering of Leadership Education at Duke University, "Andrew Walls has been described as 'the most important person you've never heard of.' Although the incredible growth of the non-Western church is now a recognized phenomenon, Walls was one of the first to realize, while working in Africa in the 1960s, that the global church was not just an inferior imitation of the "standard" Christian church but rather

---

62. Walls, "Christianity," 58–73.
63. Jehu, "Migration and the Globalization," 228.
64. Walls, *Missionary Movement*, xix.

a vital community of its own and indeed a new center of vitality."[65] His final remark is about servantshood: "I hadn't thought of it in these terms before—but yes—that make the translator, with the two sets of constraints—put on by the source language and the receptor language—a servant in very literal form."[66] Really, he realized the immigrant as diaspora in relation to mission and paved the way for Diaspora missiology.

Jehu Hanciles

Biblical Perspective of Dispersion

In his "Migration, Diaspora Communities, and the New Missionary Encounter with Western Society," Hanciles describes the biblical foundation of Diaspora as the unfolding of salvation history: "The biblical record . . . reveals a profound interconnection between human mobility or dispersion and the unfolding of salvation history. The same link is manifest throughout the history of Christian missions."[67] His significant finding concerning diaspora is that human mobility and dispersion is pivotal to the unfolding of salvation history. It shows how essential diaspora studies are to understanding God's redemptive plan.

The Southern Migration toward the Western World

Jehu argued that with the end of European colonialism, international migrations have escalated in volume, velocity, and complexity, and have transformed into a truly global phenomenon. According to him, the earlier flows with European initiatives and economic priorities, and was replaced by "a far more complex pattern of migration involving vastly greater non-European or non-white migrations from the developing and under-developed, non-Western world to the Western world—generally considered South-to-North flows";[68] "by the 1980s, Africa, Latin America, the Caribbean, and Asia had become net exporters of millions of people to Western countries, initially as labor migrants, subsequently as asylum seekers, but increasingly and predominantly as economic migrants. By 2000, non-Western migrants

---

65. Walls, "Andrew Walls: An Exciting Period," lines 1–5.
66. Ibid.
67. Hanciles, "Migration, Diaspora Communities," lines 1–4.
68. Ibid., lines 13–16.

accounted for seventy percent of immigrants into most wealthy developed nations in Europe and North America."[69]

The West as a New Missionary Frontier

For Jehu, another finding is to see the West differently from traditional scholars; he proclaims that the West is a new missionary frontier. Here is his challenging remark:

> It is a most extraordinary historical coincidence that the momentous "shift" in global Christianity's demographic and cultural center of gravity to the southern continents has occurred at almost precisely the same time as the equally momentous reversal in the direction of international migrations. *This means that, as in the previous five centuries, the continents which represent the chief sources of global migration movement are also now the main heartlands of the Christian faith.*[70]

Jehu suggests new perspectives about America and the EU. Firstly, immigrants' distinctive expressions of faith and ways of doing church, adapted to the new context of the USA, have contributed to a "de-Europeanizing of American Christianity"; secondly, in the EU, where Islam represents Europe's fastest growing religion and its second largest faith, Europe's new immigrants—a huge number of Christians—have contributed to an explosive growth in the numbers of churches.[71] This remark represents the realty of Western Christianity and churches.

Toward the "Real" Global Christianity beyond Walls's and Hanciles's Visions

From the 1960s, Walls has heralded the coming of Southern centrality in global Christianity; through the data of migration statistics, Jehu also reported the age of mobile faith centered on Southern Christianity. Nobody can ignore the prophecies and arguments of both scholars that the Southern will be a new center of global Christianity; the West can be a new missionary field. However, moving beyond the arguments of both scholars, we can suggest and consider three issues:

69. Ibid., lines 17–20.
70. Ibid., lines 29–33.
71. Ibid.

(1) Issues of Southern Contextual Theology for the Northern

If the West is the mission field, the South is the missionary church for the Western church, and the crucial question arises: How does the South contextualize the West to communicate to the West? This means that in the past, as the West tried to contextualize the gospel to the non-West, the South should contextualize the gospel in the West. The spirit of contextualization is to respect and inculturalize the culture in which the gospel is communicated. In fact, generally, immigrant churches in the West are limited to ethnic groups and identity, how do immigrant churches contextualize the West?

Here, the question is this: Have the Southern ever practiced contextual theology to communicate with the Northern? Or have the Southern been ready for inculturalizing the Western culture for the effective communication of the gospel? We worry about the future of global Christianity in which the Southern would be its center. Why? So far, the Southern continues to demand something from the West and has not tried to give something to them. This will harm a real development of global Christianity because real global Christianity is based on reciprocity or mutual give-and-take.

(2) Ministry Issue of non-Western Immigrant Churches for Western White Churches

As mentioned earlier, non-Western immigrant churches are almost all ethnic ones; how will they involve the life and faith of the Western? If immigrant churches are enclaved by their ethnicities, how can they be like "yeast that is mixed into a large amount of flour" in the world? (see Matt 13:33)

If we the Sothern are a new center of global Christianity, it is time that we the Southern start to talk about how we can be its center. Unfortunately, there have been no more detailed discussions about an agenda of the Southern to become a new center of global Christianity.

(3) The South and the West as Global Partners

In the colonial era, the West dominated the non-Western. In an anti-colonial era, the West has been under attack from the entire Southern world. In the global era, how should the relation be between the South and the West? Paul Hiebert answers this crucial question by describing the spirit of the global era as "hard love," "metaculturalism," and "complementarity," which can be called to be partnership.⁷² In fact, human beings cannot be a center; the only center of global Christianity is Jesus Christ. We all are partners for his kingdom.

This age is in crisis for the whole of Christianity; look at the many wars, terrors, and dying refugees in Africa; look at the declining churches becoming secularized and the fastest growing religion of Islam in the EU; look at the humanistic and secularized prosperity theology in the USA; and look at other religions—Hindu, Islam, Buddhism, and Judaism in the whole of Asia. Can the South be qualified as the center of global Christianity? Or can the West be its center? No we all are just partners for Jesus Christ. We all—the South and the West—prepare for world mission. The reason the South immigrates into the West is not to be the center of global Christianity, but to be partners with the West for God's kingdom in his time. The awareness of the South and the West is to hear the voice of one calling, pointing to the great discoveries of "all people" in Diaspora mission.

> Isaiah 40: 3A voice of one calling:
> "In the wilderness prepare
> the way for the Lord;
> Make straight in the desert
> a highway for our God.
> 4Every valley shall be raised up,
> every mountain and hill made low;
> The rough ground shall become level,
> the rugged places a plain.
> 5And the glory of the Lord will be revealed,
> and all people will see it together.
> For the mouth of the Lord has spoken."
> 6A voice says, "Cry out."
> And I said, "What shall I cry?"
> "All people are like grass,
> and all their faithfulness is like the flowers of the field.
> 7The grass withers and the flowers fall,
> because the breath of the Lord blows on them.
> Surely the people are grass.
> 8The grass withers and the flowers fall,
> but the word of our God endures forever."

---

72. Hiebert, *Anthropological Reflections*, 63–73.

3

Interdisciplinary Understandings of Diaspora

Diaspora is a product of complex globalization as interactions of a variety of cultures. This is why we study diaspora an interdisciplinary fashion. Diaspora is in the middle of global phenomenon. Generally, anthropology, demography, psychology, social science, political science, and so on were interested in diaspora. The understanding of diaspora calls for interdisciplinary knowledge and perspectives because diaspora is the product of globalization as interactions of different forms. An interdisciplinary approach is based on our concern to better understand diaspora in a complex situation. However, it is noted that these interdisciplinary understandings should be interconnected with the teaching of the Bible and theology to not lose its right path.

ANTHROPOLOGY

Diaspora: Ethnic Enclave

There has been much research about diaspora from anthropology. In 1963, Nathan Glazer and Patrick Moynihan published their book *Beyond the Melting Pot*, which called American assimilation metaphor into question. A study of ethnicity maintenance and ethnic enclaves in some ways helped to initiate the study of ethnicity maintenance among "white" ethnic groups. In 1969, Fredrik Barth's concept of diaspora tried to change the path of the study. He published the book *Ethnic Groups and Boundaries: The Social Organization of Cultural Difference*; he observed that "The critical focus of investigation . . . becomes the ethnic boundary that defines the group, not the cultural stuff that it encloses."[1]

In 1974, Cohen's *Urban Ethnicity* was published with contributions from several others who were doing research on immigration, urbanization, ethnicity maintenance, and identity transformation.[2] To him, ethnicity is just a useful heuristic concept tailored to make sense of particular, historically delineated processes such as urbanization in Africa, and it is the processes whereby "some interest groups exploit parts of their traditional culture in order to articulate informal organizational functions that are used in the struggle of these groups for power."[3] For him, ethnicity "involves a dynamic rearrangement of relations and of customs and is not the result of cultural conservatism or continuity."[4]

From anthropology, diaspora is an "ethnic enclave," which means any isolation from a broad context of the society; diaspora has ethnic boundaries apart from other ethnic groups. At the same time, diaspora as ethnicity is a heuristic concept, exploited by interest groups. It is essential that Diaspora missiology understand ethnic boundaries and relations to other groups.

Transnational Ties

Diasporas move outside of their own country, live in a foreign country, and become surrounded by a different culture but not assimilated to it. Diaspora have a transnational culture with their homeland country. With regard to diaspora culture, the Parliamentary Assembly of the EU states:

> Diaspora cultures exist as a result of the dispersion of communities throughout the world; this dispersion is often forced or has historical reasons. Diaspora communities represent and maintain a culture different from those of the countries within which they are located, often retaining strong ties with their country and culture of origin (real or perceived) and with other communities of the same origin in order to preserve that culture. This is an essentially cultural phenomenon and is not necessarily linked to migration.[5]

1. Barth, "Introduction," 9–38.
2. Cohen, *Urban Ethnicity*.
3. Cohen, *Two-Dimensional Man*, 91.
4. Ibid., 97.
5. Council of Europe, "Recommendation: Diaspora Cultures," lines 1–3. This text

In addition, however, this report describes little consideration of diaspora and relations with their country of origin. While much attention has been paid to the situation of migrant communities and their relations with their host countries, relatively little consideration has been given to the relations between each community and its country of origin. The Assembly recalls in this context its earlier Recommendations 1410 (1998) and 1650 (2004) on the links between Europeans living abroad and their countries of origin. A more dynamic policy is, however, necessary to promote the cultures of diaspora communities.[6]

In the anthropological circle, diasporas and transnationalism are intimately related. Ethnic diasporas have been called "the exemplary communities of the transnational moment."[7] According to Vertovec, the meaning of transnationalism has to do with a kind of social formation spanning borders, which have become the paradigm in this understanding of transnationalism. Diasporas have become today's "transnational communities," sustained by a range of modes of social organization, mobility, and communication.[8] The study of diaspora considers the aspects of transnational ties because diaspora has a strong commitment to homeland.

Cultural Identities

What is the cultural identity of diaspora? With regard to cultural identity, in *Identity, Language and Culture in Diaspora*, Maryam Jamarani deals with "diasporic identities" and suggests a new paradigm in which "becoming" rather than "being" is emphasized. She investigates changes in the identity of first generation Iranian Muslim women in Australia. Her interest lies in what affects this distinctive experience had on the linguistic, cultural, national, gender, and religious identity of diaspora within this grouping. Her aim is to identify the core values that these women continue to hold after migration.[9] Furthermore, she came to engage with contemporary theories of acculturation, and enhanced acculturation models, emphasizing the significance of the fluid and flexible nature of identity, which holds out

---

was adopted by the Standing Committee, acting on behalf of the Assembly on 23 November 2004 (see Doc. 10342, report of the Committee on Culture, Science and Education, rapporteur: Ms. Petrova-Mitevska).

6. Council of Europe, "Recommendation: Diaspora Cultures," lines 13–15.

7. Tololyan, "Nation-State and Its Others," 3–7.

8. Vertovec, "Conceiving and Researching Transnationalism," 449. Also refer to Vertovec, "Transnationalism and Identity"; and Vertovec, "Introduction: New Directions."

9. Jamarani, *Identity, Language and Culture.*

the promise of shedding new light on the acculturation process of migrants in general. This means that diaspora identity is not subjected to the host country only.

In *Cultural Identity and Diaspora*, Hall also argues that diasporic identity is based upon difference and hybridity. He rejects solely imperialist and hegemonizing forms of ethnicity.[10] Hall points out that there are two principal ways of thinking about (cultural) identity: "The traditional model views identity in terms of one, shared culture, a sort of collective 'one true self,' hiding inside them any other, more superficial or artificially imposed selves, which people with a shared history and ancestry hold in common."[11]

After describing the traditional view of identity based on one, shared culture, a sort of collective "one true self," he suggests a new way to explain the second model of the identity:

> The second model of (cultural) identity (which Hall favors) acknowledges the "critical points" of deep and significant difference which constitute "what we really are"; or rather—since history has intervened—"what we have become." From this point of view, cultural identity is a matter of "becoming" as well as of "being." It belongs to the future as much as to the past. It is not something which already exists, transcending place, time, history and culture. Cultural identities come from somewhere, have histories. But like everything which is historical, they undergo constant transformation. Far from being eternally fixed in some essentialised past, they are subject to the continuous "play" of history, culture and power.[12]

In a word, the cultural identity of diaspora is not being but becoming; it does not belong to the past, but the future. This is very essential for the identity of diaspora. We do not focus on the past, but the future, "the continuous 'play' of history, culture, and power." We see the flexibility of diaspora identity beyond fixed national identity. This type of identity has openness to different others. His view of diaspora identity represents a global and multicultural one, which should be applied to the redefinition of diaspora today.

---

10. Hall, "Cultural Identity and Diaspora," 401.
11. Ibid., 393.
12. Ibid., 394.

PSYCHOLOGY

Cultural Psychology of Immigrants: Culture Shock

Psychology plays a key role to serve as a lens for understanding diaspora in the context of cultural shock. In *Cultural Psychology of Immigrants*, Mahalingam explains the influence that transnational ties and cultural practices and beliefs have on creating the immigrant self through an interdisciplinary perspective on how intersections of race, class, gender, sexuality, and culture shape the cultural psychology of immigrants.[13] For example, Koreans still remain in Korean-ness after immigration. This is a key issue to analyze in the psychology of diaspora.

The essential issue in the cultural psychology of immigrants is cultural shock. As Hiebert puts it,

> Life in foreign culture leads to misunderstanding and ethnocentric response and also cultural shock ... the shock does not come from sights of poverty or lack of sanitation but stems rather from the fact that those in an unfamiliar culture do not know the language or even the simplest role of social behavior.[14]

Historically, it was Karl Oberg that first used the term "culture shock" to describe the difficulties people experienced as they adjusted to their new lives in foreign area.[15] For Oberg, culture shock is a mental illness that can be "cured" only when you accept that the new culture is just another way of living. So, anthropologist Dutton says, "in essence, you are either mad or you accept cultural relativism. Dismissing intellectual opponents as mad is, of course, a well-known tactic of some less than savory political regimes."[16] Without adaptation, people are prone to anxiety and frustration, which can lead to physical ailments. It is noted that cultural shock can lead to aggression. It follows, as Oberg argues, that people become aggressive, they band together with fellow countrymen and criticize the host country, its ways, and its people.[17]

In particular, the language problem and its stress in immigrant diaspora is a huge issue in cultural shock. It also is shown in the statement that

---

13. Mahalingam, *Cultural Psychology of Immigrants*. Also refer to Berry, "Psychology of Immigration," 615–31.

14. Hiebert, *Cultural Anthropology*, 39.

15. Oberg, "Culture Shock."

16. Dutton, *Culture Shock and Multiculturalism*. Dr. Edward Dutton is an anthropologist and journalist.

17. Oberg, "Culture Shock."

"culture shock subsides as students gain proficiency in the new language, become more familiar with their environment, and achieve greater success in their intercultural interactions."[18] This shows how the language issue plays a key role in forming cultural shock; cultural shock results in depression, frustration, and anger in diaspora mentality and life.

Collective Trauma in Diaspora

Cohen argued that diasporas have a collective trauma, banishment into exile and a heart-aching longing to return home.[19] Traumatic events shared by an entire society can bring up collective sentiment, often demanding a shift in the group's culture and mass actions. Diaspora itself expresses "a collective trauma" the context of which should be the starting point for understanding diaspora. In *Trauma and Human Existence*, Robert D. Stolorow describes:

> I characterized the essence of emotional trauma as a shattering of what is called by *the absolutisms of everyday life*—the illusory beliefs that allow us to experience the world as stable, predictable, and safe. The shattering of these illusions by trauma brings us face to face with our finiteness and our existential vulnerability and with death and loss as possibilities that define our existence and that loom as constant threats.[20]

The concept of collective trauma was introduced by Algerian psychiatrist Frantz Omar Fanon, who had already published his first analysis of the effects of racism and colonization, *Black Skin, White Masks* (*BSWM*). Regarding *BSWM*, the scholarly blog Postcolonial Studies @ Emory states:

> *BSWM* is part manifesto, part analysis; it both presents Fanon's personal experience as a black intellectual in a whitened world and elaborates the ways in which the colonizer/colonized relationship is normalized as psychology. Because of his schooling and cultural background, the young Fanon conceived of himself as French, and the disorientation he felt after his initial encounter with French racism decisively shaped his psychological theories about culture. Fanon inflects his medical and psychological practice with the understanding that racism generates harmful psychological constructs that both blind the black man to his subjection to a universalized white norm and alienate his

---

18. Tannen and Alatis, *Linguistics, Languages, and the Real World*, ix.
19. Cohen, *Global Diasporas*.
20. Stolorow, "Feeling, Relating, Existing on Emotion," lines 9–14.

consciousness. A racist culture prohibits psychological health in the black man.[21]

Here, one of Fanon's essential discoveries is that specific culture is normalized in psychology. According to his discovery, racial culture generates harmful psychological constructs that both blind the black man to his subjection to a universalized white norm and alienate his consciousness. In relationship to the host country, diaspora as foreigners experience the feeling of the colonizer/colonized relationship, leading to harmful psychological constructs. In particular, for Fanon, being colonized by a language, to quote from his remark, has huge implications for one's consciousness:

> To speak . . . means above all to assume a culture, to support the weight of a civilization" (17–18). Speaking French means that one accepts, or is coerced into accepting, the collective consciousness of the French, which identifies blackness with evil and sin. In an attempt to escape the association of blackness with evil, the black man dons a white mask, or thinks of himself as a universal subject equally participating in a society that advocates equality supposedly abstracted from personal appearance. Cultural values are internalized, or "epidermalized" into consciousness, creating a fundamental disjuncture between the black man's consciousness and his body. Under these conditions, the black man is necessarily alienated from himself.[22]

For Fanon, speaking a certain language means that one accepts, or is coerced into accepting, the collective consciousness of a certain nation, which identifies others with evil and sin; this comes to alienation from himself. Isolation from one's real self takes place in the life of diaspora. In the foreign culture of the host country, diaspora experience this same experience as Fanon describes regarding the language problem.

Inbom Choi, a fellow at the Institute for International Economics in Korea, describes the essential life of diaspora as a collective trauma. Eventually, however, the meaning of diaspora changed to become quite negative, to describe a forced dispersion of people out of their homeland to their countries of exile. For some groups, such as Africans, Armenians, Jews, and Palestinians, the expression acquired an even more negative and brutal meaning. For them, the word "diaspora" signified a collective trauma and banishment to live in exile against their will. The most famous such trauma,

---

21. Fanon, "Postcolonial Studies," lines 8–13.
22. Ibid., lines 14–20.

of course, is that of Jews.²³ In fact, so closely did the word "diaspora" become associated with the fate of Jews and the biblical use that usually when it is written with a capital "D," the Diaspora means "the settling of scattered colonies of Jews outside of Palestine after the Babylonian exile, or Jews living outside Palestine or modern Israel."²⁴ This is a very narrow definition of a diaspora. A little broader meaning is the dispersion of Christians isolated from their own communion and scattered across the Roman Empire before it adopted Christianity as the state religion. These definitions associated with Jews and early Christians form the classical concept of a Diaspora.

Most importantly, a collective trauma is accompanied by a physiological or emotional affect. With the development of brain scan technology, scientists can observe and examine the brain in action, which reveals that trauma actually changes the structure and function of the brain, and a "significant finding is that brain scans of people with relationship or developmental problems, learning problems, and social problems related to emotional intelligence reveal similar structural and functional irregularities as is the case resulting from PTSD (Post-Traumatic Stress Disorder)."²⁵

What then is emotional and psychological trauma? According to *Helpguide.Com*, emotional and psychological trauma is:

> The result of extraordinarily stressful events that shatter your sense of security, making you feel helpless and vulnerable in a dangerous world. Traumatic experiences often involve a threat to life or safety, but any situation that leaves you feeling overwhelmed and alone can be traumatic, even if it doesn't involve physical harm.²⁶

From the above statement it follows that the psychology of diaspora is described as stressful, helpless, overwhelmed, alone, and frightened. What then is collective trauma in a social sense? Collective trauma, first of all, impairs social bonds and community. According to sociologist Kai Erikson, it is a "blow to the basic tissues of social life that damages the bonds

---

23. Choi, "Korean Diaspora in the Making," 10.

24. Ibid.

25. Robinson et al, eds., "Emotional and Psychological Trauma," lines 1–5. This article appears on *HelpGuide.org*, in collaboration with Harvard Health Publications, the consumer health publishing division of Harvard Medical School.

26. Ibid., lines 25–27. *HelpGuide.org* explains six causes of emotional or psychological trauma. That is, an event will most likely lead to emotional or psychological trauma if. (1) It happened unexpectedly; (2) You were unprepared for it; (3) You felt powerless to prevent it; (4) It happened repeatedly; (5) Someone was intentionally cruel; and (6) It happened in childhood.

attaching people together and impairs the prevailing sense of community,"[27] which occurs in the form of a natural or human-made disaster, or discrete or chronic social disorder. Diaspora missiology fully understands psychological aspects of diaspora. This pain is like that of Job who was in despair and anger before God and his friends in the Bible.

Violent Behavior as Collective Trauma

Ethnic groups may conflict with others when contacting other ethnics. Conflicts come from relations of cultural, social, and ethnic structure and class. However, we do not lose its transnational root. For example, the Korean Diaspora is known to have conflict and divisions; why does this conflict happen severely? Jung Hwan Back, a reporter of *Korea Daily*, conducted interviews after a shooting tragedy at Oikos University, writing, "observing killing relatives, hostages . . . among Korean Americans, what happens to the Korean American society? Seeing this incident, it's not just an individual problem,"[28] said Dong Kim, publisher of the Korean-language weekly *Hyundai News USA* and long-time Oakland resident, who feels this latest shooting incident among Korean Americans highlights potentially deeper problems within the community. Jung continues:

> Pointing to increasingly *common reports out of South Korea* about the often violent bullying that occurs there, sometimes driving victims to suicide, Dong says such bullying "doesn't only happen in schools.[29] (Italics mine).

The reports of the media suggest that the "international ties" of immigrant Koreans is essential to understand their conflict and struggle; "This incident is a sad self-image of immigrant Korean society who dreamed the 'American dream.'"[30] Here the "American dream" is characterized by two characteristics: high education and economic success. These contribute to a core psyche of immigrant Koreans, the "American Dream," emphasizing high education and economic success, which are the major characteristics of *yangbanization*, the popular philosophy of all Koreans.[31]

According to *The Psychology of Attacks and Attackers* by Arieahn Matamonasa-Bennett, assistant professor DePaul University, Chicago, "Violent

27. Erickson, *New Species of Trouble*, 223.
28. Back, "Shooting Tragedy of Oikos University."
29. Lee, "*Oakland Shooting Rampage*."
30. Kang-Lee, "Killing of 7 Students."
31. Lett, *In Pursuit of Status*.

behavior is the result of a situation or combination of situations that create a perceived threat to a person or group and a response to that threat that involves egocentric, dichotomous (e.g. black or white, good or evil) and distorted thinking.";[32] it comes from everyday frustrations in our lives.[33] In societies, violence is continually reaffirmed "as the only possible solution" to conflict.[34] Thus, experiencing the failure and frustration of *yangbanization*, leading to the eruption of *han* and the psyche of attacker in a foreign nation, Korean diaspora have a tendency toward aggressive violence.

SOCIO-ECONOMICS

Sociology of Diaspora

In 2007, Ajaya Kumar Sahoo and Brij Maharaj edited *Sociology of Diaspora: A Reader*, which is a comprehensive collection of essays. This provides various answers by focusing on various themes—immigration, transnationalism, ethnicity, identity, religion, politics, citizenship, gender, sexuality, and hybridity. These themes comprise the domain of diaspora studies. This book suggests answers on why diaspora has attracted scholarly interest recently; who are the principal protagonists who have made important contributions to the field?

In particular, the concept of "transnationalism online" sheds light on the ways in which information and communication technology in the homeland and the host land functions as both a catalyst and indicator of contemporary socio-cultural change. It engages with theoretical and methodological debates regarding the shaping and transforming of migrant culture in emerging sites of sociality, including issues such as religion, citizenship, nationalism, and region as they relate to diaspora identity in global, transnational contexts.

Recent diaspora study examines issues pertaining to the political, economic, religious, social, and cultural grounding of diaspora experience in the context of postcolonial global inequality and limited citizenship. Due to this, diaspora become a major issue of sociology. In his class "Diaspora, Hegemony and Cultural Identity" for the Summer 2012 Graduate Program in Sociology, Rina Cohen, York University Faculty of Graduate Studies, argued:

---

32. Matamonasa-Bennett, "Psychology of Attacks and Attackers," lines 18–20.
33. Beck, *Prisoners of Hate*.
34. Remington, "Lars and the Real Girl," 1.

Contemporary globalization and postcolonial migration processes result in the emergence of dynamic transnational communities which both maintain lively connections to home societies and other satellite, co-ethnic communities while, at the same time, engage the places of settlement in mutually transformative ways. This course will develop understanding of international migration, transnationalism, and diaspora as both a cause and a consequence of globalization.[35]

This implies that diaspora study is the relationship between global and local sociology, which is one area of major sociology, and it involves "international migration," "transnationalism," and "a cause and a consequence of globalization."

The Spirit of Neo-liberal Capitalism

Generally, neo-liberalism is a product of globalization, and at the same time the reverse is true. Above all, diaspora is in the context of globalized world economy—neo-liberal capitalism. In his article "Globalization and Neo-liberalism," David M. Kotz, Department of Economics and Political Economy Research Institute, Thompson Hall, University of Massachusetts, argues that the progress of globalization speeds up the movement of people through global economy. He explains:

> The process of globalization, which had been reversed to some extent by political and economic events in the interwar period, resumed right after World War II, producing a significantly more globalized world economy and eroding the monopoly power of large corporations well before neo-liberalism began its second coming in the mid-1970s. . . . On the other hand, once neo-liberalism became dominant, it accelerated the process of globalization. This can be seen most clearly in the data on cross-border flows of both real and financial capital, which began to grow rapidly only after the 1960s.[36]

According to Kotz's analysis, neo-liberalism is the product of globalization; at the same time, "once neo-liberalism became dominant, it accelerated the process of globalization." Neo-liberalism accelerates the speed of migration. This feature of neo-liberalism becomes the background of migration, which has accelerated the move of people and migration. Also, Dreher's third

---

35. Cohen, "Diaspora, Hegemony and Cultural Identity," lines 10–15.
36. Kotz, "Globalization and Neoliberalism," 64–79.

volume, *Neoliberalism and Migration: An Inquiry into the Politics of Globalization*, looks at the role of neo-liberalism for capital and migration flows in the global economy.[37] This shows how neo-liberalism—an economical issue—affects migration.

What then is neo-liberalism? Neo-liberalism, in general, is about making free trade between nations easier. That is, freer movement of goods, resources, and enterprises to gain cheaper resources—to maximize profits. Kotz continues:

> Neo-liberalism is both a body of economic theory and a policy stance. Neo-liberal theory claims that a largely unregulated capitalist system (a free market economy) not only embodies the ideal of free individual choice but also achieves optimum economic performance with respect to efficiency, economic growth, technical progress, and distributional justice.[38]

An unregulated capitalist system, a free market economy, not only embodies the ideal of free individual choice, but also achieves optimum economic performance with respect to efficiency, economic growth, technical progress, and distributional justice. This spirit and flow of neo-liberalism affects the life and mind of diaspora on the move toward globalization.

Richard Robbins, in his book *Global Problems and the Culture of Capitalism*, also indicates some of the guiding principles behind the ideology of neo-liberalism:

(1) Sustained economic growth is the way to human progress.

(2) Free markets without government "interference" would be the most efficient and socially optimal allocation of resources.

(3) Economic globalization would be beneficial to everyone.

(4) Privatization removes inefficiencies of the public sector.

(5) Governments should mainly function to provide the infrastructure to advance the rule of law with respect to property rights and contracts.[39]

In particular, neo-liberalism removes boundaries between markets, regions, individuals, and companies. At the international level, it is noted that neo-liberalism translates to: (1) Freedom of the movement of people; (2) freedom of trade in goods and services; and (3) freedom of capital and investment. Here it should be noted that the spirit of neo-liberalism, a largely unregulated capitalist system, is to embody the ideal of free individual

---

37. Dreher, *Neoliberalism and Migration*.
38. Ibid.
39. Robbins, *Global Problems and the Culture*, 100.

choice, but also achieves optimum economic performance and affects the lives and choices of diaspora.

However, it should be noted that neo-liberalism causes various problems in human life. David Harvey, Distinguished Professor of Anthropology at the City University of New York, explains the problems of neo-liberalism:

> While personal and individual freedom in the marketplace is guaranteed, each individual is held responsible and accountable for his or her own actions and well-being. This principle extends into the realms of welfare, education, health care, and even pensions . . . [T]he state withdraws from welfare provision and diminishes its role in areas such as health care, public education, and social services . . . The social safety net is reduced to a bare minimum in a favour of a system that emphasizes personal responsibility.[40]

Firstly, neo-liberalism emphasizes individual freedom and responsibility for one's own actions and well-being, including the areas of welfare, education, health care, and even pensions. This situation reduced social safety to a bare minimum. It is noted that diaspora surf the wave of neo-liberalism, which is dominant in the global economy. It is remembered that diaspora pursue economic interest as their goal. Generally speaking they move here and there for economic gain. In a sense, diaspora are never stable in their mindset and life; diaspora are in the middle of global economics, focusing on money. In understanding diaspora, Diaspora missiology considers the lessons of 1 Timothy 6:9–10, teaching about the danger of the love of money.

> 1 Tim 6: 9those who want to get rich fall into temptation and a trap and into many foolish and harmful desires that plunge people into ruin and destruction. 10For the love of money is a root of all kinds of evil. Some people, eager for money, have wandered from the faith and pierced themselves with much grief.

Conflict by Middleman Minority Theory

Conflict issues prevail among diaspora communities. It is argued that diaspora conflict is related to what is called the middleman minority theory. With regard to the Korean Diaspora conflict and violence, various kinds of

---

40. Harvey, *Brief History of Neoliberalism*, 1–3.

research have already been studied (Kwon;[41] Abelmann;[42] Abelmann and Lie;[43] Kim;[44] Ikemoto;[45] Kim and Dance;[46] Lee 2000;[47] Lee 2001;[48] Norman 1994;[49] Weitzer 1997;[50] Chung 2007;[51] Hertic 2001;[52] and cf., Johnson and Oliver 1989;[53] Pogrebin and Poole 2012[54]). To explain the cause of the Korean Diaspora conflict, these research studies introduced middleman minority theory. Generally, "Because of Korean entrepreneurs' minority-oriented commercial activities, many researchers have concluded that they play a middleman minority role in the United States."[55]

Here "middleman minority," also known as "market-dominant minorities," is an ethnic group gaining prosperity in their adopted country;[56] at the same time, they are "often hated by both sides of the host society distinct status gap" (see Bonacich[57]; Portes and Manning[58]). Because immigrant Koreans like to play a middleman minority in the multiethnic society of the USA, they stand in the center of conflict and hatred (Hurh;[59] Port;[60] Zenner;[61] and Zenner[62]).

From above literature, we learn that diaspora want to become a market-dominant minority for gaining prosperity. In April 2012, a *Korea Daily* survey of the twentieth anniversary of the LA Riot, 70 percent of respondents

41. Kwon, *Korean Americans: Conflict and Harmony*.
42. Abelmann, *Intimate University*.
43. Abelmann and Lie, *Blue Dreams*.
44. Kim, "View from Below."
45. Ikemoto, "Traces of the Master Narrative."
46. Kim and Dance, "Korean–Black Relations."
47. Lee, "Striving for the American Dream."
48. Lee, "Entrepreneurship and Business Development."
49. Norman, "Black–Korean Relations."
50. Weitzer, "Racial Prejudice among Korean Merchants."
51. Chung, *Legacies of Struggle*.
52. Hertic, *Cultural Tug of War*.
53. Johnson and Oliver, "Interethnic Minority Conflict."
54. Pogrebin and Poole, "Culture, Conflict, and Crime."
55. Min and Kolodny, "Middle man Minority Characteristics," 131.
56. O'Brien and Fugita, "Middleman Minority Concept."
57. Bonacich, "Middleman Minorities and Advanced Capitalism."
58. Portes and Manning, "Immigrant Enclave."
59. Hurh, *Korean Immigrant in America*.
60. Porter, "Urban Middleman."
61. Zenner, "Middleman Minority Theories."
62. Zenner, *Minorities in the Middle*.

of the Korean-Americans in LA say the riot will explode again; 50 percent of respondents also say, "The Korean-Hispanic ethnic relationship should be developed, facing the dangerous situation of conflict and violence."[63] Each ethnic diaspora has transnational culture; the major issue of the Korean Diaspora is conflict and division, which has transnational roots. If Diaspora missiology does not understand the conflict issue of diaspora, it would be the same as total emptiness. Diaspora mission should study middleman minority theory to understand ethnic conflict related to social economics.

SOCIOLOGY AND RELIGION

What is the relationship between society and religion? What kinds of dimensions does religion have in relations to social life? This question is needed to identify the relationship between diaspora and Christianity so that we may understand diasporas in society and give them Christian care and guidance.

The Sociology of Religion

For Émile Durkheim, religion is "to yield an understanding of the religious nature of man, by showing us an essential and permanent aspect of humanity."[64] Religion is real, and an expression of society itself. Durkheim argues that the cohesiveness of society depends on the organization of its belief system (religion). For him, religion, the great binding force, is eminently social; it occurs in a social context. In *Masters of Sociological Thought: Ideas in Historical and Social Context*, Coser argues:

> Society is not at all the illogical or alogical, incoherent and fantastic being which has too often been considered. Quite on the contrary, the collective consciousness is the highest form of psychic life, since it is the consciousness of consciousness. Being placed outside of and above individual and local contingencies, it sees things only in their permanent and essential aspects, which it crystallizes into communicable ideas.[65]

Weber also gives religion credit because it shapes a person's view of the world, which affects their view of their interests, and how to decide regarding social actions.[66] His sociology of religion should be notable for its

---

63. *Korea Daily* April 28, 2012.
64. Dukeheim, *Elementary Forms*.
65. Coser, *Masters of Sociological Thought*, 136–39.
66. Weber, *Protestant Ethic*.

suggestions that religion can be a source of social change (Reinhard,[67] cf. Swatos[68]). In particular, religious rite controls the behavior of individuals in relation to others;[69] this infers that religion serves as a mechanism to solve conflicts. These literatures show how religions can involve conflict and conflict resolution.

Economics of Religion

Christian religious traditions contain a fundamental concern with economy.[70] This assumes that religion is constituted by a kind of economy as in ancient Israel and classical Christianity. That is, the knowledge of God is revealed in the accounting of an economy and, is constituted by the performances of an economy. The economics of religion uses socio-economic theory and methods to explain the religious behavior patterns of individuals or groups and the social consequences of such behavior. Its example is Adam Smith's analysis of the effect of government regulation or support for religious denominations on the quantity and quality of religious services.[71] According to the definition from the ASREC (Association for the Study of Religion, Economics, and Culture), "The economic study of religion comprises a variety of subfields, which collectively embrace all aspects of the social-scientific study of religion."[72]

Furthermore, Robert Nelson sees economics as religion.[73] He explores the genesis, the prophets, and the prophecies of the Bible, and finds a religion of economics that has come into full blossom in latter-day America. He proposes to show how the arguments of economists approve and legitimize social and economic theories by providing theories with quasi-religious justification. Finally, drawn from Nelson's terms, for diaspora, economics is religion, and sometimes it is more than this.

---

67. Reinhard, *Max Weber: An Intellectual Portrait*.
68. Swatos, *Encyclopedia of Religion and Society*.
69. Kunin, *Theories of Religions*.
70. Meeks, *God the Economist*.
71. Anderson, "Mr. Smith and the Preachers."
72. ASREC, "What is the Economic Study of Religion," lines 6–7. The Association for the Study of Religion, Economics, and Culture exists to promote interdisciplinary scholarship on religion through conferences, workshops, newsletters, websites, working papers, teaching, and research. ASREC supports all manner of social-scientific methods, but seeks especially to stimulate work based on economic perspectives and the rational choice paradigm (Ibid., lines 1–4).
73. Nelson, *Economics as Religion*.

Culture and Religion

What is the relationship between religion and culture? Under the rubric of semantic anthropology, Geertz advocates the need to widen the perspective and to accept that religion is "essentially a cultural system that gives meaning to human existence."[74] This topic is typically known as Tillich's theology of culture. In his lecture at the University of Aberdeen, Russell Re Manning argues, for Tillich, "culture and religion are within each other." Tillich called religion "the state of being grasped by an ultimate concern." In turn, he said, culture was "the form of religion" which, era by era, expresses "intimate movement of the soul" as art.[75]

Theologically, Paul Tillich, in his three-volume work *Systematic Theology* (1951–63),[76] developed his "method of correlation," an approach of exploring the symbols of Christian revelation as answers to the problems of human existence raised by contemporary existential philosophical analysis.[77] A Christian message is understood in terms of the culture of diaspora; it should be delivered in a method of answering to questions of the problems of diaspora existence.

Psychology and Religion

US psychologist and philosopher William James is the founder of the psychology of religion, and believes that individuals with healthy-mindedness tend to ignore the evil in the world and focus on the positive and the good. His title *The Varieties of Religious Experience: A Study in Human Nature* was a book originally published by Harvard University.[78] When at the University of Edinburgh in 1901, William James delivered a series of lectures on "natural religion," and he defined religion as the feelings, acts, and experiences of individual men in their solitude; so far as they apprehend themselves to stand in relation to whatever they may consider the divine. His position of religion shed a light for natural man to open his mind.

74. Morris, *Anthropological Studies of Religions*, 313.
75. Ireland, "Theology of Culture," lines 19–24.
76. Tillich, *Systematic Theology*.
77. Tillich, *Courage to Be*, 184.
78. James, *Varieties of Religious Experience*. James distinguished between institutional religion and personal religion. The first—institutional religion—refers to the religious group or organization, and plays an important part in a society's culture; the latter—personal religion—has mystical experience, and can be experienced regardless of the culture. James was most interested in understanding the latter—personal religious experience.

For Wulff (2010), Department of Psychology, Wheaton College, Norton, MA, the "psychology of religion" is to account in psychological terms for religious phenomena and to clarify the outcomes of these phenomena for individuals and larger society.[79] In fact, many areas of religion remain uncertain and unexplored by psychology, though religion and spirituality play a role in many people's lives. People are uncertain how psychology leads to outcomes that are at times positive and at other times negative. Thus, the pathways and outcomes that underlie these associations and causations need additional research. Recently some scholars examine a faith life in perspective of psychology or psychological phenomenon in terms of faith.[80]

In Jung's *Study of Psychology and Religion* (1938), religion as "collective unconscious" has a profound psychological significance.[81] He defines religion as a numinous experience that seizes and controls the human subject.[82] For him, collective unconscious means a physic reality shared by all humans.[83] Religion as "a physic reality shared by all humans" serves as the key grounds for understanding, communicating, and resolving conflicts between different parties.

DIASPORA AND PHILOSOPHY: EXISTENTIALISM

The existential understandings of diaspora call for a knowledge of existentialism. In "Diaspora Existentialism: The Psychology of Zambians in the Diaspora," George N. Mtonga states,

> A unique trend has emerged and continues to emerge as more Zambians find the financial freedom to relocate outside Zambia and raise their children abroad. Part of this unique experience has been the existentialism dilemma that members of the diaspora have come to suffer from; this is tantamount to clinical depression as their identity has been questioned.[84]

In brief, Mtonga describes the life of diaspora as falling into "the existentialism dilemma," which implies that diaspora can be well understood in lens

---

79. Wulff, "Psychology of Religion," 732–35.
80. Moriarty, "Integrating Faith and Psychology."
81. Jung, *Psychology and Religion*, 59.
82. Morris, *Anthropological Studies of Religions*, 167.
83. Ibid., 45.
84. Mtonga, "Diaspora Existentialism," lines 1–6.

of existentialism. Diaspora leave their hometown, and live in a foreign land as strangers.

Existentialism has its philosophical roots in solving the problem of human existence; existentialism searches for the "meaning of being." In other words, what does it mean to exist in this world? According to Kalamazoo Valley Community College (KVCC), existentialism has six basic themes: existence precedes essence; anxiety, or the sense of anguish, a generalized uneasiness, a fear or dread; absurdity; nothingness, or the void; the existentialist theme of death; and alienation. These six themes pertain to all humans, but especially, to diaspora.[85] Diasporas think that they are simply here, thrown into this time and place, but they question why now? Why here? These questions are also asked by Sören Kierkegaard in explaining existentialism,[86] existentialism is the philosophy that best describes the situation and questions of diasporas.

Generally, in his phenomenological pursuit of human being-in-the-world, Heidegger became the reluctant father of existentialism because he drew inspiration from two seminal nineteenth century writers: Kierkegaard and Friedrich Nietzsche. One can find anticipations of existential thought in the contemporary significance of the works of Kierkegaard and Nietzsche.[87] Kierkegaard developed the problem of existence in the context of Christian faith; however, Nietzsche tried to solve its problems in light of his thesis of the death of God. Most diaspora feel the problems of existence in a foreign land more than ever before. He stands in the crossroads of faith and unfaith.

Sören Kierkegaard: "The Single Individual"

Kierkegaard used the term "the single individual"; for him, "this singularity is, what is most my own, 'me,' could be meaningfully reflected upon while yet, precisely because of its singularity, remain invisible to traditional philosophy, with its emphasis either on what follows unerring objective laws of nature or else conforms to the universal standards of moral reason."[88] In his *Fear and Trembling*, Kierkegaard wanted to understand the anxiety in Abraham when God commanded him to offer his son as a human sacrifice; Abraham had a choice to complete the task or to forget it. Finally, Abraham gave up himself to the loss of his son, obeying and acting according to his faith. Here, Kierkegaard argued that one must be willing to give up all his or

---

85. KVCC, "Six Basic Themes of Existentialism," lines 4–9.
86. Ibid., lines 10–13.
87. Crowell, "Existentialism," 6–7.
88. Ibid. Also refer to Kierkegaard, *Fear and Trembling*.

her earthly possessions in infinite resignation, whatever it is that he or she loves more than God. In his book, Kierkegaard poses the question "What ought I do?" which is present in the anxiety of humans. His answer to the question divided into a three-fold distinction of stages on life's way:

1. The first stage is the aesthetic, which calls for the quest for sensual and intellectual pleasure. Eventually, this stage leads to "boredom and then suicide"; there is an impulse to turn to a form of life in which there is a sense of oughtness.
2. The second stage is a moral life in which we freely arrange and align ourselves with the moral law, determined to be good.
3. The third stage is a religious life in which we must accept a teleological suspension of the ethical. In the religious life, divine command is paramount and true love for God is expressed in the willingness to set aside moral habits and respond to the divine command.[89]

Kierkegaard understands the conflict between religion and ethics. He says, "If Abraham's life is meaningful, it represents, from a philosophical point of view, the "paradox" that through faith the "single individual is higher than the universal." Existence as a philosophical problem appears at this point: if there is a dimension to my being that is both meaningful and yet not governed by the rational standard of morality, by what standard *is* it governed? For unless there is some standard, it is idle to speak of "meaning."[90]

Nietzsche: "God is dead" and Nihilism

For Kierkegaard a philosophical problem of existence emerges as the struggle to think the paradoxical presence of God; however, for Nietzsche, it is found in the echo or reverberations of the slogan "God is dead," in the challenge of nihilism. "If such existence is to be thinkable there must be a standard by which success or failure can be measured. Nietzsche variously indicates such a standard in his references to 'health,' 'strength,' and 'the meaning of the earth.' Perhaps his most instructive indication, however, comes from aesthetics, since its concept of *style*, as elaborated in *The Gay Science*, provides a norm appropriate to the singularity of existence."[91] It was in his *The Gay Science* that he first proclaimed "the death of God" and he introduced his doctrine of the eternal recurrence.

---

89. Irvine, "Existentialism," lines 18–31.
90. Crowell, "Existentialism," 7.
91. Nietzsche, *Gay Science*. Also see Crowell, "Existentialism," 11.

Nietzsche's slogan "God is dead" leads to the loss of meaning, namely, nihilism; one such reaction to the loss of meaning is what he calls "passive nihilism," which he recognizes in the pessimistic philosophy of Schopenhauer, which advocates a separating oneself of will and desires in order to reduce suffering. He refers to Schopenhauer's doctrine as Western Buddhism. Nietzsche defines this fakir attitude as a "will to nothingness," whereby life turns away from itself, as there is nothing of value to be found in the world. This moving away of all value in the world is characteristic of the nihilist.[92] According to this view, our existence (living, suffering, willing, and feeling) has no meaning: this "in vain" is the nihilist's pathos.

Consistent with Nietzsche, Sartre's philosophy heads toward "God is dead." Sartre's slogan—"existence precedes essence"—may serve to introduce what is most distinctive of existentialism, namely, the idea that no general, non-formal account of what it means to be human can be given, since that meaning is decided in and through existing itself. For Sartre, existence is described as "self-making-in-a-situation."[93] Sartre's view of existence infers that the existential life of diaspora can easily fall into human atheistic life.

Alienation

Alienation or estrangement is a theme that characterizes existentialism. Originally, alienation is a theme that Hegel opened up. For Hegel, the Absolute is estranged from itself, as it exists only in the development of finite spirit in historical time.[94] In particular, Sartre's slogan—"existence precedes essence"—introduces the idea that no general, non-formal account of what it means to be human can be given, since that meaning is decided in and through existing itself. This is what is most distinctive of existentialism. For him, to "exist" is precisely to constitute such an identity of humans; "it is in light of this idea that key existential notions such as facticity, transcendence (project), alienation, and authenticity must be understood."[95]

In particular, the Heideggerian word stem *heim*, "home," often translated as "uncanny," indicates the strangeness of a world in which humans precisely do *not* feel "at home."[96] This experience, basic to existential thought, opposes the ancient notion of a *kosmos* in which human beings have a well-ordered place; it connects existential thought tightly to the

92. Nietzsche, *On the Genealogy of Morals*.
93. Fackenheim, *Metaphysics and Historicity*, 37.
94. Wheat, "Hegel's Undiscovered Thesis."
95. Crowell, "Existentialism," 17.
96. Ibid.

modern experience of a meaningless universe. Here strangers, or those who do "not feel at home," signify a typical pattern of diaspora living. In *The Essential Kierkegaard*, we find the main theme that binds the whole together, namely, Kierkegaard's overarching concern with, in his own words, "What it means to exist; . . . what it means to be a human being."[97] This main theme deals with the conflict between freedom and responsibility.

INTERDISCIPLINARY STUDIES AND DIASPORA: ITS POSSIBILITY AND LIMITATIONS

Significances of Interdisciplinary Understandings of Diaspora

Diasporas live a complex social situation; that is why we study the sociology of Christianity. That is, they ask in what meanings is Christianity understood sociologically. This question seeks how to relate Christianity to the society. Diaspora missiology should research how to respond to diaspora's sociology of Christianity. Diaspora, who live in the middle of complex globalization, are interested in the questions of what meanings Christianity has in social relations. However, interdisciplinary studies are not perfect, and thus lie under the authority of the Bible. Furthermore an interdisciplinary approach should be in terms of applications of the Bible and the contextual understanding of human beings.

In particular, we understand the concept of diaspora in terms of existentialism. Diaspora think that they were thrown into a foreign land, unknown to themselves; they have strong questions of existentialism. Existential philosophy is very helpful to understand and guide diaspora who have severe existential questions and problems. However, the existential slogan of "existence precedes essence" has a possible danger of falling to pragmatic existentialism, ignoring essence in a desperate life.

With possible danger of interdisciplinary aims becoming syncretic, the Lausanne states: "From our perspective, no area of science, society, or culture is perfect or neutral. It is essential to recognize, critique, and respond to the implicit ethics, forms of power, and/or oppression embedded in them."[98] Interdisciplinary studies for diaspora have some limitations because not all disciplines are consistent with the teachings of the Bible. That is, interdisciplinary knowledge can be used and applied under the guidance of the Bible as special revelations in reference to the knowledge of general revelations.

97. Hong, *Essential Kierkegaard*, 17.
98. Third Lausanne Congress, "Content Library: The Cape Town Declaration," lines 27–28.

Interdisciplinary Descriptions in the Bible

It is noted that the Bible describes the events or persons of the Bible interdisciplinarily. Paul, Aquila, and Priscilla, written in Acts 18:1–4 is an example. Interdisciplinary descriptions are as follows:

1. It describes geographically: Paul left Athens and went to Corinth.
2. It describes anthropologically and ethnically: Aquila, a native of Pontus, who had recently come from Italy with his wife Priscilla.
3. It describes socially, politically, and historically: Claudius had ordered all Jews to leave Rome.
4. It describes Roman law: Claudius had ordered as emperor.
5. It describes migration: Left ... went ... leave ...
6. It describes economically: Because he was a tentmaker as they were.
7. It describes religiously: Every Sabbath he reasoned in the synagogue, trying to persuade Jews and Greeks.

It should be noted that interdisciplinary descriptions of the Bible call for interdisciplinary perspectives for the interpretations and applications of the Bible. Interdisciplinary interpretations of the Bible also make possible its interdisciplinary applications, applying its teachings to the entirety of life. Interdisciplinary descriptions allow readers to read, interpret, or apply the biblical truths broadly, deeply, or exactly. In a word, the interdisciplinary interpretation and application of the Bible is the effort to try to find all lessons of God in the Bible and apply them in every area of life. The goal of the interdisciplinary approach is to interpret, understand, and reach people in the context of interdisciplinary situations.

In other words, it is based on the confession that all scripture should be interpreted and applied for salvation and every good work, including the area of the soul as well as every life.

> 2 Timothy 3: 16All Scripture is God-breathed and is useful for teaching,
> rebuking,
> correcting,
> and training in righteousness,
> 17so that the servant of God may be thoroughly equipped for *every* good work. (Italics mine)

4

Biblical Understandings of Diaspora

For doing Diaspora missiology, it is necessary to investigate its concept in the Bible; it is essential to understand its meaning through the whole text of the Bible. The word diaspora as the scattered began along with the fall of man in the garden of Eden; human beings were banished from God's presence due to his judgment over sin and scattered outside the Eden. The Old Testament (OT) is the written history of scattered humankind, culminated in the exile of Babylon. However, in the New Testament (NT), the scattered by God's judgment accepted Jesus Christ as savior, were saved and gathered in his church, and were scattered to preach the gospel. "The scattered" is the core theme of biblical theology, relating to that of the covenant and fulfillment of salvation.

THE OLD TESTAMENT

The Definition of Diaspora

The *New Bible Dictionary* defines that the term dispersion (Gk. *diaspora*) can denote either Jews scattered in the non-Jewish world, or the places in which they reside.[1] "It is difficult to know how early the voluntary dispersion of Israel began; there are hints of an early 'colony' in Damascus (1 Kgs 20:34), and Solomon's expansionist policies may well have led to earlier commercial outposts. But the conquering kings of Assyria and Babylonia

---

1. Marshall, "Diaspora," 286.

introduced a new factor, the compulsory transplantation of the population to other parts of their empire (2 Kgs 15:29; 17:6; 24:14; 25:11).[2]

It is noted that there is no technical Hebrew equivalent for the Greek word *diaspora*. However, in Deuteronomy 30:4, the Hebrew root is *ndt*, which means "expelled, driven out" in its niphal. An example of Hebrew terms that may be similar to diaspora is *golah*, or *galot*, or the emphatic *galota* (from the Aramaic root, *galo*). Here, three Hebrew words of *ndt*, *golah*, and *galota* mean the situation of "leading away," "deportation," or "exile." They have become technical terms for exile or banishment after the destruction of Jerusalem and the loss of the Palestinian homeland.[3] However, in the Greek translation (LXX or Septuagint) of the Hebrew Old Testament, "the technical term, *Diaspora*, is found in twelve passages, generally referring to the "dispersion of the Jews among the Gentiles" or "the Jews as thus scattered." This noun, *Diaspora*, is used in the LXX of the exile of the scattered people of God among the Gentiles. Moreover, Diaspora can refer to both the dispersion and the totality of the dispersed."[4]

In sum, the concept of dispersion or scattering in the Old Testament is addressed in seven root words: 1) *gôlah* (exiles) / *galah* (to remove) / *galût* (captivity); 2) *zarah* (spread, winnow, scatter); 3) *nadaḥ* (banish); 4) *naphas* (scatter); 5) *pûṣ* (disperse); 6) *paza* (scatter abroad); and 7) *parad* (separated).[5] Here, seven meanings related to the concept "scattered"—exile, remove, captivity, winnow, banish, scatter, and separated—are related to God's judgment or exile. The LCWE noted that "diaspora" is a biblical word and a vital biblical theme in redemptive history.[6]

Historical Overviews of Diaspora as Scattered

In the OT, diaspora as the scattered has been one of the major themes of the Bible. The concept of scattering appeared in the creation before the fall of man to the exile through the walks of the Bible. Here is a brief overview of the scattered:

---

2. Ibid.
3. Santos, "Diaspora Occurrences in the Bible," lines 25–29.
4. Ibid.
5. Wan, *Diaspora Missiology*, 22.
6. LCWE, *Scattered to Gather*, 15.

God's Creation: "Fill the Earth"

When God created man and woman, God blessed them. Genesis 1: "28God blessed them and said to them, 'Be fruitful and increase in number; fill the earth and subdue it. Rule over the fish in the sea and the birds in the sky and over every living creature that moves on the ground.'" Here, "fill" in "fill the earth" is the Hebrew verb מלאו (*mil'û*), which simply means *fill*. It was God's purpose that the earth should be completely inhabited. As Wenham puts it, "this command, like others in scripture, carries with it an implicit promise that God will enable man to fulfill it. It is repeated to Noah after the flood ([Gen] 9:1), and the patriarchs too are reminded of this divine promise."[7] Here the meaning of "fill the earth" means "spread over the whole earth and fill it."[8] That is, the scattering of humankind.

The LCWE of the Lausanne movement sees God's mandate as "Diaspora." It says, "Being fruitful, multiplying, filling the earth, subduing it and having dominion would also imply voluntary "Diaspora" as restated in Genesis 9:1 after the flood."[9]

Fall of Men, and God's Judgment

In Genesis 3, in the initial stage, the human committed the sin by disobeying God's command, and was banished from the garden of Eden by God's judgment over human sin.

> Gen 3: 23so the Lord God *banished* him from the Garden of Eden to work the ground from which he had been taken. 24After he *drove* the man *out*, he placed on the east side[e] of the Garden of Eden cherubim and a flaming sword flashing back and forth to guard the way to the tree of life. (Italics mine)

Here, the words "banished" and "drove out" represent the expulsion. The word they are expressed by is used in regard to divorces. Humankind is banished and driven out. In this sense, human being is diaspora being existentially. This is the first report of the human scattered. The concept of scattered was repeated again with Cain because he killed his brother and was judged by God. One of God's judgments is a scattering as wanderer:

---

7. Wenham, *Word Biblical Commentary: Genesis 1:1-15*, 33.
8. Alders, *Bible Student Commentary: Genesis*, 248.
9. LCWE, *Scattered to Gather*, 16.

> Gen 4: 14Today you are *driving* me from the land, and I will be hidden from your presence; I will be a *restless wanderer* on the earth, and whoever finds me will kill me." (Italics mine)

Here, God's judgment is to drive Cain to leave his home. "What we actually have here is God punishing Cain by condemning him to the life of a fugitive and a wanderer across the face of the earth. He must leave the land which had been his home."[10]

In the Tower of Babel, humankind recognized that they were in the process of being scattered over the face of the whole earth (Gen 11: 4); they tried to make bricks and build a city, with a tower that reached to the heavens, however, "From there the Lord *scattered* them over the face of the whole earth." (Gen 11:9, italics mine). From the beginning of the Bible, the human being was in the state of scattered by the judgment of God over sinned humans.

What was the purpose God had for man when he created man? It is to "fill the earth" (Gen 1:28). However, with the Tower of Babel mankind attempted to congregate in one place. Alders commented on this event:

> This purpose was in conflict with God's plan for mankind. At the time of creation God had specially ordered that humanity was to be fruitful and "fill the earth." This was repeated at the time they left the Ark (Gen 1:28, 9:1). Mankind was not to congregate in one small area, such as the Plain of Shinar, but was to spread over the whole earth and fill it. They now had determined to disobey this order and to crowd into one place.[11]

Here we find that humanity was supposed to be scattered over the whole world, but disobeys this fact. Finally, God himself scattered them. Genesis 11:8 says, "so the Lord scattered them from there over all the earth, and they stopped building the city." This shows that, once again, sinned humans cannot avoid scattered life, which was brought by God's judgment.

The Patriarchs: Abram, Isaac, and Jacob

Abram obeyed God's call to leave his homeland to go to the promise land (Gen 12:1–3). Jacob was trained by God in the diaspora environments of *Paddam Aram* (Gen 29–31), *Succoth* (33:17), and *Shechem* (33:18–35); later he was sent to Egypt with his whole family and lived as diaspora, "the year of the pilgrimage" (47: 9), hoping for God's exodus of his people. Joseph

---

10. Alders, *Bible Student Commentary: Genesis*, 125–26.
11. Ibid.

Biblical Understandings of Diaspora 87

was sold as slaves by his brothers, and was faithful and prospered in very difficult diaspora circumstances. As a result he not only influenced Egypt for good but also fulfilled God's purpose of blessing for Israel and through her for the whole world (Gen 37–50). Jacob also saw the life of his own and his ancestors as "pilgrimage" (Gen 47:9).

Thus Hebrews proclaims the fathers of faith as pilgrims or strangers:

> Heb 11: 8by faith Abraham, when called to go to a place he would later receive as his inheritance, obeyed and went, even though he did not know where he was going. 9By faith he made his home in the Promised Land like a *stranger* in a *foreign* country; he lived in tents, as did Isaac and Jacob, who were heirs with him of the same promise. 10For he was looking forward to the city with foundations, whose architect and builder is God. . . . 13all these people were still living by faith when they died. They did not receive the things promised; they only saw them and welcomed them from a distance, admitting that they were *foreigners* and *strangers* on earth.

Here the term of foreigner and stranger is that of diaspora as scattered. Stranger is παροικέω (*paroikeó*) in Greek, which means, "to dwell near," i.e., reside as a foreigner. "This word is translated properly, 'to dwell beside (one) or in one's neighborhood (παρά); to live near; (Xenophon, Thucydides, Isocrates, others).'"[12] In contrast, foreigner is ἀλλότριος (*allotrios*) in the Greek, which means "belonging to another (opposed to ἴδιος), not one's own: Heb 9:25; Rom 14:4; Rom 15:20; 2 Cor 10:15; 1 Tim 5:22; John 10:5."[13] We find that the two words have similar meaning; the first and the latter are common in both leaving homeland and living in a foreign land as strangers if they are different in specific conditions.

Moses: Exodus and the Law

Moses was born as a Hebrew Diaspora boy, but he grew up as the son of the Pharaoh's daughter in a foreign land, but when he became forty years old, he made a decision regarding the calling from God (Heb 11:24–5). By faith he left Egypt, not fearing the king's anger; he persevered because he saw he who is invisible. At his age of forty, Moses left Egypt and lived a median in a desert in a foreign land (Acts 7 and Exodus 3). Israel, the people of God,

---

12. Bible Hub, "Parepidémos," lines 2–3.
13. Bible Hub, "Allotrios," lines 3–4.

lived as diaspora and slaves in a foreign land, Egypt. These geographies are diasporic.

Israel lived in Egypt, the land of Gentiles; they were slaves of Egypt, the land of a foreign country. With the leadership of Moses, Israel was brought out of Egypt and entered Canaan and settled in a foreign land as a diaspora nation.

> Exod 3: 8So I have come down to rescue them from the hand of the Egyptians and to bring them up out of that land into a good and spacious land, a land flowing with milk and honey—the home of the Canaanites, Hittites, Amorites, Perizzites, Hivites, and Jebusites. Here these ethnic groups were in a land foreign to Israel. God's covenant would be accomplished in the state of diaspora.

In particular, the Law warned Israel of the captivity and their scattered punishment. Leviticus 26:33 says, "I will scatter you among the nations and will draw out my sword and pursue you. Your land will be laid waste, and your cities will lie in ruins"; in addition to this text, this word occurs two times in the OT: in Ezekiel 5:12; 12:14. This word "scatter" is זָרָה (*zarah*) in Hebrew, which means "to scatter, fan, winnow"[14] in the NASB translation; this word is translated: disperse (5), dispersed (1), disperses (1), north (1), scatter (13), scattered (7), scrutinize (1), spread (4), winnow (3), winnow them with a winnowing (1), winnowed (1), and winnows (2). "Scattered" signifies God's pursuit and judgment.

Canaan: Conquest and Settlement

As mentioned earlier, the land of Canaan was originally not Israel's property, and Canaan land was the home of the Canaanites, Hittites, Amorites, Perizzites, Hivites, and Jebusites. Canaan was the land of the Gentile; as diaspora, Israel would enter into the land of the Gentile. This shows Israel lived as a diaspora in the land of Canaan. That is, God's redemption is described as the moving of Israel as diaspora from Egypt to Canaan, which means a diasporic state. We remember that the promised land of milk and honey is the land of diaspora from Israel's perspective; redemption is described through the process of the passage from the exodus to the promised land. Here we find that diaspora is a strongly symbolic typology of God's redemption.

---

14. Bible Hub, "Zarah," lines 5–6.

Judges and Ruth

Twelve leaders appeared in Judges; they were mainly diasporic. For some examples, Ehud was sent with tribute to Elgon, king of Moab, and killed that king. Finally through the diasporic ministry of Ehud, the land had peace for eighty years. Deborah was a prophet in the hill county of Ephraim, but was sent by God into Mount Tabor in Kedesh (Judg 4). Jephthah the Gileadite was a mighty warrior, lived diaspora life in Tob, and returned and become the head of the Gileadites, and fought with the Ammonites (Judg 11). Samson also lived a diaspora life and died in a foreign land of the Philistines.

In particular, Ruth in the age of Judges was totally diasporic:

> Judg 1: 1In the days when the judges ruled, there was a famine in the land. So a man from Bethlehem in Judah, together with his wife and two sons, went to live for a while in the country of *Moab*. 2The man's name was Elimelek, his wife's name was Naomi, and the names of his two sons were Mahlon and Kilion.

They all were Ephrathites from Bethlehem, Judah. But they went to *Moab* and lived there. They moved to Moab, a foreign land, and lived as diaspora. After the death of Elimelek, Mahlon and Kilion and *Ruth*, a foreign, widowed Gentile, returned with Naomi and Ruth became a wife of Boaz, being a witness of God's salvation to the Gentiles.

The United Kingdom: David and Solomon

The United Kingdom of Israel is the safest age in its history; but the Israelites exchange pilgrim for worshiping God and offering sacrifices to God in the temple in three times in a year (see Exod 23:17; 1 Kgs 9:25). In particular, before becoming the king, David lived a diaspora life as a result of Saul's chase (1 Sam 17–31); he wandered in various areas of Philistines and Jude. In preparation for the building up of the temple, he confessed, "we are aliens and strangers" (1 Chr 29:15).

Solomon, the son of David, knew a diaspora life, expressed as captive life. In his prayer of dedication, he confessed:

> 1 Kgs 8: 46When they sin against you—for there is no one who does not sin—and you become angry with them and give them over to their enemies, who take them *captive* to their own lands, far away or near; 47and if they have a change of heart in the land where they are held *captive*, and repent and plead with you in the land of their *captors* and say, "We have sinned, we have done wrong, we have acted wickedly." (Italics mine)

Solomon's prayer saw that Israelites can be taken captive far away; these words, captive and captors represents diaspora life.

In particular, when he built the temple, Solomon made a treaty with Hiram, king of Tyre, a nation of the Gentiles, and had all the cedar and pine logs supplied from Hiram (1 Kgs 5:7-12). That is, God's temple was built with the help of the Gentiles and through diaspora works. Furthermore, the Queen of Sheba from Ethiopia visited Solomon (1 Kgs 10), which was quoted by Jesus saying, "she came from the ends of the earth to listen to Solomon's wisdom, and now one greater than Solomon is here" (Matt 12:42). It is worthy of noting that Solomon welcomed the Queen of Sheba who "came from the ends of the earth," namely, a diasporic woman.

The Divided Kingdom: the Northern and Southern Kingdoms

In 931 BC, the kingdom was divided into two kingdoms: the Northern and Southern. The Northern kingdom experienced a series of political revolts, in which its many kings were killed or murdered by opponents. In that age, God's judgment over sins had exacted; Israelites spatially continued to be scattered; the concept of diaspora prevailed. In particular, Jesus pointed out two persons selected by God—Zerephath in the region of Sidon, and Naaman the Syrian (Luke 4:25-27). These Gentile people were both of the Northern Kingdom, which connected to the prophets Elijah (1 Kgs 17:8-16) and Elisha (2 Kgs 5). These people were the result of a Diaspora ministry of two prophets. In particular, Jonah, the prophet of the Northern, was known to have been called by God for missionary preaching in the city of Nineveh, Assyria (Jonah 1-4).

Another issue here is the prophecies of many prophets who warn of the kingdom's destruction and exile. From the prophecy of Joel in 825 BC, prophecies of destruction and exile were repeated by several prophets. In particular, Jeremiah's prophecy continued for fifty-three years from 627BC to 574 BC. The Northern kingdom was destroyed in 722 BC; the Southern kingdom, Judah, was destroyed in 586 BC, along with the destruction of the temple.

Exile Age

Exile is the typical pattern of diaspora by God's judgment. In biblical studies, the term "exile" or "captivity" mainly refers to the deportation of Judah's leaders in the destruction of Jerusalem in 586 BC. Of course, the earlier leaders of the Northern kingdom had been deported by the Assyrians, following the fall of Northern kingdom in 722 BC. Samaria, the capital city of the Northern kingdom, was forcibly resettled by the king of Assyria with various ethnic groups (2 Kgs 17:24). The estimated number of exiles or deported of the Southern kingdom, Judah, varies according to the texts (Jer 52:28–30; 2 Kgs 24:14).[15] However, 2 Chronicles 36:1–20 has broad explanations.

The First Deportation

> 2 Chr 36: 5Jehoiakim was twenty-five years old when he became king, and he reigned in Jerusalem eleven years. He did evil in the eyes of the Lord his God. 6Nebuchadnezzar king of Babylon attacked him and bound him with bronze shackles to take him to Babylon. 7Nebuchadnezzar also took to Babylon articles from the temple of the Lord and put them in his temple there. 8The other events of Jehoiakim's reign, the detestable things he did and all that was found against him, are written in the book of the kings of Israel and Judah. And Jehoiachin his son succeeded him as king.

Here Nebuchadnezzar, in the fourth year of Jehoiakim (Jer. 25:1), invaded Judah, and carried away some royal youths, including Daniel and his companions (606 BC). This is the first deportation.

The Second Deportation

Second Chronicles 36 explains a second deportation in this way:

> 15. Firstly, in Jer 52:28–30, three deportations are listed, numbering 4,600 as the total exiled from Judah: "28This is the number of the people Nebuchadnezzar carried into exile: in the seventh year, 3,023 Jews; 29in Nebuchadnezzar's eighteenth year, 832 people from Jerusalem; 30in his twenty-third year, 745 Jews taken into exile by Nebuzaradan the commander of the imperial guard. There were 4,600 people in all." According to Jeremiah's report, Nebuchadnezzar took into exile 4,600 people in all.
> Secondly, in 2 Kgs 24:14, ten thousand in the second deportation alone are described: "14He carried all Jerusalem into exile: all the officers and fighting men, and all the skilled workers and artisans—a total of ten thousand. Only the poorest people of the land were left. 15Nebuchadnezzar took Jehoiachin captive to Babylon. He also took from Jerusalem to Babylon the king's mother, his wives, his officials and the prominent people of the land. 16The king of Babylon also deported to Babylon the entire force of seven thousand fighting men, strong and fit for war, and a thousand skilled workers and artisans." Here the importance is that the God's temple was destroyed, and the treasures from the temple of the Lord were removed to Babylon. The destruction of the temple is a traumatic experience for the exiled. For example, Psalm 137, the quotations from exiles in the prophets, gives the traumatic feeling and sorrow of the exile.

> 2 Chr 36: 9Jehoiachin was eighteen years old when he became king, and he reigned in Jerusalem three months and ten days. He did evil in the eyes of the Lord. 10In the spring, King Nebuchadnezzar sent for him and brought him to Babylon, together with articles of value from the temple of the Lord, and he made Jehoiachin's uncle, Zedekiah, king over Judah and Jerusalem.

In 598 BC (Jer 52:28), in the beginning of Jehoiachin's reign, Nebuchadnezzar carried away the king (2 Chr 36:10), and took captive 3,023 eminent Jews from his family and officers (2 Kgs 24:12), a large number of warriors (v. 16), many persons of note (v. 14), and artisans (v. 16), leaving behind only those who were poor and helpless. This is the second deportation.

The Third Deportation

2 Chronicles 36 also reported a third deportation:

> 2 Chr 36: 18He carried to *Babylon* all the articles from the temple of God, both large and small, and the treasures of the Lord's temple and the treasures of the king and his officials. 19They set fire to God's temple and broke down the wall of Jerusalem; they burned all the palaces and destroyed everything of value there. 20He carried into *exile* to *Babylon* the remnant, who escaped from the sword, and they became servants to him and his successors until the kingdom of *Persia* came to power." (Italics mine)

Here, Babylon and Persia were lands of diaspora for Israelites; they were carried into exile. The importance is that "They set fire to God's temple and broke down the wall of Jerusalem; they burned all the palaces and destroyed everything of value there." For the exile, God's burned temple has a huge meaning; their sorrow and hurt is related to the destruction of the temple; and at the same time, their hope will be back to the temple. Psalm 137 describes the sorrow and hope of the captive. In the exile, there were Israelites living as diaspora in a foreign land—Babylonia and Persia.

Here are several extraordinary examples of diaspora faith in the exile:

1. Daniel and his friends were outstanding examples of how to live in an alien host country (Dan 1:8; 3:18; 6:10).
2. In the citadel of Susa, Nehemiah recognized God's calling to rebuild the city in Judah; he answered the question from the king he served. (Neh 2:4–5)

3. Esther remained faithful to the calling of God for saving her people, Esther 4: "15 Then Esther sent this reply to Mordecai: 16 'Go, gather together all the Jews who are in Susa, and fast for me. Do not eat or drink for three days, night or day. I and my attendants will fast as you do. When this is done, I will go to the king, even though it is against the law. And if I perish, I perish."

As diaspora, these three worked in a foreign land. In exile, there are strong faith movements. In particular, Raitt argued that there was some paradox grace in the exile, a new era, compared to an old era.[16] That is, the exile prepared for messianic grace. He summarized this dichotomy in the following table.

Figure 3: Dichotomy of Old and New Eras

	Old Era	New Era
1	Expected standard of righteousness achieved by human efforts through obedience and by repentance.	Expected standard created by God's intervention to transform the people's natures: "heart to know," new heart and spirit."
2	Forgiveness conditional, practical.	Forgiveness unconditional, total.
3	Election grounded in events dating back to David, Moses, Abraham . . . followed by total rejection.	New election, and future even, direct between God and people, more of an idealistic "I–Thou" quality.
4	Old Covenant	"New covenant," "eternal covenant."
5	The norm for faith centers on events in the past.	The norm for faith shifts toward events in the future.

Here, the key finding is that the new covenant, the gospel, was mainly revealed in an age of exile, in the captivity of Babylonia or regarding captivity. In particular, in his life of captivity, Ezekiel (Ezek 36:22–31) wrote a new covenant:

> Ezek 36: 19I dispersed them among the nations, and they were *scattered* through the countries; I judged them according to their conduct and their actions . . . 24For I will take you out of the nations; I will *gather* you from all the countries and bring you back into your own land. . . . 28Then you will live in the land I gave your ancestors; you will be my people, and I will be your God.

---

16. Raitt, *Theology of Exile*, 213.

From verses above, this "scattered-gathered" structure represents the judgment of God and the salvation of God in Jesus Christ. This implies that "scattered," namely, diaspora, serves as the situation of the salvation of God in which scattered people are called and gathered. In this sense, diaspora, "scattered," serves as the field of God's salvation, which echoes the core value of the gospel. Here above all, it is noted that "scattered" is the result of God's judgment over sins; thusly, scattered people are called into repentance for gathering.

The Post-Exile

In 536 BC, Israel returned home as diaspora people because their land, Canaan, was under the colony of Persia and already full of several Gentile ethnic groups.[17] The post-exile community itself was composed of and Jews and Gentiles. The following verses show this:

> Ezra 10: 16So the exiles did as was proposed. Ezra the priest selected men who were family heads, one from each family division, and all of them designated by name. On the first day of the tenth month they sat down to investigate the cases, 17and by the first day of the first month they finished dealing with all the men who had married *foreign women.*

It can also be inferred that the post-exile community included interethnic groups through inter-marriage of Israelites. But as Renz points out, after the exile, there was an increase in openness to foreigners, this new Israel included ethnic groups although it emphasized the organization of its tribal line.[18]

In sum, the entire age of the OT shows that Israel was involved in diaspora identity and situations. This tendency of diaspora indicated that the Messiah would come and save all nations and ethnic groups beyond Israel, which made physical Israel a new spiritual Israel, composed of ethnic communities. Jesus Christ is the savior of the Jews as well as the Gentiles; the OT paved the way for Jesus Christ as savior for all human beings to come.

---

17. The land of Canaan was composed of various ethnic groups. They interfered with Nehemiah's project of building up the Jerusalem wall. Refer to Nehemiah 2: "19But when Sanballat the *Horonite*, Tobiah the *Ammonite* official and Geshem the *Arab* heard about it, they mocked and ridiculed us" (italics mine).

18. Renz, *Rhetorical Functions of the Book of Ezekiel*, 235.

Classifications of Diaspora in the OT: Two Types of Scatteredness

Generally speaking there are two categories of diaspora in the Old Testament: (1) diaspora by God's judgment—the exile, and (2) diaspora for mission. These two are related to each other even though they are separated in the initial stage. For example, Daniel was deported to captivity in the 606 BC pre-exile period; and based on repentance, his captivity was caused by God's judgment to Israel's sins, including his; but later he had a mission for prophesying the victorious kingdom of God and the saint's victory during the tribulation period.

Scattered by God's Judgment

The Bible said that the scattered were the result of God's judgment. In Leviticus 26:33, it is written that God warned of scattering Israel. Lev 26: "33I will scatter you among the nations and will draw out my sword and pursue you. Your land will be laid waste, and your cities will lie in ruins." "Scattered" is a symbol of God's judgment.

In Deuteronomy 4:25–27, regarding God's judgment over "doing evil in the eyes of the Lord your God and provoking him to anger," Moses warned Israel: "27The Lord will *scatter* you among the peoples, and only a few of you will survive among the nations to which the Lord will drive you" (italics mine). It is discovered that the Jewish Diaspora was the result of the sovereign outworking of the righteous judgment or justice of God.

This warning happened in history. Israel was put into the exile; "scattered" form as a culmination in the incident of the exile. Psalm 137 is one that represents a deep sorrow and hurt of the exile:

> Ps 137: 1By the rivers of Babylon we sat and wept when we remembered Zion.
> 2There on the poplars we hung our harps, 3for there our captors asked us for songs,
> our tormentors demanded songs of joy; they said, "Sing us one of the songs of Zion!"
> 4How can we sing the songs of the Lord while in a foreign land? 5If I forget you, Jerusalem,
> may my right hand forget its skill. 6May my tongue cling to the roof of my mouth
> if I do not remember you, if I do not consider Jerusalem my highest joy.
> 7Remember, Lord, what the Edomites did on the day Jerusalem fell. "Tear it down," they cried,

> "tear it down to its foundations!" 8Daughter Babylon, doomed to destruction,
> happy is the one who repays you according to what you have done to us.
> 9Happy is the one who seizes your infants and dashes them against the rocks.

These words, "remember," "tormentors," "foreign land," "tear it down," "forget," "doom to destruction," "cries," and "repay," appearing in the above psalm, represent the psyche and life of the exile, diaspora. Generally, in the Old Testament, diaspora was the product of deportation and exile. After the exiles triggered by conquests of the Assyrian, Babylonian, and Roman empires, voluntary migration was triggered by shame or by restoration of dignity. In the OT, diaspora mainly are scattered and sorrowed people by God's judgment; the heart of diaspora is full of sorrow and tears and hope for restoration.

In this sense, the OT diaspora represents the human experience of trial and sorrow under God's judgment; Reimer argued:

> That process, of expulsion and the eventual domestication of the new residence, is deeply embedded in the biblical story. Beyond that, the idea of exile is common human experience across time and cultures. It has also become an important symbol for taking about biblical theology and the life of the church.[19]

This explanation of the OT diaspora is helpful to understand contemporary diaspora around the world. As Epp Weaver puts it, "Exile names a political condition—the physical reality of stateless refugees, of violent dispossession, of enforced homelessness."[20] Exile is an experience of pain.

Gathering as Fulfilling God's New Covenant: Scattered for Mission

The Old Testament gives several positive examples of those who were faithful to God while living in a diaspora environment. There is no direct implication of sin or judgments even if all humankind is sinner and God's judgment is implicit. This type is called to be "scattered" for God's mission. That is, this type of scattered is a scattering for God's deliverance, a typology of God's gathering for the deliverance of the scattered.

In the Old Testament, the scriptures are filled with references to those who left their birthplace, and lived and made a difference in the context of

---

19. Reimer, "Exile and Diaspora," 107.
20. Epp Weaver, *State of Exile*, 15.

"Diaspora." The second pattern of diaspora is that for mission. One of the prominent precursors is Abram. He was called by God to become the father of the faith.

See Genesis 12:1–3, God said to Abram, "Go from your country, your people and your father's household to the land I will show you." Here, Abram is a typical person of diaspora: he left his country, people, father, and household, and lived in a foreign land. Why did God call Abram? Genesis 12 says:

> 2I will make you into a great nation, and I will bless you; I will make your name great, and you will be a blessing. 3I will bless those who bless you, and whoever curses you I will curse; and all peoples on earth will be blessed through you.

The Lord had a plan to bless Abram, make his name great, be a blessing, bless those who bless him, and bless all people on earth through him. The Lord called Abram to leave his place of birth and go to and bless those people that God wanted to bless by the faith of Abram. What is meant by "blessing the Gentile"? Galatians 3 says:

> 8Scripture foresaw that God would justify the Gentiles by faith, and announced the gospel in advance to Abraham: "All nations will be blessed through you." 9So those who rely on faith are blessed along with Abraham, the man of faith.

Here, blessing the Gentile means, "those who rely on faith are blessed along with Abraham, the man of faith." That is, Abram was called by God to be a diaspora of faith so that he blesses the Gentiles by faith. Being diaspora is related to being called into God's mission.

Another inspiring example of diaspora for mission is Jonah, the prophet. In Jonah 1: "1The word of the Lord came to Jonah son of Amittai: 2'Go to the great city of Nineveh and preach against it, because its wickedness has come up before me.'" Here, Jonah is the son of Amittai, who appeared in 2 Kings as a prophet, and his hometown is Gath-hepher, a few miles north of Nazareth, during the reign of Jeroboam II (786–746 BC). Jonah was a prophet who was ordered by God to go to the city of Nineveh to prophesy against it, "for their great wickedness has come up before me." He was sent by God to preach God's judgment and repentance to them. He was sent as one of temporary diaspora for mission to Nineveh.

For convenience, "the scattered" have been divided two types; however, finally these two types become one. This is because the scattered by God's Judgment is moving toward God's salvation and mission. The prophets of the OT proclaim God's new covenant in the exile. One of those prophets is

Ezekiel (36:24–27) describing God's new covenant in the exile. God's gathering present his covenant, including sprinkling clean water, putting a new spirit, removing a heart of stone, giving a heart of flesh, following decrees and keeping laws. All of these blessings were given to people in the exile. The experience of the exile is that of God's salvation.

Characteristics and Significances of Diaspora in the OT

What are characteristics of the scattered in the OT? The following are characteristics and significances of diaspora.

The Typology of God's Judgment/Salvation Motif

First of all, "scattered" signifies God's judgment over human sin; it is the result of God's judgment (Lev 26:33, Deut 4:27). At the same time, this scattered is moving for gathering as the fulfillment of God's covenant—salvation,[21] and the fulfillment of the covenant—salvation—is promised in God's judgment and curse.[22] The motive of diaspora as scattered is twofold in meaning—judgment and deliverance. God's judgment over human sin is expressed as "scattered"; the scattered is waiting for the gathering as deliverance. In this sense, the "scattered" represents both God's judgment and deliverance. Thus the scattered motif penetrates into the heart of the Bible—God's covenant.

There are twelve passages of *Diaspora* in the Septuagint (LXX), which translated the OT into the Greek. This was translated by Jewish scholars who were themselves *dispersed* in Alexandria. Surprisingly, these passages were related to the hope of the re-gathering of the believing Jewish remnant, a confession about God's covenant of salvation. This shows that God's judgment prepared for God's salvation. Two representative passages of the twelve LXX passages are Deuteronomy 30:4 and Psalm 147:2. These passages contain God's promise of both judgment and deliverance.

Diaspora as a Center of God's Deliverance and Mission

In the OT, diaspora is in the center of God's deliverance. For example, Abraham was called by God's plan of salvation and mission to leave his homeland and live a foreign land—Canaan; he became a father of the faith later. Faith

---
21. Robertson, *Christ of the Covenants*.
22. Vos, *Biblical Theology: Old and New Testaments*.

and salvation were practiced and achieved in a diasporic land. The New Covenant occurred in the context of the exile. God's promise of a new heart and a new spirit appeared in the prophecies of Ezekiel in the exile (see Ezek 36:16–31). The new covenant was given in the context of the "scattered," the state of the exile; this is a paradoxical grace.

Jesus pointed out several persons in the OT as representative examples of God's salvation. It is noted that the people of the OT that Jesus mentioned for good faith are almost all diaspora. For example, in Matthew 12:40–42, the men of Nineveh and the Queen of Sheba whose faith Jesus admired were Gentile diaspora; in Luke 4:25–27, he also admired two persons: a widow in Zarephath and Naaman the Syrian. They all were diaspora from the Gentiles. Diaspora centered ministry of God is one of the major thematic characteristics in the Old Testament.

The case of Ruth also has a strong lesson of diaspora centeredness; Ruth was from Moab, a Gentile woman. She became Boaz's wife, namely, a grandmother of David (Ruth 3). Later, she became a member of the genealogy of Jesus Christ (Matt 1). God's redemption is in the context of diaspora.

Identity of Diaspora as Foreigner and Stranger

"I am a foreigner and a stranger" is a confession of Abraham, the father of our faith. This shows that the spirit of the scattered is confessed in a life of Diaspora faith. When his wife, Sara, died, he spoke to the Hittites, Genesis 23: "4I am *a foreigner and stranger* among you. Sell me some property for a burial site here so I can bury my dead" (italics mine). This is his confession of his identity. However, in response to his confession of foreigner and stranger, the Hittites replied to Abraham, "6Sir, listen to us. You are a mighty prince among us. Bury your dead in the choicest of our tombs. None of us will refuse you his tomb for burying your dead."

In addition, there are several texts in the OT in which God's people confess that they are the following: 1 Chronicles 29:15—"For we are *strangers* before thee, and *sojourners*, as were all our fathers: our days on the earth are as a shadow, and there is none abiding" (KJV); Psalm 39:12—"Hear my prayer, O Lord, and give ear unto my cry; hold not thy peace at my tears: for I am a *stranger* with thee, and a *sojourner*, as all my fathers were" (KJV); and Psalm 119:19—"I am a *stranger* in the earth: hide not thy commandments from me" (KJV).

Here, "I am a stranger" signifies the identity of the scattered as diaspora; "foreigner and stranger" is the evidence of the scattered. Alders interprets Abraham's confession of a foreigner and stranger in this meaning: "It should be noted that Abraham approached the children of Heth with all due courtesy. In the presence of those who occupied that territory he presented himself as stranger who, although living among them, claimed no rights of citizenship or ownership. He therefore acknowledges that acquiring a burial plot was not a right but a favor."[23]

At that time, "stranger (*ger*) was a resident alien with some footing in the community but restricted right. In Israel, for example, the *ger* would be granted no land of his own, and in this chapter the keen question under the elaborate courtesies was whether Abraham was to gain a permanent foothold or not. The flattery in [verse] 6 was an inducement to remain a landless dependent. Abraham's rejoinder, naming an individual, made skillful use of the fact that while a group tends to resent an intruder, the owner of an asset welcome a customer."[24] Here the meaning of the scattered is well described.

Calling for God's Covenant

Another characteristic of diaspora in the OT is that it is intertwined with God's covenant; its example is Psalm 10:9-13.

> Ps 105: 9the covenant he made with Abraham, the oath he swore to Isaac. 10He confirmed it to Jacob as a decree, to Israel as an everlasting covenant: 11"To you I will give the land of Canaan as the portion you will inherit." 12When they were but few in number, few indeed, and strangers in it, 13they wandered from nation to nation, from one kingdom to another.

The text above indicates that Israel was in the state of strangers when God made a covenant with them.

God's covenant was made with the Israelites, who were strangers in a land. This implies that God's covenant was deeply interconnected with strangerness, namely, pilgrimage. God's promise, "To you I will give the land of Canaan as the portion you will inherit," inferred that Israel would become strangers in the land of Canaan; also the expression, "they wandered from nation to nation, from one kingdom to another," shows that God's covenant people live in diaspora.

---

23. Alders, *Bible Student Commentary: Genesis*, 56.
24. Kidner, *Tyndale Old Testament: Genesis*, 145.

Host Country: "Compassion on Strangers" as God's Command of Loving Your Neighbors

God commands his people to *love foreigners* among them, which mean to have compassion on strangers:

> Lev 19: 33when a *foreigner* resides among you in your land, do not mistreat them. 34The *foreigner* residing among you must be treated as your native-born. Love them as yourself, for you were *foreigners* in Egypt. I am the Lord your God. (Italics mine)

Here the major point is that "The *foreigner* residing among you must be treated as your native-born. Love them as yourself." This is God's commandment that God's people should love foreigners. However, it is noted that the compassion and love for strangers comes from their experience of being strangers in Egypt. This means that Israelites also were foreigners in Egypt before the exodus. We find that the host country had also been foreigners in the past. That is, the experience and memory of being strangers held by the host country serves as a source of compassion for strangers. That is, the host country should have compassion for foreigners, and God's command is based on its same experience of being foreigners in Egypt, a diasporic land.

THE NEW TESTAMENT

The Definition of Diaspora

Two Greek words in the New Testament—diaspora (dispersion, that which is scattered) and *diaspeiro* (to scatter) convey a similar idea that found in the Old Testament. A typical example is in 1 Peter 1: "1Peter, an apostle of Jesus Christ, to God's elect, exiles scattered throughout the provinces of Pontus, Galatia, Cappadocia, Asia and Bithynia." Here Peter used the word διασπορά (diaspora) for the scattered, which means "dispersion," namely, Israel in Gentile countries.

Here, diaspora is composed of both *diá* ("through") and *speírō* ("sow or scatter seed," which is the root of *sperma*, "seed"). Thus it means, "properly, thoroughly scatter, distribute seed widely." They were literally scattered throughout the Roman Empire (i.e., dispersed) and therefore called "the Diaspora," referring to the Israelites exiled to foreign lands, i.e., Jews residing outside of Palestine (see John 7:35).[25] Diaspora's twofold meaning, 1) dispersion and 2) the seed, is related to God's redemption and the gospel.

---

25. Bible Hub, "Diaspora," lines 1–5.

Finally, the NBD defines the word in this way: "It is interesting that Peter and James, both Palestinian Jews, address Christians as 'the dispersion' (Pet1:1; Jas 1:1). Like the members of the old dispersion, they are 'sojourners' where they live, they enjoy a solidarity unknown to the heathen; and they own a transcendent loyalty to the Jerusalem which is above."[26] In particular, the psychology of the scatted can be described as wounded or suffering.

Historical Overview of Diaspora:

The Four Gospels: Matthew, Mark, Luke, and John

Jesus' Diaspora Life and the Gospel of Diaspora

Jesus was God's promised Messiah incarnate in human history. Tim Naish (2008) describes the incarnation of Jesus Christ as "the stranger in our midst."[27] Jesus Christ lived a diasporic life when he was born in Bethlehem. He continued to live a diasporic life for his public ministry. Before public life, Jesus' hometown was Nazareth, but, beginning his public life, he moved to Capernaum, which became his second home (Matt 4:13). The gospel that Jesus and his disciples preached is diasporic. The first proclamation of the gospel of Jesus Christ was in a diasporic area, which represents the gospel of Diaspora:

> Matt 4: 12when Jesus heard that John had been put in prison, he withdrew to Galilee. 13Leaving Nazareth, he went and lived in Capernaum, which was by the lake in the area of Zebulun and Naphtali—14to fulfill what was said through the prophet Isaiah: 15"Land of Zebulun and land of Naphtali, the Way of the Sea, beyond the Jordan, Galilee of the Gentiles—16the people living in darkness have seen a great light; on those living in the land of the shadow of death a light has dawned." 17from that time on Jesus began to preach, "Repent, for the kingdom of heaven has come near."

These areas belong to diasporas; Galilee was called to be "Galilee of the Gentiles," because of a mixed Gentile-Jewish population.[28] Hendrickson argued that the five places mentioned here in verse 15 refer to five different sections of Greater Galilee: the "land of Zebulun" was west of the Sea of the

---

26. Marshall, *New Bible Dictionary*, "Diaspora," 287.
27. Naish, "Mission, Migration."
28. Hendriksen and Kistemaker, *Matthew*, 243.

Galilee, and was bounded on the north by the "land of Naphtali." The region "toward the Sea" was to the west of these, and extended from north to south along the Mediterranean. "Beyond the Jordan" indicates the territory east of the Jordan. The region which because of the strong pagan elements in its population is called "Galilee of the Gentiles" (*Galil* in the Old Testament) was the northernmost stretch of what used to be called *Naphtali*."[29] The land of Zebulun, land of Naphtali, toward the sea (the way of the sea), beyond the Jordan, and Galilee of the Gentiles are all lands of diaspora. These areas are signified as *darkness* and *in the shadow of death*, indicating a condition of danger, fear, and hopelessness; delusion (blindness of mind and heart, see Eph 4:18), depravity (Acts 26:18), and despondency (Isa 9:2).[30] In particular, it is noted that it was in Galilee of the *Gentiles* that Jesus' gospel was proclaimed. Here, Galilee belongs to the territory of the Israelites; the ownership of twenty towns in Galilee was delivered to Hiram, the Gentile king of Tyre, by king Solomon for his supplying of materials for building the temple (1 Kgs 9:10–14). That is why Galilee has been called of the Gentiles. At that time, the Israelites believed that "a prophet does not come out of Galilee"(John 7:52).

In addition, it is noted that Jesus' disciples left their hometowns to follow Jesus as their master. Jesus and his disciples all left their hometowns and lived as diaspora in different places. In a word, the gospel movement of Jesus and his disciples is really that of diaspora. In particular, Jesus and his disciples as diaspora leaving their hometowns to minister to Gentile areas (Mark 3:8; Luke 6:17).

Texts of Diaspora: John 7:35

In John 7:35, the Jews said to one another, "Where does this man intend to go that we cannot find him? Will he go where our people live scattered among the Greeks, and teach the Greeks?" (NIV). Here the Jews asks, will he go to the Dispersion (of)—or, among—the Greeks, and teach the Greeks?

Generally, the word "Greek" is the Gentile, the Pagan world, which means the Greek in speech at the time. Another word, "Grecian" or "Hellenist," is used for the Jews who had adopted Greek ideas, habits, and speech. Whatever may be the strict meaning of that word, here the word "Greek" is the antithesis to "Jew" in every respect.

Thus, *The Pulpit Commentary* defines "the Dispersion" (τῶν Ἑλλήνων) in two ways:

29. Ibid.
30. Ibid, 224.

(a) The Jewish dispersion among the Greeks is beyond the limits of Palestine (2 Macc 1:27). It is also found in Josephus for the outcast of Israel (see LXX. Ps 146:2; cf. Jas 1:1; 1 Pet 1:1). The Dispersion was the Greater Israel. Most intimate relations subsisted between these scattered Israelites and their political and ecclesiastical centre in the metropolis.

(b) The "Dispersion" may refer to the wide scattering of the Greeks themselves, the natural antithesis to God's covenanted people.[31]

Dispersion is literally, "the spoliation," those stripped of the temple and home of their fathers.

Diaspora refers to the scattered Jews, but if the dispersion may refer to the Greeks themselves, it is used for the Jews who had adopted Greek ideas, habits, and speech, as mentioned earlier, or it seems to me that the Greeks adapted Jewish ideas, habits, and speech, that is, converts or proselyte.

The Book of Acts: The Book of Mission and the Book of Diaspora

Acts is named as the written history of church mission. Here it should be noted that the history of Acts also is that of the Diaspora. This is because there were diaspora over there where there was Christian mission.

The Birth of the Church and Diaspora

The peculiar background of Acts 2, explaining the origin of the church, is the existence of the Diaspora. Acts 2 describes how the church was established: first of all, the Holy Spirit came from heaven and filled the whole house where they were sitting (Acts 2:1–4).

Who was there besides a group numbering about a hundred and twenty when the church started? They are the Diaspora, God-fearing Jews from every nation under heaven, the future gospel-bearer. The church started with diasporas:

> Acts 2: 5Now there were staying in Jerusalem God-fearing Jews from every nation under heaven. 6When they heard this sound, a crowd came together in bewilderment, because each one heard their own language being spoken. 7Utterly amazed, they asked: "Aren't all these who are speaking Galileans? 8Then how is it that each of us hears them in our native language? 9Parthians, Medes and Elamites; residents of Mesopotamia, Judea

---

31. Spence-Jones, et al., *Pulpit Commentary: John*.

and Cappadocia, Pontus and Asia, 10Phrygia and Pamphylia, Egypt and the parts of Libya near Cyrene; visitors from Rome 11(both Jews and converts to Judaism); Cretans and Arabs—we hear them declaring the wonders of God in our own tongues!" 12Amazed and perplexed, they asked one another, "What does this mean?"

Here, diasporas witnessed the wonders of God that the church declared, and asked one another, "What does this mean?" This means that God prepared diaspora for his redemptive plan when he established his church. John Calvin commented on Acts 2:5 about the gathering of scattered people:

> Yea, this was also a work of God worthy to be remembered and wondered at, that in so huge and horrible a scattering abroad of the people, he did always reserve some relics, yea, he caused certain strangers to adjoin themselves unto a people which were in such misery, and, as it were, quite destroyed. For although they lived here and there in exile in far countries, and being one far from another, did, as it were, inhabit diverse worlds, yet did they hold among themselves the unity of faith. Neither doth he call them unadvisedly, and without good consideration, godly men, and men fearing God.[32]

In addition, three of the major points are that, 1) the apostles preach the cross and resurrection of Jesus Christ according to the Bible (Acts 2:14–36; 1 Cor 15:1–19); and 2) they proclaimed "everyone who calls on the name of the Lord will be saved" (Acts 2:21); and 3) the apostles communicated the gospel to ethnic people from several different countries (Acts 2; 11). This is possible in the work of the Holy Spirit.

Diaspora as a Channel of Mission in Acts

The mission of God continued to spread with diaspora. That is, "the church persecuted and scattered" was the secret plan of God's mission: "Acts 8: 1On that day a great persecution broke out against the church in Jerusalem, and all except the apostles were *scattered* throughout Judea and Samaria . . . 4Those who had been *scattered preached* the word wherever they went" (italics mine).

Here the importance is that a great persecution against the church cause it to be "scattered" throughout Judea and Samaria, and spread the gospel. We see that the gospel was spread with the persecution of Christians

---

32. Calvin, "Calvin's Commentaries, Vol. 36," lines 13–16.

in Jerusalem, so Christians were "scattered" or dispersed "throughout the regions of Judea and Samaria" and "Those who had been scattered preached the word wherever they went." This is example of the interactions between "scattered" and "preached."

Here is another example:

> Acts 11: 19now those who had been scattered by the persecution that broke out when Stephen was killed traveled as far as Phoenicia, Cyprus and Antioch, spreading the word only among Jews. 20Some of them, however, men from Cyprus and Cyrene, went to Antioch and began to speak to Greeks also, telling them the good news about the Lord Jesus. 21The Lord's hand was with them, and a great number of people believed and turned to the Lord.

We see that diaspora Christians who "had been scattered by the persecution that broke out when Stephen was killed traveled as far as Phoenicia, Cyprus and Antioch, spreading the word only among Jews." Some of these diasporas, men from Cyprus and Cyrene, went to Antioch and started to speak to Greeks also, telling them the good news about the Lord Jesus. Through the work of the Diaspora, the Antioch church was planted.

The Antioch Church as Diaspora, the Center of World Mission

The Antioch church, the center of world mission in Acts, was composed of diaspora, and hearing the news of the Antioch church, the Jerusalem church sent Barnabas, a Levite from Cyprus (Acts 4:36), to serve as a key role in planting the Antioch church. Barnabas lived as a diaspora after he left Cyprus, and entered into Antioch by being sent by the Jerusalem church. He was already ready for planting the church because "He was a good man, full of the Holy Spirit and faith, and a great number of people were brought to the Lord" (Acts 11:22–24).

Furthermore, he visited Tarsus to find Saul, the second-generation diaspora of Jewish Hebrew living in the Hellenistic area, Tarsus. This city was a center of both Hellenism and Jewish spirit, a Turkish town in the city of Adana, twelve miles from the Mediterranean, on the River Cydnus. "During the Roman period it was the capital of Cilicia. It was important on account of its commerce and its textile products, and was famed for its schools of rhetoric ... The Hellenization of the city began in the days of Alexander the Great; this influence was fully felt by the Jews, who had been colonized at Tarsus by the Seleucids about 170 B.C. During the reign of Antiochus Epiphanes a revolt of these colonists proved a factor in Jewish history (2 Macc 4:30–38).[33]

Barnabas invited Saul from Tarsus to welcome him as his co-worker for planning the church (Acts 11:25–26). For a whole year Barnabas and Saul met with the church and taught great numbers of people. The disciples were called Christians first at Antioch. Here we find that there was the intercultural network of Diaspora; this network of Diaspora became more developed and advanced: "Now in the church at Antioch there were prophets and teachers: Barnabas, Simeon called Niger, Lucius of Cyrene, Manaen (who had been brought up with Herod the tetrarch) and Saul" (Acts 13:1). They were committed to worshiping the Lord and fasting; the Holy Spirit said, "Set apart for me Barnabas and Saul for the work to which I have called them" (v. 3). So after they had fasted and prayed, they placed their hands on them and sent them off (v. 4).

These workers of the Antioch church came from different geographies and cultures: Barnabas from Cyprus, Simeon, likely from Africa, Lucius from Cyrene, and Saul from Tarsus. Various backgrounds, cultures, and traditions of the workers contributed to various ministries toward various people. The merit of diaspora is the variety of cultures, ethnicities, theologies, and traditions. According to Ramsay, in a Latin work entitled *Prophet Collected from the Books*, Acts 13:1–2 was found in the African church early in the fourth century.[34] This shows the Africans and the Westerns got together at Antioch for the world mission.

Missionary Paul, one of the diasporic Antioch church leaders, confesses, "I have become all things to all people so that by all possible means I might save some," the variety of cultures and traditions contribute to saving some people in Jesus Christ who are in various cultures and traditions. This confession represents the mindset and lifestyle of diaspora.

Nevertheless, more importantly, the members all are sensitive to the work of the Holy Spirit; it is deserved to note that the Holy Spirit played a key role in leading diaspora community. Bruce comments, "The Holy Spirit made known his will to them—doubtless through the prophetic utterance of one of the number . . . There are indications that NT Christians were especially sensitive to the divine message and directed the leaders of the church to set Barnabas and Saul apart for a special work to which he had called them."[35]

---

33. Jewish Encyclopedia, "Tarsus," lines 1–11.
34. Ramsay, *St. Paul the Traveler*, 390.
35. Bruce, *New International Commentary: Acts*, 261.

Letters of Paul

Thirteen letters—Romans; 1 and 2 Corinthians; Galatians; Ephesians; Philippians; Colossians; 1 and 2 Thessalonians; 1 and 2 Timothy; Titus; and Philemon—are known as letters Paul sent to the Gentile churches or leaders. These churches appeared in biblical times; they were composed of both Jews and Gentiles. That is, these churches were diasporic; these churches were planted by Diaspora missionaries. Paul himself was a second generation Hebrew in Tarsus, Cilicia, of the Hellenistic areas, which is a distinguished city of free learning.[36] All of Paul's missionary fields were diasporic because he was diaspora. For Paul, the mission center for each local area was the synagogue. "The word 'synagogue' is a Greek word, it means a gathering or an assembly, or perhaps a congregation. The synagogue, then, was the point of communal organization of the Jews in the Diaspora."[37]

Timothy, Paul's disciple, also was diaspora. Timothy, whose name means "honoring God," was trusted coworker of Paul, whom he referred to as a "son in the faith." According to 2 Timothy 1:5 and 3:15, when Timothy was a child, his mother Eunice and his grandmother Lois taught him the Scriptures. He was a native of Lystra, and may have been converted on Paul's first missionary journey (Acts 14:6–23). But Timothy's father was a Greek though his mother was Jew, and he had not been circumcised. Timothy accompanied Paul; Paul had Timothy circumcised because Timothy's mother was Jewish (Acts 16:3).

Silas, another disciple of Paul, was diaspora. He had the Greek and Latin form of the same name, possibly derived from the Aramaic or Hebrew name Saul. He and Paul left Antioch together on a mission to Asia Minor (Acts 15:40–41). Titus, another disciple of Paul was a Gentile. He is very emphatically spoken of as a Gentile, by which is probably meant that both his parents were Gentiles (Gal 2:1–3). Titus also was a Gentile diaspora.

Finally, all teachings written in these letters are consistent with diaspora life. In his Letter to the Philippians, Paul encourages believers to live

---

36. Tarsus is "a major city in Cilicia and the birthplace and early home of Paul. Acts 9:11; 21:39; 22:3. Even in the flourishing period of Greek history it was an important city. In the Roman civil wars, it sided with Caesar and on the occasion of a visit from him its name changed to Juliopolis. Augustus made it a free city. It was renowned as a place of education under the early Roman emperors. Strabo compares it in this respect to Athens and Alexandria. Tarsus also was a place of much commerce. It was situated in a wild and fertile plain on the banks of the Cydnus. No ruins of any importance remain" (Bible Tools, "Tarsos," 1–10). It was distinguished for its wealth and for its schools of learning, in which it rivaled, nay, excelled even Athens and Alexandria, and hence was spoken of as "no mean city." (WebBible Encyclopedia, "Tarsos," lines 1–5)

37. Cohen, "Jewish Diaspora," lines 21–24.

a heavenly life: "But our *citizenship* is in heaven. And we eagerly await a Savior from there, the Lord Jesus Christ, who, by the power that enables him to bring everything under his control, will transform our lowly bodies so that they will be like his glorious body" (Phil 3:20–21). Paul reminded the Philippians of heavenly citizenship, which is one of the major characteristics of Diaspora confession.

With the concept of citizenship, William Barclay comments:

> Here was a picture the Philippians could understand. Philippi was a Roman colony. Here and there at strategic military centres the Romans set down their colonies. In such places the citizens were mostly soldiers who had served their time—twenty-one years—and who had been rewarded with full citizenship. The great characteristic of these colonies was that, where they were, they remained fragments of Rome. Roman dress was worn; Roman magistrate governed; the Latin tongue was spoken; Roman justices were administrated; Roman morals were observed. Even in the ends of the earth they remained unshakably Roman. Paul says to the Philippians, just as the Roman colonists never forget that they belong to Rome, you must never forget that you are citizens of heaven; and your conduct must match your citizenship.[38]

Here Paul tells the Philippians that they are heavenly citizens, and at the same time that they are strangers and pilgrims on earth, namely, they live diasporic lives. In sum, the epistles of Paul are diasporic. In a word, Paul had the politics of diaspora in missionary works.[39]

General/Common Letters

Eight letters—Hebrews; James; 1 and 2 Peter; 1, 2, and 3 John; and Jude—are called the general or common letters. These letters were generally written for general purposes. In particular, the way in which the author of Hebrews described faith written in Hebrews 11 is distinctively diasporic; 3 John 1:5 introduced the concern for strangers: "5Dear friend, you are faithful in what you are doing for the brothers and sisters, even though they are *strangers*[40]

---

38. Barclay, *Letters to the Philippians*, 69.
39. Charles, *Paul and the Politics of Diaspora*.
40. Here, a foreigner refers to a stranger; this word is used in this texts in two categories: 1) properly, Matthew 25:35, 38, 43; Matthew 27:7; 3 John 1:5; 2) topically, α. alien (from a person or thing); without knowledge of, without a share in: with a genitive of the thing; β. new, unheard of: διδαχαι, Hebrews 13:9; ξένον τί a strange, wonderful

to you" (italics mine). At that time, strangers referred to circuit evangelists who preached from here to there or from one nation to another. The following are the texts in which the term scattered was used.

JAMES 1:1

James 1: "1James, a servant of God and of the Lord Jesus Christ, to the twelve tribes *scattered* among the nations: Greetings." It is special that James was writing to those scattered as the recipient of his letter, even though the message is applied to all Christians. James used diaspora as a technical term to refer to Jews outside of Palestine, scattered like seed throughout the Gentile world. The main point is that James called "the scattered," "the twelve tribes." This shows that the scattered people among the nations forms the twelve tribes, representing the whole of Israel. That is, the Diaspora is not part of the twelve tribes, it is its wholeness. This represents James's theology of Diaspora, echoing through the whole of Israel who exists in diaspora.

As mentioned earlier, it is worthy of being noted that *Diaspora* is from *diaspeiro*, to scatter abroad, which is from *dia* (through) and *spora* (a sowing). This is a noun describing the condition of being scattered and thus refers to a scattering or dispersion, as one would scatter seed in a field. Here, it is important that diaspora means seed in a field. That is, diaspora is a seed in God's field through forcibly being scattered even if for various reasons, the Jews were *scattered* into foreign countries "to the outmost parts of heaven" (Deut 30:4). Some Jews had voluntarily moved to other countries for business or other reasons (cf. Acts 2:5); some of these *dispersions* were voluntary, as in the case that during the Greco-Roman period Jews voluntarily migrated to the civilized world, mainly for the sake of trade. However, on the other hand, others had dispersions involuntarily forced upon them by conquering nations such as *Assyria* (2 Kgs 17:6), and *Babylon* (2 Chr 36:10). In the history of Israel, various conquerors had deported the Jews from their homeland in Palestine to various areas. In this sense, diaspora itself is viewed in a negative way, but ironically also is seen in a positive way because it essentially carried the seed, the gospel of God.

For reference to diaspora life, James's major teachings are the following: trial and temptation (1:2–18); listening and doing (1:19–27); favoritism forbidden (2:13); faith and deeds (2:14–26); taming the tongue (3:1–12); two kinds of wisdom (3:13–17); submit yourself (4:1–12); boasting about tomorrow (4:13–17); warning to rich oppressors (5:1–6); patience in suffering (5:7–12); and the prayer of faith (5:13–20). These teachings were given

---

thing, 1 Peter 4:12. See Bible Hub, "Xenos," lines 1–7.

Biblical Understandings of Diaspora 111

to diaspora in particular even though these are applied to all Christians;[41] these are useful to forming a holy life for diaspora on earth.

1 Peter 1:1

> 1 Pet 1: "1Peter, an apostle of Jesus Christ, To God's elect, *exiles*[42] *scattered*[43] throughout the provinces of Pontus, Galatia, Cappadocia, Asia and Bithynia, 2who have been chosen according to the foreknowledge of God the Father, through the sanctifying work of the Spirit, to be obedient to Jesus Christ and sprinkled with his blood: Grace and peace be yours in abundance." (Italics mine)

The epistle of 1 Peter was written to the scattered even though the message is applied to all Christians. Here, "the strangers scattered throughout" indicates the Jews first, who had believed the gospel of Jesus outside Israel, and converted Gentiles also. In the Old Testament, the word "strangers" may refer to religious people (refer to Gen 47:9 and Ps 39:12), but in the New Testament, in particular, Hebrews 11:13, the word specially refers to those who were driven by persecution to seek refuge or religious freedom in those heathen provinces which the influence of their persecuting people did not reach. Here it is very important that Peter views scattered as exile. Exile refers to captive people who experience trauma.

In addition, Peter describes "God's elect" as "sojourners of the dispersion" (RSV). It is used here to describe Christians, and to suggest that in this world they are not only scattered but also away from their true homeland or metropolis in heaven. Such dwelling in this world is therefore

---

41. This division and summary comes from the NIV version (1984).

42. Here, exile is a translation of παρεπίδημος, παρεπίδημον (see ἐπιδημέω), properly, it refers to "one who comes from a foreign country into a city or land to reside there by the side of the natives; hence, stranger; sojourning in a strange place, a foreigner"; in the NT metaphorically, in reference to heaven as the native country, one who sojourns on earth: so of Christians, 1 Pet 1:1; joined with πάροικοι, 1 Pet 2:11, cf. 1:17. See Bible Hub, "Parepidémos."

43. The word scattered is a scattering, dispersion: ἀτομων, opposed to σύμμιξις καί παραζευξις; in the Sept. used of the Israelites dispersed among foreign nations, Deut 28:25; Deut 30:4; especially of their Babylonian exile, Jer 41:17, Isa 49:6; Jdt 5:19; abstract for concrete of the exiles themselves, Ps 146:2 (equivalent to נִדָּחִים, expelled, outcasts); 2 Macc. 1:27; εἰς τήν διασποράν τῶν Ἑλλήνων, unto those dispersed among the Greeks, John 7:35. Transferred to Christians (i.e., Jewish Christians (?)) scattered abroad among the Gentiles: Jas 1:1 (ἐν τῇ διασπορά, namely, οὖσι); παρεπίδημοι διασπορᾶς Πόντου, sojourners far away from home, in Pontus, 1 Pet 1:1 (see παρεπίδημος). See Bible Hub, "Diaspora," lines 10–15.

only a sojourning (see 1 Pet 1:17 where the world is *Parokia*, "a dwelling alongside") in a place to which they do not belong. So they are here called sojourners, *Parepidemoi*, a word that emphasizes both alien nationality and temporary residence.[44]

Hebrew 11

A meaning of stranger in the NT, exile, is summarily described in Hebrews 11:

> 8By faith Abraham, when called to go to a place he would later receive as his inheritance, obeyed and went, even though he did not know where he was going. 9By faith he made his home in the promised land like a *stranger* in a *foreign* country; he lived in tents, as did Isaac and Jacob, who were heirs with him of the same promise . . . 13All these people were still living by faith when they died. They did not receive *the things promised*; they only saw them and welcomed them from a distance, admitting that they were *foreigners* and *strangers* on earth. 14People who say such things show that they are looking for a country of their own. 15If they had been thinking of the country they had left, they would have had opportunity to return. 16Instead, they were longing for a better country—a heavenly one. (Italics mine)

Here, the important discovery is that "it was Abraham, Isaac and Jacob, however, who lived preeminently as 'strangers and pilgrims' on the earth in a sense which is inapplicable to those Israelites of later generation after the settlement in Canaan. To Abraham, Isaac and Jacob, Canaan remained a 'promised' land to the end of their days."[45] "The promised land" represents a better country—a heavenly one. We understand that, in essence, all believers, signified in the lives of the fathers of believers such as Abraham, Isaac, and Jacob, move toward a better country—a heavenly one.

Summarized from the above quotation of Hebrews 11, the core characteristics of Diaspora are as follows:

(a) The reason they move is faith in God.

(b) They left their birthplace and lived in a foreign country.

(c) They move along with being called by God to go to the place.

(d) They lived like a strangers and even strangers on earth.

---

44. Stibbs and Walls, *Tyndale New Testament Commentaries: I Peter*, 72.
45. Bruce, *Epistle to the Hebrews*, 304.

(e) They were longing for a better country—a heavenly one.

The life of Diaspora equals those of the fathers of the faith; furthermore, it equals the common life of believers. Here, we found that the life of Diaspora as strangers penetrates the core values of Christian faith, however, later generations of Abraham lost this vision and that is why they distorted and were taken away from the faith.

For reference, 1 Peter's core teachings in which Christians were called Diaspora are as follows: praise to God for a living hope (1:3–12); be holy (1:13–2:3); the living stone and a chosen people (2:4–10); to abstain from sinful desires (2:11–13); submission to rulers and masters (2:13–25); suffering for doing good (3:8–22); living for God's glory (4:1–11); suffering for being a Christian (4:12–19); be shepherds of God's flock (5:2–14).

This life is characteristic of the life of Diaspora; Diasporic life accompanies transcendent and holy life as well as submission to social orders. A transcendent Christian life can overcome the imminence of secular society through seeing heavenly hope and living out pilgrimage.

The Book of Revelation

The Revelation of Saint John began with the reports of seven Diasporic churches—Ephesus, Smyrna, Pergamum, Thyatira, Sardis, Philadelphia, and Laodicea—consisting of Gentiles and Jews. The message was revealed to Saint John. At that time, John was trapped in prison on the island of Patmos. Patmos is a small rocky island in the Aegean Sea; on account of its dreary and desolate character, this island was used by the Roman emperors as a place of confinement for criminals. St. John was banished to this island by the Emperor Domitian; "95–97 AD, the date St. John was exiled to the island of Patmos where he wrote the Book of Revelations. He stayed approximately 15 years before returning to Ephesus."[46] In Patmos, a foreign land, the Revelation was recorded by John.

The book of Revelation is the last book of the Bible, which describes the fulfillment of the biblical revelations of the Old and New Testaments. Here, the spiritual journey of scattered people will accomplish its peak in the second coming of Jesus Christ and end in heaven, the New Jerusalem. All plagues written in the seven seals (chapters 5–8), seven trumpets (chapters 11–14), and seven bowls of God's wrath (chapter 16) will be poured out in this world, and Babylon will be destroyed. Finally, the pilgrims realized that they are right.

46. PatmosIsland.com, "Patmos Island, " lines 9–11. See also Bible History Online, "Island of Patmos," 1–10.

In sum, from the Four Gospels to the Revelation, the NT is the full of the concept of Diaspora and its activities; all of Christian life can be described with the identity and mission of Diaspora.

Characteristics and Significance of Diaspora in the NT

The Gospel of Diaspora

What is the essence of the gospel Jesus preached? The gospel provided redemption through blood, the forgiveness of sins (Eph 1:7), completing in heaven. This implies that all believers live in Diaspora on earth because they ultimately move toward a heavenly country. Jesus explains his goal in coming to the earth: "in my Father's house are many rooms . . . if I go and prepare a place for you, I will come back and take you to be with me" (John 14:1–2). The promise of Jesus indicates that his disciples will soon go to heaven and will receive rooms that Jesus prepared.

There are the examples of the gospel of Diaspora Jesus proclaims; those who Jesus commended as examples of good faith in the OT are almost all diaspora, those scattered in foreign lands, Gentile or Jew. Who were people Jesus praised as those representing the spirit of the gospel in the Old Testament? See here:

> Luke 4: 24"Truly I tell you," he continued, "no prophet is accepted in his hometown. 25I assure you that there were many widows in Israel in Elijah's time, when the sky was shut for three and a half years and there was a severe famine throughout the land. 26Yet Elijah was not sent to any of them, but to *a widow in Zarephath* in the region of Sidon. 27And there were many in Israel with leprosy in the time of Elisha the prophet, yet not one of them was cleansed—only *Naaman the Syrian*."(Italics mine)

> Matt 12: 38Then some of the Pharisees and teachers of the law said to him, "Teacher, we want to see a sign from you." 39He answered, "A wicked and adulterous generation asks for a sign! But none will be given it except the sign of the prophet Jonah. 40For as *Jonah* was three days and three nights in the belly of a huge fish, so the Son of Man will be three days and three nights in the heart of the earth. 41The men of *Nineveh will* stand up at the judgment with this generation and condemn it; for they repented at the preaching of Jonah, and now something greater than Jonah is here. 42The *Queen of the South* will rise at the judgment with this generation and condemn it; for she came

from the ends of the earth to listen to Solomon's wisdom, and now something greater than Solomon is here. (Italics mine)

The gospel, typified in the OT, was preached to Gentile diaspora who visited Israel, foreigners who were Gentiles living a foreign land. In addition, he states that Gentile cities, Tyre, Sidon, and Sodom, were better off than the cities of Israel, Korazin, Bethaida, and Capernaum, on the day of judgment (Matt 11:20–24). Here it is noted that diasporas are in the center of God's salvation.

The apostles and disciples of Jesus in the church were scattered as diaspora to preach the gospel. We cannot understand the Acts and missionary journey without understanding diaspora. The church was established with a gathering of diasporas from within the country and the outside countries (Acts 2). Peter and James call Christians to be Diaspora (Jas 1:1; 1 Pet 1:1–2); Peter understands Diaspora Christians as strangers and foreigners (1 Pet 2:11–12).

This series of descriptions confirms that the gospel can be called as Diaspora. Humankind is existentially diaspora, scattered by God's judgment due to sin, and scattered voluntarily or involuntarily for preaching the gospel after accepting Jesus Christ as savior. In this sense, the gospel is Diaspora. Every page of the gospel is Diasporic. In a word, Diaspora is an isolated community of salvation, which has already experienced or is still waiting for Jesus Christ.

Diaspora as God's Choice for Salvation and Mission

First Peter 1:1 offers essential factors of the word Diaspora; he describes Diaspora (dispersion) with two words: God's elect and exile. The Greek word for "chosen" is *eklektos* from the verb *eklego*. This in middle voice, *eklegomai*, means to select or pick out for one's self, which is derived from *ek* (out) and *lego* (call), meaning literally the "called out ones" or "chosen out ones." The idea of *eklektos* is the ones who have been chosen for one's self, selected out of a larger number. The proper interpretation of the meaning of *elect* in each of these NT uses depends on the context; generally, God's election includes his mission as well as salvation. This is clearer as the word "scattered" is viewed as the seed scattered in the field. That is, Diaspora can be called the seed of the kingdom

The verb *eklego* is used in Ephesians 1:4 where it is rendered "chosen." This word refers to the act of God, in sovereign grace, choosing out certain from among mankind for himself, and in addition, the verb is in middle voice, speaking of the subject acting in his own interest. "Chosen" is for sovereign grace, namely, God's elect for salvation.

It is important to note that the words "according to" are the translation of *kata* whose root meaning is "down," meaning the idea of domination. In other words, this choice out from a number was dominated by the foreknowledge of God the Father. This word foreknowledge makes its meaning clear in its use in Acts 2: "23This man was handed over to you by God's deliberate plan and foreknowledge; and you, with the help of wicked men, put him to death by nailing him to the cross." Diaspora is God's foreknowledge beyond human knowledge and experience.

Here, God's deliberate plan explains the meaning of foreknowledge; the Greek word *boule*, "plan or counsel," refers to an interchange of opinions, the exchange of deliberative judgment. The word "deliberate; determinate" is the translation of *horismenei*, a perfect participle which refers to the past act of affecting something with the present result that some certain thing has been decreed. This means that God's foreknowledge is more than previous knowledge, and is based on the exchange of God's counsel, God's judgment through the death of Jesus Christ on the cross. Thus the word "foreknowledge" goes toward that counsel of God in which, through deliberate judgment, the Lord Jesus was to be delivered into human hands to be crucified for the cleansing of their sins. In 1 Peter 1:20, Jesus Christ is the one who was foreordained before the foundation of the world to be the Lamb who was to take away the sins of lost humanity. In this sense, God's election refers to God's plan of salvation. That is, Diaspora is called to God's salvation, which means that saved Diaspora believe in and carry the gospel they are ready for preaching.

The Church as the Gathering of the Scattered

To understand the nature of the church, we need to investigate how the church began. First of all, the church was established with diaspora. The disciples of Jesus who participated in building the church are composed of men of Galilee (see Acts 1: "11'Men of Galilee,' they said, 'why do you stand here looking into the sky? This same Jesus, who has been taken from you into heaven, will come back in the same way you have seen him go into heaven'"). As we know, these men of Galilee are diasporic.

The place in which the church was established was in an upstairs room where they were staying in Jerusalem (see Acts 1:12-13). This means that the disciples of Jesus moved from Galilee to Jerusalem, confirming that they were diaspora within a nation who had left their places of birth. In addition, the Diaspora from foreign nations was "God-fearing Jews from every nation under heaven" (Acts 2:5). In particular, the expression, "from every nation under heaven," echoes God's promise of the gathering of the scattered in Deuteronomy 34. Thus, the church was established with the fulfillment of the covenant of the scattered. The church was given birth as the gathering of the scattered.

As Acts 13 notes, the Antioch church, which become a center of world mission, was composed of culturally diverse Diaspora but there was no conflict or division because they all were led by the Holy Spirit. Diaspora's priority is to preach and spread the gospel. They all were one by obeying the work of the Holy Spirit (Eph 4:1–4). Here, the common point of Diaspora churches is that the members of the church were fulfilled by the Holy Spirit (Acts 2:4; Acts 13:1–3).

The Identity of the Scattered (Diaspora) as Exiles or Strangers.

The word "scattered" is translated to various words: exiles (ESV and NIV); temporary residents (GWT); refugees (TEV); sojourners (NAB); those away from their homes (NCV); pilgrims (NKJV); living as foreigners (NLT); those who have settled down alongside a pagan population (Wuest); those temporarily residing abroad (NET). In addition, the word exile is *Parepidemos* in the Greek, which is used three times in the NT (Heb 11:13; 1 Pet 1:1 and 2:11), and is translated in the NAS as exiles; reside as aliens; and strangers. The KJV translates it twice as "pilgrim."

Here, *parepidemos* literally means "a stranger or sojourner." This identity points to not simply one who is passing through, but a foreigner who has lived a little while next to or among the native and host people. *Parepidemos* continues to describe one who makes a brief stay in a strange or foreign place, not expecting to be regarded as a native of the place he resided. Early Christians who carried the gospel lived as Diaspora as aliens or foreigners in this world, and longed for the better world above. Phan says:

> For them [Christians], migration was an essential part of the Christian permanent self-consciousness and theological—and not merely sociological—identity. No doubt this self-description had an eschatological and spiritual overtone insofar as Christians considered themselves to be the pilgrim people of God on the march toward the Kingdom of God.[47]

---

47. Phan, "Migration in the Patristic Era," 48–9.

Diaspora as God's Strategy of Mission

In Acts, Diaspora played a key role in preaching the gospel, which often appears in Pauline missionary strategy. After being sent as missionaries by the Antioch church, the missionary strategy of Paul is to enter the synagogue, a center of Jewish Diaspora community, and preach the gospel. Aquila and Priscilla, written in Acts 18, form a typical model of Diaspora, devoting to Christian mission. In Acts 18:11, Paul stayed for a year and a half, teaching them the word of God, and Paul left the brothers and sailed for Syria, accompanied by Priscilla and Aquila. They arrived at Ephesus, where Paul left Priscilla and Aquila. Here they met a Jew named Apollos, a native of Alexandria (Acts 18:24), teaching in the synagogue. Priscilla and Aquila taught Apollos about the way of God. Acts 18:26 says: "He began to speak boldly in the synagogue. When Priscilla and Aquila heard him, they invited him to their home and explained to him the way of God more adequately."

Here it was noted that Priscilla and Aquila were Diaspora, laypeople, who were the co-workers of Paul, and the Bible teachers who taught Apollos regarding the way of God more accurately. Priscilla and Aquila host the church at Ephesus: 1 Corinthians 16: "19the churches in the province of Asia send you greetings. Aquila and Priscilla greet you warmly in the Lord, and so does the church that meets at their house." Finally, in the Letter to Romans, Paul introduced this couple: "3Greet Priscilla and Aquila, my fellow workers in Christ Jesus, 4who risked their necks for my life, to whom not only I but also all the churches of the Gentiles give thanks" (Rom 16:3–4 RSV). Paul's tribute shows how Diaspora played an enormous key role in missionary works. Diaspora are workers sent and prepared by God; the bottom line here is how Diaspora were discovered and selected for missionary networks.

CORE CONCEPTS OF DIASPORA IN THE OLD AND NEW TESTAMENTS

Diaspora as God's Grace and Salvation through Judgment

Originally, diaspora is the result of God's judgment (Lev 26:32; Deut 4:26). However, ironically God promised his redemptive plan through/after his judgment and punishment:

> Deut 30: 1When all these blessings and curses I have set before you come on you and you take them to heart wherever the Lord your God *disperses* you among the nations, 2and when you and

> your children return to the Lord your God and obey him with all your heart and with all your soul according to everything I command you today, 3then the Lord your God will restore your fortunes and have compassion on you and gather you again from all the nations where he *scattered* you. 4Even if you have been banished to the most distant land under the heavens, from there the Lord your God will *gather* you and bring you back. (Italics mine)

More importantly, God promises to gather and bring his people back whenever the Lord your God disperses you among the nations. We find that God's judgment turns to the restoration of his sinned and judged people. Of course, it is noted that God's grace works with the obedience of his people to God. Reimer asserts that exile representing the imposition of punishment turns to "a sign of grace," which is "a metaphor for God's renewing the life of faith."[48] He says:

> If exile represents the imposition of punishment which those exiled wish to reverse as quickly as possible, Diaspora on the other hand suggests a situation which can be embraced. John Howard Yoder described the scenario with typical power, finding his stimulus in the "poem-drama," *Jeremiah*, by Stefan Zweig: "dispersion is mission," was Yoder's pithy formulation. . . . The dispersal that came in judgment on Babel reasserted the divine intention of diversity, against the autonomous, absolutizing tendency of the human creatures. From this perspective, "Diaspora" is a sign of grace. The resonances between this first dispersal from "Babylon" (= Heb. "Babel") and a later dispersal to Babylon shed further light on how it is that in *galut*/diaspora in Babylon, God's people find a vocation to the wider world (Jeremiah 29:7).

It is noted that the diaspora, judged through exile, entered into God's plan that God's people find a vocation to the wider world; Jeremiah 29: "7Also, they seek the peace and prosperity of the city to which I have carried you into exile. Pray to the Lord for it, because if it prospers, you too will prosper." Diaspora scattered by God's judgment represent God's paradoxical grace. "Diaspora is a sign of grace."

---

48. Reimer, "Exile and Diaspora: Leaving and Living," 16.

Diaspora as the Seed of God's Kingdom

First of all, the Diaspora is understood as the twelve tribes. Here the twelve tribes are addressed as those who have received Jesus as their Messiah (John 1:11–13). Here the phrase "the twelve tribes" is clearly a Jewish expression denoting the Jewish people as a whole, meaning God's people. It is noted that diaspora comes from *diaspeiro*, meaning "to scatter abroad," and ultimately means scattering seed, a sowing, which is a noun describing the condition of being scattered as one would scatter seed in a field. In a word, Diaspora is a sowing, like scattering seed in a field.

It is interesting to note that Diaspora is understood as a sowing. Here, God is the sower; the seed that is scattered is his people. Here his scattered people are signified as his seed scattered in a field. In the parable of the sower in Matthew 13, the seed is the people of the kingdom, all Christians. See here:

> Matt 13: 36Then he left the crowd and went into the house. His disciples came to him and said, "Explain to us the parable of the weeds in the field." 37He answered, "The one who sowed the good seed is the Son of Man. 38The field is the world, and the good seed stands for the people of the kingdom. The weeds are the people of the evil one.

Here it is found that a Diaspora, which echoes and implies the seed in Greek, is the person who carried the gospel, compared to the seed scattered in a field of the world. This proclaims that Diaspora are the seed for the field of the world, meaning God's calling of Diaspora for mission. The experience of diaspora in diverse cultures is essential to various persons and cultures. Paul emphasizes the variety in doing mission, 1 Corinthians 9:19–23 says:

> 1 Cor 9: 19though I am free and belong to no one; I have made myself a slave to everyone, to win as many as possible. 20To the Jews I became like a Jew, to win the Jews. To those under the law I became like one under the law (though I myself am not under the law), so as to win those under the law . . . 22To the weak I became weak, to win the weak. I have become all things to all people so that by all possible means I might save some. 23I do all this for the sake of the gospel that I may share in its blessings.

The merit of Diaspora is to approach various people with various cultures. The variety becomes a ministry tool for workers. This explains why Diaspora is suitable to minister to diverse cultures and a global society. Traditional missiology is based on authoritarian or ethnocentric structure. In *Oxford*

Bibliographies, Elizabeth Elliott Cooper defines the word ethnocentrism and explains the risk of its bias.

> Ethnocentrism is a term applied to the cultural or ethnic bias—whether conscious or unconscious—in which an individual views the world from the perspective of his or her own group, establishing the in-group as archetypal and rating all other groups with reference to this ideal. This form of tunnel vision often results in: (1) an inability to adequately understand cultures that are different from one's own and (2) value judgments that preference the in-group and assert its inherent superiority, thus linking the concept of ethnocentrism to multiple forms of chauvinism and prejudice, including nationalism, tribalism, racism, and even sexism and disability discrimination.[49]

Ultimately, ethnocentrism in mission results in an inability to understand the reality of chauvinism and prejudice. It is admitted that traditional missiology has been under the influence of this tunnel vision. However, Diaspora, called "strangers," are called to "being not in charge" (to use Yoder's term),[50] which means that he/she does not matter to ethnocentrism from every nation under heaven.

Diaspora as the Model of a Christian Life—Pilgrimage

What is the meaning of a Diaspora life for Christians? What does Diaspora life signify? On the meaning of the Diasporic life, in his conclusion to "Exile and Diaspora: Leaving and Living," David J. Reimer states, "Diaspora implies a different and more complex relationship between where-I-live, and where-I-belong. Security, as the people of Genesis 11 found, is not to be found in a place, but in the presence of God." For Diaspora life, "home is not hope"; rather "it remains clear that God's people are sustained in going 'home,' which is above."[51] In Daniel 1:1–21 and 3:1–18, he found "the life of Diaspora."

Firstly, in commenting on Daniel 1:1–21, Reimer emphasizes "the essential tension of the resident alien":

> This glimpse into Diaspora life affirms the essential tension of the resident alien. It was the same tension that Augustine described first in his Psalms Commentary, before it came to full expression

---

49. Cooper, "Ethnocentrism," 1–8.
50. Smith-Christopher, *Biblical Theology of Exile*, 9.
51. Reimer, "Exile and Diaspora: Leaving and Living," 114.

> in his great *City of God*: in extended comment on psalm 62:4, he writes, "and these two cities are meanwhile mingled . . . against each other mutually in conflict . . . And sometimes . . . certain men belonging to the city of Babylon, order matters belonging to Jerusalem, and again certain men belonging to Jerusalem, order matter belonging to Babylon."[52]

Here, the life of Diaspora is characterized by conflict, as described in the two cities in Augustine's commenting on Psalm 62:4, "Surely they intend to topple me from my lofty place; they take delight in lies. With their mouths they bless, but in their hearts they curse. Here conflict issues turn on fundamental loyalties . . . Daniel's request arises from his loyalty to God." This means that Diaspora live in a conflicting coexistence of the city of God and the city of the world.

Secondly, "in Daniel 3:1–18, the story teaches that Diaspora should stand up before the threat life because of refusal to comply. Sometimes it is the moment in the furnace itself that is the focal point for reflection in this story (v. 25, "He said, 'Look! I see four men walking around in the fire, unbound and unharmed, and the fourth looks like a son of the gods'"), but significant factors for Diaspora living crop up before that."[53]

Due to the loyalty to God, Diaspora living can be thrown into the furnace. "It is not even the fact of brave resistance that is impressive: the key phrase here is in verse 18: 'But if not . . .' in Daniel 1, they 'won.' Here keeping loyalties in their proper relation is declared without regard to personal well-being."

In sum, the Diaspora is not just a specific group, who appeared and disappeared in a historically given time, indicating the pattern of ideal Christian life. As Peter well states, all Christians are called to be "aliens and strangers in the world" (1 Pet 2:11). This means that all Christians are Diaspora. All Christians are going home above through suffering and pain, like all Diaspora.

Here is a living attitude of people of faith on earth; their life is a transcendental pilgrimage toward the city in heaven.

> Heb 11: 13All these people were still living by faith when they died.
> They did not receive the things promised;
> they only saw them and welcomed them from a distance,
> admitting that they were foreigners and strangers on earth.

---

52. Ibid., 118.
53. Ibid., 119.

14People who say such things show that they are looking for a country of their own.
15If they had been thinking of the country they had left, they would have had opportunity to return.
16Instead, they were longing for a better country—a heavenly one.
Therefore God is not ashamed to be called their God, for he has prepared a city for them.

5

The Theological Foundations and Implications of Diaspora

The theological foundations and implications of Diaspora will explore how we understand the concept of Diaspora theologically, and in what aspects it is helpful toward understanding theological concepts such as the Trinity—the Father, the Son, and the Holy Spirit—human beings, salvation, church, sanctification, and mission. This offers us new light and ideas for dynamic Christian theology, leading to a formulation of Diaspora missiology. It also guides us to learn to articulate and enlarge faith in biblical revelation though the concept of Diaspora, and to understand the nature and functions of the Christian faith, the church, and mission.

THE DOCTRINE OF THE TRINITY IN DIASPORA

We begin our theological foundations of "Diaspora" with the doctrine of the Trinity: God the Father, the Son, and the Holy Spirit. The author and source of Christian mission is the Trinity; the Godhead. Who and what is God from the perspective of Diaspora?

The Doctrine of God the Father

Nothing in history happens by chance. Every geographical move of every human being who ever lived happens within the overall will and sovereignty of God. The fact that God created nations (Gen 25:23; Ps 86:10) and languages/cultures (Gen 11:1, 6, 7, and 9), and determined the place (space) and the timing (time) of our habitation. The passage in Acts 17:26–29 implies that he not only created the Diaspora, and set up and designed their time and place, but he lead to seeking to find God for the salvation of the lost. All dispersed people have a role to play in God's redemptive history.

In the doctrine of God, first of all, God the Father is that of the lost son who was living a diaspora life, away from his father's house. The diaspora life of the lost son serves to find God the Father.

> Luke 15: 21The son said to him, 'Father, I have sinned against heaven and against you. I am no longer worthy to be called your son.' 22But the father said to his servants, 'Quick! Bring the best robe and put it on him. Put a ring on his finger and sandals on his feet. 23Bring the fattened calf and kill it. Let's have a feast and celebrate. 24For this son of mine was dead and is alive again; he was lost and is found.' So they began to celebrate.

Here it is noted that God is the Father who welcomes the lost son. The concept of Diaspora as represented in the lost son's life affects the doctrine of God the Father. Here, the father who is waiting for the lost son in diaspora life sheds a new light on the understanding of who God the Father is—love, compassion, forgiveness, endurance.

The Doctrine of Jesus Christ: Christology

His Incarnation and Diaspora life

It is noted that Tim Naish described the incarnation of Jesus as a "stranger in our midst,"[1] which means that Jesus came down with the identity of diaspora. After that, Jesus lived a diasporic life all of his days. What happened in places when Jesus was born and moved by Mary and Joseph? Luke 2:2–7 said, Joseph lived in the town of Nazareth in Galilee and went to up to Judea, to Bethlehem, the town of David. After Jesus was born, Joseph went to Egypt because of Herod's attempting to kill Jesus (Luke 2:13–15).

Jesus said he had no place to lay his head: Matthew 8: "18When Jesus saw the crowd around him, he gave orders to cross to the other side of the lake. 19Then a teacher of the law came to him and said, 'Teacher, I will follow you wherever you go.' 20Jesus replied, 'Foxes have dens and birds have nests, but the Son of Man has no place to lay his head.'" This remark shows that

---

1. Naish, "Mission, Migration."

Jesus was not a permanent resident. Also, in his hometown, Jesus' ministry was never welcomed by his people. Matthew 13: "57And they took offense at him. But Jesus said to them, 'A prophet is not without honor except in his own town and in his own home.' 58And he did not do many miracles there because of their lack of faith." A prophet is without honor in his own town and in his own home. In other words, in the same way as most prophets, Jesus ministered outside the place of his birth, which is the way of Diaspora.

In particular, in preaching the gospel, Jesus visited synagogues, which are the centers of Jewish Diaspora. "The synagogue, then, was the point of communal organization of the Jews in the Diaspora."[2] Jesus visited the center of Jewish Diaspora. Cohen argues that many of our sources tell us that Jews would gather in synagogues regularly, perhaps every Saturday on the Sabbath, or perhaps more often than that, in order to read the laws, to read the Torah, the sacred book of Moses and to expound upon it. Thus Jesus lived a Diaspora life all of his days; so believers should live a Diaspora life, following Jesus Christ.

The Crucifixion of Jesus

Regarding Diaspora on Christology, the most important fact is that the cross of Jesus Christ makes Jews and Gentiles one body. That is, Jews and Gentiles were reconciled through the cross of Christ. We find that the concept of Diaspora plays key role in presenting the nature of the crucifixion of Christ. This is the message to Ephesians:

> Eph 2: 11Therefore, remember that formerly you who are Gentiles by birth and called "uncircumcised" by those who call themselves "the circumcision" (which is done in the body by human hands)—12remember that at that time you were separate from Christ, excluded from citizenship in Israel and *foreigners* to the covenants of the promise, without hope and without God in the world. (Italics mine)

Here, Gentiles were called foreigners by Jews; "those who call themselves 'the circumcision.'" Diaspora were originally separated from Christ, excluded from citizenship. However what change did the crucifixion of Christ bring about to the relations between Jews and Gentiles as foreigners?

> Eph 2: 13But now in Christ Jesus you who once were far away have been brought near by the blood of Christ. 14For he himself is our peace, who has made the two groups one and has

---

2. Cohen, "Jewish Diaspora," lines 21–22

> destroyed the barrier, the dividing wall of hostility, 15by setting aside in his flesh the law with its commands and regulations. His purpose was to create in himself one new humanity out of the two, thus making peace, 16and in one body to reconcile both of them to God through the cross, by which he put to death their hostility.

Here, one new humanity is the Jew plus the Gentile in Christ, by the blood of Christ, Jesus has made the two groups one and has destroyed the barrier, the dividing wall of hostility. Finally,

> Eph 2: 19Consequently, you are no longer *foreigners* and *strangers*, but fellow citizens with God's people and also members of his household, 20built on the foundation of the apostles and prophets, with Christ Jesus himself as the chief cornerstone. 21In him the whole building is joined together and rises to become a holy temple in the Lord. 22And in him you too are being built together to become a dwelling in which God lives by his Spirit. (Italics mine)

Thus, Gentiles, who were foreigners and strangers, became "fellow citizens with God's people" and also "members of his household," which works in principle both "already" and "yet to come"; in accepting Jesus they were no longer foreigners and strangers in principle, but this was not yet completed on earth. It was in heaven that they would totally be foreigners and strangers no more. In the cross of Christ, diaspora—foreigners and strangers—became fellow citizens with God's people and members of his household, and became a holy temple, being built together to become a dwelling in which God lives by his Spirit. The issue of Diaspora is related to a discussion of the doctrine of atonement, which is often called "the heart of the gospel."[3] This is because Diaspora were welcomed, and by the blood of Christ became the one body to reconcile both of them to God through the cross, by which he put to death their hostility.

The Doctrine of the Holy Spirit: Pneumatology

Contextualization of the Holy Spirit in Diaspora

When the Holy Spirit came over the church on the day of its birth, diaspora "from every nation under heaven" (Acts 2:5) were standing there:

---

3. Berkhof, *Systematic Theology*, 367.

Acts 2: 8then how is it that each of us hears them in our native language? 9Parthians, Medes and Elamites; residents of Mesopotamia, Judea and Cappadocia, Pontus and Asia, 10Phrygia and Pamphylia, Egypt and the parts of Libya near Cyrene; visitors from Rome 11(both Jews and converts to Judaism); Cretans and Arabs—we hear them declaring the wonders of God in our own tongues!" 12Amazed and perplexed, they asked one another, "What does this mean?"

Here, the Holy Spirit inspired diaspora to hear the disciples speaking in their own native language. This is the contextualization of language by the Holy Spirit. That is, the Holy Spirit, who communicates the gospel into various languages and cultures, is a spirit of contextualization. It should be emphasized that contextualization is basically processed by the Holy Spirit. Today, however, recent missiology does not emphasize the contextualization of the Holy Spirit. In Acts 15: "28it seemed good to the Holy Spirit and to us not to burden you with anything beyond the following requirements." The Holy Spirit enables those who hear to "[open their] heart to respond to Paul's message" (Acts 16:14), mark with a seal (Eph 1:13), or be given the Spirit of wisdom and revelation (Eph 1:17). These works make the hearer respond to the gospel. This process can be called the contextualization of the Holy Spirit.

The Sanctifying Works of the Holy Spirit on Chosen Diaspora

In 1 Peter 1:1, it is noted that the Trinitarian God works on diaspora. Three prepositional phrases describe the elected strangers of diaspora as chosen (a) according to the foreknowledge of God the Father, (b) through the sanctifying work of the Spirit, and (c) to be obedient to Jesus Christ and sprinkled with his blood.

Here, the Holy Spirit serves as the instrument for the practical working of God's electing foreknowledge in the lives of believers in Jesus Christ, distinguished from their surrounding culture for a sanctified and holy life of obedience to serving Jesus.[4]

Missionary Works of the Holy Spirit in Diaspora

Who and what is the Holy Spirit in missionary works? When he ascended into heaven, Jesus commanded to his disciples twofold: (1) "Do not leave

---

4. Elliot, *1 Peter*, 319.

Jerusalem, but wait for the gift my Father promised" (Acts 1:4); (2) "But you will receive power when the Holy Spirit comes on you; and you will be my witnesses in Jerusalem, and in all Judea and Samaria, and to the ends of the earth" (v. 8). His disciples go far to the ends of the earth with the power of the Holy Spirit. This commandment was partly accomplished by Philip, Peter, Paul, and Jesus' disciples.

In particular, Paul visited Jewish synagogues—centers of Diaspora community—in the Gentile lands, and the Holy Spirit worked there. The Holy Spirit uses Diasporas for his mission (see Acts 8:1–4).

Leaders of the church at Antioch were different in their cultural backgrounds and languages, but the Holy Spirit communicated to each of them, making them one, and led them to obey the missionary commandment of the Holy Spirit. Diaspora, with diverse cultures and languages, cannot do mission without the work of the Holy Spirit; this implies that the work of the Holy Spirit is essential and indispensable.

The Holy Spirit Forming the One Body of Christ in Jews and Gentiles

The Holy Spirit forms one body that includes various ethnic groups. First Corinthians 12: "12Just as a body, though one, has many parts, but all its many parts form one body, so it is with Christ. 13For we were all baptized by one Spirit so as to form one body—whether Jews or Gentiles, slave or free—and we were all given the one Spirit to drink." Here the Holy Spirit serves to form the oneness among various members. In the Corinthian church, there were various ethnic groups and social classes—Jews and Gentiles, slave and free.

Regarding the relationship between the doctrine of God and Diaspora, in *Scattered to Gather: Embracing the Global Trend of Diaspora*, the Lausanne Committee for World Evangelization (LCWE) concluded:

> The will and the work of God the Father, the Son, and the Holy Spirit are clearly revealed in the Scriptures, starting from creation (Genesis 1) to consummation (Revelation 22). The historical overview of the Old and the New Testament attests that "Diaspora" is intrinsically related to redemptive history and sovereignly planned and executed by the Father, Son, and Holy Spirit.

That is, the grace of the Lord Jesus Christ, the love of God, and the fellowship of the Holy Spirit are the subject and source of Diaspora missiology.

The major work of the Holy Spirit is to make many one: "13For we were all baptized by *one* Spirit so as to form *one* body—whether Jews or Gentiles, slave or free—and we were all given the *one* Spirit to drink. 14Even so the body is not made up of *one* part but of many" (1 Cor 12:13–14). The work of the Holy Spirit forms one body among many ethnic groups—Diaspora.

EXILE THEOLOGY

The Necessity of Exile Theology for Renewing Christian Theology

In 1977, there was published a comprehensive book regarding exile theology: *A Theology of Exile: Judgment/Deliverance in Jeremiah and Ezekiel*, in which Thomas M. Raitt clarifies:

> We ask not merely how God moves from wrath to love, but how do the prophets move from the oracle of judgment to the oracle of deliverance? This question is leading to the study on the existence of exile, having the same root as Diaspora.[5]

He argues that the Old Testament studies stress the theological significance of exile and it should be emphasized that the onset of the exile was not solely a problem for Israel faith; suggesting a challenge for interpretation,[6] finally, he argued that an experience of exile is necessary for Christian believers.[7]

Christian theology has continued to seek the themes of biblical theology from the Old Testament, but has failed to find the gravity of the Babylonian exile. In *Biblical Theology of Exile*, Daniel Smith-Christopher argues that the period of focus for the canonical construction of biblical thought is precisely the exile and diaspora; voices of dissent arose and articulated words of truth in the context of failed power. Exile as diaspora is the theme to understand the canonical construction of biblical thought.[8]

Furthermore, exile theology contributes to forming a theology of the Old Testament. In *Exile, Diaspora, and Old Testament Theology*, Reimer suggests how exile and diaspora serves to form the Christian project of Old Testament theology. According to his claim, a renewed appreciation for the exile offers something valuable to the Christian project of Old Testament theology. Through his closer look at the language used in relation to "exile," he suggests a different profile for the event and experience in the lives of

---

5. Raitt, *Theology of Exile*, 4.
6. Ibid.
7. Ibid., 229.
8. Ibid.

"biblical people," one that generates different theological trajectories as well. He asserts that diaspora language deserves a greater claim to our attention than it is usually given. In other words, the biblical language of exile and diaspora offers a major fundamental framework for understanding Old Testament theology.

In particular, diaspora studies contribute to understanding the relationship between Christianity, other religions, and secularity. In *On Diaspora: Christianity, Religion, and Secularity*, Daniel Colucciello Barber (2011) argues how the concept of diaspora affects Christianity, religion, and secularism.[9] He tried to overturn the previous common understanding of religion and its relationship to secularism by explaining the Christian traditions and the ancestry of both concepts. His main question is, "What is secularism?" He answers that by arguing that a theory of secularism cannot be divorced from theories of religion, Christianity, and even the concept of being; he takes up matters proper to philosophy, religious studies, cultural studies, theology, and anthropology, which are connected in a coherent manner as a result of the overarching concern with the concept of Diaspora.

In a word, for Barber, it is the concept of Diaspora that allows us to think in genuinely novel ways about the relationship between Christianity, religion, and secularism. Here we find how essentially the concept of Diaspora plays a key role to clarify critical issues of Christianity. From the above statements, it follows that exile theology reorients our stereotypes of theology and thinking, and also challenges to overturn misperceptions in our mindset.

The Major Theme of Exile Theology

It was John Howard Yoder who introduced and emphasized the meaning of Diaspora into the contemporary Christian faith community. In 1972, Yoder wrote *The Politics of Jesus*, in which he argues that church tradition painted a portrait of Jesus as separate from governmental concerns and whose teachings point to an apolitical life for his disciples . . . He asked how are we to respond today to a world so thoroughly entrenched in national and international affairs.[10] His book introduced a radical portrait of Christian ethics and life; he emphasized the value of the royal priesthood and the priestly kingdom; he saw the exile as God's calling.

Resident Aliens: Life in the Christian Colony is a memorable book authored by theologians Stanley Hauerwas and William Willimon, which is

9. Barber, *On Diaspora: Christianity, Religion*.
10. Yoder, *Politics of Jesus*.

"a provocative Christian assessment of culture and ministry for people who know that something is wrong."[11] The book deals with and discusses the nature of the church and Christians, and their relationship to surrounding society, politics, and culture. It argues that churches and Christians should focus on developing Christian life and community and living lives which model the love of Christ, rather than attempting to reform the secular culture. Hauerwas and Willimon reject the idea that any country is a Christian nation, and instead believe that the church or Christians should see themselves as "resident aliens" in a foreign land, using the metaphor of a colony to describe the church. Rather than conforming the gospel to the world and attempting to transform secular governments, they believe that Christians should focus on conforming themselves to the gospel.

One exile theologian, Walter Brueggemann, who emphasized the joy of heaven, wrote *Cadences of Home: Preaching among Exiles*, in which he views Christians as exiles, and argued that today's Christians [churchgoers] wander in a world that was once reliable, but now is recognized as meaningless and incoherent.[12] In this book, he argues for a dynamic transformation of preaching to help Christians find their spiritual home and to proclaim to the world that there is a heavenly home for all people and here is just exile. Smith-Christopher also sees the emergence of Diasporic theology in these scholars: John Howard Yoder, Walter Brueggeman, and Stanly Hauerwas.[13]

These scholars argue for new understandings of Christian faith and ethics. They try to understand the nature of church from a new perspective—the church should be station for believers to reach heaven. This does not mean that Christians give up on the world, but an encouragement that we do not lose heaven. The reason we live as Diaspora as exile is because our eternal home is above. Furthermore, we can proclaim that the transcendent life of Diaspora is an antidote to secularist focusing on earth.

Applications of a Theology of Exile for Witness for the Middle East

A theology of exile can be applied to mission for the Middle East and Asia. In his *States of Exile: Visions of Diaspora, Witness and Return*, Alain Epp Weaver applied a theology of exile to envision Diaspora and return both as integral dimensions of the churches witness for the peace of the city. In opposition to conventional views, the author argues that diaspora and return

11. Hauerwas and Willimon, *Resident Aliens*.
12. Ibid.
13. Smith-Christopher, *Biblical Theology of Exile*, 6.

need not stand in irreducible opposition and are in communion with each other. Exploring understandings in critical conversations with John Howard Yoder, Edward Said, Karl Barth, and Daniel Boyarin, Weaver presents reflections over a decade of living and working among Palestinian refugees. "In recognizing that the 'not in charge' for which Yoder calls is only a temporal, not a theological not in charge," Weaver writes, "the church in exile, as a church which is politically not in charge, should be 'theologically not in charge' as well."[14]

Weaver tries to envision the church as an exile community to learn to be 'theologically not in charge.' He argues that the church in exile should cultivate a receptiveness to the inbreaking of God's spirit from beyond the walls. Weaver tries to show both Christians and Jews how diaspora and exile can transform and redirect Christian witness befitting their own religious traditions, pointing to a sign of justice, peace, and reconciliation in a suffering land. This can be a good trial example of doing a theology of exile for a Christian mission. Here, Diaspora is the symbol of reconciliation and receptiveness; the concept of Diaspora also plays a key role in creating a new missiological model among deepening conflict and struggling regions.

THE REDISCOVERY OF ECCLESIOLOGY WITHIN A DIASPORA CONTEXT

Luther's Reformation Motif from Babylonian Captivity of the Church

Prelude on the Babylonian Captivity of the Church (1520) was one of the major treatises published by Reformer, Martin Luther. In this treatise, the term captivity is used in three regards: (1) Luther regarded the first "captivity" to be withholding the cup in the Lord's Supper from the laity; (2) the second was related to the doctrine of transubstantiation; and (3) the third was about the Roman Catholic church's teaching that the Mass was a sacrifice and a good work.[15]

This book is Martin Luther's revolutionary call to spiritual individualism. In it, Luther articulated a reformed theology that saved, and reduced the essence of Christianity to just two core elements: God's promise to man as set forth in Scripture, and man's faithful acceptance of that promise. The ecclesiastical implications of this book were momentous and incomparable. In his treatise, Luther addressed the understanding of the Roman church on

14. Boyarin, "Introduction," 9.
15. Luther, *Prelude by Martin Luther on the Babylonian Captivity*, 507–12.

sacrament and instead develops a biblically reformed conception of the sacraments and of the church. "In reading the document, it is well to remember that it was written on the eve of developments which led to the organization of Reformation churches. It represents a theological viewpoint which made the Reformation necessary."[16] In using the term captivity, Luther expressed the righteousness of the Reformation focusing on the saving grace of Christ. The experience of exile (captivity) helped to move the church toward its reformation. This exile serves as the foundation for the church reformation. Here, Luther's use of the word captivity calls for the necessity of reformation, which is represented as "the justification by faith."

In particular, *Prelude on the Babylonian Captivity of the Church* was also known as *The Pagan Servitude of the Church*.[17] This means that, to put in contemporary terms, Luther's *The Babylonian Captivity of the Church* can be interpreted as "the secularization of the church." That is, secularization of the contemporary church can be understood to call for the second Reformation. Father George Morelli, Assistant Pastor at St. George Antiochian Orthodox Church and professor of university and seminary courses in psychology and pastoral theology, describes the nature of secularism:

> Secularism is not new. Intellectual history scholars locate the emergence of secular thought in the French Enlightenment, particularly in the writings of Jean Jacques Rousseau, who rewrote the Genesis narrative by placing the locus of the Fall in Adam's socialization rather than his private decision to disobey God. Rousseau effectively shifted responsibility for sin in the world—including the deleterious social effects some sins engender—from the individual to society.[18]

In a word, secularism means rewriting or reinterpreting the Bible in terms of humanism. The works of Jean Rousseau repeated in the contemporary Christian faith and church. That is why we proclaim the second Reformation based on diaspora studies, moving beyond secular humanism.

Emphasis of Diaspora Church on the Holy Spirit

A major characteristic of Diaspora church is to emphasize the works of the Holy Spirit. In *Theology in the Russian Diaspora: Church, Fathers, Eucharist in Nikolai Afanas'ev*, Aidan Nichols describes the situation of Russian

16. Luther, *Pagan Servitude of the Church*, lines 1–8.
17. Luther, *Prelude by Martin Luther on the Babylonian Captivity*.
18. Morelli, "Secularism and the Mind of Christ," lines 5–10.

church. From his perspective, in the last half of the nineteenth century, some Russian scholars reluctantly welcome the rigidities of the scientific parameters of Westernization.[19] They also wished to move beyond the worldview dictated by science. Indigenous Russian perspectives allowed for other options. These scholars, led by I. V. Kireevski and Aleksei Khomiakov, were the Slavophiles. Here, the Slavophiles were a group of nineteenth century Russian intellectuals who were drawn together by religion, philosophy, and the problem of Russia and the West.

Vladimir Soloviev's philosophy of worldview and *Sophia* (wisdom) had a strong impact on Russian intelligents who never embraced the materialism of the scientific world. Soloviev influenced several generations of creative theologians—both East and West. His was the first generation that reached their maturity, and the second generation became the "Theologians of the Russian Diaspora." Here, the second-generation theologians of the Russian Diaspora contribute to the development of Russian ecclesiology. The freedom from intellectual oversight outside Russia created an environment in which Diaspora could make huge contributions to Russian thought in the twentieth century, including theology of the church.

Nikolai Afanas'ev (1893–1966) was one of these second generation theologians. Firstly, he worked at the Saint-Serge Institute in Paris, established by the Russian Orthodox Diaspora who left Russia after the Revolution. Aidan Nichols, a Dominican monk, has examined the ecclesiology of Afanas'ev under Diaspora life, and suggested that it represents the "convergence" of Eastern and Western theology. In particular, for Afanas'ev, the local church is the highest form of the church, equally critical of national churches and papal hierarchical organization. Afanas'ev did not hesitate to ascribe a prime role to the Holy Spirit. His church is a church without human "power" (authority of leaders to impose decisions on members). It is the "Church of the Holy Spirit." His pneumatology directly challenges modern fundamentalism. Most fundamentalists argue that the Holy Spirit works through "those in authority," but Afanas'ev insisted that the Holy Spirit works through the members.[20] Here we find that the Diaspora experience of the church offers a new perspective of ecclesiology: first of all, freedom is the environment in which scholars seek the truth beyond human oversight, and various travels and experiences of Diaspora in culture has a "stream of convergence" of Eastern and Western theology. The Russian Diaspora's contribution to ecclesiology is centered on the Holy Spirit. The

---

19. Nichols, *Theology in the Russian Diaspora*.
20. Ibid., 295.

Holy Spirit will work with doctrine that is authoritative through acceptance by the members.

Communio Sanctorum of the Church as its Essence: The Significance of the Church as "Scattered" in Contemporary Churches

What is the essence of church? The doctrine of the church in Louis Berkhof's *Systematic Theology* says:

> The essence of the church is not found in the external organization of the church, but in the church as the *communio sanctorum*. For both Luther and Calvin, the church was simply the community of the saints, that is, the community of those who believe and are sanctified in Christ, and who are joined to him as their Head. The church forms a spiritual unity of which Christ is the divine Head. It is animated by one spirit, the spirit of Christ; it professes one faith, shares one hope, and serves one king.[21]

The unity or oneness of the church is its essence; in Ephesians, it represents a becoming one body of both Jews and Gentiles through the blood of Christ (Eph 2:11–22). In addition, the unity of the church is one of the three attributes of the church—unity, holiness, and catholicity.[22] The essence of the church is the *communio sanctorum*, and the unity of the church as its attribute calls for inclusion and embrace of diaspora as foreigners.

Recently, the issue of the gathered and the scattered in the church has been discussed in contemporary churches. In *The Gathered and Scattered Church: Equipping Believers for the 21st Century*, Edward H. Hammett and Loren B. Mead distinguish the church in terms of "gathered" and "scattered."[23] They criticize the one-sidedness of the contemporary church focusing on "gathered"; they attempt to define what is called to be the "scattered church," as opposed to the "gathered church." According to them, in the past, the church has primarily conceived of itself in this "gathered" capacity, coming together for worship, but neglecting the call to be scattered to proclaim the gospel throughout the world. This book questions what the church is. In fact, most churches tend toward a "gathered" church, neglecting the aspect of a "scattered" church.

---

21. Berkhof, *Systematic Theology*, 564.
22. Ibid., 572–76
23. Hammett and Mead, *Gathered and Scattered Church*.

The Theological Foundations and Implications of Diaspora 137

Hugh Halter and Matt Smay also wrote a book entitled *AND: The Gathered and Scattered Church*;[24] Halter and Say try to balance both sides of being the church: "gathered" and "scattered." According to the authors, the church must "gather" within the church, and "scatter" into the world. Most churches just focus on one side of the "and." It is important that believers gather for the worship of God but they must scatter into the world for evangelism and service. The authors challenged, if the church focuses on gathering only, whether you are a mega-church, traditional, contemporary, or organic church, the vast majority of un-churched Christians and non-believers are not moving toward any form of church.

According to the authors, bringing together the very best of the attractional and missional models for church ministry, and catalyzing a missional movement of incarnational people into the world for Jesus Christ, the church should make balance between "gathered" and "scattered." This book also explains the significance of the scattered church in contemporary churches. Diaspora missiology will help the church to solve this problem, which causes spiritual stagnation, leading to the reduction in its numbers.

Halter and Smay continue on to state that there are two types of churches: "attractional" and "incarnational." According to the authors, most churches are "attractional"—their goal of ministry is to attract people to their service, by providing their wonderful programs, attractive worship, and various ministries. Sometimes they might go out into the world, the culture (door-to-door), but the main goal is to get more people into the church building.

In contrast, the "incarnational" model engages the culture first, forms a community, which then attracts people to a life of following Christ. The "incarnational" approach would spend more time in contacting people in the world. They proceed under the assignment, "Therefore go and make disciples of all nations, baptizing them in the name of the Father and of the Son and of the Holy Spirit, 20and teaching them to obey everything I have commanded you. And surely I am with you always, to the very end of the age" (Matt 28:19–20).

As the authors noted, most contemporary churches move toward the one side of "gathering" in the church, and attract more people to come in the church. However, the "scattered" aspect of the church is a major strategy of church ministry and mission, as noted in Acts 8:1–2; Acts 13:1–4. In Acts, God's mission in the world proceeded through scattered people—Diaspora. This shows how the concept of Diaspora contributes to a balanced formation of church—gathered and scattered. The church should get into the

---

24. Halter and Smay, *AND: The Gathered and Scattered Church*.

whole "missional" and "emergent" scene. That's the early church as written in Acts! For this, the church should restore a scattered aspect of the church and its dynamic participation into the world, signified in the life of Diaspora as scattered.

Diaspora Identity of the Church for Mission

As mentioned earlier, the mission of church is Diasporic. In *Towards a Missional Theology for African Diaspora in North America*, David Mwihia asserts that missional theology in North America is not attending to the unique needs of the African Diaspora.[25] It has failed to understand the African Diaspora's existential conditions. The African Diaspora, Mwihia argues, stands at the intersection of multiple forces affecting global Christianity. It embodies distinctive theological elements that have the potential for understanding and redefining the theology of mission and ecclesiology within a global context.

In this dissertation, he laid the groundwork for developing a missional theology that is criticized, challenged, and influenced by the experience of the African theology; he has developed a more relevant missional theology for AICs, and suggest how the experience of AICs can inform and contribute to North American missional theology. The author argued that the North American missional theology developed in the past has much to learn from the missional experiences of AICs.[26]

AN UNDERSTANDING OF HUMAN BEINGS AS DIASPORA: THE DOCTRINE OF MAN

Existential Understandings of Human Beings as Diaspora

The understanding of human beings as diaspora sheds light on existential understandings of human beings—suffering and anxiety. Human beings have banished from the garden of Eden by God's judgment on human sin; they were scattered as diaspora around the world. They have fear and trembling because of his judgment, and at same time, their deep heart was waiting for God's redemption. In this sense, all human beings are existentially diaspora.

---

25. Mwihia, *Towards a Missional Theology*.
26. Ibid.

The Theological Foundations and Implications of Diaspora

With regard to this view of man, Gordon J. Spykman suggests the necessity of existential understanding of human beings, saying:

> The surrealistic anthropologies of existentialist and nihilist commentators paint a picture of human nature starker than the grimmest old-fashioned sermons on total depravity. The future of man is not utopian peace and prosperity, but a nuclear doomsday. Human rights . . . are daily trampled in the dust.[27]

So he proposed an existentialist view of man as "shattered in a thousand irreparable pieces at our feet."[28] This existentialist view of man serves as the context of diaspora for human beings realizing the absolute necessity for God's salvation.

Suffering Trauma of Diaspora as Human Existential Problem

In Diaspora life, all human beings are fearful under sin and God's judgment; Cain, the archetype of sinful man, appealed to God in Genesis 4: "13Cain said to the Lord, 'My punishment is more than I can bear. 14Today you are driving me from the land, and I will be hidden from your presence; I will be a restless wanderer on the earth, and whoever finds me will kill me.'" According to Cohen, diaspora means a collective trauma, banishment into exile, and a heart-aching longing to return home.[29] During the early modern period, trade and labor diasporas girded the mercantilist and early capitalist worlds. He understands diaspora in terms of trauma, suffering, and brokenness. Most diasporas are caught in worry, fear, confusion, and frustration.

Naturally, human existence in sin and God's judgment and suffering, which describes diasporic human beings, leads to realizing religious aspects of life, and existential descriptions of human beings under God's judgment are open to the possibility of the Christian message of God's salvation because there is no other option in human science, morality, and philosophy. Crowell argues:

> Existentialism does not deny the validity of the basic categories of physics, biology, psychology, and the other sciences (categories such as matter, causality, force, function, organism, development, motivation, and so on). It claims only that human beings cannot be fully understood in terms of them. Nor can

27. Spykman, *Reformational Theology*, 210.
28. Ibid., 209.
29. Cohen, *Global Diasporas*.

such an understanding be gained by supplementing our scientific picture with a *moral* one. Categories of moral theory such as intention, blame, responsibility, character, duty, virtue, and the like *do* capture important aspects of the human condition, but neither moral thinking (governed by the norms of the good and the right) nor scientific thinking (governed by the norm of truth) suffices.[30]

Human existential problems and sufferings typically represented in a diaspora life can be solved on a religious level. "Neither moral thinking (governed by the norms of the good and the right) nor scientific thinking (governed by the norm of truth) suffices," is the conclusion of existentialism. This implies that existential diaspora problems lead to a religious level, the relationship with God.

In particular, existential loneliness, the sense of emptiness and void, is really a problem within every human being—a lack of meaningful relationships. We cannot ignore the suffering reality and psychology of diaspora—existential loneliness and problems—characterized as "trauma." In this sense, diasporic understandings can lead to being sympathetic with suffering, contemporary human beings.

Human Beings Scattered as Apologetic Theme

The fact that human beings are scattered diaspora offers an apologetic value to Christian evangelization. In understandings of man, Berkhof suggests four issues—the origin of man, the constitutional nature of man, man as image of God, and man in the covenant of works. The diasporic characteristics of human being are a common experience for human beings. Diaspora is an existential experience for all human beings. All human beings want to rest in God.

"Our heart is restless until it rests in you," is a famous confession of Saint Augustine of Hippo.[31] "Who will grant me to find rest?" This question lets human beings open the room of their heart in themselves for God to enter and gather them. The concept of Diaspora is powerful toward understanding human existentialism, and accessible for contextually communicating to contemporary human beings.

---

30. Crowell, "Existentialism," 2.
31. Augustine, *Confessions*.

The Identity of Christians as Diaspora

After receiving Jesus Christ as the Savior, all Christians should be willing to live a Diaspora life for the gospel; all Christians are called to be Diaspora by Peter, 1 Peter 2: "11'Dear friends, I urge you, as foreigners and exiles, to abstain from sinful desires, which wage war against your soul.'" Here Peter calls Christians foreigners and exiles, who also are called to be Diaspora. This warring is that all Christians must live the life of Diaspora as foreigners and exiles. Here, Diaspora indicates not only a specific group who has left their homeland and lived in foreign land, but all Christians, who should live like foreigners and exiles in this world.

Thus, Diaspora signifies all Christians who live as exiles and scatter for preaching the gospel. The fact that Christians are called to be Diaspora as exile offers new theological implications to the doctrine of man. Christians as Diaspora are limited to this world; this prevents Christians from keeping from falling into secularization and the prosperity gospel.

THE REDISCOVERY OF JOHN BUNYAN'S THEOLOGY OF PILGRIM: THE MAJOR THEMES OF THE PILGRIM'S PROGRESS

In 1628, John Bunyan was born to Thomas and Margaret Bunyan; in 1650, John married a young woman, an orphan, and the two books, Arthur Dent's *Plain Man's Pathway to Heaven* and Lewis Bayly's *Practice of Piety*—which she brought into the marriage—appeared to have strongly influenced John towards a religious life.

Under the influence of these two books, Bunyan wrote *The Pilgrim's Progress* (1678/1684) in two parts; he conceived this work during his first imprisonment, and probably finished it during the second. *The Pilgrim's Progress* is arguably one of the most widely known allegories ever written, and has been extensively translated. Generally, Protestant missionaries commonly translated it into local languages as the first book after the Bible. This shows how Bunyan's theology of pilgrim is essential to Protestantism.

The Themes of John's Pilgrim's Progress

First of all, one of the major themes in *The Pilgrim's Progress* is that of the pilgrimage or journey. Bunyan adapts a journey as an allegory. In general, Christian's temporal journey moves from this world to that which is to come—the City of Destruction to the City of Zion. However, "the more significant journey is the one that happens inside the pilgrim. This happens when the person realizes the blessing of their election and changes his or her life to devote it to the gospel. Ultimately, Christian must "cross the river," or die trying and join the Father in heaven, which is the ultimate achievement of the journey. However, before arriving at this point, he must face many obstacles along the way."[32]

Secondly, corruptions and limitations of human understanding is one of the main themes. For Bunyan, the human is corrupt. "Bunyan makes it clear in the text that humans are blinded by virtue of their fallen-ness, and thus, often have trouble seeing the divine truth. Indeed, every time that Christian strays from his course, it is due to the limitation of his perception."[33]

In particular, fear in faith plays a key role in processing the spiritual journey. In 1679, he wrote *the Fear of God—What it is and What it is Not*, and emphasized how much the fear of God is important. For Bunyan, the fear of God is valuable, but he clarified that fear is different from the fear that results from human cowardice. To fear God is not to be frightened, but to be in awe of and believe in his mercy, power, and grace; being frightened holds no such virtue.[34]

Thirdly, strangers and foreigners in imprisonment is one of the main concepts of pilgrimage. One of the central themes in *Pilgrim's Progress* is imprisonment and the subsequent struggle for liberation. Bunyan wrote the first part of the book while he was in jail, and therefore, the pilgrim's struggle for liberation from the temporal world is central to the text. For John, alienation is not strange for Christians.

"Alienation and community go hand in hand in *The Pilgrim's Progress*. The life of the pilgrim is a difficult one, and Christian often meets with scorn, malice, and ignorance. A pilgrim exists temporally in one world while simultaneously renouncing it and pursuing another means that the life of a pilgrim is filled with constant denial and anticipation."[35]

For Bunyan, the Christian community is alien; Christian was imprisoned and struggled for liberation. This is characteristic of the Diaspora community as strangers and foreigners. Feeling a tension, the pilgrim coexists in both worlds—here and over there.

---

32. *Grade Saver*, "Pilgrim's Progress Themes," 5–10.
33. Ibid.
34. Bunyan, *Fear of God*.
35. *Grade Saver*, "Pilgrim's Progress Themes."

John's Succession of the Reformation

The reason his faith and theology of pilgrim is essential is because it deals with the basics of Christian faith. Bunyan was faithful to Christian basics as two other successful works of his, *The Life and Death of Mr. Badman* (1680) and *The Holy War* (1682), were published; and a third book which revealed Bunyan's inner life and his preparation for his appointed work was *Grace Abounding to the Chief of Sinners* (1666). It is a classic example of a spiritual autobiography, focusing on his own spiritual journey and exalting the Christian concept of grace and comforting those passing through experiences like his own. He had a spiritual legacy of reformation teachings, which fatally lacking in contemporary church.

John Bunyan was influenced by the Reformer, Martin Luther's *Commentary on the Epistle to the Galatians*, the 1575 translation; he was involved in theological discussion in the succession of the reformation. As *Grade Saver* puts, "Bunyan draws heavily from both Luther and Calvin's ideas, and their influence is palpable in *The Pilgrim's Progress*. One of the hallmarks of Reformation theology is that it articulates a system of justification by faith alone, as opposed to justification by good works, as the Catholic Church once encouraged."[36]

An article hosted by Covenant of Grace Protestant Reformed Church (CGRC), "John Bunyan: Author of Pilgrim's Progress," introduced John Bunyan as part of the post-reformation period in Britain (1600–1700), and described him as worker of the reformation:

> Bunyan's views accurately reflect the theology of Puritans in these days. He was strong on doctrine and even satirized the Anglican Church in Mr. Worldly Wiseman, who wanted to reduce Christianity to mere ethics. He held firmly to the doctrines of grace, but preached these doctrines from the Lutheran viewpoint of justification by faith alone. But especially in his view of conversion, he reflected Puritan views, and without a solid doctrine of the covenant he had no room for the salvation of elect children in the line of the covenant, and somewhat de-emphasized the daily conversion to which a child of God is called. In his spiritual biography, *Grace Abounding to the Chief of Sinners* (1666), he spoke of conversion as involving conviction of sin, attempts to appease God with legal righteousness, subsequent despair, a long and drawn-out period of temptation and struggle, and finally peace in the way of faith in Christ. Such a conversion, though indeed the means God uses to bring some

---

36. Ibid.

to salvation, has become the norm for genuine conversion even in many Reformed circles, but in those circles where there is no biblical doctrine of the covenant.[37]

From the quotation above, his views such as justification by faith, the doctrine of grace, or the doctrine of covenant, accurately represent the theology of reformation. Particularly, in *A Discourse upon the Pharisee and the Publican*, John tried to restore the essence of the grace of the church. Here is his final conclusion:

> It is the sensible sinner, the self-bemoaning sinner, the self-judging sinner, the self-abhorring sinner, and the self-condemning sinner, whose prayers prevail with God for mercy. Hence I infer, that one reason why men make so many prayers, and prevail no more with God, is because their prayers are rather the floatings of pharisaical fancies, than the fruits of sound sense of sin, and sincere desires of enjoying God in mercy, and in the fruits of the Holy Ghost.[38]

His favor for the publican over the Pharisee is to show what a saving grace is, and has the power to reform the self-righteousness gospel of contemporary Christians.

In John's age, Kiffin and Paul published a response in *Serious Reflections* (London, 1673), in which they argued in favor of the restriction of the Lord's Supper to baptized believers, and received the approval of Henry Danvers in his *Treatise of Baptism* (London, 1673 or 1674). "The controversy resulted in the Particular (Calvinistic) Baptists leaving the question of communion with the unapprised open. Bunyan's church admitted paedobaptists to fellowship and finally became paedobaptist (Congregationalist),"[39] admitting the practice of baptizing infants or young children.

From the view of John's theology, infant baptism is biblical. Presbyterians (including Reformed Christians) believe that baptism, including infants, is a "sign and seal of the covenant of grace," and that baptism admits the party baptized into the visible church.[40] John's theological argument for infant baptism contributes to clarifying the membership of the church.

---

37. Covenant of Grace Protestant Reformed Church, "John Bunyan: Author of *Pilgrim's Progress.*"
38. Bunyan, *Discourse upon the Pharisee*, 172.
39. Bunyan, *Discourse upon the Pharisee*.
40. Westminster Confession of Faith, "Chapter 28: Of Baptism."

Bunyan's Theology of Pilgrim against Secularization

Generally, the Reformation rejected the secular spirit of the Italian Renaissance in its varying themes as Luther separated with the humanist, Erasmus. However, Luther's view of vocation moves toward secularization. In "Has Lutheranism caused secularism?" Jene Veith, Professor of Literature at Patrick Henry College, and Director of the Cranach Institute at Concordia Theological Seminary, argued:

> Lutheran Protestants are free from religiosity. For centuries, Lutheran Protestant Christianity in Northern Europe and the US taught our ancestors that there was nothing they could do to make God think better of them. Neither good deeds nor giving money to the church was seen as having importance in the eyes of God.[41]

Veith quotes from Matias Dalsgaard:

> For Protestants, life can be good just as it is. Life does not have to be lived in any particular 'religious' way in order to have a good relationship with God," says [Matias] Dalsgaard.... Lutherans, even orthodox ones, do seem to have less "religiosity." And there is quite a bit of the doctrine of vocation here: "live an ordinary life with other people"; "you should actively be the one you are, where you are–and not think so much about who you are.[42]

In 2012, Brad Gregory, a University of Notre Dame historian, examines why and how the West was propelled into its current pluralism and polarization over the long term, and wrote *The Unintended Reformation: How a Religious Revolution Secularized Society*.[43] He offers new insight into how life in North America and Europe has been shaped over the past five centuries by the Protestant Reformation. According to his opinion, the Reformation era's conflicts secularized Western society. This reminds us that we as Protestants have the peril of secularization occurring in the Christian faith and church, as contemporary protestant churches show. Here, we Protestants need to have a broad spectrum of reformation so that Bunyan's theology of pilgrim is included within the Reformation. A major mission of the contemporary church is to overcome secularization; focusing on heaven has the power to resist secularization and focusing on earth.

---

41. Veith, "Has Lutheranism Caused Secularism," 7–13.
42. Ibid.
43. Gregory, *Unintended Reformation*.

What is the antidote of Christian theology to secularism? In *Pilgrim Theology: Core Doctrines for Christian Disciples*, Michael Horton, professor of Systematic Theology and Apologetics at Westminster Seminary California, explains the reason for the title of his book, that it is meant for Christian disciples on a journey of spiritual growth, underpinned by a common Christian theology of faith. For him, Reformed Christian theology needs to dialogue with the spirit of pilgrim theology.[44]

John's Centeredness on Heaven and The Beatitudes

The Beatitudes are the foundational values of heaven for the disciples of Jesus. They should live out heavenly values and move toward heaven; they are pilgrims. "The Beatitudes of Jesus provided a description of life in the kingdom of heaven. Since to be in the kingdom of heaven means to be comforted, to be accepted, to be satisfied, to be shown mercy, to see God, to be called God's child and to reign with the messiah in his glory."[45] In the Beatitudes of Jesus (Matt 5:2–12), "Blessed" means congratulations to and reflects God's estimate rather than human emotion. The Beatitudes promise compensation at the last judgment for disciples who are "inwardly desperate, mournful, non-retaliatory, longing for divine vindication, merciful, pure, peacemaking, and righteous in the face persecution."[46] This is the life of the disciple moving toward heaven, a life of pilgrimage.

In "Pilgrims of the Cross: The Beatitude of Persecution," Jim Forest also understands the Beatitudes as the persecution and pilgrimage of the cross.[47] The book *Pilgrim: The Beatitudes* explores the Christian vision for the world, including openness to God, thirsting for what is right, peacemaking, and living as citizens of God's kingdom. The authors understand the Beatitudes as a spiritual journey toward heaven. Its contributors include Helen Ann Hartley, Emma Ineson, and Martin Warner.[48] They argue that Christian pilgrims who carry the cross accept the Beatitude of persecution. Finally, Bunyan's pilgrim theology based on the concept of Diaspora offers a new insight to the Christian faith and church. Above all, it shed light on the nature of the church as pilgrims and that of Christian life as a pilgrimage.

---

44. Horton, *Pilgrim Theology: Core Doctrines*.
45. Parson, "Beatitudes of Jesus: Recited in Hebrew," 1–10.
46. Gundry, *Survey of the New Testament*, 174.
47. Forest, "Pilgrims of the Cross."
48. Croft, et al., *Pilgrim: The Beatitudes*.

DIALOGUE BETWEEN THE CONCEPT OF DIASPORA AND KRAEMER'S THEOLOGY OF THE LAITY

Kraemer's Theology of the Laity for Mission

In principle, the theology of Diaspora is connected to a theology of the laity. Hendricks Kraemer (1958) wrote *A Theology of the Laity*, which came from his lay missionary experience. "Hendrick Kraemer considers the calling of the laity as a integral part of the Church's ministry, their functions as 'the dispersion of the Church' and the unused frozen credit for the church Christian faith they represent. Here 'dispersion' means diaspora, scattered people."[49] In this sense, Diaspora theology belongs to the theology of the laity, which defines the laity in terms of the identity and mission given by God's redemption.

Kraemer puts the significance of a theology of the laity in this way:

> Of all the voices that are raised around the laity, the call for the lay apostolate is the strongest. The churches, rediscovering their missionary obligation, and suddenly becoming aware of the hugeness of the task, turn to the laity with the argument that every Christian is *eo ipso* a witness and a missionary: to discover next that a laity which has been so long neglected and left ignorant is in its majority unable to respond to such a demand.

In chapter 5 of *A Theology of the Laity*, Kraemer outlines the core meanings of the theology of the laity:

(1) The church exists for the world, not for itself.

(2) The church mission is not only a mark of the church, but is its very essence.

(3) The church is ministry; all Christians are *diakonoi*, ministers, called to a ministry.

(4) The church is *diakonoi*, rooted in the person of Christ, the *Suffering Diakonos*.

(5) All Christians are stamped with the seal of the Holy Spirit.

(6) "All members of the *ekklesia* have in principle the same calling, responsibility and dignity; have their part in apostolic and ministerial nature and calling of the church."[50]

---

49. Kraemer, *Theology of the Laity*, front cover.
50. Ibid., 127–64.

The core of a theology of the laity is to define the laity from the perspective of mission, ministry, and *diakonia*. In a word, it is a confession that the laity is called to God's mission. This confession of the laity as *diakonia* matches with that of Diaspora as the seed of God. In this sense, both the theology of the laity and Diaspora move toward the mission of God.

Calling for the Reformation of the Church and Mission

Kraemer explains his intention in publishing *A Theology of the Laity* in this way:

> The theme of this book, *A Theology of the Laity*, calls with great emphasis for treatment in the present condition of the Christian church all over the world. It is even more adequate to say, it cries for treatment. For reasons of principle and of practical relevance.[51]

Explaining "the present condition of the Christian church," in chapter 1, "The Sign of the Times," he argues:

> The fact that a new appraisal of the place and responsibility of the laity emerges at the same time in the Roman and non-Roman worlds (the orthodox world included) with such great force, and largely arising from the same cause (the relentless secularization of modern life and resurrected missionary sense of the church) is a justification for speaking of 'the sign of the times.'[52]

The theology of Diaspora also emerges with the same cause: the relentless secularization of modern life and resurrected missionary sense of the church. Today, the church, including the laity, has been secularized and lost its missionary passion in the face of the emergent situation of world evangelization. This secularization is cruel, relentless, savage, barbarous, sanguinary, unfeeling, bloody-minded, flint-hearted, and inexorable. In this secularization, the contemporary church rediscovered the theology of the laity through Kraemer, a lay theologian and missionary. Diaspora is defined in terms of a broad understanding of social, biblical, and theological foundations, and calls more imminently for mission through the theology of the laity. This shows that Diaspora missiology should dialogue with the theology of the laity, following its understanding of the church and mission.

---

51. Ibid., 9.
52. Ibid., 46.

In a word, Diaspora missiology is an "expression of the church's spiritual strategy" that Kraemer put in his theology of the laity.[53]

> Isaiah 61: 1The Spirit of the Sovereign Lord is on me,
>   because the Lord has anointed me
>   to proclaim good news to the poor.
> He has sent me to bind up the brokenhearted,
>   to proclaim freedom for the captives
>   and release from darkness for the prisoners,
> 2to proclaim the year of the Lord's favor
>   and the day of vengeance of our God,
> to comfort all who mourn,
>   3and provide for those who grieve in Zion—
> to bestow on them a crown of beauty
>   instead of ashes,
> the oil of joy
>   instead of mourning,
> and a garment of praise
>   instead of a spirit of despair.
> They will be called oaks of righteousness,
>   a planting of the Lord
>   for the display of his splendor.
> 4They will rebuild the ancient ruins
>   and restore the places long devastated;
> they will renew the ruined cities
>   that have been devastated for generations.
> 5Strangers will shepherd your flocks;
>   foreigners will work your fields and vineyards.
> 6And you will be called priests of the Lord,
>   you will be named ministers of our God.
> You will feed on the wealth of nations,
>   and in their riches you will boast.

---

53. Ibid., 12.

6

Discoveries of the Missiological Problems and Issues in a Global Era toward the Formulation of Diaspora Missiology

The major question here is: What did current missiology discover in this global era? Due to failure of doing mission, current missiology has meditated on itself, its situation, and the church, and then rediscovered many missiological problems and issues. First of all, we need to find what happened to Christian mission in a global era, that is, we need to find missiological problems and figure out what are missiological issues we should resolve for carrying out mission. Through this process, we find out what factors should be involved the formulation of Diaspora missiology. That is, current missiological problems and issues serve as a backdrop for Diaspora missiology.

GLOBALIZATION AND CURRENT MISSIOLOGY

Emergence of Global Culture and Critical Contextualization

Globalization tremendously affects cultures and societies in which diaspora live. Local indigenous culture is inseparably linked to global culture; local cultures continue to indigenize the world system, "modified to fit the local

Discoveries of the Missiological Problems and Issues in a Global Era

culture."[1] Traditional missiology has been challenged by global issues. In an editorial note, "From the Editor's Desk: Reassessing 'Peoples' in the Global Push-and-Pull," Brad Gill called for the significance of globalization research in the *International Journal of Frontier Missiology*, a section of which he edited, entitled "The Globalization of the Frontiers," and explained the background of the edition:

> Globalization is a much contested term, but there's no debate that it's transforming civilization as we know it. The Western unidirectional flow of modernity has suddenly turned multidirectional, and the inability to predict outcomes is evident in a torrent of competing scholarship. Amidst all this analysis, our journal wishes to focus on a single question: how does globalization impact populations and peoples where a vital and authentic movement of the gospel has yet to take place?[2]

In a word, they recognized that traditional methods of mission have faced challenge from the globalization of the frontiers.

As Arjun Appadurai puts it, globalization is about a world of objects or things in motion.[3] These objects include ideas and ideologies, people and goods, images and messages, technologies and techniques. This is a world of flows, namely, disjunctive flows. These objects are not coeval, convergent, isomorphic, or spatially consistent. Disjunctive flows produce problems that manifest themselves in intensively local forms, but have contexts that are anything but local.[4] Thus in a global era, the notion of culture is ambiguous. We should recognize the fluid, unbounded, and imprecise nature of culture. If we adopt a more fluid and unbounded concept of culture and apply it to globalization, it is possible to speak of "a global culture," which creates through "deterritorialization."[5] To pull from Robertson's theory of globalization (1998), he sees globalization as problems involving comparative interactions of different forms of life and raising conflicts and violence.[6] Diaspora missiology should investigate the problems and challenges of globalization: identity, confusion, and conflict, income inequality, poverty, networks between homeland and diaspora, health, and so on. We further study how these factors affect immigrants. Doing Diaspora missiology is based on the study of global culture.

1. Kottak, *Mirror for Humanity*, 237.
2. Gill, "From the Editor's Desk," 163.
3. Appaudrai, *Modernity At Large*.
4. Appaudrai, *Globalization (A Public Culture Book)*, 6.
5. Appaudrai, *Modernity At Large*, 49.
6. Robertson, *Globalization*.

What happens to the world in an age of deterritorialization? Appaudrai continues to say:

> Central among these facts is the changing social, territorial, and cultural reproduction of *group identity*. As groups migrate, regroup in new locations, reconstruct their histories, and reconfigure their ethnic projects, the ethno in ethnography takes on a slippery, non-localized quality, to which the descriptive practices of anthropology will have to respond. The landscapes of group identity—the ethnoscapes—around the world are no longer familiar anthropological objects, insofar as groups are no longer tightly territorialized, spatially bounded, historically unselfconscious, or culturally homogeneous.[7]

Thus, in globalization, the world is no longer tightly territorialized, spatially bounded, historically unselfconscious, or culturally homogeneous; so all locals move beyond the authority of the Western experience toward "feeding off one another." Appaudrai continues:

> Central challenge for current anthropology is to study the cosmopolitan cultural forms of the contemporary world without logically or chronologically presupposing either the authority of the Western experience or the models derived from that experience. It seems impossible to study this new cosmopolitanism fruitfully without analyzing the transnational cultural flows within which they thrive, compete and feed off one another.[8]

For the study of global culture, Appaudrai proposes, "a global [cosmopolitan? macro? translocal?] ethnography." This cultural study is to look at the relationships between five dimensions of global cultural flows that can be termed: (a) *ethnoscape*, (b) *mediascape* (c) *technoscapes*, (d) *finance scape*, and (e) *ideoscapes*.[9] Similarly, this cultural study in a global age is called "urban anthropology" by Ulf Hannerz.[10]

Current missiology has been practiced in the context of these various global aspects and landscapes. However, it is not easy to evaluate and identify globalization in terms of mission; some argued that globalization brings positive things for mission; others argued that it brings negative things for mission.

---

7. Appaudrai, *Modernity at Large*, 49.
8. Ibid.
9. Ibid., 33.
10. Hannerz, *Exploring the City*.

Groody emphasizes that the core issues of globalization are poverty and social injustice.[11] However, more importantly, Diaspora missiology tries to understand globalization culture in terms of the current mission field. To pull from Brad Gill's remarks, in globalization, we need to be "reassessing 'peoples' in the global push-and-pull"; "to focus on a single question: how does globalization impact populations and peoples where a vital and authentic movement of the gospel has yet to take place?"[12] However, it is noted that there is hidden the huge package of pluralism, relativism, and secularism. Instead we need to reassess and interpret it in terms of biblical and theological teachings; we need critical contextualization, to put it in Hiebert's term.[13]

In a word, critical contextualization seeks a balanced approach. For Hiebert, the Bible is seen as divine revelation and must be kept as it is encoded in forms that are understood by the people, without making the gospel captive to cultural contexts. This is an ongoing process of embodying the gospel in an ever-changing world.[14] Thus, globalization becomes the field of critical contextualization for doing Diaspora missiology, because diaspora is the product of movement by globalization.

Understanding a Global Culture as a Multidimensional Set of Social Processes

What is the nature of the globalization? Steger defines the globalization in this way: Globalization refers to a multidimensional set of social processes that create, multiply, stretch, and intensify worldwide social interdependencies and exchanges, while at the same time fosters in people a growing awareness of deepening connections between the local and the distant.[15]

Indeed, "the transformative powers of globalization reach deeply into the economic, political, cultural, technological, and ecological dimensions of contemporary social life."[16] This shows how all areas of social life are connected. Thus, Steger suggests four distinct qualities or characteristics of globalization:

11. Groody and Campese, *Promised Land*.
12. Gill, "From the Editor's Desk," 163.
13. Hiebert, *Anthropological Reflections*.
14. Hiebert, "Gospel in Human Contexts," 84–99.
15. Steger, *Globalization*, 12.
16. Ibid., vii.

1. Globalization involves the creation of new, and the multiplication of existing, social networks and activities that increasingly overcome traditional political, economic, cultural, and geographical boundaries.
2. Globalization involves the expansion and stretching of social relations, activities, and interdependencies.
3. Globalization involves the intensified acceleration of social exchanges and activities.
4. Globalization involves the subjective plane of human consciousness. Thus, globalization refers to people becoming increasingly conscious of growing manifestations of social interdependence and the enormous acceleration of social interactions.[17]

In the last case, in particular, globalization brings about social interdependence and the enormous acceleration of social interactions. Steger states:

> Their awareness of the receding importance of geographical boundaries and distances fosters a keen sense of becoming part of a global whole. Reinforced on a daily basis, these persistent experiences of global interdependence gradually change people's individual and collective identities, and thus dramatically impact the way they act in the world.[18]

Here the major characteristic of global culture is "interdependence," namely, "connectivity." Localities are connected with the world by breaking down national boundaries, links between one society and another, and between one country and another through international transmission of knowledge, ideas, technology, culture, and information.[19]

Here it is noted that the Diaspora is in the context of these global interactions. Robertson argues that we must recognize "real world" attempts to bring the global, in the sense of the macroscopic aspect of contemporary life, into conjunction with the local, in the sense of the microscope side of life.[20] This is what Robertson refers to as "glocalization" (meaning global localization). Here, "glocalization" points to the interconnection between the local and the global. It punctures the inflated views of globalization as some mere macro-level, socio-economic process, involving world-systems that either do not touch the everyday lives of ordinary people in local places, or, if they do, merely impose alien pressures upon them. Rather, the local and

17. Ibid.
18. Ibid.
19. Tomilinson, *Globalization and Culture*.
20. Robertson, *Globalization*, 173.

the global are mutually dependent. This sets in place the broad analytical context.[21]

This means that the lives of diaspora who are in the context of globalization involve global issues: the creation of new and the multiplication of existing social networks and activities that increasingly overcome traditional political, economic, cultural, and geographical boundaries; the expansion and stretching of social relations, activities, and interdependencies; the intensified acceleration of social exchanges and activities; the subjective plane of human consciousness. Thus, globalization refers to people becoming increasingly conscious of growing manifestations of social interdependence and the enormous acceleration of social interactions.

Missiological "Problems" in a Global Era

Basically, globalization causes a variety of problems in confrontation with each other. Robertson defines globalization as problems. He argues: "the strong view advanced by Wallerstein is that the *Gemeinschaft* problem was largely produced by an increasingly worldwide, capitalist *Gessellschaft* and that obsession with the basically internal-societal problem of the transition from *Gemeinscaft* to *Gesellschaft* set the social sciences off on an entirely wrong foot."[22]

According to this dichotomy, social ties can be categorized in two ways: (1) belonging to personal social interactions, roles, values, and beliefs based on such interactions (*Gemeinschaft*, German, commonly translated as "community"), or (2) belonging to indirect interactions, impersonal roles, formal values, and beliefs based on such interactions (*Gesellschaft*, German, commonly translated as "society").[23] That is, globalization causes the transition from the dichotomy of *Gemeinscaft* to that of *Gesellschaft*, leading to an explosion of problems. This means that Diaspora is in the vortex of globalization is faced by problems.

What is the challenge of globalization to Christian mission? Thomas E. Feiertag, professor of missiology at Concordia University, argued that the contemporary issue in missiology is to handle a missiological approach to religious pluralism.[24] That is, the big problems in global mission are pluralism, relativism, and secularism, which are intimately connected to one other. He argued, "In this broad sense of the term, Christianity needs to

21. Lyon, "Wheels within Wheels," 50.
22. Robertson, *Globalization*, 13.
23. Tönnies, *Community and Society*.
24. Feiertag, "Contemporary Issues in Missiology," 35–50.

address how it is going to get along with these other religions. In the narrow sense, the above description contains the phrase '... yet equally valid.' The term 'religious pluralism' in this sense describes the slippery slope that pluralism leads to if one is not careful."[25]

There are three issues regarding globalization: pluralism, relativism, and secularization.

(1) Globalization brings about Pluralism:

In globalization, Christians face pluralism. "Something else that has brought about pluralism is 'globalization.' There is a great people movement going on in this world. Asians are moving to Africa. Africans are moving to Europe. Europeans are moving to Australia. Everybody is moving to the United States. This has caused Christians to take another look at Christianity's exclusive claims."[26]

What does Peter Berger, one of the experts of the secularization thesis, say about secularization in globalization? According to the introduction for Berger's talk at the Pew Forum's Biannual Faith Angle Conference on Religion, Politics, and Public Life in December 2006:

> Peter Berger, professor emeritus of religion, sociology and theology at Boston University, examined the globalization of religious pluralism and how the peaceful coexistence of different racial, ethnic and religious groups has become a global phenomenon. He argues that pluralism—not secularization—and the resulting emergence of religious choice is the best model for understanding religion in a globalizing world.[27]

For Berger, there is no escape of religious pluralism; "the peaceful coexistence of different racial, ethnic and religious groups has become a global phenomenon."

What, then, is the definition of religious pluralism? Here, the importance is how religious pluralism is interpreted and seen from the perspective of the world. In "Defining Religious Pluralism in America," Mark Silk states that religious pluralism "enables a country made up of people of different faiths to exist without sectarian warfare or the persecution of religious minorities."[28] If understood differently in different times and places, "it is a

---

25. Ibid.
26. Ibid.
27. Berger, "Religion in a Globalizing World," 1.
28. Silk, "Defining Religious Pluralism in America," 64.

cultural construct that embodies some shared conception of how a country's various religious communities relate to each other and to the larger nation as a whole."[29] Put simply, "each religion is understood to represent a distinctive, yet equally valid grasp of some ultimate spiritual reality, which some religions term 'God' and others define in rather more non-theistic or atheistic terms."[30] This is the basic challenge to the essential doctrine of Christianity. Globalization makes this religious pluralism nearer to us than ever before. That is, pluralism is next door. It changes our spiritual situation rapidly. Diaspora missiology should pay more attention to this spiritual challenge to the Diaspora; it should describe all kinds of problems around Diaspora in as much detail as possible. Pluralism endangers Christian mission, potentially making Christian mission itself impossible or not required.

(2) Religious Pluralism brings about Relativism, Leading to Syncretism

For Peter Berger, an authoritative sociologist, relativism is a good thing:

> Now, relativism, I would say, is the philosophical legitimization of this fact. It's a good thing, and I suppose the climax of this relativism in religion and in other things is the so-called postmodern theory. We all have our narratives. There's no way of saying that one narrative is superior to another, and the real virtue here is tolerance. We should all tolerate each other's narratives.[31]

For him, the apex of relativism is the so-called postmodern theory, which implies that this postmodern age moves toward relativism; all religions are equal. Relativism is the perspective that truth and morals are relative to societies and individuals; there are no absolute truths or morals that are true for all people of all times. Relativism is the opposite of absolutism, which asserts that there are universal truths and morals that are true for all people at all times.

Here is a very important question to relativism: what is the relativist's attitude toward God? The book of collected works, *Moral Relativism: A Reader*, edited by Paul K. Moser and Thomas L. Carson, is organized under six main topics: (1) General Issues; (2) Relativism and Moral Diversity; (3)

---

29. Ibid.
30. McGrath, *Christian Theology*, 549.
31. Berger, "Religion in a Globalizing World," 6.

On the Coherence of Moral Relativism; (4) Defense and Criticism; (5) Relativism, Realism, and Rationality; and (6) Case Study on Relativism.[32]

According to this collection, generally, relativists argue that morality and truth do not come from the absolute God, but frame social constructs. That is, societies or individuals determine what is right and wrong, but their standards are not based in God or any universal standard. Furthermore, relativists argue that because truth and morals are social constructions, they are often against one culture imposing its value system upon another culture. This means that for instance, the imposition of the Christian gospel upon unbelievers is looked on as wrong. Recently, relativism is leading to absolute relativism.[33]

However, if accepting relativism, there would be no use for doing Christian mission based on the absolution of Jesus Christ; without overcoming relativism, who would go and preach the gospel to other religions despite the sacrifice and even death? This means that we should back to biblical teachings of mission written in the Scripture before discussing mission strategies. The ultimate goal of Christian mission is to gain the lost soul into God's salvation (Acts 16:31).

Finally, it should be noted that relativism moves toward syncretism. Feiertag argues:

> The mixture of cultures in our society has had a profound effect on our society. Not only has there been a proliferation of religious groups, both Christian and non-Christian, but this has been accompanied by incredible changes in the culture and society in which we live, brought on by increased mobility, intermarrying, and the advent of the Internet and the Information Age. Syncretism and its inevitable result—relativism—are in the very air we breathe.[34]

As Feiertag puts accurately, syncretism is the inevitable result of relativism; all Christians live in the very air we breathe. Recently, public theology, which comes from a liberal reinterpretation of the gospel caused by the challenge of secularism or post-secularism, is the adaptation of secularism in the name of contextualization. However, public theology is a social ethic of Christians in a secular age, but it is not the core presentation of the saving gospel (cf. 1 Cor 1:18).

---

32. Moser and Carson, *Moral Relativism*.
33. Stefanick, *Absolute Relativism*.
34. Feiertag, "Contemporary Issues in Missiology," lines 105–12.

(3) Religious Pluralism Attempts to Accept Secularism, Leading to a new Religion of Christianity

As Feiertag puts it, another response to pluralism is "secularism." It should be noted that pluralism has a similar spirit to secularism: according to George Holyoake's *English Secularism* (1896), secularism is a code of duty pertaining to this life, and intended mainly for those who find theology indefinite, inadequate, unreliable, or unbelievable; in nature, secularism move towards the rejection of transcendent Christianity.

This secularism is intertwined with pluralism; D. L. Munby characterized secular society in pluralism: (1) refuses to commit itself as a whole to any one view of the nature of the universe and the role of man in it; (2) not homogeneous, but is pluralistic; (3) being tolerant. It widens the sphere of private decision-making.[35] As society become secularized, it become more and more pluralized.

America's founding fathers made it clear that no one religion would dominate American government or society. They believed that to avoid domination, society has to adopt a secular approach. However, secularization also resulted in the "privatization of religion"; "proselytizing" has become a bad word in America's secular society. These secularization phenomena become worse and worse.[36] Hiebert points out variants of a secular gospel: "The gospel becomes a gospel of therapy and healing, not of forgiveness and salvation"[37]

From Feiertag's analysis, in pluralism, contemporary Christians deceive; he explains,

> Pluralism is nice. It is polite. It is politically correct. It is comforting. It avoids confrontation. It elevates postmodernism's tolerance to an art form. Unfortunately, pluralism is devastating to missiology. It robs missions of its very purpose because, why bother to save people who are already saved?[38]

Diaspora missiology is being formulated in the vortex of this dangerous pluralism, relativism, and secularism, because Diaspora live in the middle of globalization, which produces and fosters these thoughts. It means that the global field in which Diaspora works is dangerous field. Thus, for its great opportunity, Diaspora missiology focuses on training, lest we fall into their traps.

35. Munby, *Idea of a Secular Society*, 14–32.
36. Ibid.
37. Hiebert and Meneses-Hiebert, *Incarnational Ministries*, 36.
38. Feiertag, "Contemporary Issues in Missiology," 20–24.

The Secularization Debate and "The Secularized Church"

In 1846, George Jacob Holyoake used the term "secularism" in order to describe "a form of opinion which concerns itself only with questions, the issues of which can be tested by the experience of this life."[39] He was a leader of the English secularist and free thought movement who became famous to the wider public for his conviction under, and larger fight against, English blasphemy laws. Later, Holyoake explained his term more explicitly:

> Secularism is that which seeks the development of the physical, moral, and intellectual nature of man to the highest possible point, as the immediate duty of life—which inculcates the practical sufficiency of natural morality apart from Atheism, Theism, or the Bible—which selects as its methods of procedure the promotion of human improvement by material means, and proposes these positive agreements as the common bond of union, to all who would regulate life by reason and ennoble it by service.

In a word, secularism is to call for "the practical sufficiency of natural morality," "the promotion of human improvement by material means," and "these positive agreements as the common bond of union." In particular, its focus is on "the immediate duty of life." From its characteristics, it follows that the concept of Diaspora as pilgrim is an antidote to secularism's focus on earthly things.

In the 1950s and 1960s, Peter Berger, Harvey Cox, and others were fearless proponents of "secularization theory." This theory held that as technology improved and modernity advanced upon culture, religion would begin to decline and we would live, according to Cox, in a "secular city." First, in 1966, Christian theologian Harvey Cox wrote *The Secular City*; in which he argued that history has revealed a progressive "process of secularization," defining secularization as "man turning his attention away from worlds beyond and toward this world and this time." He welcomed this development, since he understood secularization as a "liberating process," and suggested that it "should be welcomed as an occasion requiring maturity in man"; he argued that human beings are living in a "technopolis" that has no requirement either for religion or an afterlife, and that the task of the modern theologian is to "speak of God in a secular fashion."

In 1967, Peter Berger wrote *The Scared Canopy: Elements of a Sociological Theory of Religion*; according to him, "religion emerges within a socially-constructed nomos as that part of the nomos which serves to

---

39. Holyoake, "English Secularism," 60.

legitimate anomy by providing a well-ordered, meaningful "sacred canopy."[40] Furthermore, this theory held that as technology improved and modernity advanced upon culture, religion would begin to decline. Berger understood religion as a response to the danger *par excellence* of human existence, anomy.[41]

To speak about anomy is to return to Berger's initial presupposition that social reality is constructed in order to complete human nature. Humans crave meaning and, therefore, instinctually create meaning socially. Social reality, therefore, gives order, meaning and security to a human existence that is naturally bereft of such qualities. Social reality provides a shield against the forces of chaos—particularly death, suffering, and evil—that threaten to disorder human existence. Separation from this well-shielded world results in anomy, the danger *par excellence* of human existence. The individual who has become separated from social reality "loses his orientation in experience" and, in extreme cases, "loses his sense of reality and identity." Such an individual "becomes anomic in the sense of becoming worldless."

However, in a conversation with Albert Mohler, Peter Berger recognizes some mistakes in his thesis of secularization:

> I mean they didn't like the idea that the world is becoming more secular, but they thought it was a fact. Well it took me about twenty years or so to realize that this was a mistake. I would say secularization theory has been massively falsified and with one or two interesting exceptions, the world today including the United States is very religious, and secularists are a minority in most of the world.[42]

The reason Peter Berger changed his opinion of secularization is because there has been a renaissance of religion in secular society, which is called post-secularism. However, from the Christian perspective, there has still been a continued spirit of secularization in post-secularism, notwithstanding a religious renaissance.

Historically, through various discussions, the post-secularism debate finally came to the theory of Jurgen Habermas, where there was a more clear explanation of the post-secular; in "Notes on Post-Secular Society," Habermas believes that "the return of religion" or "the return to religion" happened in the public sphere,[43] although we don't exactly know whether

---

40. Knepper, Review of *Sacred Canopy*.
41. Berger, *Sacred Canopy*.
42. Berger, "Rethinking Secularization," lines 5–10.
43. Habermas, "Notes on a Post-Secular Society," 1.

it "signifies an increase in religious thought, feeling, and action, or merely an increase in the salience of questions about religion in politics and the media."[44] For Habermas, the term "post-secular society," "refers not only to the fact that religion continues to assert itself in an increasingly secular environment and society, for the time being, but also referred to the continuing existence of religious communities."[45] His conclusion is that: "Both religious and secular mentalities must be open to a complementary learning process if we are to balance shared citizenship and cultural difference."[46]

Post-secularism has two aspects regarding secularism. On the one hand, the post-secular is for sure on the contrary to the secularization thesis that "during secularization, religion did not disappear *tout court*. It simply disappeared from the public sphere . . . Today religion is returning to the public sphere."[47] On the other hand, as Habermas puts it, a "post-secular" society must at some point have been in a "'secular' state;" "the data collected globally still provides surprisingly robust support for the defenders of the secularization thesis,"[48] in particular, as seen in the sense of the functional differentiation and the subjectivization of religion.

Finally, it is noted that some scholars use the term "post-secular" to express resurgence of religions in a secular era; in its deep level, basically the spirit of secularism still remains the same in a post-secular era. In other words, the faith is conformed to the contents of secularism; faith has itself in name, its contents are secularized. For this reason, Charles Holt, professor in the Department of Economics at the University of Virginia, in "A Sociologist Speaks of the Secular Church," argued that the church adapts to self-centered culture–secularism, by saying:

> The expression "secular church" may be a contradiction in terms, but it is what many sociologists say is emerging on the American religious scene. The secularization process that has transformed Western civilization over the past two centuries has taken different paths in Europe and in America. In Europe, secularization has meant large-scale defection from religion and the appearance of many empty church buildings and cathedrals. In America, churches have survived, however, by adapting to secularization and by commending themselves in terms that are attractive to "secular man." This strategy has insured short-term

---

44. Beckford, "Public Religions and the Postsecular."
45. Habermas, "On the Relations between the Secular," 258.
46. Habermas, "Notes on Post-Secularism," 1.
47. Bosetti and Eder, "Post-secularism: A Return," 1
48. Habermas, "Notes on Post-Secularism," 3.

Discoveries of the Missiological Problems and Issues in a Global Era

success, but it also has meant that the church has undergone many fundamental changes. In its organization, for example, the church tends to take on the characteristics and values of contemporary secular organizations and institutions; it comes to resemble surrounding technological and bureaucratic organizations. Too frequently such churches are beehives of committee meetings, questionnaires, self-studies, memos and related paraphernalia that primarily serve to maintain institutional momentum.

The author's point is that churches have survived by adapting to secularization and by commending themselves in terms that are attractive to "secular man." That is, the church was secularized in a secular culture. This doubts that the growth or survival of contemporary churches in secular culture may be accomplished by resembling the secular culture, not by effectively communicating the gospel to secular culture through biblical contextual theologizing. In other words, contextualization of contemporary churches moves toward secularization, the text becoming secularized without transforming the context.

ISSUES OF CURRENT MISSIOLOGICAL WORKS

As mentioned earlier, there are various issues of current missiology in globalized world; my intention is not to list all issues, but four issues which are related to the core issues of Diaspora missiology.

The USA and the EU as New Mission Fields for Unreached People

Based on Pew Research Center's study of the Future of the Global Muslim Population, it is worthy of noting countries with the largest projected increase in the number of Muslims from 2010 to 2030, which is a major target of current Christian mission. Pew Research analysis on the moving of Muslims to North American and Christian EU countries has the following demographic characteristics, which will be used for Christian mission:

The Americas: America and Canada

(A) The number of Muslims in Canada is expected to nearly triple in the next twenty years, from about 940,000 in 2010 to nearly 2.7 million in 2030. Muslims are expected to make up 6.6 percent of Canada's total population in 2030, up from 2.8 percent today. Argentina is expected to have the third-largest Muslim population in the Americas, after the US and Canada. Argentina, with about one million Muslims in 2010, is now in second place, behind the United States.

(B) Children under age fifteen make up a relatively small portion of the US Muslim population today. Only 13.1 percent of Muslims are in the 0–14 age group. This reflects the fact that a large proportion of the Muslims in the US are newer immigrants who arrived as adults. But by 2030, many of these immigrants are expected to start families. If current trends continue, the number of US Muslims under age fifteen will be more than triple, from fewer than 500,000 in 2010 to 1.8 million in 2030. The number of Muslim children, ages 0–4, living in the US is expected to increase from fewer than 200,000 in 2010 to more than 650,000 in 2030.

(C) About two-thirds of the Muslims in the US today (64.5%) are first-generation immigrants (foreign-born), while slightly more than a third (35.5%) were born in the US. By 2030, however, more than four out of every ten Muslims in the US (44.9%) are expected to be native-born.

(D) The top countries of origin for Muslim immigrants to the US in 2009 were Pakistan and Bangladesh. They are expected to remain the top countries of origin for Muslim immigrants to the US in 2030.[49]

From data mentioned above, it follows that the USA and Canada should be a mission field for Muslim mission; today Muslim mission has been strongly prohibited and persecuted. However, now, the USA and Canada are next-door neighbors to Muslims. In particular, Christian mission should prepare mission strategies for the younger generation of Muslims.

Europe

(A) In 2030, Muslims are projected to make up more than 10 percent of the total population in ten European countries: Kosovo (93.5%), Albania (83.2%), Bosnia-Herzegovina (42.7%), Republic of Macedonia (40.3%), Montenegro (21.5%), Bulgaria (15.7%), Russia (14.4%), Georgia (11.5%), France (10.3%), and Belgium (10.2%).

(B) Russia will continue to have the largest Muslim population (in absolute numbers) in Europe in 2030. Its Muslim population is expected to rise from 16.4 million in 2010 to 18.6 million in 2030. The growth

---

49. Pew Research Center, "Future of the Global Muslim Population."

rate for the Muslim population in Russia is projected to be 0.6 percent annually over the next two decades.

(C) France had an expected net influx of 66,000 Muslim immigrants in 2010, primarily from North Africa. Muslims comprised an estimated two-thirds (68.5%) of all new immigrants to France in the past year (2010). Spain was expected to see a net gain of 70,000 Muslim immigrants in 2010, but they account for a much smaller portion of all new immigrants to Spain (13.1%).

(D) The UK's net inflow of Muslim immigrants in the past year (nearly 64,000) was forecast to be nearly as large as France's. More than a quarter (28.1%) of all new immigrants to the UK in 2010 were estimated to be Muslim.[50]

From the data, the EU nations draw immigrant Muslims, a huge mission field for Muslims to the degree that the number of Muslims in each nation of the EU is averagely above 10 percent of the whole population; however, churches in the EU have been secularized, and an evangelistic passion for Muslims has disappeared. Revival of the churches in the EU is urgently demanded for European mission toward Muslims.

As we all know, Muslim mission is a critical frontier of Christian mission in this era. Regarding Muslim frontier mission, Ralph Winter points out:

> Looking at 'The Globe at a Glance,' you can readily see that the bulk of the individuals who live within unreached groups (white) are within the Muslim, Tribal, Hindu, and Buddhist blocs. We need to continue to send well-trained and insightful missionaries to these challenging peoples. There have been some very encouraging people movements within a limited number of Hindu, Buddhist, and Muslim groups. These three blocs are often seen as the most resistant, but we are learning that when people seem "resistant" it may only mean our approach has been defective. Half of those living within unreached peoples are in the Muslim bloc, which is a bloc that has very favorable attitudes toward Jesus Christ.[51]

According to Winter, only 24,000 missionaries out of the global evangelical missionary force of 253,000 are working within the estimated 8,000 unreached groups. That means that nine times as many foreign missionaries work within reached people groups than those doing the more difficult work of establishing breakthroughs within unreached peoples. What an

50. Ibid.
51. Winter and Koch, "Finishing the Task," 15–25.

imbalance! It is this 10 percent of the evangelical mission force that is doing pioneering mission work among the unreached people.

Winter's point reminds us how imbalanced the world mission is and how Christian mission can cover unreached people. However, surprisingly, unreached Muslim people are moving to the US and the EU. Many immigrant Muslims are projected to go to the US or the EU—representative areas of the Northern Christian countries. What are the missiological implications for the US and the EU from this data and projection? Why is God moving Muslims, one of the final targets of Christian evangelization, to the US and the EU in this time? Is it an accident? Or is it just a socio-political phenomenon? We as Christians confess that the US and the EU should be mission fields for reaching Muslims. US and EU Christianity should prepare for the evangelism of immigrants in their home. The US and the EU Christian mission need not seek Muslims outside their countries, but welcome them with the gospel in their home. Muslim mission is one of the target challenges of Christian mission, and they are moving to the Northern Christian countries as strangers next door.

Most importantly, Pew Research reports that Muslim Americans are willing to adapt to American customs and ways of life:

> Most Muslim Americans seem well integrated into American society, and about two-thirds say that the quality of life for Muslims in the US is better than most Muslim countries. 56% of Muslim Americans say that most Muslims who come to the US today want to adopt American customs and ways of life.[52]

This is a good sign for Muslim evangelization in the US. For example, Muslims living in America or the EU are easy to be adapted into American culture, which lets them be open to Christianity; this implies that unreached people in globalized society have the chance to visit Christian societies. This serves for evangelistic opportunity towards them; that is why America and the EU are called to be mission fields.

"Missionary Church" Movement, Originating from Missio Dei

Contemporary missional church movement began within the ecumenical missions debates of the 1952 Willingen meeting. Some scholars argued that instead of missions being seen as an activity of the church, the church should be considered a part of the *Missio Dei*—God's mission on earth.[53]

---

52. Pew Research Center, "Portrait of Muslim Americans," lines 25–30.
53. Van Gelder, *Ministry of the Missional Church*, 9.

They defined *Missio Dei* as something larger than just the church and extended missions, moving beyond merely evangelism into social justice.

Lesslie Newbigin, one of these scholars, began asking the crucial question, what would be involved in a missionary encounter between the gospel and "modern Western culture"?[54] According to his perspective, the West has become "post-Christian" and pluralistic, and should endeavor for a "genuine missionary encounter" with postmodern culture.[55] After that, an ecumenical team of six noted missiologists—Lois Barrett, Inagrace T. Dietterich, Darrell L. Guder, George R. Hunsberger, Alan J. Roxburgh, and Craig Van Gelder—wrote *Missional Church: A Vision for the Sending of the Church in North America (Gospel & Our Culture)*. This book came from the result of a three-year research project undertaken by The Gospel and Our Culture Network, launched by Newbigin's theology of mission and challenge for the church to recover its missional call right here in North America. These authors argued that Christendom of a new era must (1) face reality, (2) develop a plan of action, and (3) reengage our culture.[56]

The core of this missionary church theology is a triangular model of gospel-culture relationships.

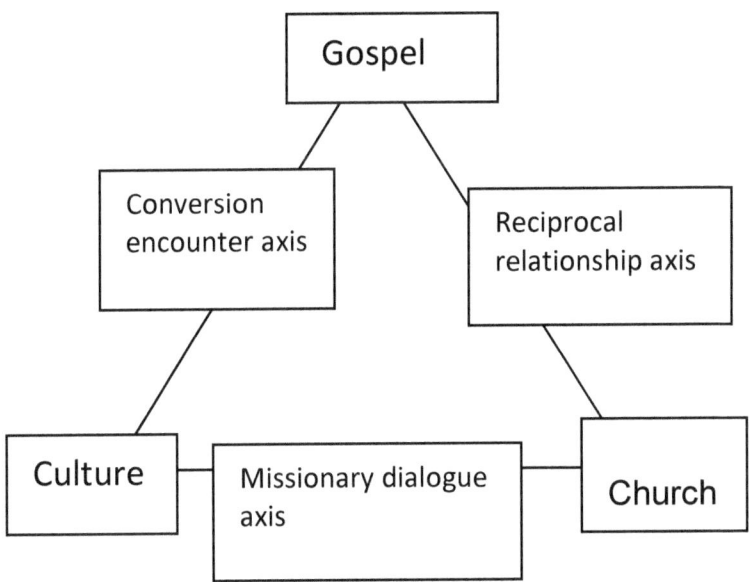

Figure 4: A Triangular Model of Gospel-Culture Relationships

54. Newbigin, *Foolishness to the Greeks*.
55. Newbigin, *Other Side of 1984*, 31.
56. Guder, et al., *Missional Church*.

The figure above was drawn according to Newbigin's theology of mission; it was processed in a theology of Christ against culture, and in a postmodern apology. In particular, the feature of Newbigin's missiological orientation is the theology of conversion, which included aspects of mind, behavior, and communal commitment.[57] However, surprisingly, there is no explanation of the Holy Spirit in these missiological orientations, in particular, the theology of conversion.

In *Shaped by God's Heart: The Passion and Practices of Missional Churches*, Milfred Minatrea, a missiologist, urban strategist, and practitioner in ministry, suggests the tools to create a new kind of church and move from merely surviving to thriving.[58] Drawing on an extensive two-year field study of two hundred churches from a variety of denominations and geographic regions, he presents the best practices for re-energizing the missionary church in a congregational setting.

This book deals with essentials related to membership, teaching, worship, purpose, measuring growth, church structures, and leadership, but these issues were analyzed in a new light, recommending an outward focus—local mission. This contributes to the growing and diverse engagement in the vision of the missional church, and draws insights from various spectrums of resources to carry out missional transformation. In particular, he argues that it's not the church's activity level that defines success, but whether its activities accomplish God's mission for his church; according to Minatrea, knowing God's purpose and pursuing it with deep passion is the first step in becoming missional. He continues to outline the nine common practices that characterize missional churches.

However, with understanding of culture by the missionary church movement, Scott Aniol, faculty at Southwestern Baptist Theological Seminary, argues that the problem occurs when some unbiblical implications and applications that naturally flow from secular anthropology also find their way into the thinking and practice of missional evangelicals. In particular, he argued that the missionary church movement promotes uncritical cultural contextualization.[59] He says:

> Contextualization is a relatively novel idea developed in recent liberal-leaning missions conversations while conservative evangelicals—including those of the missional bent—adopted the idea with reference to cultural form while nevertheless

---

57. Ibid., 12.
58. Minatrea, *Shaped By God's Heart*.
59. Aniol, "Mission of Worship," lines 16–23.

protecting the authority of Scripture by insisting that truth must never change regardless of culture.[60]

In other words, he is critical of a missionary church which does not seek for a biblical contextualization that is biblically faithful, yet culturally relevant; he argued that conservative evangelicals attempt to retain the essential message of the gospel, but everything else is merely cultural and must be contextualized.[61] Finally, the missionary church movement, based on *Missio Dei*, intends for the church to be missionary, but there have been critics among evangelical circles. In particular, contextualization in the missionary church movement is a hot issue that the evangelical church never agrees with. However, Diaspora missiology will connect the church insider and outsider because diaspora exist inside and outside of the church. Thus the subject of mission is God himself, and God can work inside the church or outside the church. I will deal with this in detail in the next section.

The Relationship between Missio Dei and the Church

Regarding the "emerging agenda for global theologizing," in "Conclusion: Global Theologizing," Craig Ott points out four missiological issues:

(1) What are the nature and implications of the *Missio Dei* in our times?

(2) How should a sequel to David Bosch's *Transforming Mission* (1991) be written, defining a biblical mission paradigm for the twenty-first century?

(3) What are the implications of the current state of world Christianity for our mandate to *fulfill the great commission* and *make disciples of all nations*?

(4) What can we as global church learn from one another regarding the encounter of Christianity and non-Christian religions and various worldviews?[62]

Here, the *Missio Dei* is the concept which is first recognized among emerging agenda for global theologizing, which shows how important the concept of the *Missio Dei* is in current missiology.

In Bosch's explanation of the *Missio Dei*, we can read some problems therein. According to the *Missio Dei*:

---

60. Aniol, *By the Waters of Babylon*, 175.
61. Ibid.
62. Ott, "Conclusion," 327–28.

> Mission was understood as being derived from the very nature of God. It was put thus in the context of the doctrine of the Trinity, not of ecclesiology or soteriology. The classical doctrine on the *Missio Dei* as God the Father sending the son, and God the Father and the Son sending the Spirit was expanded to include yet another movement: Father, Son, and Holy Spirit sending the church into world. As far as missionary thinking was concerned, the linking with the doctrine of the trinity constituted an important innovation.[63]

Put simply, the *Missio Dei* is the confession of the Father, Son, and Holy Spirit sending the church into world. It is not the church but God himself that initiated mission. Based on Moltman's explanation, "It is not the church that has a mission of salvation to fulfill in the world; it is the mission of the Son and the Spirit through the Father that includes the church."[64]

Here, the core of the debate is that there is a separation between mission and the church in the *Missio Dei*. This term was first introduced at the 1952 Willingen conference of the International Missionary Council (IMC) and developed theologically by Lutheran theologian, Georg Vicedom.[65] The real issue in the *Missio Dei* is to neglect either the essential value of ecclesiology or soteriology, even though it has dynamic mission theology emphasizing the sovereignty and centrality of the Trinity God. Jesus himself built and gave the heavenly keys to the church for preaching the gospel to gain souls—namely, mission (Matt 16); As John Calvin puts it, the church is essentially like the mother to believers.

> I shall start, then, with the church, into whose bosom God is pleased to gather his sons, not only that they may be nourished by her help and ministry as long as they are infants and children, but also that they may be guided by her motherly care until they mature and at last reach the goal of faith . . . so that, for those to whom he is Father the church may also be Mother. And this was so not only under the law but also after Christ's coming, as Paul testifies when he teaches that we are the children of the new and heavenly Jerusalem (Gal 4:26).[66]

Regarding problems of the *Missio Dei*, however, Ott explained that "the term *Missio Dei* has been so variously interpreted that its usefulness has rightly been questioned, being called a 'container' term, into which an

---

63. Bosch, *Transforming Mission*, 390.
64. Moltmann, *Church in the Power of the Spirit*, 64.
65. Vicedom, *Mission of God*.
66. Calvin, *Institutes of the Christian Religion*, 4.1.1.

out of which one can put and take whatever one wants . . . or even a Trojan horse in the theology of mission."[67] Nevertheless, for Ott, the concept of the church's mission as participation in God's mission is powerful one, worthy of further study and reflection. This shows that the *Missio Dei* is helpful to challenge and reform the institutional church for God's initiative mission. Thus, a real issue is how we can vitalize the *Missio Dei* without dismissing the church.

Generally speaking, Diaspora missiology is open to the *Missio Dei*. Diaspora missiologist Wan's response to Van Engen's "Mission Defined and Described" included this discussion of this issue.[68] Wan evaluated that Van Engel overcorrected evangelical emphasis on individual/ spiritual salvation; his paper deals with the institutional aspect of mission; his institutional focus of mission and definition of mission are narrowed down to becoming the missional church. That is, for Wan, Van Engen's definition is too institutional. He suggests his definition of mission using the *Missio Dei* like this:

> Mission is the Christian (individual) and the church (institutional) continuing on and carrying out the *Missio Dei* of the triune God at both individual and institutional levels, spiritually (saving souls) and socially (ushering in *shalom*), for redemption, reconciliation and transformation.[69]

Here we understand that the *Missio Dei* is used to carry out the mission of the triune God at both individual and institutional levels. In fact, the church is the community of believers, gathered as well as scattered. We cannot limit the scope of the church to the institutional only.

What are the nature and implications of the *Missio Dei* in our times? This question is one of the crucial tasks solved by contemporary missiology. For example, Philip initiatively preached the gospel in Samaritan areas, namely, Philip, amid a scattered situation, preached without a sending from the church. Later, the Jerusalem church heard about this and sent two apostles (Acts 8:1–14). The *Missio Dei* takes place amidst outsiders of the church; finally the *Missio Dei* is directly or indirectly connected to the church. Furthermore, it is noted that the church is not a gathering assembly only; it includes scattered people as the "scattered church."

---

67. Ott, "Conclusion," 327
68. Wan, "Mission and *Missio Dei*," 20–30.
69. Ibid.

Methodology for Doing Missiology: Interdisciplinary Studies

Globalization has challenged the research method in traditional mission. Current mission takes place in the vortex of globalization as a field of the interactions of different forms. According to Zina O'Leary:

> Process by which economic, political, cultural and environmental systems across the globe increasingly become, and are accepted as, part of an integrated and interdependent whole system. Not long ago, exploring faraway lands was left to adventurers and anthropologists who travelled for months on end to discover natives who ate bizarre foods, traded with stones, and were ruled by tribal chiefs. It's a bit different now.[70]

We realize that current missiology develops research methods on globalization, intertwined with economic, political, cultural, and environmental systems. That is, it needs the lens of interdisciplinary studies for an understanding of global mission fields.

Regarding research methodology for doing Diaspora missiology, in particular, Wan emphasizes interdisciplinary studies. He explains, "in this sense, diaspora missiology is to be interdisciplinary by integrating missiology with various related disciplines—human geography, cultural anthropology, political demography, urban and ethnic studies, communication science, etc."[71]

Recent missiological theologizing in the context of globalization, called global theologizing, moves toward interdisciplinary research. Diaspora missiology is in the center of interdisciplinary studies.

Furthermore, topics such as globalization, ethnic and race relations, conflict resolutions of ethnic and religious groups, economical issues, social justice, pluralism, and multiculturalism are involved in the research of Diaspora missiology. Major findings from these studies must be integrated with missiological understandings in ministry planning and missions strategy. The reason an interdisciplinary approach is needed for the study of doing missiology is that diaspora is the product of complex political, social, economic, cultural, and spiritual situations. The failure in much research on diaspora is due to the lack of interdisciplinary perspectives. Interdisciplinary perspectives are needed for understanding diaspora and their contexts, interpreting the Bible, and applying its messages to their mind and life.

However, interdisciplinary studies are not perfect, and lie under the authority of the Bible. Furthermore, an interdisciplinary approach should

---

70. O'Leary, "Social Science Jargon Buster," 102.
71. Wan, *Diaspora Missiology*, 109.

be mainly used as a tool for the interpretations and applications of the Bible. Regarding the risk of being interdisciplinary, the Lausanne Movement states: "From our perspective, no area of science, society, or culture is perfect or neutral. It is essential to recognize, critique, and respond to the implicit ethics, forms of power, and/or oppression embedded in them."[72] That is, interdisciplinary studies should be used critically in the light of biblical teachings. We need to develop research methods in which missiologists can research the mission field affected by global flows in terms of the Bible and various disciplines. Here in particular, it is important to study how we use interdisciplinary methodologies to interpret and apply the Bible.

According to Van Engen, the Bible should be approached as a tapestry, focusing on understanding the context of the Bible. He argues, "we are seeking an intimate interrelationship of text and new contexts through the vehicle of particular themes or motifs that bridge the text's initial context with today's contexts of mission."[73] Here we find an interdisciplinary approach works for the interpretation of the Bible. This helps to bridge the text's initial context with today's immigrant contexts; interdisciplinary interpretations of the Bible give the interpreter insights into applying its message to the problems of immigrants according to interdisciplinary factors. An interdisciplinary approach also helps us to understand the real context of human beings, and gives us contact points with biblical themes for the practical applications of the gospel. This statement shows that interdisciplinary perspectives are used to apply to the interpretations and applications of the Bible. The interdisciplinary issue is one of the important issues in current missiology.

Mission Strategies: Holistic Ministries

As mission fields become more and more holistic, the concept of mission radically moves toward holistic. Originally, the adjective *holistic* only intends to oppose and correct a one-sided approach of mission that focuses on either the vertical or the horizontal dimension of mission. To synthesize both dimensions, the word was expressed by the late W. A. Visser't Hooft in an opening speech at the Uppsala Assembly of the World Council of Churches (1968) in the following words. His address informs conflicts between "the vertical interpretation of the gospel as essentially concerned with God's saving action in the life of individuals, and the horizontal interpretation of it as

---

72. Third Lausanne Congress, "Content Library: The Cape Town Declaration," lines 25–26.

73. Van Engen, *Mission on the Way*, 42.

mainly concerned with human relationships in the world,"[74] he continues to point out Christians neglect of the responsibility that:

> A Christianity which has lost its vertical dimension has lost its salt and is not only insipid in itself, but useless for the world. But a Christianity which would use the vertical preoccupation as a means to escape from its responsibility for and in the common life of man is a denial of the incarnation, of God's love for the world manifested in Christ.[75]

First of all, holistic is used in terms of a balance between the vertical interpretation of the gospel as God's saving action in the life of individuals, and the horizontal interpretation of it as concerned with human life and relationships. This tends to point to and correct the one-sidedness of two camps—conservative and liberal—in relation to mission. Here is another example in the Lausanne Movement. Holistic mission is concerned with the whole person in all their needs, considering the meaning of the holistic gospel, how it has developed, and implications for the individual Christian. The term was used in the "Holistic Mission Occasional Paper No. 33" produced by the Issue Group on this topic at the 2004 Forum for World Evangelization hosted by the Lausanne Committee for World Evangelization in Pattaya, Thailand.

This paper was discussed by the thirty-one Issue Groups, and these new realities were taken into consideration: the HIV pandemic, terrorism, globalization, the global role of media, poverty, persecution of Christians, fragmented families, political and religious nationalism, post-modern mind set, oppression of children, urbanization, neglect of the disabled, and others.[76] In particular, the Lausanne noted, "These issues were chosen through a global research programme seeking to identify the most significant issues in the world today which are of concern in our task to take the good news to the world."[77]

A third example of holistic mission is given in the title *Holistic Mission: God's Plan for God's People*, edited by Brain Woolnough, research tutor at the Oxford Centre for Mission Studies (OCMS), and Emeritus Fellow of St. Cross College, Oxford. According to the collection of his edit, holistic mission is more emphasized in the context of global issues. For him, holistic mission, or integral mission, implies that God is concerned with the whole

---

74. LCWE Issue Group No. 4, "Holistic Mission Occasional Paper No. 33."
75. Ibid., 11.
76. Ibid., 4.
77. Ibid.

person, the whole community: body, mind, and spirit. But today, many Christians concentrate only on one aspect. This book reaffirms that to be true to the Bible, namely, to follow the example of Jesus, it considers the meaning of the holistic gospel—how it has developed and implications for the individual Christian, for the local church, for denominations and church groups, for missionary societies, and for theological training institution.[78]

Finally, the importance is that holistic mission is biblical, and more so in an era of globalization. Diaspora is the product of global phenomena; diaspora need to be cared for in all areas of life. Diaspora missiology works with this holistic mission; a holistic concern is key to Diaspora ministry because diaspora are in the middle of holistic needs. From a biblical perspective, holistic mission is the focused direction of early church mission.

The early church focused on holistic ministry and mission: spiritual and material, message and property and possession, praising God and enjoying the favor of all the people . . . holistic mission not only the ministry way of the early church, but one of the whole church to come. Mission in globalization should be more holistic, corroborating evangelism and social care and responsibility. Acts 2 gives an example of holistic ministries, focusing on God's salvation for the final goal.

> Acts 2: 42they devoted themselves to the apostles' teaching and to fellowship, to the breaking of bread and to prayer. 43Everyone was filled with awe at the many wonders and signs performed by the apostles. 44All the believers were together and had *everything in common*. 45They sold property and possessions to give to anyone who had need. 46Every day they continued to meet together in the temple courts. They broke bread in their homes and ate together with glad and sincere hearts, 47praising God and enjoying the favor of all the people. And the Lord added to their number daily those who were being saved. (Italics mine)

NEW DISCOVERIES OF DIASPORA MISSIOLOGY FOR CURRENT MISSION ISSUES

This section will deal with rediscoveries of Diaspora missiology with regard to the resolution of issues in current missiology, mentioned in part 2 of the present text. That is, this shows how Diaspora missiology gives insight to handle issues arising from contemporary missiology.

---

78. Woolnough, *Holistic Mission*.

A New Paradigm for a Global Era: Mission Based on Demographic Analysis

Recently, Diaspora missiology was introduced as a new paradigm of global mission; this approves that Diaspora missiology appeared in adapting to global culture. In a global era, diaspora, the phenomenon of massive demographic movement, offers new strategies of mission. The original word "diaspora" had a sense of a forcible dispersal of a people and their subsequent unhappiness in their countries of exile; more recently the widely used term refers to the phenomenon of the dispersion of any ethnic group.[79] Based on the *Oxford English Dictionary Online*, the first recorded usage of the word *Diaspora* in the English world was in 1876, designating "extensive *Diaspora* work of evangelization among the National Protestant Churches on the continent."[80]

Regarding Diaspora missiology, the GDN (Global Diaspora Network) introduces it in this way:

> The 21st Century has been marked by the greatest migration in world history. People are not only resettling within their own countries, but are being scattered to all four corners of the globe. U.N. experts estimate that there are over 200 million international immigrants. People from every nation and tribe are moving because of regional conflicts and wars, devastating natural calamities, urbanization, labor related opportunities, educational advancement, etc. The scattering of the people (i.e. diaspora) poses challenges and opportunities to the global Church of Jesus Christ.[81]

What then is the distinctiveness of Diaspora missiology? Tira explains in five aspects: "In contrast to traditional missions, Diaspora Missions is (1) economically sustainable; (2) benefits from travel accessibility to the target audience; (3) has less political and legal restrictions; (4) partnership among like-minded people and organizations committed to the Great Commission; and (5) missions are done not only by "few experts" or "international workers."[82]

Also, based on Wan's analysis on the shift from traditional missiology to Diaspora missiology, there are four points.

---

79. Wan, *Diaspora Missiology*, 97.

80. *Oxford English Dictionary Online*, "Diaspora," lines 1–3.

81. Global Diaspora Network, "Gatherings: 2015 Global Diaspora Forum," lines 2–5.

82. Tira, "Diaspora Missiology Part 3," 40–45.

(1) Focus Difference: Dichotomized or Holistic

Traditional missiology centers on a "polarized and dichotomized" relationship: great mission / great commandment; saving soul / social gospel; church planting / Christianity charity; and paternalism/indigenization. In a word, the mission is separated into two parts or classifications. In contrast, Diaspora missiology integrates two separated issues of the mission: integration of evangelism and Christian charity, leading to contextualization.

(2) Geographical Difference: Territorial or Deterritorialization

Traditional missiology centers on territorial polarization—here/there, local/global, foreign/local, urban/rural, state/nation, sending/receiving—in contrast, Diaspora missiology focuses on deterritorialization, "glocal," mutuality and reciprocity, hybridity, interdisciplinary, non-spatial, borderless, no boundary to debate—disciplinary difference: disciplinary compartmentalization or interdisciplinary. Traditional missiology focuses on disciplinary compartmentalization and specialization, which is separated into distinct parts, categories, or compartments. In contrast, Diaspora missiology is based on integrated and interdisciplinary missions.

(3) Orientation Difference: Polarized Coming/Going or Integration

In traditional missiology, the OT understands mission as the Gentile and proselyte's coming, and the NT understand missions as the Great Commission and going forth. In contrast, Diaspora missiology understands the mission as the activity of Diaspora in the providence of God.[83]

(4) Basic Difference: The Subject of the Mission

To traditional missiology, the subject of mission is the church; to Diaspora missiology, the subject of the mission is God himself more than the church. That is, Diaspora missiology follows the way of God who scattered in fields around the globe. Traditional missiology understands a "few specific" as missionaries; however, Diaspora understands an "unspecific many—Diaspora" as missionaries. More importantly, the biblical meaning of "scattered" in the OT and the NT becomes a dynamic field of God's redemptive plan;

---

83. This analysis is based on Wan's descriptions, but I systematized and made up these data according to my criteria and principles. See Wan, *Diaspora Missiology*, 99.

Diaspora as the seed become an instrument of God's evangelistic works. The mindset and lifestyle of pilgrimage in Diaspora serve as foundations for a holy life and evangelists. However, Diaspora missiology is not the replacement for traditional missiology, but its supplement.

Diaspora as New Concept of Mission in a Global Era

The concept of Diaspora has appeared as a hot issue in the global immigrant era. On March 8, 2012, Pew Research reported regarding "Faith on the Move" in the United States: "In the United States, for instance, more than a century of immigration by Catholics, Jews, Muslims, Buddhists, Hindus, Sikhs and others has contributed to the gradual reduction of the once-overwhelming proportion of Protestants, which has fallen from two-thirds of the U.S. public in the 1960s to about half today."[84]

This quotation shows how the United States politically and spiritually suffered from migrants of other religions. Recent influx of Muslim and other religions affects the gradual reduction of the once-overwhelming proportion of Protestants. Consistent with this trend, there are various published reports and books that deal with the decrease in Christianity in Northern Hemisphere—namely, the United States and Europe.

In *The Next Christendom: The Coming of Global Christianity*, Philip Jenkins observed that Christianity is gradually and increasingly moved toward the Southern Hemisphere of the globe.[85] Furthermore, he continues to argue that a center of gravity in the Christian world has shifted from the United States and Europe to the Southern Hemisphere. This data shows how Western Christianity would be decreased in relation to its size and resource. This decreasing phenomenon of Western Christianity and the revival of Southern Christianity finally lead to the collapse of half of global Christianity. Global Christianity hopes that the whole church of the world, neither just the Southern Hemisphere nor the Northern, catches the revival of the gospel.

Diaspora is one of the great strategies for the revival of the whole church. According to Pew Research on "The Faith on the Move—Religious Affiliation of International Migrations," "Christian migration has shifted to the United States and Europe, a major place of Western Christianity. Regional origins of Christian migrants are Latin American and Caribbean (30%), Asia-pacific (13%), Sub-Saharan African (9%) . . . two major regional destinations of Christian migrants are Northern America (34%), and

---

84. Pew Research Center, "Rising Tide," lines 4–5.
85. Jenkins, *Next Christendom*, 14.

Europe (38%)."[86] That is, Christian migrants from the Southern Hemisphere move to the Western or Northern Hemispheres. The data indicates that in global migration, the moving of Diaspora in all directions, especially from the Southern to the Northern Hemisphere, can take note of the problem of the decreased Western Christianity.

For example, in the United States, many Hispanic churches have revived. Juan Francisco Martinez authored *Walk with the People: Latino Ministry in the United States*.[87] Martinez serves in a teaching faculty position at Fuller Theological Seminary. The book claims that the majority of Hispanic churches have been "Pentecostalized," but they cover everything from Baptists to Methodists. According to a 2007 Pew Research study, 68 percent of Latinos are Catholic and 20 percent are Protestant. Interestingly, there is a generational tendency toward becoming Protestant—the percentage of Latino Protestants is higher among those who have been in the US three or four generations than among immigrants. This shows how Hispanic Christians adaptively become Protestants in the USA. Finally, the Hispanic church experienced the revival of Protestantism in the USA. It is natural that this revival of the Hispanic church affects the neighboring communities and churches in the USA.

Again, in *Los Protestants: An Introduction to Latino Protestantism in the United States*, Juan Francisco Martínez also notes marked differences that separate Latino Protestants from other US Protestants, and examines an evolving Protestant/Latino ethno-religious identity.[88] The author wants readers to understand where Latino Protestants fit in the overall picture of US religion. In particular, Martínez's the final chapter outlines critical ways in which the Latin American Protestant presence is transforming the US religious culture.

According to Martínez, 20 percent of all Latinos are Protestants, primarily Pentecostals or evangelicals; in fact, in many US Protestant denominations, the only area of growth is among Latinos. This also shows that the Diaspora church from the Southern Hemisphere can contribute to the revival of Christianity in Northern Hemisphere. However, as the Amazon book description notes, "In many US Protestant denominations, the only area of growth is among Latinos. Despite these facts, there has been nowhere for the general reader to turn for an understanding of this

---

86. Pew Research Center, "Rising Tide," lines 4–5.

87. Martinez, *Walk with the People*.

88. Martínez, *Los Protestantes: An Introduction to Latino Protestantism in the United States*.

community—until now."[89] This explains how the American church barely understands the value of the Diaspora church surrounding them.

The Incorporation of the Missio Dei and the Diaspora Mission Church

As is shown in Wan's response to Charles Van Engen, the concept of the *Missio Dei* is used to define mission in a broad sense. Wan argued that God's *Missio Dei* included individuals and the institutional church. The following picture shows this. In the *Missio Dei*, God is the imputative author of mission. The love of God the Father, the grace of the Son through his death on the cross and resurrection, and the fellowship of the Holy Spirit is the cause of mission, which is called the *Missio Dei*.

Furthermore, it should be noted that the concept of Diaspora cannot be separated from God's mission. In his article "Diaspora and Timely Hit: Toward a Diaspora Missiology," Jung explains that the Diaspora is "the seed for God's kingdom"[90] in the field, which seems to be God's secret plan in an initial stage, although it will be revealed later. Under the section heading of "Dispersion of Nations and *Missio Dei*," referring to Adolf Von Harnack, Jung suggests:

> A list wherein the Christian mission was indebted to the Jewish mission which preceded it, all of which are related to Diaspora, i.e. a field tilled all over the empire; religious community already formed everywhere in the towns; the preliminary knowledge of the Old Testament; the habit of regular worship and control of private life; an impressive apologetic on behalf of monotheism, historical teleology, and ethics; and the feeling that self-diffusion was a duty.[91]

Jung here understood Diaspora in terms of the *Missio Dei*. Diaspora is God's secret providence; sometimes, the church does not recognize the move of Diaspora; Christian mission associations also do not trace their dispersion. Diaspora missiology can be well understood in terms of the *Missio Dei*, God's own sending. The acting subject of mission here is God alone. We can suggest a Diaspora-centered church, in relation to the church and diaspora, called the Diaspora Mission Church.

---

89. Amazon.com, Book Description of *Los Protestantes*.
90. Jung, "Diaspora and Timely Hit," 65.
91. Ibid., 61–62.

Diaspora Mission Church plays a key role in carrying out the *Missio Dei* in the institutional church because the missionary church written in Acts is Diasporic. As we have seen, Diaspora is a typical pattern of the *Missio Dei*; God himself sent the Diaspora as the seed of the kingdom in his redemptive plan. However, traditionally, the *Missio Dei* has a tendency to reject the role of an institutional church for mission, and to ignore the evangelical nature of mission. The *Missio Dei* and the institutional church as the subject of mission must be reconciled in Diaspora missiology. Diaspora is a missionary subject; God is the subject of mission, sending the Diaspora as the seed in the field of the world; the church is the Diaspora community. Regarding mission, the *Missio Dei* and the church are intertwined with each other. For example, Philip and Stephen (Acts 6) were Diaspora, but were appointed as workers of the church, and their missionary works were connected to the church. Someday, the two aspects will become one, whether the church is first and Diaspora is later, or Diaspora is first and the church is later.

Therefore, the *Missio Dei* and the church as the subject of mission become one, as Philip and Stephen preached the gospel as Diaspora and gained souls for Christ. This means that Diaspora missiology satisfies the *Missio Dei* in a sense of God sending first, and the correct *Missio Dei* in a sense of preaching the gospel and gaining souls for Christ. Diaspora is not the institutional church's sending, but God's sending. In this sense, the *Missio Dei* focusing on God only represents the spirit of Diaspora missiology. However, we need to correct some aspects of *Missio Dei* theology through the concept of Diaspora. Because the Diaspora was the people God selected for his salvation and mission (1 Pet 1:1; Acts 8:1–5), Diaspora missiology will help the *Missio Dei* to discover and hold fast to God's salvation and mission, and his church as the mission agent as addressed in the Letter of First Peter, sent to the congregation of Christians as Diaspora. In the concept of Diaspora missiology, the *Missio Dei* can be refilled with God's salvation and the church as his agent.

Diaspora: The Rediscovery of a Biblical Model of Mission in the Acts

The meaning of Diaspora is the seed of God's kingdom, scattered around the field of the globe in God's redemptive, secret plan.[92] In his providence, God already scattered the Diaspora, the seed of the gospel, to the places God

---

92. Ibid., 65.

want to evangelize; this is why Diaspora missiology should be formulated in urgency as a new paradigm in twenty-first century global mission.

Acts 6 describes Diasporas that God used for his mission. This happened in the Hebrew centered church in Jerusalem. These seven were chosen in the middle of the conflict between the Hellenistic Jews and the Hebraic Jews because Hellenistic widows were being overlooked in the daily distribution of food. This is the insight and suggestion of the twelve apostles (Acts 6:2–3):

> 2So the Twelve gathered all the disciples together and said, "It would not be right for us to neglect the ministry of the word of God in order to wait on tables. 3Brothers and sisters, choose seven men from among you who are known to be full of the Spirit and wisdom. We will turn this responsibility over to them 4and will give our attention to prayer and the ministry of the word.

Finally, the proposal of the apostles pleased the church members. Here, an amazing thing is that these seven persons all were from Hellenistic groups, Diaspora living around the Roman Empire. From the name used, they are all Hellenistic. How were these Hellenistic persons chosen in a Hebrew-centered church? This is the miracle of God for his church and mission. Finally, what happened to the church and its society? Acts 6: "7so the word of God spreads. The number of disciples in Jerusalem increased rapidly, and a large number of priests became obedient to the faith."

The crucial point here is that some of the seven contributed to the developing achievement of Jesus' mandate of the mission: "But you will receive power when the Holy Spirit comes on you; and you will be my witnesses in Jerusalem, and in all Judea and Samaria, and to the ends of the earth" (Acts 1:8). The opening of mission in Samaria was commenced by Philip, one of the seven (Acts 8:4–8). Stephen preached the gospel with a broad knowledge of a long history of the Bible in Sanhedrin, and he fully understood the organic history of God's redemption. He was not an apostle, but a lay Diaspora. Hear from his final remark and prayer:

> Acts 7: 56"Look," he said, "I see heaven open and the Son of Man standing at the right hand of God." 57At this they covered their ears and, yelling at the top of their voices, they all rushed at him, 58dragged him out of the city and began to stone him. Meanwhile, the witnesses laid their coats at the feet of a young man named Saul. 59While they were stoning him, Stephen prayed, "Lord Jesus, receive my spirit." 60Then he fell on his knees and

cried out, "Lord, do not hold this sin against them." When he had said this, he fell asleep.

Stephen became the first with the honor of martyr in church history; the first martyr was not an apostle or pastor, but lay minister or evangelist. This is a huge and significant lesson for the church and its church mission. What was the influence of the martyr of Stephen on mission? Acts 8:1–4 says:

> 1And Saul approved of their killing him. On that day a great persecution broke out against the church in Jerusalem, and all except the apostles were scattered throughout Judea and Samaria. 2Godly men buried Stephen and mourned deeply for him.... 4Those who had been scattered preached the word wherever they went. 5Philip went down to a city in Samaria and proclaimed the Messiah there.

Here it is clear that the martyr of Stephan affected godly men to preach the word wherever they went, being scattered throughout Judea and Samaria. Philip is one of the seven godly men who were affected by the martyr of Stephan. Godly men were scattered and moved to other areas, and finally to Antioch. These godly men, Diaspora, went to Antioch and began to preach to Greeks as well (Acts 11:19–21). Here some of them from Cyprus and Cyrene went to Antioch and told the Greeks the good news about the Lord Jesus. This means that Gentile mission was commenced by Diaspora Christians, not the apostles. This story of the Diaspora serves as the foundation of theorizing Diaspora in terms of biblical and theological perspectives. Just as the Diaspora seven commenced a secret strategy of God's church and mission, they now still are a secret of God for his church and mission in the days of God's redemption, which now seems to face a spiritual stagnation.

Diaspora for the Reformation of the Church in a Secular Society

As expressed in *A Secular Age*, Charles Taylor sees the Reformation as a crucial movement in the formation of the "secular age"; along with their wholesale assault on ecclesial white magic, the Reformers rejected the various hierarchies between clergy and lay members or between the religious and secular.[93] The secular issue in the Protestant church has been claimed to have its root in the Reformation. Taylor argued that there have been three stages of a "nova effect," an explosion of secularity beginning with "an exclusive alternative to Christian faith."[94]

93. Taylor, C., *Secular Age*.
94. Ibid., 299.

In the immanent frame, "The whole culture experiences cross pressures, between the draw of the narratives of closed immanence on one side, and the sense of their inadequacy on the other."[95] Here, the crucial point is that transcendence is a key issue of Christians living in secular culture. For him, "The secular age is schizophrenic, or better, deeply cross-pressured."[96] Finally, against unbelief, Taylor presents a selection of recent spiritual conversions or "epiphanic" experiences.[97]

In this sense, the concept of Diaspora becomes a key word to reform and renew the secularized church, because their identities as strangers or pilgrims represents a transcendent existence. Again that is why Diaspora represents a key spirit to carry out living faith in a secular culture.

Finally, the great priority of mission is the renewal of the church excising mission, as Shenk puts, "Ever since Jesus' time, mission must precede the church. The renewal of the church is linked to recovery of this priority of mission."[98] Without the renewal of the church, there is no improvement in Christian mission. The concept of Diaspora is a driving force of renewing secular churches because the concept of Diaspora itself has a transcendent nature against secularism. Diasporas are called to God's salvation and mission; they are called to be the seed of God in the field. They are willing to be called strangers in this world, and pilgrims who walk toward heaven; they are transcendental beyond earthly things. They are the seed of the kingdom, and strangers in an existential sense without greed of the property on earth, and long for better country in heaven (Heb 11:16). At the same time, these Diaspora enter into all areas of the local society, and do "good deeds" on earth. Peter says:

> 1 Pet 2: 11Dear friends, I urge you, as aliens and strangers in the world,
>   to abstain from sinful desires, which wage war against your soul.
> 12Live such good lives among the pagans
>   that through they accuse you of doing wrong,
>   they may see your good deeds and glorify God on the day he visits us.

---

95. Ibid., 595.
96. Ibid., 727.
97. Ibid., 767.
98. Shenk, *Changing Frontiers of Mission*, 15.

7

Contextual Theologizing for Diaspora Missiology

Contextual theologizing moves toward the encounter of the text and the context, including the interpretation of the Bible and the interpretation of the context. That is, the principles and skills to communicate the gospel into the particular context—culture. What is the most important priority here? Keeping it short, it is a saving grace of Christ through faith. If we are not sure about this, why do we contextualize the gospel? This means that contextualization should focus on the cross and resurrection of Christ, and a theologizing that the Holy Spirit will be poured out. In addition, the contextualization of Diaspora missiology should gear toward the church itself, its ministries, all members, and all their ways of life.

CONTEXTUAL THEOLOGIZING OF DIASPORA MISSIOLOGY

The Definition of Contextual Theologizing

The concept of Diaspora presupposes the change of the context because they left their homelands and experienced different cultures of host nations. The core issue here is an effective communication of the message, which calls for a contextualized theologizing. Contextual theologizing can be defined as "the various process by which a local church integrates the gospel message (the text) with its local culture (the context)."[1]

Doing Diaspora missiology is a kind of contextual theologizing. The theologizing subject should be a local Diaspora church. Hiebert calls it "the fourth self," namely, "self-theologizing."[2] What are the factors for doing Diaspora missiology? For forming contextual theologies, there are three, dimensional methods: the Bible, culture, and community (Tienou; Schreiter[3]). Van Engel argues that the contextualization broadens various understanding of culture to include social, political, and economic question.[4] He states,

> The term "contextualization" includes all that is implied in indigenization or inculturation, but also seeks also to include the realities of the contemporary, secularity, technology, and the struggle for human justice. While indigenization tends to focus on the purely cultural dimension of human experience, contextualization broadens the understanding of culture to include social, political, and economic questions. In this way, culture is understood in more dynamic and flexible ways, and is seen not as closed and self-contained, but as open and able to be enriched by an encounter with other cultures and movements.[5]

In understanding the meaning of contextualization, we need to consider two essentials in addition to the definition explained above: symbolic anthropology and method of correlation.

Symbolic Anthropology

In explaining contextual theologizing, it is necessary to consider the interpretation of culture—what is called symbolic anthropology—by Clifford Geertz (1973). Here, symbolic anthropology, otherwise known as interpretive anthropology, stresses culture as meaning, expressed through symbolic means. In particular, the conceptualization of culture as symbolic implies an interpretive approach from the "native's point of view." For symbolic anthropologists, symbols carry multiple, various meanings and are used and created in public, social exchanges. In many ways, symbolic anthropology

---

1. Luzbetak, *Church and Culture*, 69.
2. Hiebert, *Anthropological Reflections*, 193–224.
3. Schreiter, *New Catholicity*, 21.
4. Van Engen, "Toward a Contextually Appropriate Methodology," 194.
5. Tienou, "Forming Indigenous Theologies," 245–52.

stands in reaction to what was being argued as the sterile scientism of both materialist and cognitive approaches.[6]

For Geertz, "Believing, with Max Weber, that man is an animal suspended in webs of significance he himself has spun, I take cultures to be those webs, and the analysis of it to be therefore not an experimental science in search of law but an interpretive one in search of meaning."[7] The important point learned from his theory of culture is: "the essential vocation of interpretative anthropology is not answer our deepest questions, but to make available to us answers that others, guarding other sheep in other valleys, have given, and thus to include them in the consultable record of what man has said."[8] His interest is not in perpetuating a specific methodology, but rather in "setting a tone or mood or agenda that people could react toward or against." This attitude should be that of contextualization researchers who study diaspora; researchers should try to find the meanings of diaspora in their own contexts.

"Method of Correlation": Answering to the Questions from the Context.

Contextual methodology can be explained in terms of Tillich's "method of correlation," which is "an approach that correlates Christian revelation with the issues and problems of human existence raised by existential, and philosophical analysis."[9] Based on Tillich's concept of a "method of correlation," the core mission of contextualization is to identify the problems of diaspora existence as context. This means that Diaspora missiology should be the answer to the problems of diaspora.

Diaspora contextualization focuses on what kind questions of diaspora have; in essence, diaspora are scattered people, existentially and spiritually, waiting for God's deliverance. "He has made everything beautiful in its time. He has also set eternity in the human heart" (Eccl 3:11). Diaspora missiology as a contextual theologizing focuses on looking for answering the problems of diaspora existence.

However, contextualization is not to follow and answer the context only, but sometimes to give the answer of the text to the context, even though the context is not interested in it or is ignorant. Sometimes, contextualization theology should ask, which is more important: the text itself or

6. Rao and Walton, *Culture and Public Action*.

7. Geertz, *Interpretation of the Culture*, 5.

8. Ibid., 30.

9. Bowker, "Tillich, Paul Johannes Oskar."

the context. Our aim to contextualize the gospel in the context is to preach the gospel to people. Contextual theologizing is useless or invalid if contextual theologians lose the essence of the gospel in its process. This is because this cannot accomplish the primary goal of the gospel saving souls.

Here, interdisciplinary perspectives should be adapted to understand their problems because "there is much complexity in the cause, process, and consequence of the phenomena of Diaspora, and no single discipline can enable researchers to explain and apply insights from the challenging undertaking."[10] It also is noted that in contextual theologizing, "Interpreters are urged to seek a broader understanding of the *human* context, both globally and historically; in so doing, they become acutely aware of themes that are in the Bible but have never figured prominently in their daily life. As a result, a multicultural perspective can help reconcile various tensions in Scripture and equip the church to develop faithful, *contextual* theologies."[11]

Contextual theologizing also is viewed as the correlation of theory and praxis. David Tracy proposed a public theology, on his basis of a "revised correlation method" in which theology is defined as a "discipline that articulates mutually critical correlations between the meaning and truth of an interpretation of the Christian fact and the meaning and truth of an interpretation of the contemporary situation."[12] Theologizing is the dialogue between theory and praxis.

Contextual Theologizing back to the Text of the Bible Itself

There are some obstacles in processing contextualization. As Van Engen puts it, there are several obstacles in our culture and our church: (1) obstacles in our culture included "the perception that God's help is not needed," the privatization of faith, and the absence of radical conversion; and (2) obstacles in our churches include a "lack of clarity in defining our task," and a "lack of clarity in understanding our faith."[13] Contextualization does not automatically communicate the gospel to culture.

Recently, due to its failure, contextualization is said to be back to the contextualization examples in the Bible. The book *Contextualization in the New Testament: Patterns for Theology and Mission* (Flemming 2005; winner of a 2006 *Christianity Today* book award!), honored as one of the "Fifteen Outstanding Books of 2005 for Mission Studies," deals with this issue of

10. Wan, *Diaspora Missiology*, 109.
11. Wu, "We Compromise the Gospel," 29.
12. Tracy, "Foundations of Practical Theology," 76.
13. Van Engen, *Mission on the Way*, 194–201.

contextualization. For Flemming, the New Testament provides numerous examples of contextualization, examines how the early church contextualized the gospel, and uncovers the patterns and parameters of Paul or Mark or John as they communicate the Word to the target, bringing these to bear on our contemporary missiological task.[14]

Philip H. Towner, Director of Translation Services, United Bible Societies, reviewed this book:

> *Contextualization in the New Testament* is a welcome addition to New Testament and missiological scholarship for several reasons. First, Dr. Flemming has brought current New Testament scholarship into an effective dialogue with missiological and cultural specialists. Second, in a balanced way, he has rightly taken contextualization as a New Testament missional concept for Paul and his first-century colleagues beyond the neutral sense of communication of the gospel into the realm of proclamation as an intentional engagement with cultural and political discourses. Third, this move promises some very fruitful rethinking of what, in the context of conflicting cultural and religious 'stories,' doing mission meant then and indeed what it should mean now. Finally, Dr. Flemming's lucid style allows easy access to a profound discussion that will impact our understanding of the church's gospel task both ancient and present.[15]

A very shocking fact is that "few have considered in depth how the early church contextualized the gospel." Contextualization is just not the task of the contemporary church, but also that of the early church written in the New Testament. If we go back to the Bible, what do we discover? We need to propose two most important principles of the Bible for contextual theology: (1) The centrality of the cross and resurrection of Christ; and (2) the role of the Holy Spirit in contextual processes.

(1) The Centrality of the Cross and Resurrection of Christ

Diasporas are the scattered by God's judgment over sins; they wait for the fulfillment of God's covenant of gathering as salvation—the cross and resurrection of Christ. That is, the very thing that the Diasporas long for is the cross and resurrection of Christ through which they were cleansed and saved. Thus the great good news the church should preach is the gospel of Jesus Christ. The gospel is the cross and resurrection of Christ (1 Cor

---

14. Flemming, *Contextualization in the New Testament*.
15. Flemming, Review of *Contextualization in the New Testament*, lines 5–10.

15:1–3). The Bible says that salvation relies on faith in the cross of Christ (1 Cor 1:18).

With regard to the centrality of the cross, Michael W. Goheen, introduces Newbigin's centrality of mission—the cross:

> Newbigin's thinking on every subject begins with the gospel and especially that event that is at the centre—the cross. From the beginning of his Christian life until the end, he believed that this was the clue that he must follow if he were to make any sense of the world. Newbigin stresses the foundational nature of the gospel in two closely related ways—as public truth and as universal history. While Hinduism and Western humanism locate truth in something unchanging outside of history, the Biblical story locates truth in a story of God's redemptive deeds and words in history that culminate in Jesus Christ. In Jesus Christ the end and meaning of cosmic history have been revealed and accomplished. At the cross God has dealt with the sin and misery of the world; in the resurrection a new world has dawned; at Pentecost the Spirit was given so men and women could begin to share in this new world.[16]

The cross and resurrection of Jesus Christ is the central theme of the contextual theologian in mission. We should come back to this essential foundation. What do we want to contextualize? It is the gospel of Jesus Christ—his cross and resurrection. More importantly, however, God made foolish the wisdom of the world, which means that human wisdom is an obstacle to understanding the cross of Christ. How surprising it is! Here is God's own way of salvation: "18For the message of the cross is foolishness to those who are perishing, but to us who are being saved it is the power of God. 19For it is written: "I will destroy the wisdom of the wise; the intelligence of the intelligent I will frustrate" (1 Cor 1:18–19).

Here, of most importance is that the Bible emphasizes that human wisdom thinks of the cross as foolish. More surprisingly, God was pleased *through the message of the cross that may seem foolish according to earthly wisdom* to save those who believe. There arises a crucial question: How do we contextualize the cross to the wisdom of the world? We should be very careful in doing contextualization not to distort God's will of the cross for salvation. That is, we study how contextualization may support God's plan to save people through the message of the cross, which seems foolish to earthly wisdom. Here we are reminded of the proclamation of Newbigin's

---

16. Goheen, "Significance of Lesslie Newbigin," 88–99.

Foolishness to the Greeks.[17] This shows that without the works of the Holy Spirit there is no acceptance of the crucified Jesus as the Savior.

(2) The Role of the Holy Spirit in Contextual Process

First of all, ironically, the church today, in contextualizing the gospel, ignores the work of the Holy Spirit. As we know, who communicated the gospel to "Jews from every nation under heaven" (Acts 2:5), as Jesus' disciples did not even have the concept of contextualization? It was the Holy Spirit. The Holy Spirit communicated with the Jews from other nations to hear and understand the gospel beyond the ability of the disciples. This does not mean that the Holy Spirit does everything and disciples do nothing in contextualization, but that we do focus on the contextual works of the Holy Spirit.

Unfortunately, in "The Holy Spirit and Contextualization," Andrew M. Lord argued that there are few studies about the Holy Spirit and contextualization:

> The Pentecostal/Charismatic movement is characterized by adaptability to different cultures: it is a "religion made to travel," to quote Harvey Cox. But despite this observation, little has been done to analyze this process of adaptation. Much research on missiology in recent decades has been done in the area of contextualization which encompasses this process of adaption, but little of this has been applied to the Pentecostal experience and no distinctively Pentecostal contribution has been made to the debate.... The role of the Spirit has received limited treatment in the literature on contextualization. It is not mentioned in the summaries of Bosch or Kirk. For Schreiter the role of the Holy Spirit in the task of contextualization is not defined, but appears to be one of a background worker of grace in the church: "One cannot speak of a community developing a local theology without its being filled with the Spirit and working under the power of the gospel."[18]

As mentioned earlier, two of the interdisciplinary understandings for Diaspora are that diaspora have suffering and trauma, and that diaspora are in multi-cultural dimensions. This implies that, by necessity, the Holy Spirit himself needs to inspire Diasporas to realize the meaning of their suffering and heal them, and communicate the gospel to various people of diaspora,

---

17. Newbigin, *Foolishness to the Greeks.*
18. Lord, "Holy Spirit and Contextualization," 201–13.

finally guiding them into all truth (John 16:13). In addition, the Holy Spirit reveals to us the things God has prepared for those love him.

> 1 Cor 2: 9However, as it is written: "What no eye has seen, what no ear has heard, and what no human mind has conceived"—the things God has prepared for those who love him—10these are the things God has revealed to us *by his Spirit.* 11For who knows a person's thoughts except their own spirit within them? In the same way no one knows the thoughts of God except the *Spirit of God.* 12What we have received is not the spirit of the world, but the Spirit who is from God, so that we may understand what God has freely given us. 13This is what we speak, not in words taught us by human wisdom but in words taught by *the Spirit,* explaining spiritual realities with *Spirit*-taught words. (Italics mine)

The Holy Spirit is the great communicator in delivering the gospel to human beings more than anyone or anything. However, we sometimes tend to ignore the work of the Holy Spirit and approach theologizing only from intellectual perspectives. This is one of the reasons for the stagnation of recent Christian mission.

THE SIGNIFICANCE OF CRITICAL CONTEXTUALIZATION IN A GLOBAL ERA

In a global era, critical contextualization has been emphasized. According to Hiebert, beyond colonization and anti-colonialism, moving toward globalism, we need critical contextualization.[19] We observed that in an anti-colonial era, anti-colonialism has taken the others seriously but fallen into theological relativism. "It [anti-colonialism] called into question Western cultural arrogance and it forced Western Christians to differentiate between the gospel and their culture." Paul Knitter wrote that "in our contemporary world, in which we are aware of the presence of others and the absence of absolutes. Christian theology, to be *truly* Christian, can no longer be *only* Christians."[20]

It is noted that Christian mission should differentiate between the gospel and the Western culture; however, it does not misunderstand the essentials of the biblical gospel as being of Western culture, and discard them as their own. All local Christianity should belong to God's word.

---

19. Hiebert, *Anthropological Reflections*, 53–92.
20. Ibid., 63.

Now it is time to call for critical contextualization in a global era beyond the anger and criticism of anti-colonialism. What are the principles of critical contextualization? It can be addressed from Hiebert's meta-culturalism and the contextual theologizing in Acts 15.

Hiebert's Meta-culturalism

Why does world Christianity need a meta-culturalism? According to Hiebert, a global perspective calls for critical contextualization, which challenges the ethnocentrism of earlier theories and leads anthropologists to understand other cultures in greater depth. Critical contextualization also requires the complementary nature of human knowledge.

Regarding significance of complementarity in anthropology, Hiebert says:

> One area of complementarity in anthropology is the relationship between *emic* (inside) and *etic* (outside) analysis.... Another area of complementarity is the relationship between anthropology, sociology, psychology, biology, the other sciences, and the humanities. Each contributes something to our understanding of humans. We need help from all of these disciplines to get a more complete picture.[21]

Here is the question: how does this complementarity work in anthropology? It calls for the meta-culturalism. Hiebert says, "Anthropologists again emphasize the underlying oneness of human beings, while recognizing diversity ... the development of a meta-cultural grid is the hallmark of anthropological and other bicultural people"[22]; "having participated deeply in other cultures, and having become both 'empathetic insiders' and 'comparing outsiders.' They developed mental perspectives that enable them to relate to any number of other cultures."[23]

The following picture is a little revised from Hiebert's idea of the meta-cultural grid. Here, four different shapes represent the perspective of each culture; each cultural perspective persists in the formation of the meta-cultural perspective. Each local culture participates in others at a deep level, forming the whole oneness.

---

21. Ibid., 68.
22. Ibid., 69.
23. Ibid.

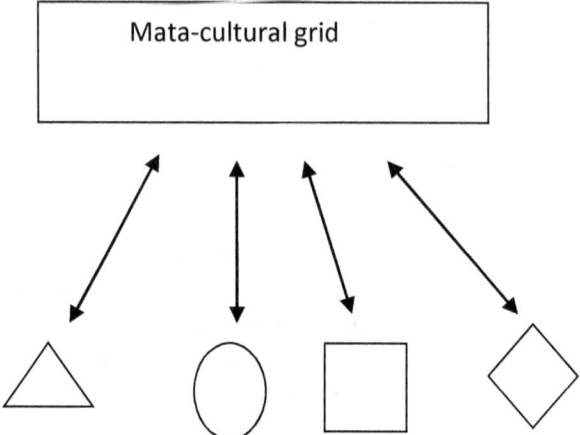

Figure 5: The Meta-cultural Grid[24]

Hiebert's meta-culturalism gives us an insight to combine different cultures for the whole. He argues:

> We must reject the relativism of the anticolonial era, but on what basis can we pass judgment on cultures without falling back into a colonial ethnocentrism? Anthropologists are increasingly aware that true participation with others at a deep level changes us. We learn to see the world through the eyes of two cultures, we are forced to develop a meta-cultural framework above these cultures that enable us to see both cultures from without, and to compare them.[25]

We try to become inside participants in, and outside observers of the culture; this inside-outside perspective enables us to translate from one to the other. This perspective is the hallmark of bicultural Diaspora.

Globalizing Hermeneutics of the Jerusalem Council in Acts 15

David K. Strong and Cynthia A. Strong propose the model of contextual theologizing in Acts 15.[26] They explain several hermeneutical principles that the Jerusalem council used for globalizing theology:

24. Ibid.
25. Ibid.
26. Strong and Strong, "Globalizing Hermeneutic," 127–39.

(1) The Scripture evaluates human experience when James said, "the word of the prophets is in agreement with this . . ." (Acts 15:15).

(2) The Jerusalem council used a legitimate but alternative Hebrew reading that corroborated the Greek text when the Antiochians used the Greek text and Judeans used the Hebrew text.

(3) The council recognized that the decision is good to the Holy Spirit and us.

(4) The hermeneutical community—the Jewish community and the multi-ethnic, Antiochian community—was united by common experience.[27]

Here it is noted that common community experience should be introduced in global theologizing. As we know, in resolving the conflict between the perspectives of Antioch and Jerusalem theologizing, the council bowed, in addition to the authority of the Bible and the guidance of the Holy Spirit, to the consensus of the two hermeneutical communities.

In "Experience—Near Theologizing in Diverse Human Context," Priest argues that experience is an essential factor for theologizing. Christian theology in essence is based on a universal and absolute nature, but has various expressions and languages in each culture. Human experience here plays an important role in understanding, feeling, and evaluating the truth in the context.[28]

As Priest quote well, "Nearly all the wisdom we possess, that is to say, true and sound wisdom, consists of two parts: the knowledge of God and of ourselves. As although they are closely connected, it is difficult say which came first.[29]" Theologizing is the dialogue of theory and praxis in which experience plays a key role in judging and evaluating the truth in the Bible and the situation.

"DOUBLE HERMENEUTICAL MODEL" BEYOND TRADITIONAL CONTEXTUAL THEOLOGIZING

Doing mission theology in principle belongs to the principle of doing practical theology, which "recognizes the interaction between theory and praxis."[30] Here, "theory is understood as a comprehensive hermeneutical-theological

---

27. Ibid.
28. Priest, "Experience–Near Theologizing," 180–95.
29. Ibid., 180.
30. Heitink, *Practical Theology: History*, 151.

statement that related the Christian tradition to experience, to the life and actions of modern human"; "Praxis is understood as the actions of individuals and groups in society, within and outside the church, who are willing to be inspired in their private and public lives by the Christian tradition, and who want to focus on the salvation of humankind and the world."[31] Here the importance is that "though at times one is unaware of it, praxis always has an underlying theory. Praxis is always, at least in part, determined by theory. Failing to recognize this leads to an ideological praxis."[32]

Generally, theological investigations occur when the outcome is not satisfactory; it begins to seek what is the problem with theology. Nowadays, Christians have faced a crisis; in particular, global flows rapidly change humankind and society. The crisis of Christian faith and mission can be divided into two: secularism and pluralism. What is the alternative to this crisis? This answer calls for theological investigations for Christian faith and mission. Generally, theology seeks to correlate Christianity with general, cultural structures of meaning.[33]

Here, the point is that theologians check praxis in dialogue between the text and context. That is, they examine praxis based on text and context. Communication of the text to the context is important, but a reverse process, namely, the context must be examined by the text. This is what we call "double hermeneutics." Through this double process, praxis should be judged by the text and the context. Here, two kinds of double hermeneutical models will be introduced in two areas—social science and practical theology. This means that the interpretative methodologies of social science and practical theology are applied to a contextualizing theology of Diaspora missiology. It will be helpful for Diaspora missiology to move toward both global society and the local church ministry setting, which is one of the major characteristics of this book, compared to other related books.

"Double Hermeneutical Model"

Generally speaking, the double hermeneutical model consists of two: hermeneutics of the Bible and the context. First, with the theory, researchers investigate the praxis; then with the situation, they investigate the praxis; and finally, they connect the theory and the situation. To make it simple, this is the dialogue between the text and the context. That is, in two ways,

31. Ibid.
32. Ibid.
33. Frei, *Types of Christian Theology*, 3.

Contextual Theologizing for Diaspora Missiology   197

the text and context have dialogue in the center of praxis. This theologizing represents double hermeneutics.

The traditional way of doing contextual theology is to consider one way of the text fitting the context, but there is no reverse process of the context fitting the text. Contextualization in extreme causes "the context losing the text phenomenon." That is, the traditional way's only way is that the text is fixed to fit the context; later theologians realized that the contextualized text is different from the original message of the text, leading to syncretism not warranting salvation and transformation.

As Bosch puts it, "in spirit of the undeniably crucial nature and role of the context, then it is not to be taken as the sole and basic authority for theological reflections"; furthermore, he argued, "people do not only need truth (theory) and justice (praxis); they also need beauty, the rich resource of symbol, piety, worship, love, awe, and mystery. Only too often, in the tug-of-war between the priority of truth and the priority of justice, this dimension gets lost."[34] This shows how fatal contextualization is out of the text and how its debate harms love in a faith community.

The "double hermeneutical model" is the two ways of contextualization, in which the text goes to the context and the context to the text, which is "a mutual, interpretative interplay" (between the text and the context). We need to set up ways of contextualization where the context is judged and fixed to fit the text. This reverse process is necessary to successfully carry out real contextualization. In double hermeneutics, the text and the context are in dialogue in with the Holy Spirit.

Originally, the concept of double hermeneutics comes from the theory of Anthony Giddens.[35] For him, every-day concepts and social theory have a two-way relationship. He explains that social scientists have considered the way "in which lay concepts obstinately intrude into the technical discourse of social science," that "few have considered the matter the other way around"; at the same time, he explains that "the concepts of the social sciences are not produced about an independently constituted subject-matter, which continues regardless of what these concepts are. The 'findings' of the social sciences very often enter constitutively into the world they describe."[36] That is, social theory and the world have a two-way dialogue.

For Giddens, the social sciences are in a subject-subject relationship with their object of study. This means not only that social scientists interact with their objects of study, but it also implies that the social world can be

---

34. Bosch, *Transforming Mission*, 431.
35. Giddens, *Social Theory and Modern Sociology*.
36. Ibid., 20.

transformed by the work of the social sciences by learning from them and changing actions accordingly. This is what is called the "double hermeneutic" by Giddens, which is defined as "a mutually interpretative interplay between social science and those whose activities compose its subject matter."[37]

To put it simply, Sayer explains it this way: "social phenomena can be changed intrinsically by learning and adjusting to the subject's understanding; this implies that social science is embedded in its subject matter—society—and is therefore unavoidably involved in interaction with it."[38] This principle is the same with the relationship between the text and the context. Furthermore, In *Salience, Credibility, Legitimacy and Boundaries: Linking Research, Assessment and Decision Making*, David Cash, William Clark, Frank Alcock, Nancy Dickson, Noelle Eckley, and Jill Jäger co-wrote on the interaction between social science and its subject matter—society. They argued:

> The boundary between science and policy is only one of several boundaries that hinder the linking of scientific and technical information to decision making. Managing boundaries between disciplines, across scales of geography and jurisdiction, and between different forms of knowledge is also often critical to transferring information. The research presented in this paper finds that information requires three (not mutually exclusive) attributes—salience, credibility, and legitimacy—and that what makes boundary crossing difficult is that actors on different sides of a boundary perceive and value salience, credibility, and legitimacy differently.[39]

These authors focus on how the gap between theory and context is filled; they suggest three attributes of theory: salience, credibility, and legitimacy.

Here, "salience" refers to the relevance of information for an actor's decisions; "credibility" refers to whether an actor perceives information as meeting standards of scientific plausibility and technical adequacy. Sources of knowledge must be deemed trustworthy and/or believable, along with the facts, theories, and causal explanations invoked by these sources; "legitimacy" refers to whether an actor perceives the process in a system as unbiased and meeting standards of political and procedural fairness. Legitimacy involves the belief that science and technology systems are "fair" and

---

37. Ibid., xxxii.
38. Sayer, *Method in Social Science*, 28–29.
39. Cash, et al., "Salience, Credibility, Legitimacy," 4–5.

Contextual Theologizing for Diaspora Missiology 199

consider appropriate values, interests, concerns, and specific circumstances from multiple perspectives.[40]

Here, three attributes are used to judge how research information is appropriate to decision making. In the same way, information presented in the contextualization process also is to be judged by the Christian hermeneutical community on whether it has salience, credibility, and legitimacy in the context and the text as well. The misreading and distortion of the text is more dangerous than the failure of communication in contextualizing the text. That is why we need double hermeneutics in contextualization theology.

The double hermeneutical model in the area of social science deserves to be applied to the contextualization in mission. The world became urbanized more and more; social structure is more complex than ever; most diaspora live the context of urbanized areas. In this sense, contextualization for mission needs to involve social polices as well.

Example of the Revised Adaption of Zerfass's Model as "Double Hermeneutical Model"

Rolf Zerfass proposed a two-way hermeneutical model, which influenced subsequent practical theologies;[41] his theologizing is a process through two ways of hermeneutic workings, of the Bible and the context. According to the process of his model, Heitink states:

> He [Zerfass] showed in this study how practical theology starts from the description of a concrete, and usually unsatisfactory, praxis. Something must be done! Reflecting on this situation solely on the basis of church tradition does not lead to any real improvement. Praxis must first be examined with the use of a series of instruments from the social sciences. As a result, tensions become visible, leading to the emergence of impulses to act, with a view to renewal and improvement of the existing praxis.[42]

There are double hermeneutical principles in this statement: the praxis, the context (situation), and the church traditions (theory). In other words, praxis (the act of faith in believers) is examined for why it is not satisfactory. This theologizing sees dialogue between the text and the context, pivoting

40. Ibid.
41. Zerfass, "Praktische Theologie," 167.
42. Heitink, *Practical Theology*, 113.

on the praxis. The double hermeneutical model requires the study of the interpretative interaction between the praxis, theory—biblical/theological traditions, and situational analysis to develop a new, satisfactory praxis. The double hermeneutic process involves the interpretation of the Bible and the context, pivoting on praxis. Thus, this double hermeneutics prevents the dogmatic contextualization of the Bible in relating to the context and the absolutization of the context syncretizing the message of the Bible.

In the process of double hermeneutics, the guidance and empowerment of the Holy Spirit is essential, because it is only the Holy Spirit who can guide the church into the truth, the gospel of salvation.

> John 16: 13But when he, the Spirit of truth, comes, he will guide you into all the truth. He will not speak on his own; he will speak only what he hears, and he will tell you what is yet to come. 14He will glorify me because it is from me that he will receive what he will make known to you. 15All that belongs to the Father is mine. That is why I said the Spirit will receive from me what he will make known to you.

The contextualization of the Holy Spirit, guiding into and speaking all truth, is within the Trinity—the Father, the Son, and the Holy Spirit. The Holy Spirit is Christ centered, and truth centered; so the contextualization of the Holy Spirit should be discerned by Christ and the truth. He also empowers and guides the church to preach the gospel: "But you will receive power when the Holy Spirit comes on you; and you will be my witnesses in Jerusalem, and in all Judea and Samaria, and to the ends of the earth" (Acts 1:8). These verses show how the Holy Spirit works in the process of contextualization, in which the gospel is communicated into various cultures in order that hearers believe in Jesus Christ as Savior; He works so that the text and the context are communicated to each other beyond human knowledge and explanation.

Zerfass's model is composed of thirteen steps, but it can be summarized in seven processes; there are descriptions of seven processes in the following figure; this process proceeds under the principle of double hermeneutics. The goal of this hermeneutics is to check how the text and the context have a dialogue, pivoting on praxis in the Holy Spirit.

Contextual Theologizing for Diaspora Missiology   201

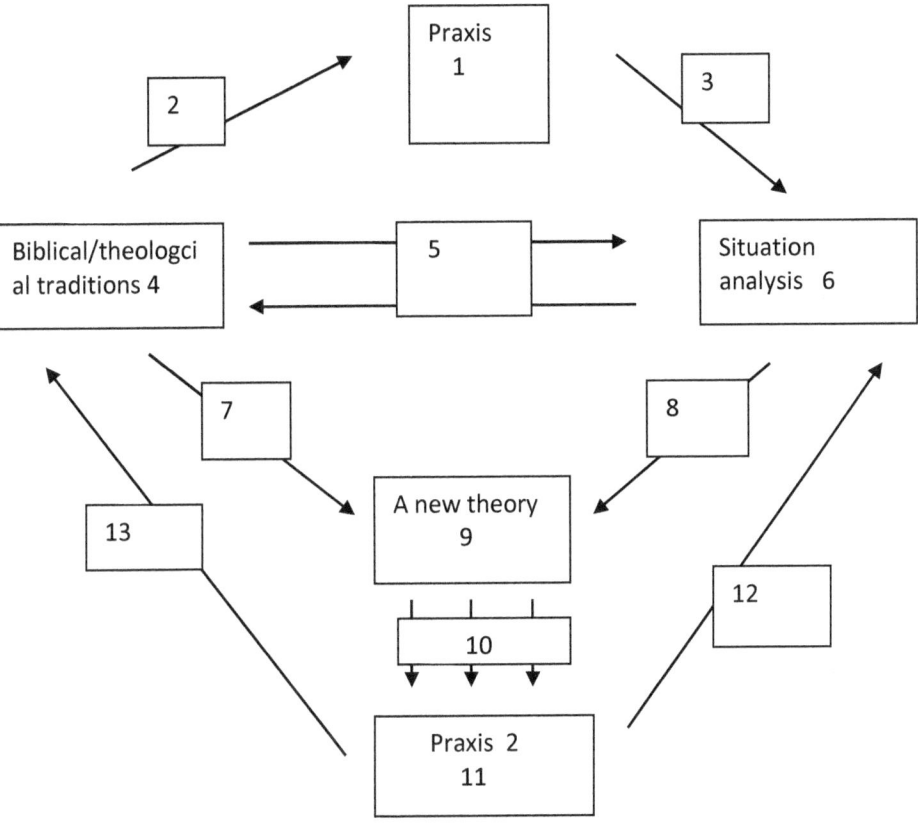

Figure 6: R. Zerfass's Practical Theology Model[43]

The following are the summaries of the processes of the double hermeneutical model by Zerfass:

1. Praxis: (1)
   The process starts with "praxis 1," which is the existing praxis; generally, it is unsatisfactory when a new theologizing is required. The hermeneutic community (referring to the Diaspora church) judges and evaluates their praxis, finds some problems therein, and decides to start doing theologizing.

2. Biblical/Theological Investigations: (2) and (4)
   The current praxis is examined from traditional theological viewpoints and theories; praxis is examined by the standards of biblical/

43. Ibid., 114.

theological viewpoints. It investigates how the praxis involves the teachings of Bible.

3. Situational Analysis: (3) and (6)
   A situational analysis must be carried out by researching the current situations and involving the insights of interdisciplinary studies.[44] The main contemporary situation can be described as global fields, flows, and culture. Furthermore, the research on people will include studies from interdisciplinary perspectives—sociology, anthropology, psychology, philosophy, and law.

4. Theory-Situation Dialogue: (5)
   The situational analysis takes place throughout the research process in keeping a constant interaction/dialogue with and comparison to the biblical/theological traditions. Here, theory should be in dialogue with the situation. Here the importance is by what criteria we judge the situation, what kind of theory is used, and what priority principle is applied.

5. Discovering a New Theory: (7), (8), and (9)
   Based on both the biblical/theological traditions and the results from the situational research/analysis, a new Diaspora theory [paradigm] is developed so that it can overcome the problems of the current praxis.

6. Applying the New Theory to the Praxis: (10)
   When a new theory is discovered, it then must be developed into creating "praxis 2," overcoming and resolving the barriers to effective mission in praxis 1, including the formation of detailed values, goals, ministries, and programs.

7. Final Examination: (11), (12), and (13)
   Creating the new praxis must be a goal of doing theology, leading to praxis 2, which then should be examined by theological investigations (13) on the one hand, and also must be examined to ensure effectiveness in given situation (12) on the other hand.

In sum, the above theologizing processes move from the discovery of problems to creating a new model. In particular, a final examination step is needed to check the whole process again and the contextualized theologizing in terms of the result. This model deserves to be applied to doing Diaspora missiology and Diaspora mission church.

---

44. Zerfass approaches the checking in a series of instruments from the social sciences. But I used interdisciplinary knowledge and instruments for checking.

Seven Steps for Adapting Zerfass's Model into Creating the New Perspective of Diaspora Missiology, including Diaspora Mission Church

Until now, Diaspora missiology was mainly based on Wan's theory and the Lausanne Movement's leadership on Diaspora, which is characterized by demographic phenomenon—diaspora, people on the move in a global era. However, our mission needs to move beyond Wan's and Lausanne's as the LCWE admitted. In 2014, the Torch Center for World Mission in Korea published *World Mission Vision of Korean Diaspora*, which focused on biblical perspectives, including the OT and the NT. This collection covers various subjects of biblical teachings of Diaspora—biblical theology, systematic theology, Christian ethics, mission theology . . .[45] This collection is helpful to investigate the meaning of diaspora in relation to various topics in the Bible.

Diaspora missiology needs to move forward toward applying church ministry in local settings, because diaspora live amid our next-door neighbors. Thus, by applying the concept of Diaspora to the local church, it needs to develop towards doing practical theology in a church ministry setting. Now the local church will become the missionaries.

At the same time, this attempts to redefine Diaspora missiology as in a dialogue between the concept of Diaspora in the Bible and that of diaspora in a global situation. It is an attempt to move beyond the concept of diaspora as a demographical phenomenon toward that of the Bible focused Diaspora church ministry, with the lens of interdisciplinary studies in a global situation. Zerfass's original process is revised and reconceptioned by the intention of the author. For clarifying Diaspora missiology, the double hermeneutical process proceeds as the following:

1. The First Stage: Current Praxis of Traditional Missiology—Praxis 1
   Current Christian mission has found that traditional missiology cannot function in the contemporary missiological situation; its praxis has been challenged by globalization, secularism, pluralism, relativism, and so on. The hermeneutic community (referring to the Diaspora church) judges and evaluates their current praxis (praxis 1), and finds some problems therein, and decides to start doing contextualization.

2. The Second Stage: Biblical/Theological Investigations: (2) and (4)
   The current praxis is examined from traditional theological viewpoints and theories; praxis is examined by the standards of biblical/

---

45. Kim, *World Mission Vision*.

theological viewpoints. In investigating the praxis 1, the most important fact is Christian strategy and methods, the subject of mission, rather than missional theology. For example, the subject of mission in the early church was Christians filled with the Holy Spirit. The situation or context is worse than that now. We find that first of all, we need to focus on the subjects of mission, Christians or missionaries. The Bible, in particular, Acts shows that Diaspora serve as agents of God's mission (Acts 8:4; 13:1–3).[46]

Through investigating biblical/theological teaching, the term of diaspora helped to rediscover its value as the field for God's redemption, and find the strategy of Diaspora regarding the nature, ministries, and mission of church.

3. The Third Stage: Global/Interdisciplinary Analysis on Diaspora—(3) and (6)

   The Diaspora church carries out situational analysis and involves the insights of interdisciplinary studies. Here, global analysis should be carried out; globalization should be understood in terms of local culture, including trans-international culture. A global phenomenon of the twenty-first century is "the movement of people spatially at unprecedented scale."[47] The research on people should be conducted according to interdisciplinary perspectives. Diaspora is the socio-cultural and political product of globalization. Diaspora church research figures out interdisciplinary aspects of diaspora—sociology, anthropology, psychology, philosophy, demography, politics, law, and so on. At the same time, as Schreiter puts it, global culture contributes to the fullness of faith, a new catholicity.[48]

4. The Fourth Stage: Text-Context Dialogue—(5)

   As mentioned earlier, the situational (context) analysis of diaspora takes place throughout the research process, however, this process keeps a constant interaction/dialogue with and comparison to the biblical/theological traditions (text). Here, an essential work in the analysis of diaspora is to distinguish socio-cultural and political aspects of diaspora from biblical and theological aspects of Diaspora. If not, diaspora is just limited to a social and political phenomenon, but no more a spiritual, biblical, and missiological phenomenon. In a word, the importance is to see diaspora in the situation from the

---

46. Refer to chapters 3 and 4 regarding biblical meanings of diaspora in the OT and the NT.
47. Wan, *Diaspora Missiology*, 3.
48. Schreiter, *New Catholicity*, 130.

lens of the biblical portrait of Diaspora. Diaspora, scattered, become a field of God's gathering, God's redemption (Ezek 36:19–31). Thus we see the concept of Diaspora as ecclesiastical and missiological paradigm shift, which brings about the practice of church ministry and mission for his redemptive purpose.

5. The Fifth Stage: Discovering a New Theory—(7), (8), and (9)
   Based on both the biblical/theological tradition and the results from the situational research/analysis, a new missiological theory is discovered and it is called Diaspora missiology as a practice of God's redemption. Diaspora missiology is believed to resolve the problems of church, its ministry, and its traditional missiology in a global era in which people are on the move.[49] Furthermore, it is helpful towards transforming a distortion of the Christian faith, church, and mission that is intertwined with secular, plural, and relative tendencies, because the term of diaspora as "stranger" (1 Pet 1:1) has a transcendent nature of faith and church, and becomes a strategy to overcome secularism and worldliness, which hinder Christian mission. "Resident aliens" serve as "a proactive Christian assessment of culture and ministry for people who know that something is wrong."[50]

6. The Sixth Stage: A New Praxis of Diaspora Missiology—(10)
   Diaspora missiology, a new theory, must now be applied and developed into creating the new praxis 2, creating new values, goals, ministries, and programs of biblical Christianity. Diaspora as the field of God's redemption affects creating praxis 2, overcoming praxis 1, which brings about the reformation of a secularized church and missiology, leading to creating a missional church. In particular, Diaspora is representative of early church Christians who were scattered as foreigners, and preached the gospel in any place where they entered. They were longing "for a better country—a heavenly one" (Heb 11:16), originating in the spirit of Diaspora which became a powerful strategy of Christian mission.

7. The Seventh Stage: Final Examination—(11), (12), and (13)
   The new praxis (praxis 2) must be considered to be examined by theological investigations and checks again, and confirm how it is adjusted will ensure effectiveness in a given situation. After the final step, the hermeneutical community should one more time examine

---

49. Wan, *Diaspora Missiology*.
50. Haurwas and Willimon, *Resident Aliens*, 24–29.

whether the new praxis (praxis 2) is biblical and relevant. This feedback process continues until the Lord comes back.

In final remarks, the double hermeneutical process above is presented to give a new perspective of Diaspora missiology beyond Wan's, although the same words are used to describe the meaning of Diaspora missiology; it moves toward the application of Diaspora missiology to the development of local church ministry. This is a kind of a new definition of Diaspora missiology, including the missional church.

In defining Diaspora missiology, Wan adapted the definition from the LCWE's "The Seoul Declaration on Diaspora Missiology," "a missiological framework for understanding and participating in God's redemptive mission among diaspora groups."[51] Yet I try to define the term of diaspora in the biblical perspectives, and understand the history of his redemption through the concept of Diaspora. That is, the biblical meaning of Diaspora is the starting point for Diaspora missiology, and then it is applicable to its missional strategies. In this sense, Diaspora missiology in the present book covers a faith of Christians as strangers, life in the Christian colony, the mission of Diaspora church, leading to a transcendent transformation of a Christian faith and a reformation of the church and its mission, which is captivated with secular humanism and relative pluralism. I tried to understand a Bible-focused meaning of Diaspora missiology along with interdisciplinary studies in a global era by using the double hermeneutical model.

FOUR PROCESSES OF CONTEXTUAL THEOLOGY FOR DOING DIASPORA MISSIOLOGY

What then is the process of contextual theology for doing Diaspora missiology? It follows the contextual theologizing process. It starts with (1) the theologizing subject, the church; (2) the church understanding the context—Diaspora in globalization; (3) the church interpreting the Bible and applying it to the context from the interdisciplinary perspectives; and finally (4) we confirm the guidance of the Holy Spirit for the theologizing process.

51. Wan, *Diaspora Missiology*, 5.

A Theologizing Subject

Diaspora Church as the Hermeneutic Community in the Presence of God the Trinity

The Trinity God is the subject of mission, the *Missio Dei*, which is not the traditional view which rejects or ignores the church, but a newly revised, incorporated way of the Trinity God's mission and church in the concept of Diaspora; the love of the Father, the grace of Son, and the fellowship of the Holy Spirit work in the church as his people, his body, and his temple. The mission of God was delegated into his agent, the church, which was built up to preach the gospel. The church as a hermeneutic community is referring to the Diaspora church, in which the churches exist for the gospel, having heavenly citizenship and living foreigners.

Participation of the Host Churches in Diaspora

It is more biblical that this faith community invites and includes host churches, representing the whole church. Acts 15 provides a good example of forming Diaspora theology. In verses 1-2, we see that a problem happens in the Antioch church, a local church in the Hellenistic culture. It decides to send its delegates—Paul, Barnabas, and some other believers—to the Jerusalem church, the sender in the Hebrew culture (v. 3). Then they—including the Antioch church from Hellenistic world-view and the Jerusalem church from the Hebrew world-view—discuss and make the decision (vv. 4-21). Here we see that the relationship between the Antioch church and the Jerusalem church is not one of paternalism but brotherhood, even though the latter sent emissaries to the former.

The Significance of Emphatic Hospitality of the Host Church on Diaspora

It is noted that, generally speaking, the host churches have a responsibility for welcoming strangers or foreigners, one of which is immigrants, as written in Leviticus 19:33-34 and Deuteronomy 10:17-19.

> Lev 19: 33When a foreigner resides among you in your land, do not mistreat them. 34*The foreigner residing among you must be treated as your native-born. Love them as yourself, for you were foreigners in Egypt.* I am the Lord your God.

Deut 10: 17For the Lord your God is God of gods and Lord of lords, the great God, mighty and awesome, who shows no partiality and accepts no bribes. 18He defends the cause of the fatherless and the widow, and *loves the foreigner residing among you, giving them food and clothing. 19And you are to love those who are foreigners, for you yourselves were foreigners in Egypt.* (Italics mine)

God is a god of foreigners; his people should love them as themselves. Hospitality to foreigners is the covenant of God with his people. Here we find that the host church's relationship with immigrant foreigners affects their relationship with God. Hospitality to the immigrant church from the host church is why host churches should involve in partnership with immigrants doing missiology. It is noted that the partnership between the host church and the immigrant church is for global mission.

Partnership between Hosted Diaspora and Host Country

In an interview with Enoch Wan on Diaspora missiology, he argues that the immigrant church should call for the host church to do Diaspora missiology:

> If an English-speaking congregation is planning to be involved in China (i.e., the largest mission field with one of the most receptive peoples of the 21st century), it is strategic to enter into partnership with a neighboring diaspora Chinese congregation to empower their church members to reach their own kinsmen in their country of birth.[52]

This shows that the immigrant church's partnership with the host church serves as the strategy of global mission. The partnership between immigrant and host churches is essential to ministering to immigrants. However, there are the issues that cause problems in the partnership relations among churches around world: (1) cultural differences, (2) lack of effective communications, (3) financial issues, (4) personality conflicts, and (5) lack of clear objectives.[53]

Immigrant and host churches need to overcome these issues that hinder partnership between both churches for the sake of global mission. Actually, host churches can provide practical help—such as ESL programs, mentoring, public services, and translating services—for immigrant problems.

---

52. Wan, "Interview with Enoch Wan," 5–10.
53. Taylor, *Kingdom Partnerships*, 10–11.

Diaspora as the Revival Principle of the Host Church

It is noted that the host churches should have a partnership with the hosted immigrant churches from the principle of the biblical church. We need to remember the day of the Acts 2 Pentecost, the birth of the church; "there were staying in Jerusalem God-fearing Jews from every nation under heaven" (Acts 2:5). And then God poured the Holy Spirit out upon the host Hebrew Christians, and let them preach the gospel to and care for these gathering "scattered" people, representing today's diaspora immigrants. That is, gathering "scattered" people is the sign to host churches for calling and partnering for the world mission. Likewise, host churches should stand with immigrant churches for his redemptive works and mission, as shown in Acts 2. Diaspora partnership with the host churches of the USA is the first step of Diaspora missiology; American hospitality with immigrant strangers is the first step of global Christianity and mission in US churches.

Interpreting the Context: Diaspora in a Global Society

Here, the term "interpretation" is to understand the real meaning of the context, as expressed in *The Interpretation of Culture* by Clifford Geertz.[54] The context needs to be interpreted to find its hidden meanings behind external phenomena and forms. Thus, interpreting the context is to see the suffering of diaspora, an existential pattern of human being under God's judgment and toward God's redemption in the context. This is like God's way to see his people in the context of suffering under Egypt and the Pharaoh, which is written in Exodus:

> Exod 3: 7The Lord said, "I have indeed seen the misery of my people in Egypt. I have heard them crying out because of their slave drivers, and I am concerned about their suffering. 8So I have come down to rescue them from the hand of the Egyptians and to bring them up out of that land into a good and spacious land, a land flowing with milk and honey—the home of the Canaanites, Hittites, Amorites, Perizzites, Hivites and Jebusites. 9And now the cry of the Israelites has reached me, and I have seen the way the Egyptians are oppressing them. 10So now, go. I am sending you to Pharaoh to bring my people the Israelites out of Egypt."

---

54. Geertz, *Interpretation of Culture*.

Thus in interpreting the context of diaspora, it is important to see (1) diaspora from lens of the Bible, and then continue to see (2) the global context of diaspora living.

Seeing Diaspora from the Lens of the Biblical Diaspora

From lens of the Bible, Diaspora have three characteristics and experiences: Diaspora as an experience of exile; Diaspora identity: salvation and the mission—the seed of the kingdom; Diaspora as pilgrimage.

Diaspora as Experience of Exile

First of all, a diaspora is a scattered person in or through God's judgment knowingly or unknowingly. This means that diaspora have suffering, hurt, and trauma. The word diaspora itself has suffering, hurt, and trauma because this word implies the "scattered people by God's judgment." Thus, the essence of diaspora can be described as hurt, suffering, and trauma. Regarding the hurt memories of diaspora, Reimer explains: "Exile is punishment; this is what Solomon feared. Today's reading reports with brutal simplicity the deportation of Judeans to Babylon in 587 BC. The encompassed account barely hints at the claustrophobia of siege and panic of flight."[55]

Here "the claustrophobia of siege and panic of flight" portrays the mentality of diaspora; this includes emotions of fear, loneliness, hatred, and anger. Generally suffering was stored as hurt. He continues: "Exile is punishment, and today's reading portrays a wide range of suffering, affecting not just those removed but also those remaining. This passage is not overtly theological; that will come. For the moment, we gaze on the human tragedy and weep with those who weep."[56] Here, suffering, punishment, tragedy, and weeping subsist in the emotions of diaspora.

Diaspora Identity: Salvation and the Mission—The Seed of the Kingdom

The essential identity of Diaspora is the called to God's elect; the Diaspora is called to God's salvation. This confession is very important to formulate Diaspora missiology. Peter described the Diaspora in terms of "soteriological perspectives": "To God's elect, strangers in this world, scattered through

---

55. Reimer, "Exile and Diaspora," 109.
56. Ibid., 110.

Contextual Theologizing for Diaspora Missiology 211

. . . who have been chosen according to the foreknowledge of God the Father, through the sanctifying work of the Holy Spirit, for obedience to Jesus Christ and sprinkling by his blood" (1 Pet 1:1-2). Diaspora were called to being his elect, strangers in this world. Thus, it is important we confess that Diaspora anywhere are called by God to be saved; this means that the Diaspora is the object of mission for God's salvation.

The Diaspora is also called to be God's mission. Regarding Diaspora as the subject of mission, in *Korean Diaspora and Christian Mission,* there was introduced an awareness of the role of Diaspora Christians as both missionaries and subjects of mission.[57] This book presents an especially interesting example of how the Korean Diaspora can be utilized in mission. This shows that Diaspora is the subject of mission as well as the object of mission. Here we should distinguish Diaspora in terms of two levels: first, the object of mission; and second, the subject of mission.

Diaspora should be understood in terms of the subject of mission. For example, the recipients of the Letter of First Peter are Diaspora, as explained 1 Peter 1:1-2. Thus the whole message of 1 Peter 1 was given to Diaspora. With regard to the mission of Diaspora, Peter pointed out:

> 1 Pet 1: 9but you are a chosen people, a royal priesthood, a holy nation, God's special possession, that you may declare the praises of him who called you out of darkness into his wonderful light. 10Once you were not a people, but now you are the people of God; once you had not received mercy, but now you have received mercy.

The major mission of Diaspora is to "declare the praises of him who called you out of darkness into his wonderful light." Diaspora's mission is to call people out of darkness into a wonderful light of Jesus Christ. The Diaspora is the seed of God's kingdom.

Diaspora as Pilgrimage

As mentioned earlier, in 1 Peter 1:1, Peter calls Diaspora as "pilgrims."[58] This shows the identity of Diaspora is related to that of a pilgrim. In 2004, Craig

---

57. Kim and Ma, *Christian Mission and Korean Diaspora.*

58. There are various versions of pilgrim. American King James Version: "Dearly beloved, I beseech you as strangers and pilgrims, abstain from fleshly lusts, which war against the soul"; American Standard Version: "Beloved, I beseech you as sojourners and pilgrims, to abstain from fleshly lust, which war against the soul"; Douay-Rheims Bible: "Dearly beloved, I beseech you as strangers and pilgrims, to refrain yourselves from carnal desires which war against the soul"; Darby Bible Translation: "Beloved, I

Bartholomew and Fred Hughes edited *Explorations in a Christian Theology of Pilgrimage*, which described the nature of Christian faith in pilgrimage.[59] Also Forrest J. Clingerman, Associate Professor of Religion and Philosophy in the Department of Religion and Philosophy at Ohio Northern University, offers a contemporary theological interpretation of pilgrimage, "how might we describe the meaning of journeying and illustrate its spiritual depth? Integrating insights from the theology of culture and the theology of place, a philosophical theology of pilgrimage defines spiritual journeying as a uniquely dialectical movement of place and movement, being and action, dwelling and mobility."[60] Pilgrimage provides us a "dialectical movement of place and movement, being and action, dwelling and mobility."

John Bunyan's *The Pilgrim's Progress* offers the explicit essentials of Protestant theology, which made it much more popular than its predecessors. It was reprinted in colonial America, and was widely read in the Puritan colonies. In particular, John's concept of pilgrim contributes to the reformation of the church and faith through the concept of "pilgrim" itself. In his *Pilgrim's Progress,* Bunyan describes a giant who confronts Christian at the end of the Valley of the Shadow of Death that is explicitly named "Pope": "Now I saw in my Dream, that at the end of this Valley lay blood, bones, ashes, and mangled bodies of men, even of pilgrims that had gone this way formerly: And while I was musing what should be the reason, I espied a little before me a cave, where two giants, *Pope* and *Pagan*, dwelt in old time, by whose power and tyranny the men whose bones, blood, ashes, etc. lay there, were cruelly put to death."[61]

Christian pilgrims, who Bunyan describes, overcome the attack of Pope and move toward heaven. This shows that pilgrims defeat the attack of unbiblical doctrines and succeed in arriving at heaven. This image of pilgrim echoes the reformation of doctrine and church; also, the image of pilgrim is the dialectic movement that pilgrims meet the two giants and feel fear, but finally get through the attack of the two giants, and continue to move toward heaven: "They go by."

---

exhort you, as strangers and sojourners, to abstain from fleshly lusts, which war against the soul"; English Revised Version: "Beloved, I beseech you as sojourners and pilgrims, to abstain from fleshly lusts, which war against the soul"; Webster's Bible Translation: "Dearly beloved, I beseech you as strangers and pilgrims, abstain from fleshly lusts, which war against the soul"; Weymouth New Testament: "Dear friends, I entreat you as pilgrims and foreigners not to indulge the cravings of your lower natures: for all such cravings wage war upon the soul"; World English Bible: "Beloved, I beg you as foreigners and pilgrims, to abstain from fleshly lusts, which war against the soul."

59. Bartholomew and Hughes, *Explorations in a Christian Theology.*
60. Clingerman, "Walking into the Frame," 18–32.
61. Bunyan, *Pilgrim's Progress*, 299.

Seeing the Global Context of a Diaspora living

This has three descriptions: (1) social trauma of Diaspora; (2) cultural identity of Diaspora with heterogeneity, diversity, and hybridity; and (3) identifying spiritual meanings behind globalization.

SOCIAL TRAUMA OF DIASPORA

A prominent phenomenon of global culture is neoliberal economics. According to neoclassical economics theory based on globalization, capital moves from high wage countries to low wage countries.[62] Flows of labor follow this financial opportunity. That is, people who seek wealth mostly follow this opportunity for their own interest and well-being. At the same time, diaspora have transcultural ties with their homeland culture.

With cultural shock in an alien area, they experience a feeling of a stranger—brokenness, wounding, fear, desperation, isolation—in a strange land. In a word, the life of the immigrant is trauma. According to Cohen, diaspora means a collective trauma, banishment into exile, and a heartaching longing to return home.[63] During the early modern period, trade and labor diasporas girded the mercantilist and early capitalist worlds. He understands diaspora in terms of trauma, suffering, and brokenness. Importantly, Diaspora missiology pays more attention to the suffering and hurt of immigrants, which can lead to mental distortion and hindrance to Diaspora mission.

Diaspora missiology cannot ignore the reality and psychology of immigrant diaspora, characterized as "trauma." Most immigrants are caught in worry, fear, confusion, and frustration; thus we ask: can they live their life of Diaspora mission? The real question is: are they healed from the hurt of the heart? Diaspora missiology should study ethnography of immigrants and find out real data of the mental health and lives of immigrants as it concerns Diaspora mission.

CULTURAL IDENTITY OF DIASPORA WITH HETEROGENEITY, DIVERSITY, AND HYBRIDITY

Diaspora has acquired new meanings if it is related to notions such as global deterritorialization, transnational migration and cultural hybridity. Here in

---

62. Aspromourgos, "On the Origins of the Term 'Neoclassical.'"
63. Cohen, *Global Diasporas*.

particular, the meaning of religion plays a key role as a factor in forming diasporic social organizations, shaping and maintaining diasporic identities, and the appropriation of space and place in history.[64] Diaspora identity is not viewed as being but becoming. In "Cultural Identity and Diaspora," Stuart Hall (1993) argues that there are two kinds of identity, (1) identity as being (which offers a sense of unity and commonality), and (2) identity as becoming (or a process of identification, which shows the discontinuity in our identity formation). Hall uses the Caribbean identities to explain how the first one (identity as being) is necessary, but the second one (identity as becoming) is truer to the postcolonial conditions.[65]

According to Hall, the diaspora is defined, not by essence or purity, but by the recognition of a necessary heterogeneity and diversity; by a conception of "identity" which lives with and through, not despite, difference; by *hybridity*. Diaspora identities are those which are constantly producing and reproducing themselves anew, through transformation and difference.[66] Diaspora identity is not fixed, but fluid. In particular, religion plays a role in transcending the worldly identity.[67] Religion is a powerful force for immigrants in the formation and preservation of personal and group identity because it provides transcendent grounding for identity. Basic religious affirmations and commitments pit the individual and group against external forces that would precipitate either chaos or homogeneity, they provide a base for resistance to mainstream values. Many immigrants affirm that "they are more religious following immigration than their native place, even though their participation and their religious roles in Western countries are substantially different."[68]

Identifying Spiritual Meanings behind Globalization

As mentioned earlier, globalization brings spiritual challenges to a Christian faith; we need to identify spiritual meaning behind globalization: secularism, pluralism, and relativism, undermining Christianity. Some scholars argued for the opposite to this opinion. They say, "Old assumptions about modernization and modernity as undermining religion are now being questioned; the secularization thesis once widely accepted by Western scholars as the dominant narrative pointing to religion's demise is under considerable

---

64. Alfonso, et al., *Diaspora, Identity and Religion*.
65. Hall, "Cultural Identity and Diaspora," 401–2.
66. Ibid.
67. Jacobsen and Raj, *South Asian Christian Diaspora*, 255.
68. Ibid.

scrutiny."[69] However, this is just trickery; the real damage of secularization is happening to the Christian faith and church on a deep level. Thus, global culture should be judged from the criteria of living the gospel.

At same time, global justice is a major issue in global life. In *Globalization, Spirituality, and Justice*, Groody offers a vision of justice as an integral part of Christian spirituality in the complex, globalized world.[70] At the same time, Groody analyzes that faith and spirituality have an integral role in the struggle to achieve a more just social order in global era. Specially designed for the classroom, this text will help all readers understand the facts and values from which a just world must be fashioned. In his nine chapters, Groody introduces readers to the core of the biblical worldview, the Christian message on justice and human liberation in its historical context, and the challenge of Catholic social teaching.

The Interpretations and Applications of the Bible

The Interdisciplinary Interpretation of the Bible

As Hiebert puts it, "Theologizing must begin with Scripture. It is God's revelation to us, not human reflections about God, although it contains these."[71] This means that propositional theology or philosophical theology should not be the starting point for local theologizing. That is, the interpretation of the Bible, not foreign theology, is the foundation for forming a Diaspora missiology. The church considers incarnational ministry when it interprets and applies the Bible and plants churches in immigrant societies.[72] This means that Diaspora theologizing deliberates diasporas and their context.

As we know, theology is a product of the community, not of individuals. This means that the Diaspora church and lost church should be involved in hermeneutical theologizing, and community should include everyday life. Hiebert says, "Theology must be done in the community. It is ultimately the task not of individuals but of the church. This corporate nature of the hermeneutical task guards us against the privatization of faith and from our personal misinterpretations of Scripture."[73] As many people as possible should participate in doing theology, which means that theology includes everyday life of Diaspora.

69. Roof and Caron, "Shifting Boundaries," 12.
70. Groody, *Globalization, Spirituality, and Justice*.
71. Hiebert, *Anthropological Reflections*, 70.
72. Hiebert and Meneses-Hiebert, *Incarnational Ministry*.
73. Hiebert, *Anthropological Reflections*, 70.

William A. Dyrness calls it "a theology of people."[74] The church doing theology should remember that their audience is immigrants, in fear and emptiness. In interpreting the Bible, understanding of the context of Diaspora is essential. As Sadiri Joy Tira puts it:

> Diaspora missiology necessitates interdisciplinary study of academic fields related to who, what, when, where, and how populations are moving (e.g., anthropology, demography, economics, geography, history, law, political science, and sociology), and classic missiological study (e.g., theology, missiology, biblical studies, evangelism).[75]

Interdisciplinary study is a lens to better understand Diaspora in the complex global context. They include anthropology, demography, economics, geography, history, law, political science, and sociology; in addition, psychology, therapy, philosophy, and so on can be included. However, of most importance is that the Word of God is the central principle and source of incorporating interdisciplinary applications in the light of the Holy Spirit.

Finally, the church should try to find the models of the immigrant persons in the Bible for today's immigrants. For an example, in case of Joseph living in Egypt, out of his own land of Canaan, he learned the Egyptian culture, assimilated to its dress and appearance (Gen 41:14), and became involved in its governmental affairs; finally, he was "in charge of the whole land of Egypt" (Gen 41:41). Later, he welcomes and cares his father and brothers in the famine crisis. To his brothers he confessed, "And now, do not be distressed and do not be angry with yourselves for selling me here, because it was to save lives that God sent me ahead of you" (Gen 45:5). Joseph confessed that he came to Egypt because of God's redemptive mission. Their brokenness and wounds were healed, and they embraced one another from God's perspectives. Joseph's life through this was incarnational without any change of the essentials as "the Word became flesh and made his dwelling among us" (John 1:14).

The Centrality of the Gospel: The Cross and Resurrection of Christ

Hiebert emphasizes taking the Bible seriously as the rule of faith and life. "First, critical contextualization takes the Bible seriously as the rule of faith and life. Contextualized practices, like contextualized theologies, must be biblically based. This may seem obvious, but we must constantly remind

---

74. Dyrness, *Learning about Theology*.
75. Tira, "Diaspora Missiology," 34.

ourselves that biblical revelations are the standard against which all practices are measured."[76] Here we find that, for Hiebert, contextualization focuses on the Bible as the rule of faith and life.

What is the purpose of Christian mission? For example, let's take Pauline mission. Why did Paul want to preach the gospel to Rome?

> Rom 1: 14I am obligated both to Greeks and non-Greeks, both to the wise and the foolish. 15That is why I am so eager to preach the gospel also to you who are in Rome. 16For I am not ashamed of the gospel, because it is the power of God that brings salvation to everyone who believes: first to the Jew, then to the Gentile. 17For in the gospel the righteousness of God is revealed—a righteousness that is by faith from first to last,[e] just as it is written: "The righteous will live by faith."

The goal of mission for Paul is to preach the gospel because it is the power of God that brings salvation to everyone who believes. In relation to Christian mission, the major finding of Romans is that many Romans already believed in Jesus; Paul proclaimed, "your faith is being reported all over the world" (Rom 1:8). Why then did Paul want to preach the gospel to Romans again? His answer is: "in order that I might have a harvest among you, just as I have had among the other Gentiles" (Rom 1:13). His explanation implies that there was not a harvest in the Romans yet even if their faith was reported all over the world. This statement gives a deep consideration to Christian mission; also this explains why we preach the gospel again to so-called believers.

And in a specific way, salvation comes from believing in the cross of Christ only: "for the message of the cross is foolishness to those who are perishing, but to us who are being saved it is the power of God" (1 Cor 1:18). That is, the message of the cross is the power of God, which saves those who believe. For this, Paul proclaimed, "for I resolved to know nothing while I was with you except Jesus Christ and him crucified" (1 Cor 2:2).

Finally, the major goal of contextualization is to communicate the gospel of the cross to people and let those who believe be saved more than anything else. What is more important than this? The point here is that missionaries and church leaders should make their best effort to contextualize the gospel of the cross for salvation. The purpose of the Bible is: "But these are written that you may believe that Jesus is the Messiah, the Son of God, and that by believing you may have life in his name" (John 20:31). Contextualization should serve for this main purpose of the Bible—"life"; effective communication itself is not the final goal of contextualization, "having life in his name" is its goal.

---

76. Hiebert, *Anthropological Reflections*, 91.

Interdisciplinary Applications of the Bible toward "Incarnational Ministry"

Recently, interdisciplinary studies have become essential to understanding and doing mission. In "What in the World is Missiology?" R. Priest states that missiology itself is interdisciplinary:

> But missiology is also, at a fundamental level, interdisciplinary. Historically those teaching missiology have often had doctorates in other disciplines—like anthropology (Miriam Adeney, Paul Hiebert, Louis Luzbetak, Enoch Wan, Darrell Whiteman, myself), communications (David Hesselgrave, Del Tarr), comparative religions / philosophy of religion (Robert Hunt, Terry Muck, Harold Netland, J. Dudley Woodberry), history (Jehu Hanciles, Dana Robert, Lamin Sanneh, Wilbert Shenk, Andrew Walls), educational studies (James Plueddemann, Duane Elmer, Robert Ferris), linguistics / linguistic anthropology (Eugene Nida, Charles Kraft, Dan Shaw), or theology (Frances Adeney, Robert Schreiter, Gary Simpson). But what differentiates these scholars from others with similar doctoral degrees, is that we connect our work self-consciously to the discipline of missiology and to the ends which it serves.[77]

For Priest, missiology is interdisciplinary: anthropology, communications, comparative religions, philosophy of religion, history, educational studies, linguistics, linguistic anthropology, and theology. These interdisciplinary subjects contribute to forming Diaspora missiology; also these should be used as ministry tools for the church.

Quoting from Caroline B. Brettell and James H. Hollifield's explanation that migration studies are interdisciplinary, Tira states that each discipline focuses on specific aspects of migration, but all work together to provide the bigger picture. Practitioners of these disciplines interact to explain and develop migration theory for Diaspora missiology:

> (A) Anthropologists are interested in the immigrant experience and the results of social and cultural changes.
>
> (B) Demographers project the future of population movements by analyzing the nature of population change. They document the pattern and direction of population shifts.
>
> (C) Economists use human capital terms and labor market patterns to chart population shifts.

---

77. Priest, "What in the World is Missiology?" 23–33.

(D) Geographers study the spatial patterns of migration (e.g., employment patterns and residential patterns; the development of ethnic enclaves; segregation patterns of ethnic and racial groups).

(E) Historians study past immigrant experiences.

(F) Lawmakers and researchers of migrant law study and develop national immigration policies related to migration.

(G) Political scientists study the relationship between migration and a nation's policies.

(H) Sociologists are interested societal changes that occur with migration.[78]

According to Tira, Diaspora missiology is based on eight disciplines—anthropology, economics, geography, history, law, political science, and sociology. Ultimately, interdisciplinary application of the Bible contributes to incarnational ministry. Incarnational principles should be kept not only in interpreting the Bible but also in applying it to teachings. In addition, it should be noted that interdisciplinary principles of biblical application lead to holistic mission. Interdisciplinary applications cover all areas of life of Diaspora.

78. Tira, "Diaspora Missiology," 35.

220 Doing Diaspora Missiology Toward "Diaspora Mission Church"

Contextual Issues & Concerns	Interdisciplinary Lens	Interpretation	Bible	Exegetical Message	Interdisciplinary Lens	Contextual Issues & Concerns
suffering	anthropology		B		anthropology	Healing
poor	politics		I		politics	Compassion on poor
isolation	psychology				psychology	
	economics		B		economics	Fellowship
sorrow	demography				demography	
	law		L		law	Joy
cultural shock	history				history	Justice
	philosophy				philosophy	
injustice			E			Mission

Figure 7: Interdisciplinary Interpretation and Application of the Bible

The above picture shows how interdisciplinary perspectives work in contextual theologizing.

First of all, an interpreter has interdisciplinary concerns and questions from the context; secondly, with this lens, they enter into the Bible and interpret the Bible; thirdly, they get biblical messages; then they begin to apply the message to the context with interdisciplinary lens.

In sum, an interpreter understands the context with an interdisciplinary perspective and sees the Bible with its same lens, and finally applies the biblical message to the context. However, the interdisciplinary perspective works together with the work of the Holy Spirit and the teachings of the Bible.

Holistic/Incarnational Ministries from Interdisciplinary Interpretations and Applications of the Bible

Interdisciplinary interpretations and applications of the Bible make Diaspora missiology move toward holistic mission. The spirit of holistic mission is "love and repentance in all areas of life." The "Holistic Mission Occasional Paper No. 33" from the LCWE describes its nature like this:

> The Oxford meeting Micah adopted, as a matter of practicality in network communication, a distinctive term to refer to the Biblical model of mission that it advocates, namely, "integral

> mission," which was understood as pointing to "the proclamation and demonstration of the gospel." It went on to explain that it is not simply that evangelism and social involvement are to be done alongside each other. Rather, in integral mission our proclamation has social consequences as we call people to love and repentance in all areas of life. And our social involvement has evangelistic consequences as we bear witness to the transforming grace of Jesus Christ. If we ignore the world we betray the word of God, which sends us out to serve the world. If we ignore the word of God we have nothing to bring to the world. Justice and justification by faith, worship and political action, the spiritual and the material, personal change and structural change belong together. As in the life of Jesus, being, doing and saying are at the heart of our integral task.[79]

Here, holistic mission is not that evangelism and social involvement are to be done alongside each other, but that "our proclamation has social consequences as we call people to love and repentance in all areas of life." This means social consequence is an integral part of the gospel; social involvement is processed by the transforming grace of Jesus Christ. As its evidence, the Pentecost experience of the church in Acts 2 shows the event of holistic mission. LCWE states:

> In Acts 2:41–47, it clearly shows that the result of the Pentecost experience is no ghetto-church devoted to cultivating individualistic religion and an exclusive, separatist church only. On the contrary, it is a community of the Spirit, a community that becomes a centre of attraction, "having the good will of all the people" (v. 47) because it incarnates the values of the kingdom of God and affirms, by what it is, by what it does and by what it says, that Jesus Christ has been exalted as Lord over every aspect of life. It is a missionary community that preaches reconciliation with God and the restoration of all creation by the power of the Spirit. It is a Community which provides a glimpse of the birth of a new humanity, and in which can be seen, albeit "in a mirror, dimly" (1 Corinthians 13:12), the fulfillment of God's plan for all humankind.[80]

From the above quotation, it follows that holistic mission is biblical, and that biblical mission is practiced in spiritual as well as physical aspects.

---

79. LCWE Issue Group No. 4, "Holistic Mission Occasional Paper No. 33," 15.
80. Ibid., 18.

Today, mission involves various areas of life because contemporary people live in complex networks of cosmopolitan cities.

The Guidance, Checks, and Empowerment of the Holy Spirit for Theologizing

(1) The Guidance of The Holy Spirit in Contextual Theologizing

Acts 15 provides a good example for forming global theology. The Jerusalem community confessed, "It is seems good to the Holy Spirit and to us not to burden you with anything beyond the following requirements" (v. 28). Here we understand that the product of local theology is checked by the Holy Spirit and "us," namely, the whole church (cf. v. 22). The universal checking criterion of theologizing is the conviction of the Holy Spirit. Here the importance is that the community becomes the one body in the Holy Spirit. Fee states, "Just as Christ's death made the 'one body' a possibility by abolishing what divided Jew and Gentile, so now through Christ both 'have access to the Father *in one Spirit*.'"[81]

Hiebert also states, theologizing must be led by the Holy Spirit, who instructs us in the truth. We need also to recognize that the same Holy Spirit at work in us is also at work in the lives of believers in other contexts.[82] To deny them the right to interpret the Scriptures for themselves is to deny this fact. This work of the Spirit guards us from cultural parochialism, and from theologies based on human reason alone.

When Martin Luther stood before the Holy Roman Emperor at the Diet of Worms, "His interrogator asked: Martin, how can you assume that you are the only one to understand Scripture?" In response, Luther asserted that interpretive tradition alone would not sway him. Only Scripture could *convict*: my conscience is captive to the Word of God.'"[83] Luther believed that the truth comes from the conviction of the Holy Spirit through the word of God. We should confess that the Holy Spirit supervises indigenous theologizing. The Holy Spirit is the spirit of the truth; contextualization theology depends on the Holy Spirit to move it toward the truth. This implies that the Holy Spirit serves as the universal check for local theologizing. The Holy Spirit prevents local theologizing from falling into parochialism or syncretism. Jesus promises that the Holy Spirit leads us all into the truth (John 14:16).

---

81. Fee, *God's Empowering Presence*, 873.
82. Hiebert, *Anthropological Reflections*, 70–71.
83. Vanhoozer, *Is There a Meaning in This Text*, 466.

However, the work of the Holy Spirit guiding us into the truth should be judged and confirmed according to the truth—the gospel of the salvation (Eph 1:13). Luzbetak proclaims the primacy of the Holy Spirit, that (1) "the mission of the church is essentially a spiritual activity—the work of the Holy Spirit"; and (2) "the most important and most desirable ingredient in a person engaged in mission is genuine and deep spirituality."[84] Here we learn that doing contextual theology should be inspected, supervised, and monitored by the Holy Spirit. Those involved in contextual processes should have a holy faith because contextualization itself is a holy process. If this principle is broken, contextual theology does not represent God's biblical salvation.

(2) The Guidance and Empowering Power of the Holy Spirit in Mission

It is the Holy Spirit that plans the ministry and sends the workers for mission (Acts 13:1–3). The work of the Holy Spirit in the Diaspora church and ministry is crucial; he commissioned the church, set it apart, and sent missionaries according to his own plan. The Holy Spirit does the things we cannot do in mission. That is, it is the Holy Spirit who appointed and sent missionaries for his own plan; the Holy Spirit is the master of mission.

In "The Role of the Holy Spirit in Mission," Robertson McQuilkin suggests eight roles of the Holy Spirit in mission: (A) The Holy Spirit gave the message; (B) The Holy Spirit created the method: the church; (C) The Holy Spirit is the guide for the missionary enterprise; (D) The Holy Spirit calls the messenger; (E) The Holy Spirit energizes the messenger; (F) The Holy Spirit confirms that the message is his by miracle signs that follow; (G) The Holy Spirit convicts of sins; and (H) The Holy Spirit regenerates.[85]

The above list shows how the Holy Spirit is essential to Christian mission. By necessity, the Holy Spirit works with the gospel; whenever the gospel is preached, the works of the Holy Spirit should be there. Without recognizing the work of the Holy Spirit, there is no missiological evangelism.

See how the Holy Spirit works with the gospel! The gospel begins to be preached along with the anointing work of the Holy Spirit. Jesus Christ, our master and master of mission, quoted this passage when inaugurating his public ministries.

---

84. Luzbetak, *Church and Cultures*.
85. McQuilkin, "Role of the Holy Spirit," 23–32.

Isa 61: 1 The Spirit of the Sovereign Lord is on me,
    because the Lord has anointed me
    to proclaim good news to the poor.
He has sent me to bind up the brokenhearted,
    to proclaim freedom for the captives
    and release from darkness for the prisoners,
2 to proclaim the year of the Lord's favor
    and the day of vengeance of our God,
to comfort all who mourn,
    3 and provide for those who grieve in Zion—
to bestow on them a crown of beauty
    instead of ashes,
the oil of joy
    instead of mourning,
and a garment of praise
    instead of a spirit of despair.
They will be called oaks of righteousness,
    a planting of the Lord
    for the display of his splendor.

8

The Transcendent Nature of the Church, the Missional Frameworks of 'Diaspora Mission Church', and its Three Ministry Areas

How does Diaspora missiology challenge the Christian faith, church, and mission? In particular, how is Diaspora applied to the church ministry? In principle, the church was built for Jesus' plan of salvation, and it was composed of diaspora. This diaspora-centeredness challenges and restores the transcendent nature of the church and its framework because the church presents heavenly reality. In addition, Christians can be understood as pilgrims, as "alien and strangers," and "the seed of the kingdom." A biblical portrait of the pilgrim moving toward heaven represents transcendence. Finally, the church exists as Diaspora, who live mission, creating a Diaspora mission church. This church is defined as the church of the Diaspora, which exists as mission, lives as the seed of the kingdom and moves as pilgrims toward heaven.

THE CRUCIAL QUESTION: WHAT IN THE WORLD IS THE CHURCH?

The Priority of the Gospel before the Church

The church is built on the foundation of the gospel (Eph 2:20); thus to understand the church, we need to know the gospel of Jesus Christ first. Here, the crucial question is: what is the gospel that Jesus himself, the son of the God, proclaimed first? Put simply, it is in Matthew 4: "17From that time on Jesus began to preach, 'Repent, for the kingdom of heaven has come near.'" Jesus' gospel was composed of two elements—repentance and the kingdom of heaven. In *The Kingdom of God: The Biblical Concept and its Meaning for the Church*, John Bright argued that the people of God were released from the Babylonian exile, and hoped for the dawn of a new thing—the holy commonwealth and apocalyptic kingdom.[1] Here, "apocalyptic" means "revelation." Specifically, it is a revelation couched in the critical language of the great end events. It tells how "God will intervene to wind up the affairs of this earth, to judge his foes and to set up his kingdom."[2] Here, the condition for the kingdom of heaven is repentance: "the Israelite state is not the kingdom of God, and God will not defend it if it were. The hope of Israel began thus to be broken irrevocably from the nation, and to be made something not realizable in terms of it."[3] Repentance only is the great entrance to the kingdom of God: a remnant shall repent.[4]

How was this kingdom of heaven explained and detailed? This was in the Beatitudes in Matthew 5:3-12, which is called the constitution of heaven.

> 3Blessed are the poor in spirit,
>   for theirs is the kingdom of heaven.
> 4Blessed are those who mourn,
>   for they will be comforted.
> 5Blessed are the meek,
>   for they will inherit the earth.
> 6Blessed are those who hunger and thirst for righteousness,
>   for they will be filled.
> 7Blessed are the merciful,
>   for they will be shown mercy.

---

1. Bright, *Kingdom of God*, 156.
2. Ibid., 163.
3. Ibid., 71.
4. Ibid., 71-97.

> 8 Blessed are the pure in heart,
>   for they will see God.
> 9 Blessed are the peacemakers,
>   for they will be called children of God.
> 10 Blessed are those who are persecuted because of righteousness,
>   for theirs is the kingdom of heaven.
> 11 Blessed are you when people insult you, persecute you and falsely say all kinds of evil against you because of me. 12 Rejoice and be glad, because great is your reward in heaven, for in the same way they persecuted the prophets who were before you.

Here, the kingdom of heaven exists in eight blessings; these blessings represent the kingdom of heaven, which are called the constitution of the heavenly kingdom; this was accomplished in the cross of Jesus Christ. Now this kingdom of God exists in the heart and life of those who believe in Jesus as the Savior. The point here is that eight kinds of virtue represent the mind and life of believers and at the same time, essentially belong to the transcendent heaven. In this sense, these kinds of virtue are transcendent although they are immanent in living.

Transcendence is a powerful way of living and communicating an immanent life as the disciples of the early church did. There is no more powerful penetration than transcendence in this world. The poor in spirit, moan, meek, hunger, and thirst for righteousness, and mercy, purity of heart, peacemaking, and persecution because of righteousness are the signs of a transcendent life, God's transcendent intervention in history. These kinds of virtues serve as the salt of the world and the light of the world (Matt 5:13–16)

In addition, it is remembered that this kingdom exists in repentance. Repentance, a change of mind about sin and about God, resulting in turning from sin to God, makes possible a kingdom life, and to put it another way, the eight blessings of the kingdom of God are the signs of repentance. Thus in the birth of church, Peter proclaimed to those who asked, "what shall we do?": "Repent and be baptized, every one of you, in the name of Jesus Christ receive the gift of the Holy Spirit." (Acts 2:37–38)

Representative Texts for the Church in the Bible

The Church as Preachers of Transcendent Heaven through Jesus Christ—Matthew 16

The story of Jesus promising to build his church is recorded in Matthew 16:13–20. The church starts with the question of who is Jesus. The next item of significance here is the promise of Jesus to the church and its members:

> Matt 16: 17Jesus replied, "Blessed are you, Simon son of Jonah, for this was not revealed to you by flesh and blood, but by my Father in heaven. 18And I tell you that you are Peter, and on this rock I will build my church, and the gates of Hades will not overcome it. 19I will give you *the keys of the kingdom of heaven*; whatever you bind on earth will be bound in heaven, and whatever you loose on earth will be loosed in heaven." 20Then he ordered his disciples not to tell anyone that he was the Messiah. (Italics mine)

The key role of the church is to preach the kingdom of heaven through confessing Jesus Christ as the Messiah or Savior. The church, the congregation of believers, has the keys of the kingdom of heaven. What is the function of key? It is to open the way and let somebody in. We discard complex theological discussion on it, but very seriously acknowledge why Jesus built his church in this world—to open the way to the kingdom of heaven. That is, the church in nature is transcendent, which represents transcendent heaven even though it was built in this world; also, the church is the gathering of pilgrims who walk through the world to eternal heaven.

The Community of God's People as Agents of the Holy Spirit for Diaspora Mission—Acts 2

Before the church was built, Jesus promised two things to his disciples: firstly, "4Do not leave Jerusalem, but wait for the gift my Father promised, which you have heard me speak about. 5For John baptized with water, but in a few days you will be baptized with the Holy Spirit" (Acts 1:4–5). Secondly, "But you will receive power when the Holy Spirit comes on you; and you will be my witnesses in Jerusalem, and in all Judea and Samaria, and to the ends of the earth" (v. 8).

That is, the church was built in history along with Jesus' two promises: receiving the Holy Spirit and becoming a witness for the gospel. These two promises of Jesus were actualized in the birth of the church in history (Acts 2).

Of most importance is that church was built from diaspora; when the church was built, the Diaspora, "the Jews from every nation under heaven" (Acts 2:5), heard the gospel, were converted, and became involved in the church and mission. As Acts 2:41 tells us, "those who accepted his message were baptized, and about three thousand were added to their number that day." As we know, the original number of the church was about a hundred and twenty (Acts 1:15). Of course, we don't know if these thousands included homeland Jews or not; however we cannot help but believe that they were almost all diaspora because Acts 2:6–7 indicates that "when they ['the Jews from every nation under heaven'] heard this sound," and that "each one heard them speaking in his own language." This implies that they were diaspora, living a foreign land.

What percentage was three thousand to the total number? About 96 percent. That is, the first church in the Bible came from diaspora. This Diaspora is a pilgrim for Zion, signifying the heavenly Jerusalem. We also remember that 120 disciples were from Galilee; the church was built in a foreign place, not Galilee but Jerusalem. More importantly, it should be confirmed that the church was composed of diaspora, in which it exists as mission. It is what we call Diaspora mission church. Its main characteristic is transcendence, representing heaven.

From the above text, the church was built as a community of Diaspora on earth, but its origin is heaven, the other world. This co-existence of this world and the other world, the interactions between transcendence and immanence, is essentially a main characteristic of the church in this world. The church is moving and moving because it will be a witness for the gospel in Jerusalem, in all Judea and Samaria, and to the ends of the earth. In this sense, the church is Diasporic.

DIASPORA MISSION CHURCH FOR THE REVIVAL IN AND FOR CHRISTENDOM

The Decline of Church in Christendom and Missional Church Movement

In 1983, Lesslie Newbigin warned the Western church that it is hopeless; that it should be understood as a mission field as India has been. His book is interpreted as "an invitation to the church to be bold in offering to the men and women of our culture a way of understanding which is based unashamedly on the revelation of God made in Jesus Christ and attested in Scripture and the tradition of the church." It explained that because no church or culture is an island, an invitation to adopt "an authentically missionary approach to modern culture" needs to be extended to all Christians everywhere.[5]

Thirteen years after Newbigin's book was published, American scholars published a book regarding missional church entitled, *The Church between Gospel and Culture: The Emerging Mission in North America* (1996), edited by George R. Hunsberger. This is an excellent collection of essays, written by a diverse group of Christian leaders working on the frontier of mission in North America, and laid the groundwork for a recently emerging missionary encounter of the gospel with North American society and culture.[6] It is very worthwhile for American scholars to be awakened by Newbigin's warning and to try to find effective evangelism in the postmodern society of the USA. After one year, they suggested a model of a "missional church," quoting from Newbigin's theory.[7] Following the missional church movement, there have been various movements for the adapting of the church into new contexts. One of these movements, The Missional Network (TMN), declaims: "We are a people of hope-in-action learning to participate in what God is doing in the local. TMN cultivates safe spaces, robust resources and processes to re-orient our Christian communities for the sake of the gospel and the transformation of God's world."[8]

The core values of the missional church are those such as "learning," "participation," "reorienting," "gospel," and "transformation." The missional church is kind of a contemporary movement of the reformed church and theology, which is shown in "New Calvinists," who participate in the missional church movement. To understand what the characteristics of New Calvinism are, it is worthwhile to note John Piper's explanation:

Twelve Features of the New Calvinism:

(1) The New Calvinism, in its allegiance to the inerrancy of the Bible, embraces the biblical truths behind the five points (TULIP), while having an aversion to using the acronym or any other systematic packaging, along with a sometimes qualified embrace of limited atonement. The focus is on

---

5. Newbigin, *Other Side of 1984*.
6. Hunsberger, *Church between Gospel and Culture*.
7. Guder, *Missional Church*.
8. Inhabit Conference, "Missional Network."

Calvinistic soteriology but not to the exclusion or the appreciation of the broader scope of Calvin's vision.

(2) The New Calvinism embraces the sovereignty of God in salvation, and in all the affairs of life in history, including evil and suffering.

(3) The New Calvinism has a strong complementarian flavor as opposed to egalitarian, with an emphasis on the flourishing of men and women in relationships where men embrace a call to robust, humble, Christ-like servant leadership.

(4) The New Calvinism leans toward being culture-affirming rather than culture-denying, while holding fast to some very culturally alien positions, like positions on same-sex practice and abortion.

(5) The New Calvinism embraces the essential place of the local church. It is led mainly by pastors, has a vibrant church-planting bent, produces widely sung worship music, and exalts the preached word as central to the work of God locally and globally.

(6) The New Calvinism is aggressively mission-driven, including missional impact on social evils, evangelistic impact on personal networks, and missionary impact on unreached peoples of the world.

(7) The New Calvinism is inter-denominational with a strong (some would say oxymoronic) Baptismal element.

(8) The New Calvinism includes charismatics and non-charismatics.

(9) The New Calvinism puts a priority on pietism or piety in the Puritan vein, with an emphasis on the essential role of affections in Christian living, while esteeming the life of the mind and being very productive in it, and embracing the value of serious scholarship. Jonathan Edwards would be invoked as a model of this combination of the affections and the life of the mind more often than John Calvin, whether that's fair to Calvin or not

(10) The New Calvinism is vibrantly engaged in publishing books and even more remarkably in the world of the internet, with hundreds of energetic bloggers and social media activists, with Twitter as the increasingly default way of signaling things new and old that should be noticed and read.

(11) The New Calvinism is international in scope, multi-ethnic in expression, and culturally diverse. There is no single geographic, racial, or cultural governing center. There are no officers, no organization, nor any loose affiliation that would encompass the whole. I would dare say that there are outcroppings of this movement that nobody (including me) in this room has ever heard of.

(12) The New Calvinism is robustly gospel-centered and cross-centered, with dozens of books rolling off the presses, coming at the gospel from every conceivable angle, and applying it to all areas of life with a commitment to seeing the historic doctrine of justification, finding its fruit in sanctification personally and communally.[9]

According to John Piper, the New Calvinism is the production of the critical contextualization of the gospel for postmodernism; this kind of movement should continue to spread among world Christianity because it fell into severe decline in the church. For him, there is no area in the Christian world that excludes the necessity of church reformation and revival. This New Calvinism involves the missional church movement. In a word, New Calvinism is adaptation to postmodern society, consistent with Kuyper's New Calvinism.[10]

In his article, "The Missional Church," Tim Keller, senior pastor of Redeemer Presbyterian church and one of the New Calvinists, argues that the missional church movement aims to reform stigmatized Christianity in Christendom. He argued:

> In the West for nearly 1,000 years, the relationship of (Anglo-European) Christian churches to the broader culture was a relationship known as "Christendom." The institutions of society "Christianized" people, and stigmatized non-Christian belief and behavior. Though people were "Christianized" by the culture, they were not regenerated or converted with the gospel. The church's job was then to challenge persons into a vital, living relation with Christ.[11]

---

9. This article comes from John Piper, who spoke at Westminster Seminary, and delivered at the seventh annual Gaffin Lecture on "The New Calvinism and the New Community: The Doctrines of Grace and the Meaning of Race." See also Piper, "John Piper's Twelve Features of the New Calvinism," 11–56.

10. Kuyper, *Lectures on Calvinism*, 9–40. This section deals with Calvinism as lifestyle.

11. Keller, "Missional Church."

A major issue of the missional church movement is that current Christianity has already fallen into the phenomenon of "Christendom"; "the institutions of society "Christianized" people, and stigmatized non-Christian belief and behavior." This shows why the missional church movement has recently appeared. In consistence with the purpose of the missional movement, Diaspora movement focuses on the revival of church and mission in a secularized society, which is through rediscovering the concept of Diaspora as the field of the gospel and God's redemption.

"Diaspora Mission Church" in consistence with "Missional Church"

First of all, "Diaspora mission church" moves toward mission as its final goal. That is, it is a succession of missionary church. How then does the church become missionary? Introducing Newbigin's theology of mission, Michael W. Goheen comments on Newbigin's method of doing missiology in this way: "If the gospel was to be liberated from this syncretism, the religious beliefs at the centre of western culture needed to be unmasked"; "If the gospel is true, if it tells us where all of history is going, then mission must follow: it must be made known."[12] Following this logic, Newbigin employed the tools of his missionary training to bring new light to bear on the topic. This task is fourfold: cultural, theological, ecclesiological, and epistemological.

These four topics of Newbigin's missionary training, remaining profoundly relevant for our day, are relayed to be used for the renewal of the church, leading to the missional church. The core point in the logic of mission is that the church itself should be missional; all members should live a mission-oriented life; and all life should be mission. This can be called a missionary church, a biblical church.

Likewise, Diaspora mission church asserts that for becoming missional, the church should restore the nature of the church as Diaspora, based on the gospel. The concept of Diaspora should be applied to all life in the church. A Diaspora-centered church is missional as well as pilgriming; like pilgrimage, Diaspora mission church is moving toward salvation, mission, and heaven. The identity of church members as Diaspora plays key role in carrying out holiness and mission. In this sense, Diaspora mission church can be defined as the transcendent church of the Diaspora who were elected and called by the Trinity, live as the seed of the kingdom and as pilgrims, preach the gospel, and move toward heaven.

12. Goheen, *Significance of Lesslie Newbigin*, 88–99.

Van Engen suggested seven criteria for becoming a missionary church. These characteristics of a missionary church are included in Diaspora mission church. Here is a comparison between Van Engen's criteria and characteristics of a Diaspora mission church.

Figure 8: Comparison of Missionary Church and Diaspora Mission Church[13]

	Missionary Church	Diaspora Mission Church
1 *Contextual*	A missional church understands itself as part of a larger context of a lost and broken world, so loved by God.	A Diaspora mission church understands itself as part of a larger context of a hurt, suffering, and broken world, scattered around the world, called by God—the love of the Father, the grace of the Son, and the fellowship of the Holy Spirit.
2 *Intentional*	A missional church understands itself as existing for the purpose of following Christ in mission.	A Diaspora mission church understands itself as existing for the purpose of being gathered and saved by God's calling through preaching the gospel.
3 *Proclaiming*	A missional church understands itself as intentionally sent by God in mission to announce in word and deed the coming of the kingdom of God in Christ.	A Diaspora mission church understands itself as the seed of the kingdom, providentially scattered by God to preach Jesus' message, "repent, for the kingdom of heaven is near" (Matt 4:17).
4 *Reconciling*	A missional church understands itself to be a reconciling and healing presence in its contexts, locally and globally.	A Diaspora mission church understands itself to be reconciling and healing agents, "to reconcile both of them to God through the cross, by which he put to death their hostility" (Eph 2:16). Reconciling takes place when the "scattered" encounter with Jesus Christ and others as well, locally and globally.

---

13. Van Engen, "Mission Defined and Described," 1–29.

5 *Sanctifying*	A missional church understands itself as a faith community gathered around the Word preached, thus personally living out its truth and serving as a purifying influence in society.	A Diaspora mission church understands itself as a faith community to be holy through the sanctifying work of the Spirit, and "as aliens and strangers in this world, to abstain from sinful desires, which wage war against your soul" (1 Pet 2:11).
6 *Unifying*	A missional church understands itself as an embracing, enfolding, gathering community of faith, anxious to receive persons into its fellowship.	A Diaspora mission church understands itself as the one unified body of Christ, through "making the two one," and as foreigners and aliens becoming God's people and members of God's household (Eph 2:13–22) through making room in itself for others in the Word, and the work of the Holy Spirit (1 Cor 12:13).
7 *Transforming*	A missional church is the salt of the earth (Matt 5:13), a transforming presence as the body of Christ in mission, called to be, embody, and live out in the world the following of biblical concepts of mission, among others: koinonia, kerygma, diakonia, maertyria, prophet, priest, king, liberator, healer, sage.	A Diaspora mission church understands itself as the gathering of "pilgrims" who walk through the world toward heaven. In walking toward heaven, the pilgrim lives the kingdom of heaven, signified in the Beatitudes, which serve as a transforming power to live according to the values and morality of God's kingdom.

As the above figure shows, Diaspora mission church understands its members as "gathered people (God's salvation)," "pilgrims," and "the seed of the kingdom" as well; it moves toward a living missionary church. In this sense, Diaspora mission church is naturally and intentionally moving toward a Diaspora missiology guided by the Holy Spirit. That is, without the renewed emergence of this Diaspora-centered church, Diaspora missiology would not be successful.

Mission is not just one of the activities of the church, but the pattern of existence for the church. This vision can be accomplished when all members are understood as gathered Diaspora who are the seeds of the kingdom and pilgrims. In particular, the overseas mission of the church should essentially be geared toward the witness of Diaspora networks scattered around the world. Therefore, what we call "Diaspora church-mission" means that the church should live a Diaspora life based on God's salvation—a pilgrimage as the seed of the kingdom.

Ten Core Values of Diaspora Mission Church: Pilgrimage

Diaspora mission church, scattered and called in God's providence of salvation, based on the love of the Father, the grace of the Son, and the fellowship of the Holy Spirit (1 Pet 1:1-3), is committed to living as pilgrims who move toward heaven. Psalm 105:12 says that the chosen of Israel who made the covenant with God were called strangers, namely, pilgrims; the covenant of his salvation describes the status of the chosen ones, "they wandered from nation to nation, from one kingdom to another" (v. 13). Diaspora, scattered foreigners, is the premise for God's covenant, representing the nature of the gospel, church, and mission. In particular, Diaspora mission church has ten core values representing the pilgrimage toward heaven, which is the final destination of the faith (1 Pet 1:9).

(1) Encountering with Christ: Salvation of the Pilgrim

Human beings were scattered as diaspora in God's judgment (Lev 26:33); God promised the scattered a gathering for salvation in the new covenant (Ezek 33:19-31). When they encounter with Jesus Christ as Savior, a Diaspora's guilt of sin is removed; their wandering is ceased; they are full of the joy of salvation—amazing grace. In this encounter, it is not "I" that lives, but Christ that lives in us (Gal 2:20). Hebrews 11:13-16 proclaims that all who believe in Jesus are aliens and strangers, pilgrims.

(2) Healing: Heart of the Pilgrim

After receiving forgiveness in Christ, the heart of the believer is separated from sin and the world, understanding the meaning of the suffering in a scattered life and its pain is gone. So are Diaspora reconciled with God and neighbors in Christ who died for our sin on the cross. This healing is expressed in a Samaritan woman (John 4:1-26). In the Bible, two of the persons who dramatically encountered with Jesus are Zacchaeus (Luke 19:1-10) and a criminal (Luke 23:39-43) whose sins were forgiven and healed.

(3) Church Membership: Belongings of the Pilgrim

The church—the congregation of called Diaspora—is separated from the world, called to be holy (1 Cor 1:2), baptized by one Spirit into one body (1 Cor 12:13), and called to worship the Trinity in thanksgiving for his salvation; it has an encouraging fellowship with other believers in faith and life, and exists in a pilgrim life that practices and hopes for the spread of the kingdom of heaven. The church is the place in which heaven is opened with the key given to church by Jesus. In this sense, all saints in the church are called to be pilgrims who walk toward heaven (Matt 16:13–20).

(4) Spiritual Growth: Holiness of the Pilgrim

Spiritual growth legally represents the life of pilgrim. First Peter 2:1 says, "Dear friends, I urge you, *as foreigners and exiles*, to abstain from sinful desires, which wage war against your soul" (italics mine). Pilgrims as foreigners and exiles seek a sanctified life because they know their God and heaven; the pilgrim does not fall into greed on earth because it goes to heaven. They live their lives as strangers here, in reverent fear (2 Pet 1:17).

(5) Service: Servanthood of the Pilgrim

Another issue of the pilgrim is service, doing good to others. First Peter 2:12 says, "Live such good lives among the pagans that, though they accuse you of doing wrong, they may see your good deeds and glorify God on the day he visits us." The book of Revelation, written to the saints who wait for Jesus' second coming and hope for heaven, calls the saints as "servants": "1The revelation from Jesus Christ, which God gave him to show his *servants* what must soon take place. He made it known by sending his angel to his *servant* John, 2who testifies to everything he saw—that is, the word of God and the testimony of Jesus Christ" (Rev 1:1–2, italics mine). This shows how essential the service of the pilgrim walking for heaven is.

(6) Embracing: Open Arms of the Pilgrim

Embracing represents the room in ourselves for others; this room is made and opened in the cross of Jesus Christ who died for our all sins. This heart is first shown in the Father who embraced the lost son, based on not moral judgment but on gracious embrace through the love of God (Luke 15). In Leviticus 19:33–34, the Lord commanded Israel to not mistreat aliens, because they were aliens in Egypt. This shows that the virtue of aliens is to open their arms to others.

(7) Evangelism: The Pilgrim as the Seed of the Kingdom

Evangelism is the Great Commission of Jesus Christ, the purpose of the church and his disciples (Matt 28:18–20); as the seed of the kingdom, Diaspora are committed to live and preach the gospel. Jesus referred to his disciples as "good seed," namely, "the people of the kingdom" (Matt 13:38); they are scattered in unknown places according to God's provident plan. Also taught in John 12:24, "unless a kernel of wheat falls to the ground and dies, it remains only a single seed. But if it dies, it produces many seeds." Once again, Diaspora voluntarily scatter, and "die" for the gospel, to produce many fruits. The seed exists for dying to produce many seeds. In particular, the great commitment to evangelism is proclaimed in the missionary life of Paul (Acts 20:23–24; 21:13–14).

(8) Leadership: Influence of the Pilgrim

The sense and confession of "pilgrim" serves as leader. Abraham, called the father of the faith, confessed: "I am a foreigner and stranger among you. Sell me some property for a burial site here so I can bury my dead" (Gen 23:4). The Hittites replied to Abraham, "Sir, listen to us. You are *a mighty prince among us*" (v. 6, italics mine). He is a foreigner and stranger among the Hittites, yet he is a mighty prince among them, a mighty leader. This shows that the sense of the pilgrim is not irresponsible to this world, and instead is recognized as an influential leader, though they walk through to heaven. In Acts 13, the leaders of Antioch church are all from diaspora: Barnabas, Simeon (called Niger), Lucius of Cyrene, Manaen (who had been brought up with Herod the tetrarch), and Saul. Pilgrims shine like light around the world.

(9) World Christians: Visionary Parish of the Pilgrim

A "world" Christian refers to the vision of Christians for world evangelization; the parish of all Christians as Diaspora is both local and global. The world is a field in which seeds are scattered and the harvest will be reaped (John 4:35). More importantly, God may already have worked in the field through somebody or something unknowingly. That is, the seeds were already scattered in God's providence; it is enough that disciples as reapers obey and go there (John 4:38). A typical pattern of a world Christian is Joseph, who was healed from pains, forgave and embraced his brothers who betrayed him, and set up the kingdom of God (Gen 45).

(10) Heaven: Eternal Home of the Pilgrim

Heaven is the final destination, toward which all Christians as pilgrims who believe in Jesus must move throughout their whole life. Jesus promises his disciples:

> 1 Do not let your hearts be troubled. You believe in God; believe also in me. 2 My Father's house has many rooms; if that were not so, would I have told you that I am going there to prepare a place for you? 3 And if I go and prepare a place for you, I will come back and take you to be with me that you also may be where I am. (John 14:1–3)

When he comes back, Jesus will take his people into heaven; all believers will end their wandering and scattered journey in heaven. Moreover, we will be poured out like a drink offering, and know that the time for our departure is near; if we have fought the good fight, finished the race, and kept the faith. We are sure there is in store for us the crown of righteousness (2 Tim 4:6–8). When we arrive in heaven, the house of Father, all believers will cry, "Father, I am home."

These ten core values of Diaspora mission church represent and echo the nature, ministry, and mission of biblical Christianity. These core values are like the pattern of the pilgrimage journey in John Bunyan's *The Pilgrim's Progress from this World to that which is to Come*. Diaspora mission church also has the same purpose as the pilgrim's progress from this world to that which is to come. That is, the spiritual journey of Diaspora mission church is to guide people toward heaven; its ten core values are reinterpreted from basic Christian theology in terms of Diaspora mission church and with regard to contemporary issues of the church and mission.

A main point here is that we Christians exist as Diaspora on the move, scattered around the world as the seed of the kingdom for world evangelism, and finally continue to move as pilgrims in this world toward heaven. The church always considers this ultimate concern of believers, regardless of their approval or not, and does its best to inspire them about and guide them toward eternal life in heaven. Here we know that eternal life was the plan of God before the beginning of time. Human beings were created for his plan—eternal life; this world is full of God's calling into eternal life. In a word, this world and life serves as a chance for God's calling.

Paul says, "1 Paul, a servant of God and an apostle of Jesus Christ to further the faith of God's elect and their knowledge of the truth that leads to godliness—2 in the hope of eternal life, which God, who does not lie, promised before the beginning of time" (Tit 1:1–2). We find that the calling of Christians and church leaders and the nature of faith is *"in the hope of eternal life,* which God, who does not lie, promised before the beginning of time" (v. 2, italics mine). The eternal life God promised before the creation of the world is partially accomplished on earth, but will be completely accomplished in heaven someday. Thus, eternal life should be the hope of life in all believers.

Also, in Ephesians 1:3–5, Paul explains that God predestined us to be adopted as his sons through Jesus Christ before the creation of the world. Once again, the goal of God's creation is related to practicing his plan of redemption; thus Christian mission must never lose this crucial point. Diaspora mission church is intertwined with these essential values of biblical Christianity.

REORIENTING THE DIRECTIONS OF THE CURRENT CHURCH FOR DIASPORA MISSION CHURCH

How can a new concept of the Diaspora mission church be applied to the church? In a brief, the first step is to restore the transcendent nature of the church through applying the concept of Diaspora into the secularized church; the second is to apply the Diaspora scattered around unreached people in the globalized world. These two applications can open the door of reorienting the direction of the church for Diaspora mission church.

The Transcendent Spirit of Diaspora for the Church

Against Secularizations

Secularization is a theory relating to the idea that religion becomes less powerful as a social institution with the progress of "modernity." Berger defines the term as meaning: "The process by which sectors of society and culture are removed from the domination of religious institutions and symbols."[14] In general, various secularization theories state that modernity tends to erode religion's plausibility, intensity, and authority; they tend to posit the retreat of sacred institutions, the privatization of faith, and the "progressive shrinkage and decline of religion" in public life.[15] Finally, religious preferences are becoming more privatized and individualized; also the post of orthodox

---

14. Berger, *Sacred Canopy*, 107.
15. Casanova, *Public Religions*.

religious authorities is prominently diminishing, and growing proportions of people seek a spirituality separated from traditional religion.[16]

Edward H. Hammett and Loren B. Mead strongly warn Christians of the church's secularization: "Secularization is at the threshold of every church because it is in most Christian households. There is more to Christianity than attending church and serving on church committees. In a secular age, ministry for Christians in the daily world is as significant as their ministry inside the church walls."[17] In nature, Christian mission should be against secularization. This is because secularization hinders the principle and practices of Christianity. This is why, today, Christian mission focuses on Diaspora missiology. Min Young Jung argues, "the Diaspora nature of the Christian religions is in stark contrast with secularization and/or world religions as the table below."[18]

Figure 9: Contrast between World Religions and Christianity

Secularism / World Religions	Christianity
Human centered	God centered
Human desire: fortress earth	God's plan: pilgrimage (Diaspora)
Tower of Babel	Dispersion (Diaspora)
Security in self/world; e.g., "American dream"	Security in God/heaven: "Kingdom Dream"
Restless wanderers (Gen 4:12, 14)	Purpose-driven pilgrim/Diaspora
Settlement in Mesopotamia, one of the four major human civilizations	Covenant call (Heb 11:8) to live in a foreign country (Heb 11:9)
Settlement in Goshen	Exodus
Settlement Canaan	Exile (Diaspora)

According to the figure above, the factors against secularism are mainly related to the concept of Christian Diaspora; anti-secular factors have root in the characteristics of diaspora. For Jung, Christian mission is against this secularization of the society and people, exile experience of diaspora as foreigner shatters through all the limiting structures of religious institutions in modern secularization. He says, "Man, like every living being, is concerned about many things, above all about those which condition his very existence . . . If [a situation or concern] claims ultimacy it demands the total surrender of him who accepts this claim . . . it demands that all other

16. Lambert, "Turning Point in Religious Evolution."
17. Hammett and Mead, Review of *Gathered and Scattered Church*.
18. Jung, "Diaspora and Timely Hit," 65.

concerns . . . be sacrificed."[19] Here a faith is transcendent and sacrificing;[20] this transcendence to sacrifice anything is helpful to overcome secularism. To pull from Augustine's thought on two cities of God, believers do not belong to the world because they see eternal happiness. This is the very concept of transcendence.[21]

In addition, Diaspora who experience exile experience the liberation of God. Raitt says, "The exile was a time for the liberation of God, for the awesome power and the holy heat of God's goodness to shatter through all the limiting structures of Israel's religious conceptions and religious institutions";[22] at the same time, "what is crucial to realize is that we have no institutional claims on God. We are not an elect people. Persons who take their Christianity with consistent seriousness will soon be cultural exiles within American society. Believers who are not ideologically pluralistic usually find themselves to be exiles within churches. Exiled people are attractive to God."[23] Here, the liberation of God is beyond this world moving toward God's deliverance.

Exile experience sets Christians to be against modern, worldly, limiting structure of secularization, and to move to God. "By that judgment they are stripped of facades. They are forced to be mobile, to travel light, to stand naked before God. They have no enduring worldly roots, no enduring worldly security. They are vulnerable."[24] This characteristic of "exile" contributes to forming a spirit of Christian mission in modern society. "They are forced to be mobile, to travel light, to stand naked before God." These lives of the exiled are exactly a life of the missionary. In particular, Diaspora-centeredness attempts a "Copernican" transition shift of the church ministry framework, including church administration, education, worship, ministry, and evangelism. However, the crucial thing is that diaspora as foreigners against and beyond secularization calls for a transcendent identity of Diaspora. Transcendent aspects of the gospel overcome secularization in paradoxical ways.

---

19. Tillich, *Dynamics of Faith*, 1–2.
20. Ibid, 8–9.
21. Augustine, *City of God*.
22. Raitt, *Theology of Exile*, 228.
23. Ibid., 228–29.
24. Ibid., 229.

Transcendent Identity beyond National Identity

What is a Christian identity? According to Paul, Christian identity is beyond particular ethnicities: Jew or Greek (Gal 3:28). Furthermore, "Therefore, if anyone is in Christ, the new creation has come: the old has gone, the new is here!" (2 Cor 5:17). Paul proclaims that "our citizenship is in heaven" (Phil 3:20). This means that Christian identity as heavenly citizenship is transcendent beyond particular ethnicity.

For Christians, the word "transcendence" usually refers to that attribute of God that describes his difference and distance from the world. In contrast, this attribute of God is always paired with that other attribute of his immanence that describes his closeness and involvement in reality. Both transcendence and immanence form a royal pair, which always needs to be kept in balance, and always runs the risk of falling out of balance. In nature, transcending experience can be understood when much of our life is concerned with the material, un-safety, frustration, and anxiety. In this way, the yearning for transcendent experiences could be interpreted as a way of living a reality, not as mere escapism. That is, transcendence is not to escape from but strongly engage in the world, because transcendence fills Christians with power from God above.

The Transcendent Nature of the Church

With the recovering of the church from secularization, sociologist Halt suggests the significance of transcendence:

> Recovering the way is always a difficult task. For the secular church, recovery will depend upon a painfully honest recognition of the problem. It will demand nothing short of a recovery of transcendence, an openness to the biblical record of God's shattering and unpredictable incursions into human history. This, in turn, will rekindle near-forgotten memories that "his ways are not our ways." It will remind us that God is worshipped not because he is useful but because he is God. Only such a turn to the God above our countless false gods can free us from our self-imprisonment within a web of illusions and fantasies.[25]

Here a recovery of transcendence serves as an antidote to secularization; it represents "an openness to the biblical record of God's shattering and unpredictable incursions into human history." If God shatters unpredictable

---

25. Holt, "Secular Church," 15–20.

incursions into human history, who can live offhandedly? This shows how transcendence can responsibly engage in this world. According to Tillich:

> The essence of religious attitudes is what he calls "ultimate concern." Separate from all profane and ordinary realities, the object of the concern is understood as sacred, numinous or holy. The perception of its reality is felt as so overwhelming and valuable that all else seems insignificant, and for this reason requires total surrender.[26]

Today, faith and church fall into profane and ordinary realities in which Christians are not different from non-Christians in terms of lifestyle and the goal of life. Transcendent separation "from all profane and ordinary realities," causing total surrender, moves toward being real Christians based on the teachings of the Bible, and to reforming the profane church.

According to Halt, "For the secular church, recovery will depend upon a painfully honest recognition of the problem. It will demand nothing short of a recovery of transcendence, an openness to the biblical record of God's shattering and unpredictable incursions into human history."[27] Diaspora as pilgrims, who walk through this world into heaven, is a crucial Christian identity, contributing to the recovery of transcendence in faith, church, and mission. On the other hand, the pilgrim is faithfully responsible for this world because: "I will give to every one according to what he has done" (Rev 22:12).

The Participation of the Local Church in Globalizing Theology: The Necessity of its Responses to Emerging Agenda for Global Theologizing

As mentioned earlier, sixteen missiological scholars recently contributed to formulating global theology. This collection of papers was published under the title *Global Theologizing*. In the conclusion of the book, Ott proposes an urgent agenda for global theology missiologically, ecclesiologically, historically, and ethically.[28] In missiological circles, round tables will be prepared, peer review will be submitted, and the playing field between Western and non-Western Christianity will be more leveled. In fact, Diaspora missiology is a part of global theologizing, because it was formulated to find the most

---

26. Wainwright, "Concepts of God," 1–10.
27. Holt, "Secular Church," 23–40.
28. Ott, "Conclusion," 327–29.

effective missiology in the context of globalization. We hope that Diaspora missiology contributes to the formulation of a global theology.

More importantly, however, global theologizing should pivot on Diaspora missiology in the local church setting. At the same time, the church ministry should embody the emerging agenda of global theologizing. That is, the church should be transformed and revived through the concept of Diaspora, moving toward a global missiology. To be Diaspora mission church, the church frameworks should be geared toward the vision of a global Diaspora missiology.

The Urgent Mission of Diaspora Missiology for Unreached People

One of the missiological issues is the "great imbalance," put forth by Ralph Winter; there is a great imbalance in Christian mission between reached people and unreached people. The following figure shows what Winter explains:

Figure 10: The Great Imbalance[29]

Regions of:	Reached Peoples	Unreached Peoples
Number of People Groups:	16,000	8,000
Non-Christians:	40%	60%
Practicing Christians:	99%	1%
Evangelical Missionaries:	90%	10%

First of all, it is noted that a "People Group" is "a significantly large grouping of individuals who perceive themselves to have a common affinity for one another because of their shared language, religion, ethnicity, residence, occupation, class or caste, situation, etc., or combinations of these." For evangelistic purposes it is "the largest group within which the gospel can spread as a church planting movement without encountering barriers of understanding or acceptance."[30] In contrast, "An Unreached People Group is "a people group within which there is no indigenous community of believing Christians able to evangelize this people group."[31] It is also noted that "reached" does not mean "converted to Christianity" and "unreached" does not mean "the gospel has not been shared," but rather that this is a difference of having an indigenous presence of Christianity among the people groups.

29. Winter and Koch, "Finishing the Task," 24.
30. Ibid., 19.
31. Ibid.

Based on this great imbalance, Winter challenges the church to focus on unreached peoples. "Today there is only an estimated 8,000 unreached (unimax) peoples, and a dynamic global movement is now in full swing that is committed to seeing Christ worshipped and obeyed within every one of them."[32] What then is the strategy? Winter suggests Patrick Johnston's theory of utilizing a "church planting indicator," ranking the progress within a particular people group:

0–No known believers.

1–No churches, some believers.

2–One known church.

3–Group of churches.

4–Reproducing church movement.

5–Widespread, discipled churches.[33]

Here, the variable used to decide an indicator number is the number of "believers." That is, the church-planting indicator relies on the believers—Diaspora Christians in a surrounding place. Diasporas are scattered around the world; they belong to "widespread, discipled churches," as a high church-planting indicator. Diasporas live in the same culture as unreached peoples; they are accustomed to their culture and lifestyle. This shows how important Diaspora is to reaching unreached people. Diaspora missiology should contribute to reaching unreached people around the world. The church should first seek for Diaspora to be scattered in unreached areas for unreached people and teach them about God's providence for his redemption and their missional identity.

THE SIX FRAMEWORKS OF DIASPORA MISSION CHURCH

Diaspora mission church is a mission-oriented church through applying the concept of Diaspora, doing Diaspora missiology; it is originally rooted in the biblical confession of believers as Diaspora. All believers, existentially, biblically, and theologically, are Diaspora; the churches also are based on Diaspora scattered around the world as the seed of the kingdom; they are called to be God's elect and mission. The following are practical processes making up the six frameworks of Diaspora mission church.

---

32. Ibid., 15–17.
33. Ibid., 21.

1) The Identity of the Church as the Congregation of Diaspora

The church is the gathering of believers who were called by the Trinity—God the Father, God the Son, and God the Holy Spirit. The gathering comes from the scattered in God's judgment and waiting for God's deliverance. In this sense, all churches in the world are composed of Diaspora spiritually and theologically. As mentioned earlier, God's deliverance occurred in the context of Diaspora, in particular, exile. Thus, the church is a gathering of scattered people; it always has the nature and characteristics of Diaspora.

"We are Diaspora." That is the identity of the church. In this sense, every Christian is called to be a pilgrim who moves toward heaven;[34] migrant-ness is an eternal nature of the church. The church was called to be "missional migration" or "missional mobility."[35] Diaspora mission church refers to the church of Diaspora who were scattered in God's judgment and called for God's salvation, scattered as the seed of the kingdom to preach the gospel and live as pilgrims who move toward heaven. That is, Diaspora mission church exists in mission.

2) Diaspora Mission Church as the Missio Dei

Diaspora as the Missio Dei

Diaspora missiology agrees with the confession that God is the author of mission.[36] "Mission is, primarily and ultimately, the work of the Triune God, Creator, Redeemer, and Sanctifier, for the sake of the world, a ministry in which the church is privileged to particulate";[37] mission has its origin in the heart of God. God is a fountain of sending love. This is the deepest source of mission. It is impossible to penetrate deeper still; there is mission because God loves people.[38] This love of God providently scattered Diaspora, the seed of the kingdom in the field, unknowingly, and in time the seed will arise and bear fruit. The church sometimes does not know the whole process. That is, Diaspora is the timely hit of God, characterized by Diaspora missiology, as Jung puts. Diaspora is the agent of mission God sent in his secret plan.

---

34. Elliot, *Home for the Homeless*.
35. Phan, "Migration in the Patristic Era."
36. Jung, "Diaspora and Timely Hit," 61.
37. LCWE, *Scattered to Gather*, 6–10.
38. Bosch, *Transforming Mission*, 392.

Doing Diaspora Missiology Toward "Diaspora Mission Church"

The Missio Dei: Delegated to the Church, Gathered and Scattered

God's mission was delegated to the church as the community of Diaspora. In John 20:21-22, God's sending Jesus included Jesus' sending of his disciples into the world: "21Again Jesus said, 'Peace be with you! As the Father has *sent* me, I am *sending* you.' 22And with that he breathed on them and said, 'Receive the Holy Spirit.'" Before the creation, God's sending included Jesus "sending," leading to the disciples sending members of the church. This shows how the mission of God was delegated to the church. Acts 1 details Jesus' promise: "8But you will receive power when the Holy Spirit comes on you; and you will be my witnesses in Jerusalem, and in all Judea and Samaria, and to the ends of the earth." The presence of the Holy Spirit is the sign which shows that the church is the subject of mission.

The church as the congregation of Diaspora is always open to mission. The history of mission written in Acts was related to the church; mission went with the church. Even when a person individually preached the gospel, later this event was connected to the church as the mission center. The Diaspora church always follows and monitors Diaspora on the move, in which the *Missio Dei*, the imitation of God in mission, is accomplished. Here, Diaspora is an agent of doing the *Missio Dei*, which is conformed to be in relation with the church.

This principle was affirmed in Acts 8 also: without the direction of the church, Philip personally preached the gospel in Samaria, and he was guided by the Holy Spirit, but later the Jerusalem church sent the Apostles Peter and John to support and monitor that mission (Acts 8:14-24). Here we note that the church in principle is Diaspora, tending toward "moving" by the Holy Spirit. As mentioned earlier, the church was connected to Diaspora, which were ready for scattering or being scattered for his redemptive providence. The Diaspora church is not satisfied with gathering congregations; it breathes the air of mission through the scattered church. Diaspora mission church understands its members as gathered as well as scattered Diaspora; Diaspora are planted as the seed of the kingdom in the world, which is called the scattered church.

3) The Purpose of Diaspora Mission Church: World Evangelization

Toward being missional, Diaspora mission church teaches that the church exists for world evangelization. In Acts, the Diaspora is an agent of God's redemptive plan; Acts 2:5 shows that in the birth of the church, Diaspora were invited as its members for his mission; Acts 8:4 states, "those who had been scattered preached the word wherever they went. 5 Philip went down to a city in Samaria and proclaimed the Messiah there." This shows that God uses Diaspora as agents for his mission. Thus the church was planted here for his plan of evangelism, gathered from the scattered people, who were scattered in God's judgment and now voluntarily scatter to preach the gospel in his providence and for his redemptive plan. This is the confession of Diaspora mission church. Here are two ways of Diaspora mission for world evangelism.

The Great Opportunity of Mission: Social Networks between Christians and Non-Christians (Unreached People)

With regard to world mission, Ott asks, what are the implications of the current state of world Christianity for our mandate to fulfill the Great Commission and make disciples of all nations? As we see, Diaspora are scattered around the globe; the world is full of migrating people. Diaspora missiology uses mobile people for world mission; this globalization offers new opportunity toward world evangelization. To actualize this new opportunity, first of all, the church should build up social networks around the globe. Todd M. Johnson, research fellow in the Study of Global Christianity and Director of the Center for the Study of Global Christianity at Gordon-Conwell Theological Seminary, argues for the necessity of global contact between Christians and non-Christians in a global era. He says:

> In Christian–non-Christian relations we also see these dynamics at work. People of different religious backgrounds are forming new social networks to relate to each other. These networks are taking on broader mandates in international relations. They are also intensifying as peoples live in closer proximity in both the Global North and the Global South. Finally, many religionists are sensing commonalities across the religious spectrum based on universal human experiences and challenges.... Globalization often increases contact between humans, with a resulting tension between the local and the global. Frontier missions exist to bridge the possibility of a fully indigenous form of Christianity and one that is tied into the whole of Christianity around the world and throughout human history.[39]

---

39 Johnson, "Globalization, Christian Identity," 165–69.

This shows us in what way globalization was given a new opportunity for world mission. That is, globalization offers a new opportunity through contacts with non-Christians.

Diaspora stands in the middle of great opportunity for social networks between Christians and non-Christians. What then is the strategy of Christian mission in the global era? Wan sees mission as "glocal," non-spatial, and borderless in a global era. Wan describes how traditional missiology moves toward Diaspora missiology in terms of the change from polarized/dichotomized to holistic Christianity, territorial here-and-there to deterritorialzation, and from geographically divided to a non-spatial, borderless, and coming-going mission structure according to God's way of providentially moving.[40] This means that the church tries to make social networks as "glocal," non-spatial, and borderless as well as holistic on a global level. This social network will be the mission field for Diaspora.

Mission as Care and Counsel, proclaimed in Lausanne's Cape Town Declaration

Recently, the concept of mission has focused on healing the hurt. In "The Cape Town Declaration on Care and Counsel as Mission," the Lausanne Movement recognizes the suffering and brokenness, and proclaimed the value of healing:

> We live in a world of unprecedented suffering and brokenness. These human conditions include different types and levels of social and psychological suffering which are often minimized, neglected or, because they are beyond what local people can cope with at a given time, left unattended or addressed from out-of-context perspectives. We believe these omissions are both unjust and costly to individuals and communities. Virtually all of the major public health problems in the world have a psychosocial component. There is no complete health without physical, communal and psychological health . . . It is imperative that we respond to these needs in ways consistent with our Christian commitments and with culturally sensitive, holistic, systemic, and collaborative approaches.[41]

The first confession of the Lausanne Movement is for healing: "We believe that true healing includes reconciliation with God, oneself, one's neighbor,

---

40. Wan, *Diaspora Missiology*, 99.
41. Third Lausanne Congress, "Content Library: The Cape Town Declaration."

one's enemy, and creation through Christ." In consistence with Lausanne's confession, Diaspora missiology focuses on care and counsel, leading to healing the wounded souls. Diaspora should develop the program of healing souls. The church should develop healing programs to approach unreached people. The world is full of hurt and suffering. The church provides mission for healing people.

Here is evidence of how healing is essential in the mission field. The Reverend Dr. Kenneth Bailey, a longtime missionary in the Middle East and renowned contextual theologian, interpreted the Scriptures through plays, poems, and other forms of literature. He wrote a poem in the Palestinian context, which offers us a vivid picture of pain and healing. It is called, "Resurrection: Ode on a Burning Tank." This poem was written in the Holy Land, in October 1973, during the time of a major, but short, twenty-day war between Israel, Egypt and Syria. This is part of his poem:

> I am a voice,
> The voice of spilt blood
> crying from the land.
>
> The life is in the blood
> And for years my blood flowed in the veins of a young man.
>
> . . .
>
> And I was spilt into the earth—
> Into the holy earth
> of the Holy Land.[42]

This poem signifies how essential healing ministry is in relation to mission; all the world has been covered by blood, war, killing, losing beloved family, disease, famine, injustice . . . Christian mission should have the spiritual power to heal in addition to physical aids.

Finally, Peter Makari concluded his article like this: "This poem is an illustration of mission as healing. When we comprehend the pain of people—our neighbors—in the world and commit to do something about it, in a dignified and respectable way."[43] The church should hear the voices of pain from the mission field; so the church should be filled with a compassionate heart to heal them. In particular, refugee diaspora, next-door neighbors, is an urgent mission field that Diaspora mission church should pay attention to.

---

42. This poem was quoted from Makari, "Mission as Healing," 9–10.
43. Ibid.

4) Strategy of Diaspora Mission Church: Becoming Global Diaspora

How does Diaspora engage in world evangelism? It is possible in that all members are Diaspora, the seed of the kingdom scattered in many fields around the world. The strategy of Diaspora mission church in world evangelism is that all Diaspora become a global Diaspora who were scattered in fields for God's redemption globally. That is, world evangelism starts with the confession and living of Diaspora as the seed of God. In particular, any place in the global era is full of strangers next door, which implies that every place is mission field. This also implies that all members at anytime can preach the gospel to unreached people in any place. This is the reality of contemporary mission.

Diaspora as the Seed of God

Diaspora are people who left the place of their birth and live in different countries around the world. Diaspora formed the Diaspora and see them as potential missionaries. As mentioned earlier, Diaspora are the seed of the kingdom: they are called to be his elect and mission from the biblical/theological perspective. However, as Johnson puts it, "Christians have little significant contact with Muslims, Hindus, and Buddhists. Recent research reported in the Atlas reveals that as many as 86% of all Muslims, Hindus, and Buddhists do not personally know a Christian. This is surprising in light of the more than 200 million people who are now on the move across national borders—putting diverse peoples in closer proximity."[44]

In this circumstance, the concept of Diaspora, a seed of the kingdom, plays a key role in world evangelization, and Diaspora community should be networked and built up for world evangelization. In Acts 2, when God gave birth to the church, he gathered Diaspora around the world that no one knew, and scattered them again for his redemptive plan. Diaspora is God's secret strategy of mission. That is the church in the Bible; we must turn to this text for the restoration of church and mission.

Diaspora as the Secret of God's Mission

In Acts 6, the apostles selected seven Diasporas and laid their hand upon them; God sent them to break through the frontiers of mission—Samaritan

---

44. Johnson, "Globalization, Christian Identity," 166.

and the Gentile; Philip was used to open Samaritan mission, and the blood seed of Stephan was used to open the frontier of the Gentile. These events affirm why we should turn back to Diaspora missiology. Diasporas are sometimes the ones who God hides from human eyes or the church's ministrations. How can the institutional church cover all areas of the world for mission? It is almost impossible. Thus, the church should look for Diaspora missionaries more and train them for God's secret time. We don't know where and how God will use them as the seed of the kingdom. We just know God himself uses them for his redemptive plan in his own time. This is the dynamics of Diaspora mission.

Originally, Philip and Stephan were appointed not for evangelism, but for the daily distribution of food (Acts 6:2). Surprisingly, however, the church later found out that God used them for his plan of evangelism. "8Now Stephen, a man full of God's grace and power, performed great wonders and signs among the people" (Acts 6:8). Of most importance is that at that time, no one in that church knew or forecast that seven people would be used for God's plan of mission, in which he used Philip for Samaritan mission and Stephan for a martyrdom seed for Gentile mission. The only thing that the church did was to proclaim high-level spiritual qualities for church ministers, and recruit and set them up over congregation. It was God that used them in his own time and according to his own way. Therefore, the church focuses on suggesting high-level criteria for church ministry, recruiting, and training, and later God will use them for his eternal plan. That is the secret of God in mission.

5) Interdisciplinary Methodology

Diaspora can be understood in interdisciplinary lens because diaspora is in the context of global flows. This shows that studies and understandings of diaspora are indispensable. The following is to explain why we need the lens of interdisciplinary studies.

Church Frameworks from Lens of Interdisciplinary Perspectives

Diaspora mission church practices all processes of its ministry with the lens of interdisciplinary perspectives. Diaspora church-mission recognizes that diaspora live in contexts of interdisciplinary needs; this means that the church frameworks—worship, evangelism, education, ministry—should be transformed to help diaspora with interdisciplinary needs. For this, first of all, the church focuses on interdisciplinary interpretations and applications of the Bible:

(A) Interdisciplinary studies should offer new insights for interpretations of the Bible. That is, interdisciplinary studies make an interpreter understand diaspora interdisciplinarily for deep and broad understandings of diaspora in the complex of globalization, "involving comparative interaction of different forms."[45]

(B) Interdisciplinary studies of diaspora offer ways in which the messages of the Bible can be applied. The gospel should be applied holistically to all areas of human being.

(C) Interdisciplinary understandings of diaspora through the interpretation and application of the Bible offer ideas for holistic ministries regarding diaspora.

After interdisciplinary interpretations of the Bible are made, the church is operated in the understandings of interdisciplinary perspectives: anthropology, communications, comparative religions, philosophy of religion, history, educational studies, linguistics, linguistic anthropology, and theology. These interdisciplinary subjects contribute to forming Diaspora mission church. In particular, ministries to diaspora are interdisciplinary because they are intertwined with interdisciplinary contexts; healing ministry calls for the varied knowledge of social psychology, therapy theory, sociology, social behaviors, social relations, conflict theory, and so on.[46]

Interdisciplinary Approach for Global Ministries

Globalization is an interdisciplinary phenomenon, as Johnson defines the globalization: "Globalization is best thought of as a multidimensional set of social processes (economic, political, cultural, technological, and ecological) that resists being confined to any single thematic framework."[47] It is this complexity in globalization that has strong implications, both for Christian identity and for frontier missions."[48] This shows how missiology is essentially conducted in the global era. In particular, because diaspora is the product of globalization, intertwined with various interdisciplinary phenomena, interdisciplinary approaches should be considered.

---

45. Robertson, *Globalization*, 27.
46. Spradly and McCurdy, *Conformity and Conflict*.
47. Johnson, "Globalization, Christian Identity," 166.
48. Ibid.

The church should always remember that the global Christian community is in the complexity of globalization; for this, we need interdisciplinary approaches to its complex phenomena, which increase communions and networks for relating both within and outside of their traditions. Many of these networks have expanded their activities through deeper and broader cooperation. Recently, the *Global Interdisciplinary Studies Series* was published, edited by Professor Sai Felicia Krishna-Hensel, FRGS, Interdisciplinary Global Studies Research Initiative, and Auburn University, USA.[49] This series reflects a global study tendency: "Comparative and comprehensive in concept, this series explores the relationship between transnational and regional issues through the lens of widely applicable *interdisciplinary* methodologies and analytic models" (italics mine).[50] This series shows how interdisciplinary global studies are. For reference, the interdisciplinary research methodology that Wan introduced for studying Diaspora missiology is eightfold: anthropology, demography, economics, geography, history, law, political science, and sociology.[51] Imagine how these interdisciplinary studies and knowledge make the ministry of the church abundant!

6) Ministry: Incarnational/Holistic Ministries

On a final level, Diaspora church-mission transforms the frameworks of ministry. This means that the church should create ministries pivoting on a centeredness of Diaspora. This can be viewed in terms of the following of three issues.

(1) Contextualized Ministries

Theological implications of contextual theologizing should finally go to the ministry. As Hiebert puts it, theologizing accompanies contextualized ministry. He says, "Here the incarnation is our model. Just as the infinite creator became incarnate as a human to reach finite people, so the divine revelation must take flesh in human language and cultures. Just as Christ chose to live in a particular time and setting, so we must incarnate our ministry in the context of the gospel we serve."[52] Sometimes we are satisfied with intellectual

---

49. Krishna-Hensel, "Global Interdisciplinary Studies Series," 1–6.
50. Ibid.
51. Wan, *Diaspora Missiology*, 111.
52. Hiebert and Hiebert, *Incarnational Ministries*, 370.

contextualization for communications only, without applications based on newly discovered theory.

As mentioned earlier, the concept of Diaspora finds many contextualizing factors: transcendence, embracing, reconciliation, identity, heaven ... a biblical contextualization makes for effective communications. Hiebert continues:

> True contextualization is more than communications. It is God working in the heart of people, making them new and forming them into a new community ... it is his word transforming their lives, their societies and their cultures ... incarnation takes place when the gospel and the messenger become a part of the life of a community.[53]

Real contextualized ministries bring about what Hiebert said above; it is remembered, "True contextualization is more than communications." That is, the goal of contextualization is not just communication; it can communicate the Bible into the context, and bring about transformation trough the Word and the Holy Spirit.

(2) Incarnational Ministries

The goal of incarnational ministry is not that people understand the gospel. It is that they respond to God's invitation and are transformed by his power. They become new creatures through Christ and members of a new community, the church. Gibbs and Bolger, Fuller Seminary researchers, spent five years collecting data in both the US and UK from 2000 to 2005, interviewing fifty leaders to uncover important patterns among emerging churches. Here, "emerging church movement represents a rapidly evolving scenario."[54]

The authors found the insight that the "emerging church" seeks to end the dualistic spilt between sacred and secular so that all of life becomes sacred.[55] Based on this finding, the church is in decline is because of the incarnation. They state:

> Those who call themselves Christians must take seriously the incarnation of Jesus Christ. He took our culture and our practice; he became one of us. He participated in the local life of the Jews in all their cultural variety. He made himself accessible. "The

---

53. Ibid.
54. Gibbs and Bolger, *Emerging Churches*, 7.
55. Ibid., 80.

Word became flesh and made his dwelling [literally 'pitched his tent'] among us" (John 1:14).

As Jesus did, we must immerse ourselves in the local culture of our time. As Jesus did, we must provide a critique, but that evaluation must come from within rather than be imposed from outside the cultural context.[56]

The authors propose that the church must study the culture, and immerse in the culture, which is the meaning of being incarnational. This research shows how the incarnational approach is essential to the church ministry. One of the fifty leaders said, "You say the gospel by living it. Changing worship might be interesting but the focus must be the incarnation. I won't live or die for worship meeting, but I would give my life for living incarnationally, and ultimately Christianity is about what you live and die for."[57]

(3) Holistic Ministry based on the Holistic Gospel and the Cross of Christ

What in the world is holistic mission? Brian E. Woolnough and Wonsuk Ma find the basis of holistic mission in holistic gospel:

> Holistic mission, or integral mission, implies God is concerned with the whole person, the whole community: body, mind and spirit. Many Christians concentrate only on one aspect ... It considers the meaning of the holistic gospel, how it has developed, and implications for the individual Christian, for the local church, for denominations and church groups, for missionary societies, for Christian NGOs, and for theological training.[58]

Sometimes, however, holistic ministries are suspect of loose relation to the gospel centeredness in mission; in this situation, Chris Wright, Chair of the Lausanne Theology Working Group, argues that holistic ministry is based on the cross of Christ. He interestingly remarks:

> The redemptive work of God through the cross of Christ is good news for every area of life. In short, we need a holistic gospel because the world is in a holistic mess. By God's incredible grace we have a gospel big enough to redeem all that sin and evil has touched. And every dimension of that good news is good news only because of the blood of Christ on the cross. Holistic mission

---

56. Ibid., 16.
57. Ibid., 80.
58. Woolnough and Ma, *Holistic Mission: God's Plan*.

must have a holistic theology of the cross. The cross must be as central to our social engagement as it is to our evangelism. There is no other power, no other resource, no other name, through which we can offer the whole gospel to the whole person and the whole world, than Jesus Christ crucified and risen.[59]

For Wright, the reason that holistic mission comes from the cross of Christ is because the cross of Christ reaches all areas of life. The cross of Christ should be the center of holistic ministry.

THREE AREAS OF DIASPORA CHURCH-MISSION

How do we distinguish Diaspora church-mission? According to Tira's explanation of Diaspora missiology, it includes three areas: "Missions to the Diasporas," "Missions through the Diasporas," and "Missions beyond the Diasporas."[60] Here the point is that there is no separation of these three ministries; they are organically connected to one another. The classification of the three areas is made according to the spiritual development level of Diaspora. I will apply these classifications to three ministry areas of Diaspora mission church; I borrow the classifications, but the contents are filled by the present author's own intentions.

1) Missions to the Diasporas

The first area of Diaspora church-mission is the mission to the diaspora. This means that the church and Christians reach diaspora for the Great Commission, which is the open door to the lost people. J. D. Payne says:

We must reach the unreached who have migrated into our neighborhoods. Many of the world's unreached peoples have migrated not only to the West but also to many countries of the Majority World, offering the Church there wonderful Great Commission opportunities to respond in love, service, and sharing the faith. Many of the strangers next door are the keys to unlocking doors into the lostness of people you and I will never be able to meet.[61]

---

59. Wright, "Re-affirming Holistic Mission," 100–123.
60. LCWE, *Scattered to Gather*, 27–30.
61. Payne, "Mission To, Through, and Beyond."

What is included in the mission to diaspora? The church is a second home for diaspora. For example, according to Min and Kim, over 70 percent of Korean Americans regularly attend approximately 3,500 Korean churches every Sunday.[62] This shows how important the church is to the diaspora. For the "Mission to the Diasporas," there are key issues and training curriculum, pulled from principles mentioned earlier.

Key Issues

- Diasporas live in contexts in which they left their homeland and live a foreign country.
- Diasporas experience cultural shock, language and cultural issues, and diaspora trauma.
- Diasporas experience anger, un-safety, and fear.
- Diasporas have an international tie with their homeland.
- Diasporas want to have a new identity and belonging in their host country.
- Diasporas come here by God's redemptive plan.

Training Curriculum

- Diasporas need to accept Jesus Christ as their savior.
- Diasporas need to understand why they are here.
- Diasporas need to be provided with safety in Christ and a new country.
- Diasporas need to have a fellowship and reconciliation with other diaspora, and their host country.
- Diasporas need to have a new transcendent identity of Diaspora beyond national identities.
- Diasporas need to be healed regarding their hurt emotions and sufferings.
- Diasporas need to be provided with cultural adaptation—multiculturalism.[63]

---

62. Min and Kim, *Religions in Asian America*, 205.

63. Here, "Multiculturalism is a body of thought in political philosophy about the proper way to respond to cultural and religious diversity. Mere toleration of group differences is said to fall short of treating members of minority groups as equal citizens;

260　Doing Diaspora Missiology Toward "Diaspora Mission Church"

Case Study 1: OMF International

OMF International (formerly the China Inland Mission and Overseas Missionary Fellowship) was founded by James Hudson Taylor in 1865. Its vision is, "Through God's grace, we aim to see an indigenous, biblical church movement in each people group of East Asia, evangelizing their own people and reaching out in mission to other peoples."[64] In particular, the OMF has Diaspora ministries and tries to reach out to East Asian peoples who are scattered around the globe. The OMF explains its Diaspora ministry like this:

> There are over 200 million migrants around the world today. 85 million of these come from East Asia. OMF Diaspora ministries seek to reach out to these East Asian People who are *scattered* around the globe, living outside their home countries. This means reaching Mainland Chinese in the USA, Japanese in Germany and Thais in Australia. As the people of East Asia move around the world we will seek to reach them with the life-saving message of Jesus Christ *so that they can return to their home country and take the gospel to their friends and families.*[65] (Italics mine)

Here the important point is that the OMF ministers to diaspora for "mission through the diaspora." The reason this strategy is so important is that it can contribute to mission to unreached people in Asia. Furthermore, the OMF suggests several ways to welcome diaspora and train them for mission:

- Start a Bible study for international students.
- Attend international holiday events (e.g., Chinese New Year, Japanese Spring Festival, and Oktoberfest) and meet people.
- Host events to celebrate Christmas, Thanksgiving, Canada Day, etc.
- Partner with organizations such as International Student Ministry Canada (www.ismc.ca) or Inter-Varsity.
- Adopt a newcomer to Canada.
- Offer English classes for internationals through your church.
- Offer students help with rides for groceries and other errands.

---

recognition and positive accommodation of group differences are required through "group-differentiated rights," a term coined by Will Kymlicka (1995). Multiculturalism will make diaspora be reformed along with diverse cultures and identities. This will serve foundation for multicultural ministries. See Song, "Multiculturalism," lines 3–5.

64. OMF International, "About OMF International," lines 5–10.

65. OMF International, "Diaspora Ministries," lines 10–19.

- Host an "around town" event: take internationals new to your area on a tour of different points of interest.[66]

There is a special way to minister to diaspora: "partnership." The OMF ministers to diaspora in partnership with Christian organizations such as International Student Ministry Canada or Inter-Varsity. Furthermore, the OMF supports church partnerships; through church partnerships, OMF International desires to partner with mission-minded churches . . . its goals are threefold.

. . . To better support missionaries that you know . . .

. . . To develop strategic missions plans . . .

. . . To help church leaders inform and inspire church members . . . by providing people and resources!

The OMF lists what it calls the "Three P's of Partnership": prayer, provide, and participate. In particular, the OMF *provides resources* and logistical support to those who are working to bring Christ to the peoples of East Asia. It provides funds for field projects and field workers who can help to evangelize to East Asia; it provides support and training for those who feel called by God to serve East Asia; and it provides the following programs: sending short term service teams, long term service teams, volunteer projects, and observation programs.

In a word, OMF International ministers to East Asian diaspora by providing programs for diaspora, building up local church partnership for East Asian evangelization. Finally, the OMF provides training courses for Diaspora. The training covers some of the following issues:

- How to befriend and welcome East Asians into your church.
- How to understand their mindset, culture, religion, and worldview.
- How to evangelize to East Asians.
- How to disciple, mentor, and do Bible studies with East Asians.
- How to prepare someone who's returning to East Asia as a Christian.[67]

These issues that the OMF uses to approach diaspora are applicable to Diaspora ministry and the mission of the local church; or local churches can build social organizations outside the church, i.e., can do Diaspora ministries through specialized organizations in partnership with the parachurch, for example, ethnic group-based parachurch ministries.

---

66. Ibid.
67. OMF International, "Training for Churches," lines 1–10.

Case Study 2: Korean Diaspora Church

In a dissertation on Korean Diaspora ministry, Sinyil Kim did a study on Korean immigrants with a mission to investigate the way Scripture, self-identity, and mission are understood among Korean immigrants in the United States and Canada.[68] The study's methodology utilizes interviews and onsite visits; six Korean immigrant churches were analyzed: (A) Grace Korean Church of Vancouver, (B) Community Church of Seattle, (C) Seoul Baptist Church of Houston, (D) Young Nak Korean Church of Toronto, (E) Ken Bit Korean Church of Toronto, and (F) Sarang Community Church of Los Angeles.

The following are the conclusions of the dissertation; three major findings are significant toward understanding Korean Diaspora churches and ministries.

IDENTITY TRANSFORMATION

Regarding his identity transformation, the author confesses:

> For nearly three years, this passive and negative marginality-related struggle continued taking place until something happened, until I experienced my self-transcending moment, a significant "identity transformation." Through this experience, suddenly everything around me changed: my meaning and motivation for life, my attitude toward life's context, my pastoral goals in the church, and so on. What was this experience and how did it happen? My identity transformation began when I started to read the Scriptures through the eyes of an immigrant.[69]

This confession implies that the identity transformation solves every struggle and problem: "suddenly everything around me changed: my meaning and motivation for life, my attitude toward life's context, my pastoral goals in the church, and so on." Here identity transformation changes Diaspora consciousness and thinking.

---

68. Kim, "Korean Immigrants and their Mission."
69. Ibid, 109–10.

The Importance of Bible Study for Identity Transformation

Regarding the importance of Bible study for identity transformation, the author introduced his experience:

> One day I discovered that the Bible relates many important frameworks of moving: moving of Abraham to Canaan, moving of Jacob's family (70 people) into Egypt, moving of the Israelites from Egypt to the wilderness under Moses' leadership, moving and conquering into Canaan under Joshua's leadership, Israel's moving out and returning because of exile and recovery, Jesus' moving into history (incarnation) and his itinerant ministry, believers' spreading from Jerusalem to the Gentile lands, Paul and other church leaders' moving around the world for mission, and similar examples.[70]

Here it is noted that he found the key concept of "moving" in the Bible; the theme of the Bible is Diaspora. A major tool to transform the identity of diaspora is the Bible study. The author asserts that a new context of Diaspora is a place of God's calling, God's training and a new beginning. He sates:

> I also realized that my new context, the margin of a new society, can be a place of God's calling (Genesis 28:10–20; Exodus 3:1–12; Judges 10:2–3), a place of God's training (Daniel 1:8–17; Jonah 2:1–10; Matthew 4:1–11), and a place for a new beginning (1 Kings 19:1–18; Acts 8:26; 1 Timothy 3:16).[71]

That is, the context of diaspora as marginal is a place of God's calling, a place of God's training, and a place for a new beginning. This shows that immigrant churches are exactly diaspora centered.

Diaspora's Missional Potential out of Immigrant Experience

It can be argued that God has blessed Korea immensely during the last century through remarkable church growth and mission expansion and that God wants to raise Koreans to be an increasingly effective instrument for world mission today. Many Korean Christians believe that God has been

---

70. Ibid, 111.
71. Ibid.

active in Korean history, church growth, and global dispersion, preparing them for a key role in Christian mission.[72]

Here, of most importance is that the Korean Diaspora "discovers their missional potential as they build constructively upon their unique immigrant experiences." Korean immigrant Christians see a self as pilgrims, and see their context as marginal. Korean Christians have self-consciousness under God's providence; their ultimate purpose of immigrant life is a "kingdom dream" rather than an "American/Canadian dream." Finally, the church tries to teach that the church also should be Diaspora spiritually and theologically. All human beings were banished from the garden of Eden by God and scattered, longing for God's redemption. All Christians are scattered as the seed of the kingdom, and now wait for the second coming of Jesus and move toward heaven. This is evidence that we are all Diaspora. The feeling of this identity environs all Christians to do mission for diasporas, namely, immigrants.

2) Missions through the Diasporas

The second area of Diaspora missiology is "mission through the Diasporas." This stage comes after the evangelizing and sanctifying of Diaspora. At this level, Diaspora can be called as missionaries. Jason Mandryk noted, "Nearly every country is a missionary-sending country. What used to happen 'from the West to the rest' is now an extensive and expanding global activity. Missionary vision is alive even in those countries where the Church is young, small or under persecution."[73] Tira calls Diaspora Christians "the largest self-supporting contingency of missionary force."[74] Tira continues:

> Missions through the Diaspora refer to the Diasporas believers returning to their countries to share the good news and plant churches among their peoples. According to the Lausanne Diaspora Leadership Team, "Christians living in the Diaspora context represent the largest self-supporting contingency of missionary force which has been located within many of the so-called 'unreached peoples' and accessible to practically all people-groups of the world today.[75]

---

72. Ibid., 113.
73. Mandryk, *Operation World*, 949.
74. Ibid.
75. LCWE, *Scattered to Gather*, 28.

The Transcendent Nature of the Church

According to the Lausanne Diaspora Leadership Team, Tira argues, "Christians living in the Diaspora context represent the largest self-supporting contingency of missionary force which has been located within many of the so-called 'unreached peoples' and accessible to practically all people-groups of the world today." In principle, this statement is biblical and missional; but in reality most diaspora suffer and hurt in a foreign land in every day; they worry about children, education, and financial problems. Thus, for the Diaspora context to represent the largest self-supporting contingency of missionary force, with Christian educational curriculum, Diaspora missiology provides systematic training on their missionary identity and ministries. Wan also argues that missions through the Diasporas are the new paradigm of twenty-first century missiology. Diaspora mission is global mission, wherever Diaspora live around the world.

Here, the essential awareness in Diaspora missiology is to define Diaspora as potential missionaries. In contrast to professional missionaries, Diaspora missionaries were, in advance, brought to a mission field by God; they already had an advanced language skills, understood the context, and were familiar with the community and its neighbors; they were ready and used for God's mission only if they were given a minimum proper training for mission. How much money is invested before a professional missionary is trained and begins to minister in a mission field? However, Diaspora missionaries are already there. With a low cost financially, mission works can be activated.

There is an important report regarding ministry through the Diaspora. Ellen Oxford and Lynellyn D. Long report that of the thirty million people who migrated to the United States between 1900 and 1980, ten million (one-third) returned home; according to the United Nations High Commission for Refugees, from the 1990s to 2004, there was a steady rise in the number of return refugees as well.[76] This shows how a high percentage of diaspora return home; and diaspora are not permanent residents. Why did they immigrate into a Christian nation? It is God's providence for the redemption of his elect if it is not the case with all immigrants. The crucial issue lies in how Diaspora missiology is interested in equipping Diaspora for evangelism and preaching the gospel when returning home. Here are the key issues and training curricula for doing "mission through the Diaspora."

---

76. Oxfeld and Long, *Coming Home*, 1–2.

Key issues

- Diaspora can understand diaspora culturally and psychologically better than anyone else.
- Diasporas feel disappointed in a diaspora community situation, and they experience conflict and division within the members, and bitterness grows.
- Diaspora should be equipped before entering ministry.
- Diaspora are in pursuit of cultural plausibility—language.
- Diasporas will return home someday.
- Diaspora churches should have fellowship with homeland people and churches in both the homeland and diaspora countries.

It is noted that "mission through Diaspora" is not easy; it presupposes the being born again and God's calling of Diaspora. Immigrant diaspora are the secret field of God's redemptive consummation. Mission is next door; the issue is whether the church and its members see the missional vision of God through Diaspora or not. The church in Jerusalem preached the gospel to diaspora and helped them to become missionaries for God's world evangelization (Acts 2).

Training Curriculum

- Diaspora need to be provided with the core biblical teachings from the overview of the Bible.
- Diaspora need to have studied cultures and other major religions from Christian perspectives.
- Diaspora need to have a knowledge of presenting the gospel with their own personal testimony of God's guidance, salvation, and blessing.
- Diaspora need to have a knowledge of counseling others.
- Diaspora need to have English classes for effective communication.
- Diaspora need to know how to build networks with others.
- Diaspora churches need to encourage Diaspora to have personal fellowship with their family, relatives, and friends.
- Diaspora churches need to have a global network for evangelical mission and with their homeland churches.

Here it deserves to be noted that refugees are diaspora; Christian mission includes them in the category of Diaspora. The UN refugee agency reports annual statistics, showing that more than fifty-one million people were forcibly displaced at the end of 2013; this was the largest number since the end of World War II.[77] In particular, recent wars in the Middle East brought about many refugees. Diaspora mission should provide any aid for them, which is good chance for unreached people mission.

3) Missions beyond the Diasporas

Regarding the relationship of "Ministering through and beyond Diaspora," Wan and Tira state:

> Ministering *through* and *beyond* diaspora are two other aspects of practicing diaspora missions. These two approaches are to be employed in order to seize new opportunities created by the phenomenon of diaspora. Diaspora congregations are to be mobilized for the Great Commission when individual Christians are motivated and empowered to carry out their missionary duties. This is what is meant by minister *through* the Diaspora. When members of the Diaspora groups have acquired the language and are adjusted to the culture of the host society, they are the natural bridges for minister *beyond* them to reach others of host societies and countries.[78]

Here, the ministry through Diaspora means Diaspora's ministry to host countries. This implies that members of the Diaspora have acquired the language and are adjusted to the culture of the host society, and become the natural bridges to reach others of the host societies and countries. The second area is missions beyond the Diasporas in which Diaspora cooperate with host churches and Christians, leading to cross-cultural missionary labors through their partnership. The third area is based on the awareness that the Diaspora is a partner with host Christians.

"Mission beyond Diaspora" encourages Diaspora believers to see themselves as missionaries who are to evangelize to host countries. According to J. D. Payne, the concept of "missions beyond the Diasporas" implies that Diaspora believers are not only called to reach their own peoples but are also to be involved in cross-cultural missionary works. But many Americans

---

77. Guterres, "World Refugee Day," lines 1–10.
78. Wan and Tira, "Diaspora Missiology and Mission," 56.

are not aware of the mission perspective that there are a large number of followers of Jesus sent by God.[79]

Now it is time to see mission in terms of everyday life; in fact, we see the target people of missions living as our neighbors. Here and now, global networks of Diaspora for world evangelization are possible any time and any place. Mission is as near as next door and in our everyday life, but the real issue is that we have no awareness of it. Here are the key issues and training curricula for "mission beyond Diaspora."

Key Issues

- Diaspora [church] as foreigners live in a host country.
- Diaspora should obey the social and legal order of the host country.
- The responsibility of the host people and church toward Diaspora is hospitality.
- Diaspora and host people are next-door neighbors to witness the gospel.
- Diaspora and host people are partners for his kingdom.
- Partnership between Diasporas and host churches is evangelization for global evangelization.
- Diaspora is the secret of the growth and revival of the host church.

For example, the church in Jerusalem selected seven workers for the daily distribution of food, but God used these people for his mission (Acts 6). Philip was used to preach the gospel in Samaria; in preaching the gospel, Stephan died, stoned by Jews, and his blood paved the way for preaching the gospel in Antioch, one of the major Hellenistic cities (Acts 11:19–20).

Training

- Diaspora need to study and learn the social order and law of the host country.
- Diaspora need to understand why God guided them to the host country.
- Diaspora and host people and churches need to meet periodically and regionally for worship, fellowship, and evangelization.

79. Payne, *Strangers Next Door*.

The Transcendent Nature of the Church 269

- Each Diaspora and host needs to present and explain each culture, and help each other understand the culture of the other.
- Host churches need to show compassion and love to Diaspora through various events.
- Global mission teams seek Diaspora for unreached people.
- How to build global networks.
- Understanding other cultures—mutual understanding.

"Mission beyond Diaspora" is related to world evangelization; here one of the major objectives is to understand and embrace other cultures and build up a global network. How we become humble and incarnated in the lives others is the most essential class for mission beyond Diaspora.

Case Study: Partnership between the Korean Diaspora and Korean Homeland Churches for Global Diasporas in Korea

In "From Edinburgh 1910 to Tokyo 2010," David Chul Han Jun asserts that Korean church mission is developed through Korean Diaspora mission: "Korean mission movements rise from recent mission forum and network on Korean diasporas and from major Korean mission meetings. The followings are such movements: Korea Students All Nations (KOSTA, 1985), Mission Korea (MK, 1988), Korean World Mission Council for Christ (KWMC, 1988), Korean World Missions Association (KWMA), Korea Diaspora Missions Network (KODIMNET), etc. Various mission meetings have emphasized the importance of the Korean diaspora mission and its network."[80]

Introducing the memorandum of the ninth Korea mission of leader forum, declared by the KWMA in December 2009, Han argues that world mission should be developed by Diaspora. The following is the statement:

> We need to notice the significance of world mission through Diasporas, and especially the Korean Diaspora because of their church development through "three-self formula": self-supporting, self-propagating, and self-governing.[81]

This Korean Diaspora church development should become a model to other nations for Diaspora church establishment. All Diaspora churches should become self-supporting, self-propagating, and self-governing, so that they

---

80. Jun, "World Christian Mission," 171–73.
81. Ibid.

will become missional churches wherever they are. Here is the process of partnership between the Korean Diaspora and homeland church.

Development of Korean Diaspora Church, Supported by Korean Homeland Churches

Korean homeland churches are paying attention to the Korean Diaspora churches. They were dispersed all over the world due to historical, economic, and military reasons. Wherever they have gone, they have voluntarily established churches and have become missionary sending stations. The Korean Diaspora churches have been approved by missionaries for their great contribution to world mission. The Korean Diaspora churches and missionaries should co-operate; in other words, lay leaders in the Korean Diaspora churches and missionaries should support each other by taking different roles to fulfill world mission.

Here, for mission through the Diaspora, it is essential that there should be an intimate connection between Korea Diaspora and the homeland; generally speaking, the Diaspora church and homeland church need partnership for world mission. For example, the president of the Global Mission Society (GMS) at the Korean Presbyterian church [*Hapdong* Denomination] says, "because we have an American communications office in the west area of the USA, we need to nominate corporate directors from the west, and include Korean American pastors with permanent residence or citizenship to make North and South America a bridgehead of mission for world mission."[82] This is a case example of the partnership between Korean Diaspora and the homeland.

Involvement of Korean Diaspora Mission within the Republic of Korea

Recently, Korean Diasporas who return home have ministered to the Korean homeland; regarding the rush of Korean immigrant pastors to return to Korea, they show both positive and negative responses to it. Surprisingly, senior pastors of mega-churches were invited from the Korean immigrant church; the biggest mega-church in Korea, Yoedo Full Gospel church, invited immigrant pastor Lee Young Hoon, who ministered in an immigrant Korean church.[83] This shows how the Korean Diaspora affects its homeland

---

82. Gu, "Opening of American Office of GMS," 11–15.
83. Yun, "How does Immigrant Church," lines 20–23.

churches. Also it shows that in a global era, there are global networks of churches around the world, without boundary lines.

Partnership between Korean Diaspora Churches and the Korean Homeland: Mission for Foreigners (Global Diaspora) in Korea.

Korean Diaspora who live in the homeland are involved global Diaspora ministry, focusing on ministries to other ethnic diasporas living in Korea. Korean Diaspora have the same feeling as other ethnic diaspora living and suffering in a Korean foreign land because they had the same suffering in a foreign land, the USA. Leviticus 19:34 is on their heart: "The foreigner residing among you must be treated as your native-born. Love them as yourself, for you were foreigners in Egypt. I am the Lord your God." The teaching of the verse inspires Korean Diaspora more than Korean homeland people, and mission and ministry to other diaspora in Korea has begun recently. This is an example of the Korean Diaspora's mission to the homeland.

It is worthwhile to take notice of Korean and other Diasporas in the world, and we should use Diasporas within the Republic of Korea for world mission. We have to take a careful look at various types of Diasporas within Korea in order to develop appropriate training programs for them. Our goals for Diaspora mission in South Korea are witnessing, discipleship, and missionary training because they are future missionaries for their own countries. We need to continuously develop worship services for diasporas in Korea according to their major tribal groups and languages. Korean mission society should provide workers for this ministry. For this migrant mission, we also need to have various networks to have more effective ministries.[84]

ADVENTURE TOWARD DOING DIASPORA MISSION CHURCH IN A SECULARIZED CRISIS OF CHRISTIANITY

World Christianity has suffered from a secularized society, faith, and church; generally speaking, Christian theology in the West become deistic, which rejects the biblical God and churches, and instead relies on reason and experience only. The Christian world is filled with secularism, pluralism, relativism, atheism . . . Asian churches also are in the same situation; the Korean church, one of the leading churches in Asia, suffered from religious pluralism, secularism, and the moral corruption of churches and the

84. Ibid, 172.

rise of anti-Christians. What is the revival of Christian faith and church in secularized society? Now we do not limit our concern to mission only, but it is time to reconsider Christianity itself for its revival.

Voices of Crisis from Contemporary Secularized Churches

Recently, Ex-Archbishop George Carey in England warned of a crisis in Christianity, saying "Church 'is on the brink of extinction.'" Here are three points he warns of:

(1) "We ought to be ashamed of ourselves. We are one generation away from extinction—if we do not invest in young people there is going to be no one in the future."

(2) The series of high-level warnings about a looming crisis comes at a time when Christian belief and the Church of England appear under attack on a number of fronts.

(3) The Archbishop of York, who told the General Synod that compared to the need to attract new worshippers, "everything else is like re-arranging furniture when the house is on fire."[85]

This reality is echoed around world Christianity; a major reason for it is a secularization of the faith and church. Thus, firstly, the church focuses on reviving the faith, church, and ministries; and then the revived church can do mission. Without the revival of the church, there is no hope of world mission. That is why American churches turn their interest to homeland mission, missional church movement. Diaspora mission church involves this principle; the church all stands at the valley of dry bones (Ezek 37).

A Sociologist's Warning against the Secular Church: Seeking a Real Transcendence of the Church

Here is a sociologist's warning of the secular church.[86] He sees a secular domination in apparent successes of the church, he points out:

> Behind the many problems of the secular church, however, lies a fundamental problem: there is little place for the God of the Bible in the secular church. In a secular world that must quantify, manage, program and manipulate, the unfathomable mystery and majesty of the biblical God simply does not

---

85. Carey, "Church 'is on the Brink,'" lines 11–13.
86. Holt, "Secular Church," 35–40.

fit. The so-called transcendence of the secular church is a false transcendence which merely uses the Creator in a thinly veiled adoration of and infatuation with the creature.[87]

In a word, essentially secularization does not fit "the unfathomable mystery and majesty of the biblical God." Diasporas essentially are transcendent because they move toward heaven. The spirit of Diaspora can overcome secular minds focusing on earthly things. This does not mean that Christianity does not engage with this world—rather, live like yeast that works all through the dough of the world (Matt 13:33)—but that first of all, its priority is to abstain itself "from sinful desires, which wage war against your soul" (1 Pet 2:11). The transcendent nature of Diaspora mission church in pilgrimage will be an antidote to secularized churches, which strongly have been dominant and wasted the essential functions of the church.

The Renewal of Faith, Church, and Mission through the Concept of Diaspora

As mentioned earlier, the Diaspora is powerfully existent in the biblical church and mission of Philip and Stephan as expressed in Acts 6. Originally, these Diaspora are missionary leaders, foresighted and provided by God himself beyond human knowledge. The church should be provided with these Diaspora for secular culture. It is amazing to see the power of the gospel in Stephen's testimony to the Sanhedrin. As writ in the Bible, "but they could not stand up against the wisdom the Spirit gave him as he spoke" (Acts 6:10). Jesus' gospel could be preached by people such as these; when we believe that, God will provide them. Our real problem is not believing God's promise and methods written in the Bible.

Now is the time to rise up and train Diaspora for living and preaching the gospel in a secular/anti-Christian society. Average or mere Christians could not stand against this secular spirit. We should stop just following secular culture, because faith intertwined with this secularization cannot avoid being compromised or false. Rather the church should focus on calling, discovering, and training Diasporas for his salvation and mission. Diaspora mission church is God's method that can live and preach the gospel in any circumstance. "If only the Holy Spirit will work . . ." This hope, the vision, will be our prayer in this time alone.

In a deep despair, Ezekiel stood in the valley of dry bones. Here is a conversation between God and Ezekiel:

87. Ibid.

> Ezek 37: 1 The hand of the Lord was on me, and he brought me out by the Spirit of the Lord and set me in the middle of a valley; it was full of bones.
> 2 He led me back and forth among them, and I saw a great many bones on the floor of the valley, bones that were very dry.
> 3 He asked me, "Son of man, can these bones live?"
>
> ...
>
> 12 Therefore prophesy and say to them:
> 'This is what the Sovereign Lord says: My people, I am going to open your graves and bring you up from them; I will bring you back to the land of Israel.
> 13 Then you, my people, will know that I am the Lord, when I open your graves and bring you up from them.
> 14 I will put my Spirit in you and you will live, and I will settle you in your own land. Then you will know that I the Lord have spoken, and I have done it, declares the Lord.

9

Healing Empowerment of 'Diaspora Mission Church'

The success and failure of Diaspora mission church depends on the healing and empowering of diaspora, because diaspora are deeply and existentially hurt with scattering and suffering. First of all, diaspora should be healed in the love of the Father, the grace of the Son, and the fellowship of the Holy Spirit. When healed, Diaspora have a new transcendent identity in Christ for making room in themselves for others, and multiculturalism is essential for embracing mentalities and lifestyles. "Healed and empowered Diaspora" tend toward reconciliation and evangelization. Without embracing different others, there is no evangelizing power. Finally, the Diaspora is called to build up a local and global network with the partnership of Diasporas, host and homeland.

HEALING AND RECONCILIATION BEYOND CONFLICT

Cultural Shock of Diaspora

Every diaspora experiences cultural shock in their mindset and life. Culture shock is also called transition shock. Transition shock is a state of loss and disorientation predicated by a change in one's familiar environment that requires adjustment. There are many symptoms of transition shock, some of which include:

- Excessive concern over cleanliness

- Feelings of helplessness and withdrawal
- Irritability
- Anger
- Mood swings
- Glazed stare
- Desire for home and old friends
- Physiological stress reactions
- Homesickness
- Boredom
- Withdrawal
- Getting "stuck" on one thing
- Suicidal or fatalistic thoughts
- Excessive sleep
- Compulsive eating/drinking/weight gain
- Stereotyping host nationals
- Hostility towards host nationals[1]

Diaspora mission church should always acknowledge that diaspora experience transition shock, which is experienced in the seventeen above mentioned symptoms. These symptoms hinder the mentality and life that Diaspora focuses on toward understanding and following the gospel. Thus, it seeks to heal the mental and psychological illnesses of diaspora.

Empathetic Understanding of Suffering in Diaspora

As Safran states, diasporas believe that they are not fully accepted by their host society; they therefore feel partly alienated and insulated from it.[2] For Ember, Ember, and Skoggard, the word "diaspora" refers to historical dispersions of people with common roots that are of an involuntary nature, such as the expulsion of Jews from the Middle East, the African Trans-Atlantic slave trade, the southern Chinese during the coolie slave trade, or the century-long exile of the Messenians under Spartan rule.[3] Generally,

---

1. Steger Center, "Dealing with Culture Shock," lines 20–36.
2. Safran, "Diasporas in Modern Societies," 83–99.
3. Ember, et al., *Encyclopedia of Diasporas*.

migration movements are described as "alienated and insulated," whether the migration is involuntary or voluntary.

The literature above shows that diaspora experience brokenness, alienation, and suffering, which are the essential phenomena of a Diaspora event. It should be remembered that in 1 Peter 1:1, the Apostle Peter uses the word "scattered" along with the word "exile." The scattered are exiles, but also are God's elect. We understand the word "Diaspora" as conveying the calling of God and the experience of exiles. However, current Diaspora missiology literature tends to minimize or ignore the suffering aspect of the Diaspora, and considers the Diaspora community as a missionary to the host nation. Here it is important to have compassion and understanding of Diaspora; compassion is the channel to communicate with suffering Diaspora; it also is a channel to engage the hearts and lives of Diaspora; it is also a channel to bring a strong commitment to God's grace and mission.

For example, the Korean Diaspora church has experienced severe conflict and division among themselves, and many are leaving their homogeneous churches for American churches or for not attending the church at all. These Korean Diasporas are filled with brokenness and suffering; they have an extreme wounded bitterness [*sangcheo*] in their hearts and minds. We think: "Do they themselves become involved in Diaspora mission in this spiritual situation?" Nevertheless, in middle of this suffering, the Korean Diaspora church has a strong commitment to mission, which shows how God's grace works in weak and problematic human beings paradoxically.

Logotherapy's Search for "Meaning" by Viktor Frankl for Healing Diaspora

Dr. Viktor Frankl authored the book, *Man's Search for Meaning: An Introduction to Logotherapy*, in which he "gives a moving account of his life amid the horrors of the Nazi death camps, chronicling the harrowing experience that led to his discovery of his theory of Logotherapy. A profound revelation born out of Dr. Frankl's years as a prisoner in Auschwitz and other concentration camps, logotherapy is a modern and positive approach to the mentally or spiritually disturbed personality. Stressing man's freedom to transcend suffering and find a meaning to his life regardless of his circumstance."[4]

Frankl argues that human beings hold fast to "tragic optimism,"[5] which means that one is and remains optimistic in spite of the "tragic triad," as it is called in logotherapy, a triad which consists of those aspects of human

4. Frankl, *Mans' Search for Meaning*, book cover.
5. Ibid., 139.

existence which may be circumscribed by: (1) pain; (2) guilt; and (3) death. Logotherapy is what is essential to those who are vulnerable to conflict and violence, originating from anger and hatred. If human beings find meaning in life, they overcome stress, anger, and mental disturbance. This therapy is a kind of healing for the heart and personality. In fact, immigrants experience existential frustration, and to apply Frankl's theory, existential frustration can also result in neuroses.[6] The existential analysis is the key to understanding the problems in human being.

Regarding existential analysis, in his collection of works at the Viktor Frankl Institute, Frankl explains, "basically, existential analysis means analysis with respect to existence, or 'explication of existence' with consideration of a self-responsible, self-realized and humane life. In 'general existential analysis,' the pursuit of meaning is discussed and identified as a basic motivation in humans, and arguments are provided that demonstrate the fundamental possibility of finding meaning in life. On this basis the therapeutic effects of a successful search for meaning may be explained."[7]

In this special existential analysis, the specific, individual life of a person or a group is probed for the possible existential roots of a mental or psychological disorder. In this context, it provides the basis for a logotherapy as a specific therapy proceeding via the "existential core." Thus the therapeutic value of existential analysis lies in the elucidation of the concrete existential situation and the preparation for giving assistance in the—autonomous—search for meaning. Ultimately, we can learn from the theory of Frankl that immigrants vulnerable to being wounded are given "assistance in the—autonomous—search for meaning." It looks like Joseph's confession about the meaning of Diaspora:

> Gen 45: 7But God sent me ahead of you to preserve for you a remnant on earth and to save your lives by a great deliverance. 8So then, it was not you who sent me here, but God. He made me father to Pharaoh, lord of his entire household and ruler of all Egypt.

The core content of Joseph's confession is that "it was not you who sent me here, but God." He understands his experience of wounded Diaspora in terms of God's providence and mission. Here, his hurt and wounds were cleansed and removed from his memories and heart. The finding of the meaning helps wounded Diaspora overcome the possible existential roots of a mental or psychological hurt.

---

6. Ibid., 106.

7. Batthyany, "What is Logotherapy," lines 15–21.

Healing: Preaching the Gospel in the Holy Spirit

A main characteristic of diaspora life is stress, leading to conflict and anger, which occur as a result of being exposed to a stressor. Stress changes the brain.[8] This mental and behavioral process is explained in the discipline of neuropsychology, which is the study of the structure and functions of the brain as related through lesion studies in humans. Sometimes, knowledge of neuropsychology is helpful to understand and analyze mental issues, and show application skills, but it has a limitation from healing the hurt soul. The church is the unique place that can give hurt persons the gospel. In particular, it is helpful to understand and analyze the hurt of *yangbanization* on the psyche and brain of immigrant Koreans;[9] the historically long-rooted bitterness-spirit of *yangbanization* and a psyche of *Han* are not well healed by cultural dimensions. Only the gospel brings about repentance. "Repentance is a central theme in the Christian faith. Without it new relationships are not possible."[10] Repentance comes from hearing of the gospel.

For this, first of all, the church needs to preach the gospel to heal the brokenhearted people as Jesus did. This is the first priority of the immigrant church. The gospel itself has healing power. In Isaiah 61:1–3, "the poor," "the brokenhearted," "darkness for the prisoner," "all who mourn," "those who grieve," "mourning and a spirit of despair," are representations of immigrant souls and lives. God has sent a Messiah "to bind up the brokenhearted, to proclaim freedom for the captives, and release from darkness for the prisoners, 2to proclaim the year of the Lord's favor and the day of vengeance of our God, to comfort all who mourn, 3and provide for those who grieve in Zion—to bestow on them a crown of beauty instead of ashes, the oil of joy instead of mourning, and a garment of praise instead of a spirit of despair" (Isa 61:1–3).

Jesus Christ can heal every kind of problem—social, political, psychological, economic, and cultural. Christian psychotherapist Larry Crabb detailed a new methodology of healing a wounded soul. "The idea is this: When two people *connect*, when their beings intersect as closely as two bodies during intercourse, something is poured out of one and into the other that has the power to heal the soul of its deepest wounds and restore it to health. The one who receives experiences the joy of being healed. The one who gives knows the even greater joy of being used to heal. Something good

---

8. DePaulo, *Psychology of Dexter*.
9. Rains, *Principles of Human Neuropsychology*.
10. Kirk, *What is Mission*, 161.

is in the heart of each of God's children that is more powerful than everything bad."[11]

For Crabb, connection is developed into four levels:

(1) Connection with God, bringing belief—he is that good.

(2) Connection with self, bringing "embraced longings and godly consciousness."

(3) Connection with others, bringing "spiritual (self-denying) dynamics as we meet life."

(4) Connection with others, bringing "basic life strategy: yield to the good, resist the bad."[12]

Here the importance is that when a Diaspora connects with God first, they lead to the connection with the self, being healed, and then connect with others, helping them be healed. In this theory, connection is very essential to healing the wounded soul. Based on Luke 15, Volf explains, "the healing by connection" as "the will to embrace," making room for others in ourselves through the cross of Jesus Christ. Ultimately, healing comes by connecting with God, the self, and then others.[13]

DIASPORA IDENTIFY FORMATION: TRANSCENDENT MULTICULTURALISM

Identity Confusion and Transnationalism

As Kibria puts it, immigrants today, rather than severing their ties to their home countries, are sustaining economic, political, and religious ties to their homelands.[14] For the example of Koreans, some literature approaches the issue of immigrants from a transnational perspective.[15] Thus, the essential understanding of Korean immigrant identity is from its transnational study, focusing on its cultural root of nationality. "Transnational ties" serve as a framework to understand and study immigration. This means that without understanding the transnational roots of immigrants, there is no effective policy of immigration.

---

11. Crabb, *Connecting*, xi.
12. Ibid., 81.
13. Volf, *Exclusion & Embrace*.
14. Kibria, "Of Blood, Belonging."
15. Cha, *Koreans in Central California*.

After leaving their homeland, diaspora experience identity confusion and crisis; its resolution does more than address material clashes of interest; it speaks to social reintegration, restoration and redemption, existential security, personal transcendence, and transformation. These concepts are drawn from the backdrop of the sacred, which may be defined as any process that explicitly connects us to the largest possible context to which we belong.[16] This shows how Christian ideas should seek ways in which they function as the agent of conflict resolution.[17]

In particular, Shore examines the ambiguous role that Christianity played in South Africa's Truth and Reconciliation Commission (TRC).[18] Her book has two objectives: (1) to analyze the role Christianity played in the TRC, and (2) to highlight certain consequences that may contribute to conflict resolution processes. Here, an essential issue is to create a self-identity. As Said and Funk put it, it is essential to recognize that the experience of conflict evokes a deep-seated need for affirmation of identity and restoration of meaning.[19]

With regard to Christian identity, as Bloemraad, Korteweg, and Yurdakul put it, in understanding immigration policy, we should go beyond nation-state boundaries and look at transnational, post national, and multi-nationality.[20] That is, it identifies methodological and theoretical challenges in the immigration field, noting the need for a more dynamic and comprehensive understanding of the inter-relationships between the dimensions of citizenship and immigration. It is important that living immigrant Koreans create a transcendent Christian identity beyond national identities which exclude others. In particular, the identity is understood in terms of dynamic change: "Yet what if identity is conceived not as a boundary to be maintained but as a nexus of relations and transactions actively engaging a subject?"[21]

Identity of Diaspora in terms of Interdisciplinary Perspectives

According to Nico Israel, the identity of Diaspora is mainly understood in terms of exile experience:

---

16. Said, et al., *Concepts of International Politics*.
17. Guinn, *Protecting Jerusalem's Holy Sites*.
18. Shore, *Religion and Conflict Resolution*.
19. Said, et al., *Peace and Conflict Resolution*.
20. Bloemraad, et al., "Citizenship and Immigration," 153–79.
21. Clifford, "Diaspora," 344.

Drawing on texts from literary theory, philosophy, psychoanalysis, anthropology, and geography, the author explores what he calls the "rhetoric of displacement"—the struggle to assert identity out of place. He reads this writing predicament against the backdrop of the century's salient economic and technological changes, political upheavals, and mass migrations. In doing so, he draws attention to those aspects of exile and diaspora that have remained insufficiently considered: their relation to nationalism and colonialism, to authority and institutionality, and, above all, to broader questions of subjectivity, "race," location, and language, as these concepts themselves subtly change over the course of the century.[22]

Here, the identity of Diaspora can be understood in terms of the interactions of interdisciplinary studies and approaches to change; the identity of Diaspora, characterized by the "rhetoric of displacement" and the struggle to assert identity out of place, hints to how the struggle is for Diaspora in forming identity. What is the definition of identity? Generally, the identity is "the collective aspect of the set of characteristics by which a thing is definitively recognizable or known"; identity "refers to the ways in which individuals and collectivities are distinguished in their social relations with other individuals and collectivities";[23] or identity is "people's concepts of who they are, of what sort of people they are, and how they relate to others."[24]

Transcendent Identity of Diaspora for Multiculturalism: Making Room in Themselves for Others

Regarding Christian identity, as Bloemraad, Korteweg, and Yurdakul put it, in understanding immigration policy, we should go beyond nation-state boundaries and look at transnationality, post nationality, and multi-nationality.[25] That is, it identifies methodological and theoretical challenges in the immigration field, noting the need for a more dynamic and comprehensive understanding of the inter-relationships between the dimensions of citizenship and immigration. It is important that living immigrant Diaspora create a transcendent Christian identity beyond national identities which exclude others.

22. Israel, *Outlandish*. The quotation is from the inside flap of the book.
23. Jenkins, *Social Identity*, 4.
24. Hogg and Abrams, *Social Identifications*, 2.
25. Bloemraad, et al., "Citizenship and Immigration."

Healing Empowerment of 'Diaspora Mission Church'

Every Christian has room in themselves for others. This room is made through the cross, leading to forgiveness and embrace. As Volf puts it, the most basic thought that it seeks to express is important: *"the will to give ourselves to others and "welcome" them, to readjust our identities to make space for them is prior to any judgment about others, except that of identifying them in their humanity."*[26]

Volf argues that Christian identity shown in the cross should include "self-giving love which overcomes human enmity and the creation of space in him to receive estranged humanity."[27]

The four structural elements in the movement of embrace are as follows:

(1) Opening the arms: opening arms are a gesture of the body reaching for others. They are a sign of discontent with one's own, self-enclosed identity; a code of desire for the others.

(2) Waiting: the open arms reach out but stop before touching the others, waiting for desire to arise in the others.

(3) Closing the arms: closing the arms is the goal of embrace, the embrace proper, which is unthinkable without *reciprocity*.

(4) Opening them again: embrace does not make two bodies one by transforming the boundary between bodies into the seam that hold together one body, it represents all Christians participating in the one body of Christ.[28]

Volf's model of reconciliation with God, self, and others contributes to forming a Christian identity in a Diaspora situation. Diaspora identity is making space in ourselves for others, embracing others, and making reconciliation. The great kingdom workers in the Bible—Abraham, Joseph, Daniel and his three friends, Nehemiah, Ezra, Esther, the seven evangelists (Acts 6), and Paul—come from diaspora. This shows that Diaspora are called to make room in themselves for others. This also shows how essential and urgent to the identity of Diaspora it is to make room in themselves to embrace others for God's redemptive plan.

---

26. Volf, *Exclusion & Embrace*, 29.
27. Ibid, 127.
28. Ibid, 141–44.

DIASPORA EVANGELISM

The Seed of the Kingdom: Diaspora with Lay Apostles

For Christians, what is the great question? It is: Who am I? To Diaspora, who left their homeland and live in different, strange country, the most important question is, who am I? Peter defines Diaspora in terms of "God's elect, exiles scattered throughout . . . who have been chosen according to the foreknowledge of God the Father, through the sanctifying work of the Spirit, to be obedient to Jesus Christ and sprinkled with his blood." This is the identity of Diaspora.

There are God's hidden blessings in Diaspora: his elect, his choice according to the foreknowledge of God the Father, through the sanctifying work of the Spirit, to be obedient to Jesus Christ and sprinkled with his blood. This explains the distinctive privilege of Diaspora, those who were brought to exile and entered into God's choice for his purpose.

John Stott emphasizes the significance of every believer, who has apostolic authority in the body:

> The Christian presbyter is no more a New Testament apostle than he is an Old Testament priest, and the exercise of ecclesiastical discipline belongs to the whole congregation, not to the leaders only. See for example, Our Lord's injunction, "tell it to the church," and the apostle's instructions to the Corinthian Church to take action as a body to excommunicate the incestuous offender: "When you are assembled . . . you are to deliver this man to Satan . . ." and again, "Drive out the wicked person from among you."[29]

Stott here emphasizes that the exercise of ecclesiastical discipline belongs to the whole congregation. This means that the whole laity, not the leaders only, has an *apostolic succession*, which is called lay apostle.

Regarding the significance of the lay apostolate, Hendrick Kraemer says, "their burning apostolic zeal presses them to be recognized as a laity in which a specific mission, a special vocation is inherent on account of their membership of the church, and impels them occasionally, notwithstanding their loyalty to the church, to an independence which evokes inevitable tensions with the hierarchy."[30] Here, even the laity has "burning apostolic zeal" and a "specific mission"; this impels them "to an independence which evokes inevitable tensions with the hierarchy."

---

29. Stott, *One People: Laymen and Clergy*.
30. Kraemer, *Theology of the Laity*, 62.

The hurt emotions of the laity are more severe in Diaspora. Furthermore, Diaspora feel more tension with the church and pastor as those who were scattered and banished in a foreign country than in the homeland. The most important question for Diaspora is: why and for what are they there? This is about the self-identity of Diaspora. For example, in the case of the Korean Diaspora church, almost all believers had *sangcheo*, in Korean, a hurt emotion. This *sangcheo*, an unhealed knowledge, emotion, and will, serves as a bitterness of the heart and hinders relationship, spiritual growth, and ministry. This *sangcheo* affects a division between believers and makes them partisan.

Joseph, one of the Diaspora in Egypt, was sold by his brothers and was dragged as slave to Egypt. We guess that his heart had been hurt with painful memories of his past. After thirteen years, God had made him lord of all Egypt; after nine more years he met his brothers, "4Then Joseph said to his brothers, 'Come close to me.' When they had done so, he said, 'I am your brother Joseph, the one you sold into Egypt! 5And now, do not be distressed and do not be angry with yourselves for selling me here, because it was to save lives that God sent me ahead of you'" (Gen 45:4–5).

He continued, "So then, it was not you who sent me here, but God. He made me father to Pharaoh, lord of his entire household and ruler of all Egypt" (v. 8). From Joseph's confessions, we found that his hurt, *sangcheo*, was removed and remained no more. He comforted his brothers who had unmercifully sold him, rather than blaming them. Taking from Kraemer's *A Theology of the Laity*, Joseph was one person who was a lay apostle.

Interdisciplinary Evangelism toward Aggressive Diaspora

Generally speaking, the mental psychology of diaspora is full of stress, conflict, anger, and violence. It is difficult to preach the word to people with this kind of mentality. This means that evangelism for diaspora calls for interdisciplinary understandings of the immigrant self and life. In fact, conflict, aggression, and violence involve various factors surrounding Diaspora. For example, aggression and violence are not just personal and mental issues, but related to various areas of society. Aggression is a ubiquitous phenomenon, present in both animals and humans. It refers to a variety of behaviors (verbal and physical) that may be caused by different factors such as personal (medical, psychological), situational (provocative or aversive situations), and socio-cultural influences (socio-economic, political, and cultural), with the immediate intent to cause or threaten harm, destruction, or damage to self or other organisms. On the other hand, violence is a severe form of physical aggression conducted mainly by humans. All violence is aggression, but not all aggressive behavior is necessarily violence.[31]

This statement shows that the issue of violence should be treated in the contexts of interdisciplinary areas; furthermore, the gospel should be applied in the contexts of these areas. The gospel is interpreted and applicable not only to the soul, but to the physical, psychological, socio-economic, political, ethnic, and social relations and the world. Conflict and violence issues need to involve in interdisciplinary areas of the gospel. With the lens of interdisciplinary studies, for example, we can develop prevention programs for conflict and violence. First of all, prevention of violence is valuable, as Lausanne states, prevention of bio-psycho-social-spiritual distress and the promotion of well-being in the person and community is for us a critical priority; in addition, we give priority to the most vulnerable in society, including the poor and underserved, and those who serve them sacrificially.[32]

Diaspora as the minority of the country experienced conflict and division based on ethnocentrism of other ethnic groups. In particular, the Korean Diaspora has experienced and suffered from conflict and violence. What is an effective principle of evangelism for this Diaspora? It is peacemaking evangelism. Peacemaking is a way to evangelize the gospel to Diaspora surrounded by social stress and conflicts.

For example, the "Urban Improv" program serves as rehearsal for real situations. The Freelance Players organization says: "The program strategically uses improvisational theater to provide young people a realistic and compelling forum to engage in self-exploration, critical decision making, and practice self-expression. By participating in an innovative, interactive curriculum, students develop the necessary skills of problem solving, cooperation, and leadership."[33]

This curriculum includes: Violence/conflict resolution, friendship, self-esteem, imagination, peer pressure, fairness, and family; prejudice, fear, substance abuse, coping, physical challenges, bullying and scapegoating; bystander issues, gangs, drugs, teen pregnancy, homophobia, and racism. These topics are used to understand and prevent conflict and violence.[34] Here the important concept is the use of "improvisational theater to provide young people a realistic and compelling forum" to handle violence provoking situations. Generally, most violence happens in cases of unintentional and improvisational situations. "Young people witness the consequences of their

---

31. Siever, "Neurobiology of Aggression," 429–42.
32. Third Lausanne Congress, "Content Library: The Cape Town Declaration."
33. Freelance Players, "Urban Improv: A Rehearsal for Life," lines 20–24
34. Ibid.

choices unfold right before their eyes. The methodology taps participants' creativity to address issues such as violence, bullying, racism, peer pressure, and homophobia. Rehearsal for real violence gives better room to handle violence."[35]

The University of Chicago also launched a one million dollar youth anti-violence program that will include a rare component: a rigorous, scientific evaluation to determine whether it is cost-effective. It questions: Do violence-prevention programs work? The University of Chicago study hopes to find out. Researchers will take hard look at results of the education and counseling project. The program, called "Becoming a Man—Sports Edition," aims to help adolescent boys in Chicago public schools curb their impulse to use fists and guns to settle disagreements. It addresses the problem on two fronts, by using character education and counseling, as well as training in Olympic sports, such as archery and fencing.[36]

This program is helpful to promote positive development "as a catalyst for violence prevention and social change." This design is a rehearsal for life in some of its most challenging moments. This program is to inspire and empower at-risk youth to transform their own lives and real practices and contribute to reducing violence. Diaspora church introduces neuropsychology to the understanding and resolutions of human conflict. Neuropsychology, the study of the structure and functions of the brain as they relate to specific psychological processes and behaviors and to lesion studies in humans, is helpful to understand and analyze the hurt mind and brain of immigrants.[37]

> Theories of neuropsychological vulnerabilities have emerged as a robust predictor of antisocial behaviors, especially with regard to human aggression and violence. This biopsychosocial theory posits that neurological impairments and trauma that impact an individual's central nervous system are positively associated with acts of interpersonal violence and homicide.[38]

Neuropsychological knowledge is necessary to understand violence. A man named One Goh, who killed seven people, is an example. On Tuesday, January 8, 2013, the Associated Press reported: "A man accused of killing seven people at a small Northern California Christian college is not mentally fit for trial, a judge ruled before temporarily suspending criminal proceedings until the defendant is deemed competent. Alameda County Superior Court

---

35. Ibid.
36. Banchero, "Do Violence-Prevention Programs Work," lines 5–11.
37. Beaumont, *Introduction to Neuropsychology*.
38. Boots, "Neuropsychological Perspective," 21–66.

Judge Carrie Panetta on Monday put on hold the criminal case against One Goh. Two psychiatric evaluations concluded that Goh suffers from paranoid schizophrenia."[39]

How is it beneficial if Christian ministers or friends know that Goh suffered from paranoid schizophrenia before the awful event? By dictionary definition, *paranoid schizophrenia* is "a form of schizophrenia characterized by delusions (of persecution or grandeur or jealousy); symptoms may include anger and anxiety and aloofness and doubts about gender identity; unlike other types of schizophrenia the patients are usually presentable and (if delusions are not acted on) may function in an apparently normal manner."[40] If an evangelist knew of symptoms of paranoid schizophrenia in Goh's behavior and life, they could have helped to stop Goh from killing, which is one of the evangelistic tasks.

BECOMING A GLOBAL NETWORK BUILDER

Involving Global Fields

Diaspora have various networks with different Diaspora. One of the major missions of Diaspora is to build the network with various people culturally. As Robertson puts it, "globalization involves comparative interaction of different forms of life";[41] globalization refers, in this particular sense, to the coming into conjunction, often problematically, of different forms of life. Robertson also explains globalization in terms of "the global field," in which "[there are] four major components, or reference points, of the conception of globality, the basic ways in which we are able as empirically informed analysts to 'make sense' of globality, as well as the form in terms of which globalization has in last few centuries actually proceeded."[42] Based on analysis by Robertson on globalization, the world is full of problematic conjunctions of different forms of life in four levels of the global fields—selves, national societies, world system of societies, and humankind. Each component comes into problematic conjunction with or relativizes one another. This shows how problematic factors of globalization may affect Diaspora mentality and life.

This shows how difficult it is for Diaspora to make global networks in a global field. There are many variables affecting the relationship. Actually,

39. Sakuma, "One Goh, Suspect Accused," lines 1–6.
40. Ekern, "Paranoid Schizophrenia," lines 12–15.
41. Robertson, *Globalization*, 26.
42. Ibid.

Healing Empowerment of 'Diaspora Mission Church' 289

for making global networks, we consider basic four variables—Diaspora self, host, homeland, and the world. When each is connected to each other, problems always arise. Differences fight against each other, which is called "relativization,"[43] later leading to "cultural *syncretization*."[44] The global field is filled with differences; global networks depend on how to handle them. We fully understand that the global field in which global networks are practiced is full of different ideas, things, persons, and interactions from not only Christians but also non-Christians. Christian networks should be careful to be biblical.

Cross-cultural Interactions for Relationship Building

For Diaspora's building relationship with difference, cross-cultural understanding is needed. It includes the understanding of how cultural factors influence human thinking and behavior. Adequate and comprehensive cross-cultural understanding calls for the help of cross-cultural psychology. According to the *Psychology Dictionary*, cross-cultural psychology is defined in the following way: "a department of psychology which examines likeness and difference in human actions spanning various cultures and recognizes the varying psychological structures and explanatory designs employed by said cultures. Commonly referred to as ethnopsychology."[45]

That is, cross-cultural psychology demonstrates that psychological phenomena are manifested differently in different locales, and it has identified certain cultural factors that foster these diverse manifestations.[46] However, it has theoretical and methodological limitations, which have hindered and curtailed the progress of cross-cultural psychology. These limitations must be identified and corrected if we are to comprehend cultural and psychological bias.

The International Online Training Program on Intractable Conflict, Conflict Research Consortium, University of Colorado, suggests the major key to cross-cultural communication.[47] The key to effective cross-cultural communication is knowledge. First, it is essential that people understand the potential problems of cross-cultural communication, and make a conscious effort to overcome these problems. Second, it is important to assume

43. Ibid., 27.
44. Ibid, 41.
45. *Psychology Dictionary*, "What is Cross-Cultural Psychology," lines 1–5.
46. Ratner and Hui, "Theoretical and Methodological Problems," 67–94.
47. Conflict Research Consortium, "International Online Training Program," lines 5–7.

that one's efforts will not always be successful, and to adjust one's behavior appropriately. For example, one should always assume that there is a significant possibility that cultural differences are causing communication problems, and be willing to be patient and forgiving, rather than hostile and aggressive, if problems develop. One should respond slowly and carefully in cross-cultural exchanges, not jumping to the conclusion that you know what is being thought and said.

William Ury's suggestion for a heated conflict is to stop, listen, and think, or as he puts it "go to the balcony" when the situation gets tense. By this he means withdraw from the situation, step back and reflect on what is going on before you act. This helps in cross-cultural communication as well. When things seem to be going badly, stop or slow down and think. What could be going on here? Is it possible that I misinterpreted what they said, or they misinterpreted me? Often, misinterpretation is the source of the problem. Active listening can sometimes be used to check this out, by repeating what one thinks he or she heard, one can confirm that one understands the communication accurately. If words are used differently between languages or cultural groups, however, even active listening can overlook misunderstandings.[48]

William Ury, cofounder of a Harvard Law School program on negotiation, presents a five-step agenda to deal successfully with opponents. His strategies mainly focus on self-discipline, or tactics for defusing the adversary's attacks, and suggestions for developing options designed to lead to a mutually satisfactory agreement. He defines negotiations as "the art of letting the other person have your way." In *Getting to Yes*, Ury stresses the need to understand the other's character and motivation.[49]

In *Cross-Cultural Servanthood: Serving the World in Christlike Humility*, Duane Elmer emphasizes "servanthood" in cross-cultural communication. This can be a model for Diaspora's cross-cultural communication. The process of cross-cultural servanthood is as follows:

1. Openness: welcome others into your presence.
2. Acceptance: communicate respect for others.
3. Trust: building confidence in relationships.
4. Learning: seeking information that changes you.
5. Learning: biblical foundations for change.
6. Understanding: seeing through the other's eyes.

---

48. Ratner and Hui, "Theoretical and Methodological Problems," 67–94.
49. Ury, *Getting to Yes*.

7. Serving: becoming like Christ to others.[50]

The criterion of cross-cultural communication for Diaspora is servanthood. This means that a Diaspora has respect for others. A Diaspora is careful about ethnocentrism. Kottak defines ethnocentrism as: "The tendency to view one's own culture as superior and apply one's own cultural values to judging the behavior and beliefs of people raised in other cultures."[51]

Generally speaking, ethnocentrism is a cultural universal; people everywhere assume that "familiar explanations, opinion, and customs are true, right, proper and moral."[52] However, self-perspective is not always right. A Diaspora lives in a diversity of culture; they should never be soused into ethnocentric attitudes and statements.

Establishing Global Diaspora Networks and its Steps

In a global level, a major skill for Diaspora ministry is establishing global networks. This is because Diaspora live in global networks, composed of Diaspora, homeland, and host country. What are its principles when Diaspora establishes global networks? Establishing global networks is necessary for doing Diaspora mission and ministry. In *Global Matters: Global Diaspora Strategies Toolkit*, Kingsley Aikins and Nicola White introduce the methods for establishing global Diaspora networks of Kutznetsov, senior economist at the World Bank;[53] he suggests three important points to consider when establishing global Diaspora networks:

(1) It is essential that there is a formal framework in place to maintain relationships and make sure that ideas are followed through.

(2) However, if you formalize a network too much, you can kill it off. That has also been a common mistake of many developing countries, they try to put together a program that is very formal and it kills all the spirit of entrepreneurship and intrinsic motivation. People will only get involved in a network like this if they want to, not because someone tells them to.

(3) Organizations should avoid launching a network in a blaze of publicity with a big conference before it has been tried and produced some

---

50. Elmer, *Cross-Cultural Servanthood*.
51. Kottak, *Mirror for Humanity*, 30.
52. Ibid.
53. Aikins and White, *Global Matters*.

successes. Rather, a conference should be a way of celebrating credibility through showcasing proven successes.[54]

Here, the essentials are a formal framework in place, not formalizing framework too much, and avoid launching a network in a blaze of publicity. Above all, global networks should avoid the fireworks of publicity and should be launched frugally.

In addition, he introduces that successful Diaspora networks combine the following three main features:

(1) Networks bring together people with strong intrinsic motivation.

(2) Members play both direct roles (implementing projects in the home country) and indirect roles (serving as bridges and antennae for the development of projects in the home country).

(3) Successful initiatives move from discussions on how to get involved with the home country to transactions (tangible outcomes).[55]

For Paul, in particular, establishing a network with others in different tradition and culture is to keep the other-centered principle. Acts 16 shows how to establish the network with different others:

> 1 Paul came to Derbe and then to Lystra, where a disciple named Timothy lived, whose mother was Jewish and a believer but whose father was a Greek. 2 The believers at Lystra and Iconium spoke well of him. 3 Paul wanted to take him along on the journey, so he circumcised him because of the Jews who lived in that area, for they all knew that his father was a Greek. (Acts 16:1–3)

Here, Paul did not strictly stick to his theology of circumcision; he circumcised Timothy because of the Jews who lived in that area. However, according to Acts 15:1–2, Paul did not agree with the circumcision for the salvation: "1 Certain people came down from Judea to Antioch and were teaching the believers: Unless you are circumcised, according to the custom taught by Moses, you cannot be saved. 2 This brought Paul and Barnabas into sharp dispute and debate with them." Nevertheless, Paul was willing to circumcise Timothy due to the neighboring Jews. This shows that Paul has an other-oriented tendency to make networks with Jewish friends.

For a detailed guideline for the process of establishing networks, here is a four-step process to networking the Diaspora—research, cultivation, solicitation, and stewardship. This four-step process can be applied to

---

54. Kuznetsov, "Global Role Model."
55. Kuznetsov, *Diaspora Networks*, 48–49.

Diaspora ministry to establish global networks in different cultures for redemption. Two steps will be added to the four-step process in the following.

Step 1: The Guidance of the Holy Spirit in Prayer

Global Diaspora networks are not a human idea and work; the Holy Spirit guides Christians to get where God wants for his redemptive plan. This is typical of Paul's missional trips. Acts 16:6–8 shows these characteristics:

> 6Paul and his companions traveled throughout the region of Phrygia and Galatia, having been *kept by the Holy Spirit from preaching* the word in the province of Asia. 7When they came to the border of Mysia, they tried to enter Bithynia, but *the Spirit of Jesus would not allow them to*. 8So they passed by Mysia and went down to Troas. (Italics mine)

With the guidance of the Holy Spirit, Paul traveled to Philippi and encountered "a woman from the city of Thyatira named Lydia, a dealer in purple cloth. She was a worshiper of God" (v. 14). The Bible then says, "The Lord opened her heart to respond to Paul's message. 15When she and the members of her household were baptized, she invited us to her home. 'If you consider me a believer in the Lord,' she said, 'come and stay at my house.' And she persuaded us" (vv.15–16). Here, missional networks between Paul and Lydia, with her family, were built up through the guidance and inspiration of the Holy Spirit. This network is not one that Paul ever imagined, but only the Holy Spirit.

Step 2: Interdisciplinary Research

Prospect research helps us to examine and understand Diaspora in their contexts; getting as much information as possible to decide the right time, project, setting, and person to ask to become an ambassador within the Diaspora.[56] Network builders should understand the persons, culture, problems, worldview, history, traditions, suffering, relationship patterns, psychology, political or social interests, and so on. Interdisciplinary studies help network builders to see what kind of needs people call for, which serves as a starting point. The felt need for a Samaritan woman was water; Jesus began a dialogue with her from this issue of water (John 4). With a felt need, a network builder has a relationship with people; this relationship becomes

---

56. Aikins and White, *Global Matters*, 55–57.

deeper and broader over time. An interdisciplinary lens helps to see what is in need for people from various angles.

Step 3: Empowering Development/Cultivation

"Cultivation is the process of moving people from a state of unawareness to informed understanding, sympathetic interest, engagement, commitment and, finally, passionate advocacy."[57] Relationship building always needs cultivation to inform many of things and knowledge so that they commit to the network. This includes building their awareness, increasing their knowledge, and generating their interest in, involvement with, and, finally, commitment to the network.

In Nehemiah, he had vision to build the wall of Jerusalem; Neh 2:13 says: "By night I went out through the Valley Gate toward the Jackal Well and the Dung Gate, examining the walls of Jerusalem, which had been broken down, and its gates, which had been destroyed by fire." Here we see that he gains information and knowledge of the broken wall of Jerusalem, moving his heart and emotions. Here is Nehemiah's message to Israel: "17Then I said to them, 'You see the trouble we are in: Jerusalem lies in ruins, and its gates have been burned with fire. Come, let us rebuild the wall of Jerusalem, and we will no longer be in disgrace.'" He empowered and cultivated the Israelites to arise for rebuilding the wall. This is called empowerment; empowerment is defined "as a multi-dimensional social process that helps people gain control over their own lives. It is a process that fosters power in people for use in their own lives, their communities and in their society, by acting on issues they define as important."[58]

Step 4: Solicitation for His Redemptive plan

Key Diaspora members need to be engaged in small groups with specific projects over a limited time frame. "It is critical to solicit Diaspora members for specific projects. A Diaspora network should not just be a network in which to network, it should be a network which strategically engages its members."[59] Therefore, with tangible activities or outcomes, Diaspora seeks to harness a Diaspora to engage in the networks. Solicitation is needed for his redemptive plan.

57. Ibid, 56.
58. Page, "Empowerment."
59. Ibid, 57.

Acts 16:9–10 show how important solicitation is:

> 9During the night Paul had a vision of a man of Macedonia standing and begging him, "Come over to Macedonia and help us." 10After Paul had seen the vision, we got ready at once to leave for Macedonia, concluding that God had called us to preach the gospel to them.

When Paul heard the voice, "help us," he concluded, "God had called us to preach the gospel to them."

Step 5: Stewardship for God

The word "stewardship" is defined as "the conducting, supervising, or managing of something; especially: the careful and responsible management of something entrusted to one's care."[60] For the purposes of Diaspora engagement, stewardship means thanking and recognizing the contributions made by Diaspora members to the homeland. Generally, Diaspora have been hurt in the deepest heart; they need to be encouraged, loved, and motivated.

However, there often appear conflicts between members of networks. Philippians 4 gives a good example of conflict resolution, as Paul appealed to Euodia and Syntyche for steadfastness and unity, see the text carefully:

> Phil 4: 1Therefore, my brothers and sisters, you whom I love and long for, my joy and crown, stand firm in the Lord in this way, dear friends! 2I plead with Euodia and I plead with Syntyche to be of the same mind in the Lord. 3Yes and I ask you, my true companion, help these women since they have contended at my side in the cause of the gospel, along with Clement and the rest of my co-workers, whose names are in the book of life.

Look at the language Paul uses: "my brothers and sisters, you whom I love and long for, my joy and crown," "dear friends!" "I plead," "I ask," "my true companion," "at my side in the cause of the gospel," "my co-workers," and "names are in the book of life." These words strengthen the relationship between self and others.

---

60. Merriam-Webster, "Stewardship," lines 6–8.

Step 6: The Identity of Pilgrimage in Human Networks

Generally, over time, organization becomes bureaucratized; in "Bureaucratic Form According to Max Weber—His Six Major Principles," Ken Johnston describes the multiple and various meanings of the word "bureaucracy."

1) A group of workers (for example, civil service employees of the US government), is referred to as "the bureaucracy."
2) Bureaucracy is the name of an organizational form used by sociologists and organizational design professionals.
3) Bureaucracy has an informal usage, as in "there's too much bureaucracy where I work." This informal usage describes a set of characteristics or attributes such as "red tape" or "inflexibility" that frustrate people who deal with or who work for organizations they perceive as "bureaucratic."[61]

In the same way, Christian missional networks also have the possibility of falling into "inflexibility that frustrates people" without the refreshing works of the Holy Spirit. Thus, network builders have an identity of pilgrim. They are those who walk through this world toward heaven. Pilgrimage never falls into "bureaucracy." This is because they look to heaven.

Here is the great multitude in white robes in heaven, which is a final and ultimate vision of Diaspora missiology:

> Rev 7: 9after this I looked, and there before me was a great multitude that no one could count, from every nation, tribe, people and language, standing before the throne and before the Lamb. They were wearing white robes and were holding palm branches in their hands.
> 10And they cried out in a loud voice:
> "Salvation belongs to our God,
> who sits on the throne,
> and to the Lamb."
> 11All the angels were standing around the throne and around the elders and the four living creatures. They fell down on their faces before the throne and worshiped God, 12saying:
> "Amen!
> Praise and glory
> and wisdom and thanks and honor
> and power and strength
> be to our God forever and ever.
> Amen!"

---

61. Weber, "Bureaucratic Form."

Bibliography

Abelmann, Nancy. *The Intimate University: Korean American Students and the Problems of Segregation*. Durham, NC: Duke University Press, 2009.
Abelmann, Nancy, and John Lie. *Blue Dreams: Korean Americans and Los Angeles Riots*. Cambridge: Harvard University Press, 1995.
Aikins, Kingsley, and Nicola White. *Global Matters: Global Diaspora Strategies Toolkit*. Dublin: Impress, 2011.
Alders, G. C. *Bible Student Commentary: Genesis*. Translated by William Heynen. Grand Rapids, MI: Regency Reference Library, 1981.
Alfonso, Carolin, et al., eds. *Diaspora, Identity, and Religion: New Directions in Theory and Research*. Routledge Research in Transnationalism 14. Florence, KY: Routledge, 2004.
Amazon.com. Book Description of *A Promised Land, A Perilous Journey: Theological Perspectives on Migration*, edited by Daniel G. Groody and Gioacchino Campese. http://www.amazon.com/Promised-Land-Perilous-Journey-Perspectives/dp/0268029733.
———. Book Description of *Los Protestantes: An Introduction to Latino Protestantism in the United States*, by Juan Francisco Martínez. http://www.amazon.com/Los-Protestantes-Introduction-Latino-Protestantism/dp/0313393133.
———. Editorial Review of *Contextualization in the New Testament: Patterns for Theology and Mission* by Dean Flemming. http://www.amazon.com/Contextualization-New-Testament-Patterns-Theology/dp/0830828311.
Anderson, Gary M. "Mr. Smith and the Preachers: The Economics of Religions in the Wealth of Nations." *Journal of Political Economy* 96 (1988) 1066–88.
Aniol, Scott. *By the Waters of Babylon: Worship in a Post-Christian Culture*. Grand Rapids, MI: Kregal, 2015.
———. "The Mission of Worship: An Assessment of the Missional Church Movement's Impact Upon Evangelical Worship Philosophy and Practice." http://religiousaffections.org/articles/articles-on-worship/the-mission-of-worship-an-assessment-of-the-missional-church-movements-impact-upon-evangelical-worship-philosophy-and-practice/.
Appaudrai, Arjun. *Modernity At Large: Cultural Dimensions of Globalization*. Minneapolis, MN: University of Minnesota Press, 1996.
———. ed. *Globalization*. Durham, NC: Duke University Press, 2001.
Aspromourgos, Tony. "On the Origins of the Term 'Neoclassical.'" *Cambridge Journal of Economics* 10 (1986) 265–70.

Association for the Study of Religion, Economics, and Culture. "What is the Economic Study of Religion?" http://www.thearda.com/asrec/.
Augustine, Saint. *The City of God*. Translated by Marcus Dods. Peabody, MA: Hendrickson, 2009.
———. *The Confessions*. Translated by Henry Chadwick. Oxford, NY: Oxford University Press, 1992.
Back, Jung Whan. "The Shooting Tragedy of Oikos University: He Suffered Bullying due to English." *Korea Daily* (April 2012). http://www.koreadaily.com/news/read.asp?art_id=1387096.
Backford, James A. "Public Religious and the Post-Secular: Critical Reflections." *Journal for the Scientific Study of Religion* 51 (2012) 1–19.
Ball, Arnetha, ed. *With More Deliberate Speed: Achieving Equity and Excellence in Education*. Malden, MA: Blackwell, 2006.
Banchero, Stephanie. "Do Violence-Prevention Programs Work? University of Chicago Study Hopes to Find Out." *Chicago Tribune* (November 18, 2009). http://www.chicagotribune.com/news/chi-school-violence-prevention-1nov18-story.html.
Barber, Daniel Colucciello. *On Diaspora: Christianity, Religion, and Secularity*. Eugene, OR: Cascade, 2011.
Barclay, William. "The Letters to the Philippians, Colossians, and Thessalonians." Louisville, KY: Westminster John Knox, 2003.
Barth, Fredrik. "Introduction." In *Ethnic Groups and Boundaries: The Social Organization of Culture Difference*, edited by Fredrik Barth, 9–38. Boston, MA: Little, Brown & Co., 1969.
Bartholomew, Craig, and Fred Hughes, eds. *Exploration in a Christian Theology of Pilgrimage*. Aldershot, Hants, UK: Ashgate, 2004.
Batthyany, Alexander. "What is Logotherapy and Existential Analysis?" *Viktor Frankl Institute*. http://www.viktorfrankl.org/e/logotherapy.html.
BBC News. "Muslims in Europe: Country Guide." http://news.bbc.co.uk/2/hi/europe/4385768.stm.
Beaumont, J. G. *Introduction to Neuropsychology*. New York: Guilford, 1983.
Beck, Aaron. *Prisoners of Hate: The Cognitive Basis of Anger, Hostility, and Violence*. New York: Harper Collins, 1999.
Beckford, James A. "Public Religions and the Postsecular: Critical Reflections." *Journal for the Scientific Study of Religion* 51 (2012) 1–19.
Ben-Sasson, H. H. *A History of the Jewish People*. New York: Harvard University Press, 1976.
Berger, Peter. "Religion in a Globalizing World." *Pew Research Center: Religion & Public Life* (December 4, 2006). http://www.pewforum.org/2006/12/04/religion-in-a-globalizing-world2/.
———. "Rethinking Secularization: A Conversation with Peter Berger." *AlbertMohler.com* (October 11, 2010). http://www.albertmohler.com/2010/10/11/rethinking-secularization-a-conversation-with-peter-berger-2/.
———. *The Sacred Canopy*. New York: Anchor, 1967.
Berkhof, Louis. *Systematic Theology*. Grand Rapids, MI: W. B. Eerdmans, 1984.
BIAMS. "Day Conference 2012: Marginalisation and the Reign of God—Issues and Questions from the Perspectives of Biblical Studies, Mission Studies and Theology." http://www.globalconnections.co.uk/aboutthenetwork/.../biams.pdf.
Bible Hub. "Allotrios." *Strong's Concordance* 245. http://biblehub.com/greek/245.htm.

———. "Diaspora." *Strong's Concordance* 1290. http://biblesuite.com/greek/1290.htm.
———. "Parepidémos." *Strong's Concordance* 3927. http://biblesuite.com/greek/3927.htm.
———. "Xenos." *Strong's Concordance* 3581. http://biblesuite.com/greek/3581.htm.
———. "Zarah." *Strong's Concordance* 2219. http://biblehub.com/hebrew/2219.htm.
Bible Tools. "Tarsos." http://www.bibletools.org/index.cfm/fuseaction/Lexicon.show/ID/G5019/Tarsos.htm.
Bloemraad, Irene, et al. "Citizenship and Immigration: Multiculturalism, Assimilation, and Challenges to the Nation-State." *Annual Review of Sociology* 34 (2008) 153–79.
Bonacich, Eden. "Middleman, Minorities, and Advanced Capitalism." *Ethnic Group* 2 (1980) 211–19.
Boots, Denise Paquette. "Neuropsychological Perspective of Human Violence, Aggression, and Homicide." In *Public Issues Research Trends*, edited by Sophie J. Evans, 21–66. New York: Nova Science, 2008.
Bosch, David. *Transforming Mission: Paradigm Shifts in Theology of Mission*. American Society of Missiology 16. Maryknoll, NY: Orbis, 2011.
Bosetti, Giancarlo, and Klaus Eder. "Post-secularism: A Return to the Public Sphere." *Eurozine* (August 17, 2006). http://www.eurozine.com/articles/2006-08-17-ederen.html.
Bowker, John, ed. "Tillich, Paul Johannes Oskar." In *The Concise Oxford Dictionary of World Religions*. Oxford Reference Online: Oxford University Press, 2000. http://www.oxfordreference.com/view/10.1093/acref/9780198158967.001.0001/acref-9780198158967-e-5267?rskey=uNrGVK&result=13.
Boyarin, Daniel. "Introduction." *American Imago* 54 (1997) 103–104. http://muse.jhu.edu/login?auth=0&type=summary&url=/journals/american_imago/v054/54.2boyarin.html.
Braziel, Jana E., and Anita Mannur. *Theorizing Diaspora: A Reader*. Hoboken, NJ: Wiley-Blackwell, 2003.
Brenner, Frédéric. *Diaspora: Homelands in Exile, Voices*. New York: HarperCollins, 2003.
Bright, John. *The Kingdom of God*. Nashville, TN: Abingdon, 1980.
Brubaker, Rogers. "The 'Diaspora' Diaspora." *Ethnic and Racial Studies* 28 (January 2005) 1–19. http://www.sscnet.ucla.edu/soc/faculty/brubaker/Publications/29_Diaspora_diaspora_ERS.pdf.
Bruce, Frederick F. *The New International Commentary on the New Testament: Acts*. Grand Rapids, MI: W. B. Eerdmans, 1984.
———. *The New International Commentary on the New Testament: The Epistle to the Hebrews*. Grand Rapids, MI: W. B. Eerdmans, 1987.
Brueggemann, Walter. *Cadences of Home: Preaching among Exiles*. Louisville, KY: Westminster John Knox, 2007.
Bulmer, Martin, and John Solomos, eds. *Diasporas, Cultures, and Identities*. Ethnic and Racial Studies. Florence, KY: Routledge, 2011.
Bunyan, John. *A Discourse upon the Pharisee and the Publican*. Charleston, SC: Nabu, 2011.
———. *The Fear of God*. New York: Cosimo Classics, 2012.
———. *The Pilgrim's Progress*, edited by W. R. Owens. Oxford World's Classics. Oxford: Oxford University Press, 2003.

Bibliography

Cady, Linell E., and Elizabeth Shakman Hurd. *Comparative Secularisms in a Global Age.* New York: Palgrave Macmillan, 2010.

Calvin, Jean. "Calvin's Commentaries, Vol. 36: Acts, Part I." http://www.sacred-texts.com/chr/calvin/cc36/cc36018.htm.

———. *Institutes of the Christian Religion.* 1536 Edition. Grand Rapids, MI: W. B. Eerdmans, 1986.

Carey, George. "Church 'is on the Brink of Extinction': Ex-Archbishop George Carey Warns of Christianity Crisis." *DailyMail.com* (November 18, 2013). http://www.dailymail.co.uk/news/article-2509379/Church-brink-extinction-Ex-Archbishop-George-Carey-warns-Christianity-crisis.html.

Casanova, Jose. "Globalization, Religions, and the Secular." *Berkley Center for Religions, Peace & World Affairs.* http://berkleycenter.georgetown.edu/programs/globalization-religions-and-the-secular.

———. *Public Religions in the Modern World.* Chicago, IL: University of Chicago Press, 1994.

Cash, David, et al., "Salience, Credibility, Legitimacy and Boundaries: Linking Research, Assessment and Decision Making." *SSRE* (2003). http://papers.ssrn.com/sol3/papers.cfm?abstract_id=372280.

Cha, Marn J. *Koreans in Central California (1903-1957): A Study of Settlement and Transnational Politics.* Lanham, MD: University Press of America, 2010.

Charles, Ronald. *Paul and the Politics of Diaspora.* Minneapolis, MN: Fortress, 2014.

Choi, Inbom. "Korean Diaspora in the Making: Its Current Status and Impact on the Korean Economy." *The Institute for International Economics.* http://www.iie.com/publications/chapters_preview/365/2iie3586.pdf.

Chung, Angie Y. *Legacies of Struggle: Conflict and Cooperation in Korean American Politics.* Redwood City, CA: Stanford University Press, 2007.

Clifford, J. "Diaspora." *Current Anthropology* 9 (1994) 302–38.

Clingerman, Forrest J. "Walking into the Frame: A Theological Exploration of Pilgrimage along Anton Mauve's A Dutch Road." *Literature and Theology: An International Journal of Religion, Theory and Culture* 23 (March 2009) 18–32.

Cohen, Abner. *Two-Dimensional Man: An Essay on the Anthropology of Power and Symbolism in Complex Society.* Oakland, CA: University of California Press, 1977.

Cohen, Abner, ed. *Urban Ethnicity.* New York: Tavistock, 1974.

Cohen, Rina. "Diaspora, Hegemony and Cultural Identity." *York University Faculty of Graduate Studies SOCI 6615 3.0: Summer 2012 Graduate Program in Sociology.* http://www.yorku.ca/gradsoci/documents/SOCI6615.pdf.

Cohen, Robin. *Global Diasporas: An Introduction.* Florence, KY: Routledge, 1997.

Cohen, Shye I. D. "The Jewish Diaspora." *Frontline* (April 1998). http://www.pbs.org/wgbh/pages/frontline/shows/religion/portrait/diaspora.html.

Conflict Research Consortium. "International Online Training Program on Intractable Conflict." *University of Colorado* (1998). http://www.colorado.edu/conflict/peace/links_page.htm.

Cooper, Elizabeth Elliott. "Ethnocentrism." *Oxford Bibliographies* (January 11, 2012). http://www.oxfordbibliographies.com/view/document/obo-9780199766567/obo-9780199766567-0045.xml.

Coser, Lewis A. *Masters of Sociological Thought: Ideas in Historical and Social Context.* Long Grove, IL: Waveland, 2003.

Covenant of Grace Protestant Reformed Church. "John Bunyan: Author of Pilgrim's Progress." http://www.prca.org/books/portraits/bunyan.htm.

Crabb, Larry. *Connecting: Healing for Ourselves and Our Relationships: A Radical New Vision.* Nashville, TN: Word, 1997.

Croft, Steven, et al. *Pilgrim, Follow Stage: Book 4, The Beatitudes.* London: Church House, 2014.

Crowell, Steven. "Existentialism." *Stanford Encyclopedia of Philosophy.* https://leibniz.stanford.edu/friends/members/view/existentialism/sc/.

DellaPergola, Sergio, et al., eds. "World Jewish Population, 2010." *Current Jewish Population Reports* 2 (2010). http://www.jewishdatabank.org/studies/downloadFile.cfm?FileID=3031.

DePaulo, Bella, ed. *The Psychology of Dexter (Psychology of Popular Culture).* New London, CT: Smart Pop, 2010.

Dreher, Sabine. *Neoliberalism and Migration: An Inquiry into the Politics of Globalization (Politik, Gemeinschaft und Gesellschaft in einer Globalisierten Welt).* Münster, Germany: LIT Verlag, 2007.

Dukeheim, Emile. *The Elementary Forms of the Religious Life (1912).* Translated by Karen E. Fields. New York: Free, 1995.

Dutton, Edward. *Culture Shock and Multiculturalism: Reclaiming a Useful Model from the Religious Realm.* Newcastle, UK: Cambridge Scholars, 2012.

Dyrness, William A. *Learning about Theology from the Third World.* Grand Rapids, MI: W. B. Eerdmans, 1990.

Eckert, Carter. "Korea's Transition to Modernity: A Will to Greatness." In *Historical Perspective on Contemporary East Asia,* edited by Merle Goldman and Andrew Gordon, 119–54. Cambridge, MA: Harvard University, 2000.

Ekern, Jacquelyn. "Paranoid Schizophrenia." *Addiction Hope* (April 16, 2013). http://www.addictionhope.com/mood-disorder/schizophrenia.

Elliott, John H. *A Home for the Homeless.* London: SCM, 1982.

———. *1 Peter.* The Anchor Bible Commentaries. New Haven, CT: Yale University Press, 2001.

Elmer, Duane. *Cross-Cultural Servanthood: Serving the World in Christlike Humility.* Downers Grove, IL: InterVarsity, 2006.

Ember, Melvin, et al, eds. *Encyclopedia of Diasporas: Immigrant and Refugee Cultures around the World.* 2 vols. Berlin: Springer, 2005.

Erickson, Kai T. *A New Species of Trouble: The Human Experience of Modern Disasters.* New York: Norton, 1994.

Fackenheim, Emil L. *Metaphysics and Historicity.* Milwaukee, WI: Marquette University Press, 1961. http://academic.udayton.edu/LawrenceUlrich/LeaderArticles/Fackenheim_Metaphysics%20and%20Historicity.PDF.

Fanon, Frantz. "Postcolonial Studies." *Postcolonial Studies @ Emory.* https://scholarblogs.emory.edu/postcolonialstudies/2014/06/19/fanon-frantz/.

Feagin, Joe R., and C. B. Feagin. *Racial and Ethnic Relations.* Upper Saddle River, NJ: Prentice Hall, 1992.

Fee, Gordon D. *God's Empowering Presence: The Holy Spirit in the Letters of Paul.* Peabody, MA: Hendrickson, 1994.

Feiertag, Thomas E. "Contemporary Issues in Missiology: A Missiological Approach to Religious Pluralism." *Concordia University Wisconsin Theology Journal*

(October 31, 2012). http://blog.cuw.edu/tj/2012/10/31/contemporary-issues-in-missiology-a-missiological-approach-to-religious-pluralism/.

Fernandez, Jane, ed. *Diasporas: Critical and Inter-Disciplinary Perspectives*. Oxford: Inter-Disciplinary, 2009. http://www.inter-disciplinary.net/wp-content/uploads/2009/10/DCIP-1.1b.pdf.

Flemming, Dean. *Contextualization in the New Testament: Patterns for Theology and Mission*. Downers Grove, IL: InterVarsity, 2006.

Forest, Jim. "Pilgrims of the Cross: The Beatitude of Persecution." *The Chuck Colson Center for Christian Worldview* (November 2001). http://www.breakpoint.org/search-library/search?view=searchdetail&id=15748.

Frankl, Viktor. *Man's Search for Meaning: An Introduction to Logotherapy*. New York: Simon & Schuster, 1984.

Freelance Players, Inc. "Urban Improv: A Rehearsal for Life." http://www.urbanimprov.org/.

Freer, Regina. "Black–Korean Conflict." In *The Los Angeles Riots: Lessons for the Urban Future*, edited by Mark Baldassare, 175–203. Boulder, CO: Westview, 1994.

Frei, Hans W. *Types of Christian Theology*. Edited by George Hunsinger and William C. Placher. New Haven, CT: Yale University Press, 1992.

Geertz, Clifford. *The Interpretation of Cultures: Selected Essays*. New York: Basic, 1977.

Gibbs, Eddie, and Ryan K. Bolger. *Emerging Churches: Creating Christian Community in Postmodern Cultures*. Grand Rapids, MI: Baker Academics, 2005.

Giddens, Anthony. *Social Theory and Modern Sociology*. Cambridge: Polity, 1987.

Gill, Brad. "From the Editor's Desk: Reassessing 'Peoples' in the Global Push-and-Pull." *IJFM* 27 (2010) 163. http://www.ijfm.org/PDFs_IJFM/27_4_PDFs/IJFM_27_4_SP.pdf.

Glazer, Nathan, and Daniel P. Moynihan. *Beyond the Melting Pot: The Negroes, Puerto Ricans, Jews, Italians, and Irish of New York City*. Rev. 2nd ed. New York: MIT Press, 1970.

Global Diaspora Network. "Gatherings: 2015 Global Diaspora Forum." *Lausanne Movement*. http://www.lausanne.org/gatherings/issue-gathering/2015-global-diaspora-forum.

Global Policy Forum. "Globalization of Culture." *Globalpolicy.org*. http://www.globalpolicy.org/globalization/globalization-of-culture.html.

Goheen, Michael W. "The Significance of Lesslie Newbigin for Mission in the New Millennium." *Third Millennium* 7 (2004) 88–99.

Gorsevski, Ellen W. "The Spitfire Grill: Nonviolence as Social Power." *Online Journal of Peace and Conflict Resolution* 2 (1999). http://replay.waybackmachine.org/20011027134314/http://members.aol.com/peacejnl/2_1gorsev.htm.

Gottheil, Richard, and S. Kahn. "Ghetto." *JewishEncyclopedia.com*. http://www.jewishencyclopedia.com/articles/6653-ghetto.

Grade Saver. "Pilgrim's Progress Themes." *Gradesaver.com* http://www.gradesaver.com/pilgrims-progress/study-guide/themes.

Gregory, Brad S. *The Unintended Reformation: How a Religious Revolution Secularized Society*. New York: Belknap, 2012.

Gregory, James N. *The Southern Diaspora: How the Great Migrations of Black and White Southerners Transformed America*. Chapel Hill, NC: University of North Carolina Press, 2005.

Groody, Daniel G. *Globalization, Spirituality, and Justice: Navigating the Path to Peace*. Maryknoll, NY: Orbis, 2007.

Groody, Daniel G., and Gioacchino Campese, eds. *A Promised Land, A Perilous Journey: Theological Perspectives on Migration*. Notre Dame, IN: University of Notre Dame Press, 2008.

Gu, Gyunhyo. "Opening of American Office of GMS (Korean Missional Institute of *Hapdong* Denomination)." *NewsNJoy*. http://www.newsnjoy.or.kr/news/articleView.html?idxno=192631.

Guder, Darrell L., et al. *Missional Church: A Vision for the Sending of the Church in North America*. Gospel and Our Culture. Grand Rapids, MI: W. B. Eerdmans, 1998.

Guinn, David. *Protecting Jerusalem's Holy Sites: A Strategy for Negotiating a Sacred Peace*. Cambridge: Cambridge University Press, 2006.

Gundry, Robert H. *A Survey of the New Testament*. 5th ed. Grand Rapids, MI: Zondervan, 2012.

Guterres, António. "World Refugee Day: 42 Million Uprooted People Waiting to Go Home." *UNHCR* (June 19, 2009). http://www.unhcr.org/4a3b98706.html.

Habermas, Jürgen. "Notes on a Post-Secular Society." *SignandSight.com* (June 18, 2008). http://www.signandsight.com/features/1714.html.

———. "On the Relations between the Secular Liberal State and Religion." In *Political Theologies: Public Religions in a Post-Secular World*, edited by Hent de Vries and Lawrence E. Sullivan, 251–60. Bronx: Fordham University Press, 2006.

Hall, Stuart. "Cultural Identity and Diaspora." In *Colonial Discourse & Postcolonial Theory: A Reader*, edited by Patrick Williams and Laura Chrisman, 392–420. New York: Columbia University Press, 1994.

Halter, Hugh, and Matt Smay. *AND: The Gathered and Scattered Church*. Exponential Series. Grand Rapids, MI: Zondervan, 2010.

Hammett, Edward H. *The Gathered and Scattered Church: Equipping Believers for the 21st Century*. Macon, GA: Smyth & Helwys, 1999.

Hanciles, Jehu J. *Beyond Christendom: Globalization, African Migration, and the Transformation of the West*. Maryknoll, NY: Orbis, 2009.

———. "Migration and the Globalization of Christianity." In *Understanding World Christianity: The Vision and Work of Andrew F. Walls*, edited by William R. Burrows, et al., 227–42. Maryknoll, NY: Orbis, 2011.

———. "Migration, Diaspora Communities, and the New Missionary Encounter with Western Society." *Lausanne World Pulse Archives* 7 (2008). http://www.lausanneworldpulse.com/themedarticles-php/975/07-2008.

———. "Mission and Migration Megatrends." *YES Trinity* (2008) 6–8.

Hannay, H. J. *Experimental Techniques in Human Neuropsychology*. New York: Oxford University Press, 1986.

Harnnez, Ulf. *Exploring the City: Inquiries Toward an Urban Anthropology*. New York: Columbia University Press, 1980.

Harvey, David. *A Brief History of Neoliberalism*. Oxford: Oxford University Press, 2005.

Hauerwas, Stanley, and William Willimon. *Resident Aliens: Life in the Christian Colony*. Nashville, TN: Abingdon, 2008.

Hazen, Don. *Inside the Los Angeles Riots: What Really Happened and Why It Will Happen Again*. New York: Institute for Alternative Journalism, 1993.

Heisler, Barbara Schmitter. "The Sociology of Immigration: From Assimilation to Segmented Integration, from the American Experience to the Global Arena." In

Migration Theory: Talking Across Disciplines, edited by Caroline B. Brettell and James F. Hollifield. New York: Routledge, 2000.

Heitink, Gerben. *Practical Theology: History, Theory, Action Domains.* Grand Rapids, MI: W. B. Eerdmans, 1999.

Hendriksen, William, and Simon J. Kistemaker. *Matthew.* New Testament Commentary. Grand Rapids, MI: Baker, 1973.

Hertic, Young Lee. *Cultural Tug of War: The Korean Immigrant Family and Church in Transition.* Nashville, TN: Abingdon, 2001.

Hiebert, Paul. *Anthropological Reflections on Missiological Issues.* Grand Rapids, MI: Baker, 1998.

———. *Cultural Anthropology.* Grand Rapids, MI: Baker, 1999.

———. *The Gospel in Human Contexts: Anthropological Explorations for Contemporary Missions.* Grand Rapids, MI: Baker Academic, 2009.

Hiebert, Paul G., and Eloise Hiebert Meneses. *Incarnational Ministry: Planting Churches in Band, Tribal, Peasant, and Urban Societies.* Grand Rapids, MI: Baker, 1999.

Hiskey, Michelle. "Fighting Education Stereotypes." *Georgia State University Foundation* (December 5, 2011). http://netcommunity.gsu.edu/Page.aspx?pid=1031.

Hogg, Michael, and Dominic Abrams. *Social Identifications: A Social Psychology of Intergroup Relations and Group Processes.* New York: Routledge, 1988.

Holt, Charles. "The Secular Church." *The Examiner.* http://www.theexaminer.org/volume1/number6/secular.htm.

Holyoake, George Jacob. *English Secularism: A Confession of Belief.* Chicago, IL: Open Court, 1896.

———. *The Principles of Secularism Illustrated.* Charleston, SC: Nabu, 2010.

Hong, Howard V., and Edna H. Hong, eds. *The Essential Kierkegaard.* Princeton, NJ: Princeton University Press, 2000.

Hortense, Pillers, ed. *Comparative American Identities.* New York: Routledge, 1991.

Horton, Michael. *Pilgrim Theology: Core Doctrines for Christian Disciples.* Grand Rapids, MI: Zondervan, 2013.

Hunsberger, George R., ed. *The Church between Gospel and Culture.* Gospel and Our Culture. Grand Rapids, MI: W. B. Eerdmans, 1996.

Hurh, Won Moo. *Korean Immigrant in America: A Structural Analysis of Ethnic Confinement and Adhesive Adaptation.* Rutherford, NJ: Fairleigh Dickinson University Press, 1994.

Ikemoto, Lisa. "Traces of the Master Narrative in the Story of African American / Korean American Conflict: How We Constructed 'Los Angeles.'" *Southern California Law Review* 66 (1993) 1581–98.

Inhabit Conference. "The Missional Network." *Seattle School of Theology.* http://inhabitconference.com/partners/the-missional-network/.

Institute for Latino Studies. "Center for Latino Spirituality and Culture." *University of Notre Dame.* http://latinostudies.nd.edu/about/institute-staff/daniel-groody/.

Inter-Disciplinary. "6th Global Conference (2013): Diasporas: Exploring Issues." *Inter-Disciplinary.net.* http://www.inter-disciplinary.net/at-the-interface/diversity-recognition/diasporas/project-archives/conference-programme-abstracts-and-papers/.

International Society for Frontier Missiology. "Global Peoples: Gates, Bridges and Connections across the Frontiers." *Eventbrite* (September 2013). http://www.eventbrite.com/e/isfm-2013-tickets-5606354758.

Ireland, Corydon. "A Theology of Culture." *Harvard Gazette* (November 15, 2011). http://news.harvard.edu/gazette/story/2011/11/a-theology-of-culture/.
Israel, Nico. *Outlandish: Writing Between Exile and Diaspora*. Redwood City, CA: Stanford University Press, 2000.
Jacobs, Joseph, and Samuel Krauss. "Tarsus." *JewishEncyclopedia.com*. http://www.jewishencyclopedia.com/articles/14255-tarsus.
Jacobsen, Knut A., and Selva J. Raj, eds. *South Asian Christian Diaspora: Invisible Diaspora in Europe and North America*. Farnham Surrey, UK: Ashgate, 2008.
Jamarani, Maryam. *Identity, Language and Culture in Diaspora: A Study of Iranian Female Migrants to Australia*. Clayton, VIC: Monash University Publishing, 2012.
James, William. *The Varieties of Religious Experience: A Study in Human Nature*. Eastford, CT: Martino Fine, 2012.
Jenkins, Philip. *The Next Christendom: The Coming of Global Christianity*. Future of Christianity Trilogy. Oxford: Oxford University Press, 2001.
Jenkins, Richard. *Social Identity*. Key Ideas. New York: Routledge, 2008.
Jo, Moon H. "Korean Merchants in the Black Community: Prejudice among the Victims of Prejudice." *Ethnic Racial Studies* 15 (1992) 396–411.
Johnson, James H., Jr., and Melvin L. Oliver. "Interethnic Minority Conflict in Urban America: The Effects of Economic and Social Dislocations." *Urban Geography* 10 (1989) 449–63.
Johnson, Todd M. "Globalization, Christian Identity, and Frontier Missions in the Globalization of the Frontiers." *The Journal of the International Society for Frontier Missiology* 27 (2010) 165–69.
Jun, David Chul Han. "World Christian Mission through Migrant Workers in South Korea and Through the Korean Diaspora." *Tokyo 2010: Global Mission Consultation* (2010) 171–73.
Jung, Carl Gustav. *Psychology and Religion*. New Haven, CT: Yale University Press, 1960.
———. "From Civil Relations to Racial Conflict: Merchant–Customer Interactions in Urban America." *American Sociological Review* 67 (2002) 77–98.
———. "Beyond Conflict and Controversy: Blacks, Jews, and Koreans in Urban America." In *Immigration and Crime: Race, Ethnicity, and Violence*, edited by Ramiro Martinez and Abel Valenzuela, 140–63. New York: New York University Press, 2006.
Jung, Kum-Chul. "The Poetics of Korean Traditional Emotion: 'Han.'" *Kangwon National Humanities Institute—Human Sciences Research* 21 (2009) 107–31.
Jung, Min-Yong. "Diaspora and Timely Hit: Toward a Diaspora Missiology." In *Korean Diaspora and Christian Mission*, edited by S. Hun Kim and Wonsuk Ma, 59–71. Eugene, OR: Wipf and Stock, 2011.
Kang-Lee, Jong Haeng. "Killing of 7 Students by Korean 40 year old, Oikos University established by Korean Immigrants in North Oakland." *Korea Daily* (April 2012). http://www.koreadaily.com/news/read.asp?art_id=1386311.
Kalamazoo Valley Community College. "Six Basic Themes of Existentialism." http://classes.kvcc.edu/jcorbin/PHI106/OptRdngs/SixBasicThemesExistentiali.htm.
Keely, Charles B. "Demography and International Migration." In *Migration Theory: Talking Across the Disciplines*, edited by C. B. Brettell and J. F. Hollifield, 43–60. London: Routledge, 2000.
Keller, Timothy. "The Missional Church." *Redeemer Presbyterian Church* (2001). http://download.redeemer.com/pdf/learn/resources/Missional Church-Keller.pdf.

Kibria, Nazli. "College and the Notions of 'Asian American': Second Generation Chinese and Korean Americans Negotiate Race and Ethnicity." *Amerasia Journal* 25 (1999) 29–52.

———. "The Construction of 'Asian American': Reflection on Intermarriage and Ethnic Identity among Second-Generation Chinese and Korean Americans." *Ethnic and Racial Studies* 20 (1997) 77–86.

———. "Of Blood, Belonging, and Homeland Trips: Transnationalism and Identity among Second-Generation Chinese and Korean Americans." In *The Changing Faces of Home: The Transnational Lives of the Second Generation*, edited by Peggy Levitt and Mary C. Waters, 295–311. New York: Russell Sage Foundation, 2002.

———. "Race, Ethnic Options, and Ethnic Binds: Identity Negotiations of Second-Generation Chinese and Korean Americans." *Sociological Perspectives* 43 (2000) 77–95.

Kidner, Derek. *Tyndale Old Testament: Genesis—Introduction & Commentaries*. Edited by D. J. Wisenan. Downers Grove, IL: InterVarsity, 1967.

Kim, Dae Young, and Lori Dance. "Korean–Black Relations: Contemporary Challenges, Scholarly Explanations, and Future Prospects." In *Blacks and Asians: Crossings, Conflicts, and Commonality*, edited by Hazel McFerson, 17–26. Durham, NC: Carolina Academic, 2005.

Kim, Illsoo. *New Urban Immigrants: The Korean Community in New York*. Princeton, NJ: Princeton University Press, 1981.

Kim, Nadia Y. "Critical Thoughts on Asian American Assimilation in the Whitening Literature." In *Racism in Post-Racism America: New Theories, New Directions*, edited by Charles A. Gallagher, 53–66. Chapel Hill, NC: Social Forces, 2008.

———. "Finding Our Way Home: Korean Americans, Homelands Trips, and Cultural Foreignness." In *Diasporic Homecomings: Ethnic Return Migrants in Comparative Perspective*, edited by Takeyuki Tsuda, 305–24. Redwood City, CA: Stanford University Press, 2009.

———. "Patriarchy is so Third World: Korean Immigrant Women and Migrating White Western Masculinity." *Social Problems* 53 (2006) 519–36.

———. "A Return to More Blatant Class and 'Race' Bias in US Immigration Policy?" *The Du Bois Review* 4 (2008) 469–77.

———. "'Seoul-America' on America's 'Soul': South Koreans and Korean Immigrants Navigate Global White Racial Ideology." *Critical Sociology* 32 (2006) 381–402.

———. "A View from Below: An Analysis of Korean Americans' Racial Attitudes." *Amerasia Journal* 30 (2004) 1–24.

Kim, Sang-bok. *World Mission Vision of Korean Diaspora*. Seoul: Torch Center for World Mission, 2014.

Kim, Sang Jun. "Interpreting Confucian Modernity in Late Joseon Korea." *Korean Studies Information Service System* 42 (2003) 59–92.

Kim, Sinyil. "Korean Immigrants and their Mission: Exploring the Missional Identity of Korean Immigrant Churches in North America." DMiss diss., Asbury Theological Seminary, 2008.

Kim, Su[set breve over u]ng-hun and Wonsuk Ma. *Korean Diaspora and Christian Mission*. Eugene, OR: Wipf & Stock, 2011.

King, Joyce E. "'If Justice is our Objective': Diaspora Literacy, Heritage Knowledge, and the Praxis of Critical Studyin' for Human Freedom." *Yearbook of the National Society for the Study of Education* 105 (2006) 337–360.

Kingsley, Aikins, and Nicola White. *Global Matters: Global Diaspora Strategies Toolkit.* Dublin: Impress, 2011.
Kirk, J. Andrew. *What is Mission? Theological Explorations.* Minneapolis, MN: Fortress, 2000.
Kirshenblatt-Gimblett, Barbara. "Space of Dispersal." *Cultural Anthropology* 9 (1994) 339–44.
Knepper, Tim. Review of *The Sacred Canopy: Elements of a Sociological Theory of Religion* by Peter Berger, 2001. http://people.bu.edu/wwildman/relexp/reviews/review_berger01.htm.
Knott, Kim and Seán McLoughlin. "*Diasporas: Concepts, Intersections, Identities.*" London: Zed, 2010.
Kottak, Conrad Phillip. *Mirror for Humanity: A Concise Introduction to Cultural Anthropology.* Blacklick, OH: McGraw-Hill College, 1999.
Kotz, David M. "Globalization and Neoliberalism." *Rethinking Marxism* 12 (2002) 64–79.
Kraemer, Hendrick. *A Theology of the Laity.* Philadelphia, PA: Westminster, 1958.
Krishna-Hensel, Sai Felicia, ed. "Global Interdisciplinary Studies Series." *Ashgate.* https://www.ashgate.com/default.aspx?page=5097&series_id=256&calcTitle=1.
Kunin, Seth D. *Theories of Religions: A Reader.* Chapel Hill, NC: Rutgers University Press, 2006.
Kuyper, Abraham. *Lectures on Calvinism.* CreateSpace, 2009.
Kuznetsov, Yevgeny, ed. *Diaspora Networks and the International Migration of Skills: How Countries Can Draw on Their Talent Abroad.* WBI Development Studies. Washington, DC: World Bank, 2006.
———. "The Global Role Model—Global Scot's Interview with Yevgeny Kuznetsov." *The World Bank* (August 2007). http://www.worldbank.org.
Kwon, Ho-Youn, ed. *Korean Americans: Conflict and Harmony.* Chicago, IL: North Park College and Theological Seminary, 1994.
Lalaki, Despina. "Class Syllabus: Diaspora, Race, and Identity: Re-imaging the Community." *Academia* (2006). http://www.academia.edu/1748509/Diaspora_Race_Identity_Re-Imagining_the_Community.
Lambert, Yves. "A Turning Point in Religious Evolution in Europe." *Journal of Contemporary Religion* 19 (2004) 29–45.
Lausanne. "Consultations on Diaspora Missions: The Roadmap to Cape Town for People on the Move." *Lausanne Movement.* http://www.lausanne.org/gatherings/issue-gathering/consultations-on-diaspora-missions.
Lausanne Committee for World Evangelization. *Scattered to Gather: Embracing the Global Trend of Diaspora.* Manila, Philippines: Life Change, 2010.
———. "The Seoul Declaration on Diaspora Missiology." *Lausanne Movement* (November 14, 2009). http://www.lausanne.org/content/statement/the-seoul-declaration-on-diaspora-missiology.
Lausanne Committee for World Evangelization Issue Group No. 4. "Holistic Mission Occasional Paper No. 33." Edited by Evvy Hay. Delhi, India: Horizon, 2004.
Lausanne Committee for World Evangelization Issue Group No. 26 A and B: Diasporas and International Students. "Lausanne Occasional Paper No. 55: The New People Next Door." Edited by D. Clayton. Delhi, India: Horizon, 2005.
Lee, Aruna. "Oakland Shooting Rampage Forces Korean-Americans to Search for Answers Within The Community." *Highbrow Magazine* (April 2012). http://

www.highbrowmagazine.com/1078-oakland-shooting-rampage-forces-korean-americans-search-answers-within-community.

Lee, Byung Ryang, et al. "Diagnosis and Interpretation of the Social Conflict Structure in Korea: Its Level, Causes, and Alternatives." *The Korean Association for Public Management* 22 (2008) 49–72.

Lee, Jennifer. "Entrepreneurship and Business Development among African Americans, Koreans, and Jews: Exploring Some Structural Differences." In *Transnational Communities and the Political Economy of New York City in the 1990s*, edited by Héctor R. Cordero-Guzmán et al., 258–78. Philadelphia, PA: Temple University Press, 2001.

———. "Striving for the American Dream: Struggle, Success, and Intergroup Conflict among Korean Immigrant Entrepreneurs." In *Contemporary Asian America*, edited by Min Zhou and James V. Gatewood, 278–94. New York: New York University Press, 2000.

Lee, Young Hun. "Conflict Society: Its Discussions and Resolutions." *Current Mentality Monthly* (Summer 2011). http://www.sdjs.co.kr/read.php?quarterId=SD201102&num=486.

Lett, Denise Potrzeba. *In Pursuit of Status: The Making of South Korea's New Urban Middle Class*. The Harvard-Hallym Series on Korean Studies 4. Cambridge, MA: Harvard University Press, 1998.

Long, Lynellyn D. and Ellen Oxfeld, eds. *Coming Home? Refugees, Migrants, and Those Who Stayed Behind*. Philadelphia, PA: University of Pennsylvania Press, 2004.

Lord, Andrew M. "The Holy Spirit and Contextualization." *Asian Journal of Pentecostal Studies* 4 (2001) 201–13.

Lundy, David. *Borderless Church: Shaping the Church for the Twenty-First Century*. Waynesboro, GA: Authentic, 2005.

Luther, Martin. *A Prelude by Martin Luther on the Babylonian Captivity of the Church*. Originally published in *Works of Martin Luther with Introductions and Notes*, translated by Albert T. W. Steinhaeuser, 167–293. Philadelphia, PA: A. J. Holman, 1915. http://www.projectwittenberg.org/etext/luther/babylonian/babylonian.htm.

———. *The Pagan Servitude of the Church*. http://divdl.library.yale.edu/dl/FullText.aspx?qc=AdHoc&q=3157.

Luzbetak, Louis J. *The Church and Cultures: New Perspectives in Missiological Anthropology*. Maryknoll, NY: Orbis, 1996.

Lyon, David. "Wheels within Wheels: Globalization & Contemporary Religion." In *A Global Faith: Essays on Evangelicalism & Globalization*, edited by Marks Hutchinson and Ogbu Kalu, 47–68. Sydney: Centre for the Study of Australian Christianity, 1998.

Mahalingam, Ramaswami, ed. *Cultural Psychology of Immigrants*. Florence, KY: Psychology, 2006.

Makari, Peter. "Mission as Healing." *Global Ministries*. http://www.globalministries.org/resources/mission-study/college-of-mission/mission-as-healing.html.

Mandryk, Patrick. *Operation World: The Definitive Prayer Guide to Every Nation*. Colorado Springs, CO: Biblica, 2010.

Marshall, Howard, ed. *The New Bible Dictionary*. 3rd ed. Downers Grove, IL: InterVarsity, 1996.

Martínez, Juan Francisco. *Los Protestantes: An Introduction to Latino Protestantism in the United States*. Westport, CT: Praeger, 2011.

———. *Walk with the People: Latino Ministry in the United States*. Nashville, TN: Abingdon, 2008.
Matamonasa-Bennett, Arieahn. "The Psychology of Attacks and Attackers." *DePaul University, Chicago, IL*. http://www.aspcapro.org/sites/pro/files/understanding_the_nature_of_attacks_and_attackers_1.pdf.
McGrath, Alister E. *Christian Theology: Introduction*. Hoboken, NJ: Wiley Blackwell, 2010.
McQuilkin, Robertson. *The Role of the Holy Spirit in Mission*. Pasadena, CA: William Carey Library, 1997.
Meeks, M. Douglas. *God the Economist: The Doctrine of God and Political Economy*. Minneapolis, MN: Fortress, 1980.
Mercer, Kobena, ed. *Exiles, Diasporas and Strangers*. Annotating Art's Histories: Cross-Cultural Perspectives in the Visual Arts. Cambridge, MA: MIT Press, 2008.
Merriam-Webster. "Stewardship." *Merriam-Webster.com*. http://www.merriam-webster.com/dictionary/stewardship.
Min, Pyong Gap. "Cultural and Economic Boundaries of Korean Ethnicity: A Comparative Analysis." *Ethnic and Racial Studies* 14 (1991) 225–41.
Min, Pyong Gap, and Andrew Kolodny. "The Middle Man Minority Characteristics of Korean Immigrants in the United States." *Korean Journal of Population and Development* 23 (1994) 179–202.
Min, Pyong Gap and Jung Ha Kim, eds. *Religions in Asian America: Building Faith Communities*. Walnut Creek, CA: AltaMira, 2002.
Minatrea, Milfred. *Shaped by God's Heart: The Passion and Practices of Missional Churches*. San Francisco, CA: Jossey-Bass, 2004.
Moltmann, Jurgen. *The Church in the Power of the Spirit: Contribution to Messianic Ecclesiology*. Minneapolis, MN: Fortress, 1993.
Morelli, George. "Secularism and the Mind of Christ and the Church." *The Self-Ruled Antiochian Orthodox Christian Archdiocese of North America*. http://www.antiochian.org/content/secularism-and-mind-christ-and-church-some-psycho-spiritual-reflections.
Moriarty, Glendon, ed. "Integrating Faith and Psychology." Downers Grove, IL: IVP Academic, 2010.
Morris, Brain. *Anthropological Studies of Religions*. Cambridge: Cambridge University Press, 2000.
Moser, Paul K. and Thomas L. Carson. *Moral Relativism: A Reader*. New York: Oxford University Press, 2000.
Mtonga, George N. "Diaspora Existentialism: The Psychology of Zambians in the Diaspora (An Interview)." *Lusakatimes.com* (April 11, 2014). http://www.lusakatimes.com/2014/04/11/diaspora-existentialism-psychology-zambians-diaspora-interview/.
Munby, Dennis L. *The Idea of a Secular Society*. New York: Oxford University Press, 1963.
Mywihia, David. *Towards a Missional Theology for African Diaspora in North America*. Saarbrücken, Germany: Lap Lambert Academic, 2011.
Naish, Tim. "Mission, Migration and the Stranger in Our Midst." In *Mission and Migration*, edited by Stephen Spencer, 7–30. Derbyshire, UK: Cliff College Publishing, 2008.

Nayyar, Deepak. *Governing Globalization: Issues and Institutions.* Oxford / New York: Oxford University Press, 2002.

Nelson, Robert H. *Economics as Religion: From Samuelson to Chicago and Beyond.* University Park, PA: Pennsylvania State University Press, 2002.

Newbigin, Lesslie. *Foolishness to the Greeks: The Gospel and Western Culture.* Grand Rapids, MI: W. B. Eerdmans, 1986.

———. *The Other Side of 1984: Questions for the Churches.* Risk Book Series 18. New York: World Council of Churches, 1990.

Nichols, Aidan. *Theology in the Russian Diaspora: Church, Fathers, Eucharist in Nikolai Afanas'ev (1893-1966).* New York: Cambridge University Press, 2008.

Nietzsche, Friedrich W. *The Gay Science.* Translated by Thomas Common. New York: Digireads.com, 2009.

———. *On the Genealogy of Morality.* Translated by Moudemarei Clark and Alan J. Swensen. Indianapolis, IN: Hackett, 1998.

Norman, Alex J. "Black-Korean Relations: From Desperation to Dialogue, or from Shouting and Shooting to Sitting and Talking." *Journal of Multicultural Social Work* 3 (1994) 87–99.

Oberg, Kalervo. "Cultural Shock: Adjustment to New Cultural Environments." *Curare* 29 (2006) 142–46. http://www.transkulturellepsychiatrie.de/pdf/cu29,2+3_2006_S%20142-146%20Repr%20Oberg%20%25.pdf.

O'Brien, David J. and Stephen S. Fugita. "Middleman Minority Concept: Its Explanatory Value in the Case of the Japanese in California Agriculture." *The Pacific Sociological Review* 25 (1982) 185–204.

Ohmae, Kenichi. *The Borderless World.* New York: McKinsey & Co., 1991.

O'Leary, Zina. *The Social Science Jargon Buster.* Boston, MA: Saga, 2007.

O'Malley, Steven J. *Revitalization Amid Diaspora: Explorations in World Christian Revitalization Movements.* Lexington, KY: Emeth, 2013.

OMF International. "About OMF International." https://omf.org/about-omf/.

———. "Diaspora Ministries." http://omf.org/asia/diaspora/.

———. "Training for Churches and Universities." http://omf.org/asia/diaspora/training-for-diaspora-returnee-ministry/.

Ott, Craig. "Conclusion." In *Globalizing Theology: Belief and Practice in an Era of World Christianity,* edited by Craig Ott and Harold A. Netland, 309–36. Grand Rapids, MI: Baker Academic, 2006.

Ott, Craig, and Harold A. Netland, eds. *Globalizing Theology: Belief and Practice in an Era of World Christianity.* Grand Rapids, MI: Baker Academic, 2006.

Oxford English Dictionary Online. "Diaspora." http://www.oxforddictionaries.com/us/definition/american_english/diaspora.

Page, Nanette. "Empowerment." *Journal of Extension* 37 (1999). http://www.joe.org/joe/1999october/comm1.php.

Parliamentary Assembly. "Recommendation 1688: Diaspora Cultures." *Council of Europe* (November 23, 2004). http://assembly.coe.int/Documents/AdoptedText/ta04/EREC1688.htm.

Parson, John. "The Beatitudes of Jesus: Recited in Hebrew." http://www.hebrew4christians.com/Scripture/Brit_Chadashah/Beatitudes/beatitudes.html.

PatmosIsland.com. "Patmos Island." http://www.patmos-island.com/.

Payne, J. D. "Missions To, Through, and Beyond the Diasporas." *Missiologically Thinking* (March 20, 2012). http://www.jdpayne.org/2012/03/20/missions-to-through-and-beyond-the-diasporas/.

———. *Strangers Next Door: Immigration, Migration and Mission*. Downers Grove, IL: InterVarsity, 2012.

Pew Research Center. "Faith on the Move: The Religious Afflictions of International Migrants." http://www.pewforum.org/2012/03/08/religious-migration-exec/.

———. "The Future of the Global Muslim Population." http://www.pewforum.org/2011/01/27/the-future-of-the-global-muslim-population/.

———."A Portrait of Muslim Americans." http://www.people-press.org/2011/08/30/a-portrait-of-muslim-americans/.

———. "Rising Tide of Restrictions on Religion: Preface." http://www.pewforum.org/2012/09/20/rising-tide-of-restrictions-on-religion-preface/.

———. "U.S. Population Projections: 2005–2050." http://www.pewhispanic.org/2008/02/11/us-population-projections-2005-2050/.

Phan, Peter. "Migration in the Patristic Era." In *A Promised Land, A Perilous Journey: Theological Perspectives on Migration*, edited by Daniel G. Groody and Gioacchino Campese, 35–61. Notre Dame, IN: University of Notre Dame Press, 2008.

Pieterse, Jan N. *Globalization and Culture*. New York: Rowman & Littlefield, 2003.

Pogrebin, Mark R., and Eric D. Poole. "Culture Conflict and Crime in the Korean-American Community." *Criminal Justice Policy Review* 4 (1990) 69–78. *Sage Journals*. http://cjp.sagepub.com/content/4/1/69.abstract.

Porter, Jack N. "The Urban Middleman: A Comparative Analysis." *Comparative Social Research* 4 (1981) 199–215.

Portes, Alejandro, and Robert Manning. "The Immigrant Enclave: Theory and Empirical Examples." In *Competitive Ethnic Relations*, edited by Susan Olzak and Joane Nagel, 47–68. New York: American, 1986.

Posner, M. I., and G. J. DiGirolamo. "Cognitive Neuroscience: Origins and Promise." *Psychological Bulletin* 126 (2000) 873–89.

Priest, R. "Experience—Near Theologizing in Diverse Human Context." In *Globalizing Theology: Belief and Practice in an Era of World Christianity*, edited by Craig Ott and Harold A. Netland, 180–95. Grand Rapids, MI: Baker Academic, 2006.

———. "What in the World is Missiology?" *Missiological Matters*. http://www.missiologymatters.com/2012/03/07/what-in-the-world-is-missiology/.

Pritchett, L. "Divergence, Big Time." *Journal of Economic Perspectives* 11 (1997) 3–18.

Project Muse. *Diaspora: A Journal of Transnational Studies* (1991–2009). http://muse.jhu.edu/journals/diaspora_a_journal_of_transnational_studies/.

Psychology Dictionary. "What is Cross-Cultural Psychology?" *PsychologyDictionary.org*. http://psychologydictionary.org/cross-cultural-psychology/#ixzz2e4BPp8JG.

Rains, G. Dennis. *Principles of Human Neuropsychology*. New York: McGraw-Hill, 2001.

Raitt, Thomas M. *A Theology of Exile: Judgment/Deliverance in Jeremiah and Ezekiel*. Philadelphia, PA: Fortress, 1977.

Ramsay, W. *St. Paul the Traveler and the Roman Citizen*. London: Hodder & Stoughton, 1920.

Rao, Vijayendra, and Michael Walton, ed. *Culture and Public Action*. Stanford, CA: Stanford University Press, 2004. http://www-wds.worldbank.org/external/default/WDSContentServer/IW3P/IB/2004/08/19/000160016_20040819153703/Rendered/PDF/298160018047141reoandoPublic0Action.pdf

Ratner, Carl and Lumei Hui. "Theoretical and Methodological Problems in Cross-Cultural Psychology." *Journal for the Theory of Social Behavior* 33 (2003) 67–94.

Reimer, David. "Exile and Diaspora: Leaving and Living." *Guideline* 23 (2007) 6–19.

———. "Exile, Diaspora, and, Old Testament Theology." *Scottish Bulletin of Evangelical Theology* 28 (2010) 1–8.

Reinhard, Bendix. *Max Weber: An Intellectual Portrait*. Oakland, CA: University of California Press, [1960] 1970.

Remington, Ted. "Lars and the Real Girl: Lifelike Positive Transcendence." *SAGE Open* (2011). http://sgo.sagepub.com/content/spsgo/1/1/2158244011408346.full.pdf?ijkey=HUO8IwlDqtCts&keytype=ref&siteid=spsgo.

Renz, Thomas. *The Rhetorical Function of the Book of Ezekiel*. Leiden, Netherlands: Brill, 1999.

Robbins, Richard. *Global Problems and the Culture of Capitalism*. Boston, MA: Allyn & Bacon, 1999.

Robertson, O. Palmer. *The Christ of the Covenants*. Phillipsburg, NJ: P & R, 1981.

Robertson, Roland. *Globalization*. New York: Sage, 1992.

Robinson, Lawrence, et al. "Emotional and Psychological Trauma: Symptoms, Treatment, and Recovery." *HealthGuide.org*. http://www.helpguide.org/mental/emotional_psychological_trauma.htm.

Roof, Wade C., and Nathalie Caron, "Shifting Boundaries: Religion and the United States: 1960 to the Present." In *The Cambridge Companion to Modern American Culture*, edited by Christopher Bigsby, 113–134. Cambridge: Cambridge University Press, 2006.

Safran, William. "Diasporas in Modern Societies: Myths of Homeland and Return." *Diaspora: A Journal of Transnational Studies* 1 (1991) 83–99.

———. "The Jewish Diaspora in a Comparative and Theoretical Perspective." *Israel and the Diaspora: New Perspectives* 10 (2005) 36–60. http://www.jstor.org/stable/30245753?seq=1#page_scan_tab_contents.

Sahoo, Ajaya K., and Brij Maharaj. *Sociology of Diaspora: A Reader*. 2 vols. Jaipur, India: Rawat, 2007.

Said, Abdul Aziz, et al., eds. *Concepts of International Politics in Global Perspective*. 4th ed. Upper Saddle River: Prentice Hall, 1995.

Said, Abdul Aziz, et al., eds. *Peace and Conflict Resolution in Islam: Precept and Practice*. Lanham, MD: University Press of America, 2001.

Sakuma, Paul. "One Goh, Suspect Accused of Killing Seven at Oakland Christian College in April, Ruled Unfit for Trial." *Associated Press* (January 2013). http://www.nydailynews.com/news/national/oakland-college-slayer-ruled-unfit-trial-article-1.1235471.

Santos, Narry. "Diaspora Occurrences in the Bible and Their Contexts in Missions." *Lausanne World Pulse Archives* 3 (2009). http://www.lausanneworldpulse.com/themedarticles.php/1104?pg=all.

Sayer, Andrew. *Method in Social Science: A Realist Approach*. 2nd ed. New York: Routledge, 1992.

Schmerhorn, R. A. *Comparative Ethnic Relation*. New York: Random House, 1970.

Schreiter, Robert. *The New Catholicity: Theology between the Global and the Local*. Maryknoll, NY: Orbis, 1999.

Senior, Donald. "Beloved Aliens and Exile in a Christian Ethic of Immigration." https://www.usfca.edu/uploadedFiles/Destinations/Institutes_and_Centers/Lane/Events/documents/Heyer%20Lecture%201(1).pdf.
Sheffer, Gabriel. *Diaspora Politics: At Home Abroad.* New York: Cambridge University Press, 2006.
Shenk, Wilbert R. *Changing Frontiers of Mission.* American Society of Missiology Series. Maryknoll, NY: Orbis, 1999.
Shore, Megan. *Religion and Conflict Resolution: Christianity and South Africa's Truth and Reconciliation Commission.* Burlington, VT: Ashgate, 2009.
Siever, L. J. "Neurobiology of Aggression and Violence." *The American Journal of Psychiatry* 165 (2008) 429–42.
Silk, Mark. "Defining Religious Pluralism in America: A Regional Analysis." *Annals of the American Academy of Political and Social Science* 612 (2007) 64–81.
Smith-Christopher, Daniel L. *Biblical Theology of Exile.* Overtures to Biblical Theology. Minneapolis, MN: Augsburg Fortress, 2002.
Soerens, Matthew. Review of *Strangers Next Door*, by J. D. Panyne. http://www.ivpress.com/cgi-ivpress/book.pl/review/code=6341.
Song, Sarah. "Multiculturalism." *Stanford Encyclopedia of Philosophy* (September 24, 2010). http://plato.stanford.edu/entries/multiculturalism/.
Spence-Jones, H. D. M., et al., eds. *The Pulpit Commentary: Volume XVII: John.* Peabody, MA: Hendrickson, 1985. http://biblehub.com/john/7-35.htm.
Spencer, Stephen. *Mission and Migration: Papers Read at the Biennial Conference of the British and Irish Association for Mission Studies at the Westminster College.* Cambridge: Cliff College, 2007.
Spillers, Hortense, ed. *Comparative American Identities.* New York: Routledge, 1991.
Spradly, James, and David McCurdy. *Conformity and Conflict: Readings in Cultural Anthropology.* Needham Heights, MA: Allyn & Bacon, 2000.
Spykman, Gorden J. *Reformation Theology: A New Paradigm for Doing Doctrines.* Grand Rapids, MI: W. B. Eerdmans, 1992.
Stefanick, Chris. *Absolute Relativism: The New Dictatorship and What to Do about It.* El Cajon, CA: Catholic Answers, 2011.
Steger Center. "Dealing with Culture Shock." *Virginia Tech: CESA* (2010). http://www.oired.vt.edu/cesa/currentstudents/cs_culturalshock.htm.
Steger, Manfred B. *Globalization: A Very Short Introduction.* New York: Oxford University Press, 2003.
Stewart, Ella. "Communication between African Americans and Korean Americans: Before and After the Los Angeles Riots." *Amerasia Journal* 19 (1993) 23–53.
Stibbs, Alan M., and Andrew F. Walls. *Tyndale New Testament Commentaries: 1 Peter.* Grand Rapids, MI: W. B. Eerdmans, 1987.
Stolorow, Robert D. "Feeling, Relating, Existing: On Emotion and the Human Dimension." *Psychology Today.* https://www.psychologytoday.com/blog/feeling-relating-existing.
Stott, John R. W. *One People: Laymen and Clergy in God's Church.* Downers Grove, IL: InterVarsity, 1968.
Strong, David K., and Cynthia A. Strong. "The Globalizing Hermeneutic of the Jerusalem Council." In *Globalizing Theology: Belief and Practice in an Era of World Christianity*, edited by Craig Ott and Harold A. Netland, 127–39. Grand Rapids, MI: Baker Academic, 2006.

Suh, Kwang-Sun. "Minjung Theology in Korea: A Biographical Sketch of an Asian Theological Consultation." In *Minjung Theology: People as the Subjects of History*, edited by Kim Yong-Bok, 15–37. Singapore: CTC/CCA, 1981.

Swatos, William H. Jr., ed. *Encyclopedia of Religion and Society*. Lanham, MD: Altamira, 1988.

Tannen, Deborah, and James E. Alatis, eds. *Linguistics, Language, and the Real World: Discourse and Beyond*. Georgetown University Round Table on Languages and Linguistics. Washington, DC: Georgetown University, 2001.

Taylor, Charles. *A Secular Age*. New York: Harvard University Press, 2007.

Taylor, William. *Kingdom Partnerships for Synergy in Missions*. World Evangelical Fellowship Series 2. Pasadena, CA: William Carey Library, 1994.

Third Lausanne Congress on World Evangelization. "The Cape Town Commitment: A Confession of Faith and a Call to Action." *Lausanne Movement*. http://www.lausanne.org/en/documents/ctcommitment.html#p2-3.

———. "Content Library: The Cape Town Declaration on Care and Counsel as Mission." *Lausanne Movement*. http://www.lausanne.org/content/care-and-counsel-as-mission.

Tienou, Tite. "Forming Indigenous Theologies." In *Toward the 21st Century in Christian Missions*, edited by James M. Phillips and Robert T. Coote, 245–52. Grand Rapids, MI: W. B. Eerdmans, 1993.

Tillich, Paul. *The Courage to Be*. New Haven, CT: Yale University Press, 2000.

———. *Dynamics of Faith*. New York: HarperOne, 2009.

———. *Systematic Theology*. 3 vols. Chicago, IL: University of Chicago Press, 1963.

Tira, Sadiri Joy. "Diaspora Missiology." *The Lausanne Movement* (2010). http://conversation.lausanne.org/en/conversations/detail/11103#.UXrk4MokQro.

———."Diaspora Missiology Part 3: Interview with Sadiri Joy Tira." *Missiologically Thinking* (May 4, 2010). http://www.jdpayne.org/2010/05/04/diaspora-missiology-part-3-interview-with-sadiri-joy-tira/.

Thomas, T. V., et al. "Ministering to the Scattered Peoples." *Lausanne Movement*. http://www.lausanne.org/content/ministering-to-the-scattered-peoples.

Tololyan, Kachig. "The Nation-State and Its Others: In Lieu of a Preface." *Diaspora* 1 (1991) 3–7.

Tomlinson, John. *Globalization and Culture*. Chicago, IL: The University of Chicago Press, 1999.

Tönnies, Ferdinand. *Community and Society*. Translated by Charles Price Loomis. East Lansing, MI: Michigan State University Press, 1957.

Towner, Philip H. Review of *Contextualization in the New Testament: Patterns for Theology and Mission*, by Dean Flemming. http://www.amazon.com/Contextualization-New-Testament-Patterns-Theology/dp/0830828311.

Tracy, David. "The Foundations of Practical Theology." In *Practical Theology: The Emerging Field in Theology, Church, and World*, edited by Don S. Browning, 61–82. San Francisco, CA: Harper & Row, 1983.

Turner, Jonathan, and Edna Bonacich. "Toward a Composite Theory of Middleman Minorities." *Ethnicity* 7 (1980) 144–58.

UNESCO. "Trans-nationalism." http://www.unesco.org/new/en/social-and-human-sciences/themes/international-migration/glossary/trans-nationalism/.

University of Missouri, St. Louis. "Santa Claus—Secularization and Globalization." http://www.umsl.edu/~naumannj/Globalization.html.

Ury, William. *Getting Past No: Negotiating with Difficult People*. New York: Bantam, 1991.

Van Engen, Charles. "Mission Defined and Described." In *Mission Shift: Global Mission Issues in the Third Millennium*, edited by David Hesselgrave et al., 1–29. Nashville, TN: B&H Academic, 2010.

———. *Mission on the Way: Issues in Mission Theology*. Grand Rapids, MI: Baker, 1996.

———. "Monday is for Missiology: Mission, Described and Defined: A Discussion around MissionSHIFT." http://www.christianitytoday.com/edstetzer/2011/january/monday-is-for-missiology-mission-described-and-defined.html.

———. "Toward a Contextually Appropriate Methodology in Mission Theology." In *Appropriate Christianity*, edited by Charles H. Kraft, 203–26. Pasadena, CA: William Carey Library, 2005.

Van Gelder, Craig. *The Ministry of the Missional Church: The Community led by the Spirit*. Grand Rapids, MI: Baker, 2007.

Vanhoozer, Kevin J. *Is There a Meaning in This Text? The Bible, the Reader, and the Morality of Literary Knowledge*. Grand Rapids, MI: Zondervan, 2009.

Veith, Gene. "Has Lutheranism Caused Secularism?" *Patheos* (March 22, 2012). http://www.patheos.com/blogs/geneveith/2012/03/has-lutheranism-caused-secularism/.

Vertovec, Steven. "Conceiving and Researching Transnationalism." *Ethnic and Racial Studies* 22 (1999) 447–62.

———. "Introduction: New Directions in the Anthropology of Migration and Multiculturalism." *Ethnic and Racial Studies* 30 (2007) 961–78.

———. "Transnationalism and Identity." *Journal of Ethnic and Migration Studies* 27 (2001) 573–82.

Vicedom, Georg F. *The Mission of God: An Introduction to a Theology of Mission*. Translated by Gilbert A. Thiele and Dennis Hilgendorf. Saint Louis, MO: Concordia. 1965.

Volf, Miroslav. *Exclusion & Embrace: A Theological Exploration of Identity, Otherness, and Reconciliation*. Nashville, TN: Abingdon, 1996.

———. "Faith and Globalization: Secularization & Religious Resurgence." *Yale University: Faith & Globalization Initiative*. https://www.youtube.com/watch?v=oKCT-4lZHKc&list=PL003CE0429CAE4E19&index=6.

Vos, Geerhardus. *Biblical Theology: Old and New Testaments*. Carlisle, PA: Banner of Truth, 1975.

Wainwright, William. "Concepts of God." https://leibniz.stanford.edu/friends/members/view/concepts-god/sc/.

Walls, Andrew F. "Andrew Walls: An Exciting Period in Christian History." *Faith & Leadership* (June 5, 2011). https://www.faithandleadership.com/multimedia/andrew-walls-exciting-period-christian-history.

———. "Mission and Migration: The Diaspora Factor in Christian History." *Journal of African Christian Thought* 5 (2002) 3–11.

Wan, Enoch. *Diaspora Missiology: Theory, Methodology, and Practice*. Portland, OR: Institute of Diaspora Studies, Western Seminary, 2011.

———. "Interview with Enoch Wan on Diaspora Missiology." *Missiologically Thinking* (February 27, 2012). http://www.jdpayne.org/2012/02/27/interview-with-enoch-wan-on-diaspora-missiology/.

———. "Mission and *Missio Dei*: Response to Charles Van Engens Mission Defined and Described." *Global Missiology English* 3 (2011). http://ojs.globalmissiology.org/index.php/english/article/view/580/1467.

Wan, Enoch and Sadiri Joy Tira. "Diaspora Missiology and Mission in the Context of the 21st Century." *Torch Trinity Journal* 13 (2010). http://www.enochwan.com/english/articles/pdf/Diaspora%20Missiology%20in%2021st%20Century.pdf.

———. "The Pilipino Experience Diaspora Missions: A Case Study of Mission Initiative from the Majority World Churches." *Evangelical Missiological Society* (April 5, 2008) http://www.enochwan.com/english/articles/pdf/The%20Filipino%20Experience%20In%20Diaspora%20Missions%20-%20EMS.pdf.

Watson's Biblical & Theological Dictionary. "Patmos." *StudyLight.org*. http://www.studylight.org/dic/wtd/view.cgi?n=1231.

Weaver, Alain Epp. *State of Exile: Visions of Diaspora, Witness and Return*. Scottsdale, PA: Herald, 2008.

WebBible Encyclopedia. "Tarsos." http://www.christiananswers.net/dictionary/tarsus.html.

Weber, Max. "Bureaucratic Form According to Max Weber—His Six Major Principles." http://www.bustingbureaucracy.com/excerpts/weber.htm.

———. *The Protestant Ethic and the Spirit of Capitalism*. Translated by Talcott Parsons. New York: CreateSpace, 2002.

Weitzer, Ronald. "Racial Prejudice among Korean Merchants in African American Neighborhoods." *Sociological Quarterly* 38 (1997) 587–606.

Wenham, G. J. *Word Biblical Commentary: Genesis 1–15*. Waco, TX: Word, 1987.

Westminster Confession of Faith. "Chapter 28: Of Baptism." *The Covenant of Grace*. http://www.covenantofgrace.com/westminster_chapter28.htm.

Wheat, Leonard F. *Hegel's Undiscovered Thesis-Antithesis-Synthesis Dialectics: What Only Marx and Tillich Understood*. Amherst, MA: Prometheus, 2012.

Wholesome Words, "John Bunyan: English Author and Preacher." Copied from *Dictionary of National Biography*. London: Smith, Elder, & Co., 1886. http://www.wholesomewords.org/biography/bbunyan.html.

Winter, Ralph D., and Bruce A. Koch. "Finishing the Task: The Unreached Peoples Challenge." *International Journal of Frontier Mission* 19 (2002) 15–25.

Woolnough, Brian. *Holistic Mission: God's Plan for God's People*. Regnum Edinburgh 2010 series. Eugene, OR: Wipf & Stock, 2010.

Wright, Chris. "Re-affirming Holistic Mission: A Cross-Centered Approach in All Areas of Life." *Lausanne World Pulse Archives* 10 (2005). http://www.lausanneworldpulse.com/themedarticles.php/61/10-2005.

Wu, Jackson. "We Compromise the Gospel when we settle for Truth: How Right Interpretations Lead to Wrong Contextualization." *Global Missiology English* 2 (2013). http://ojs.globalmissiology.org/index.php/english/article/viewFile/1130/2613.

Wulff, D. M. "Psychology of Religion." In *Encyclopedia of Psychology and Religion*, edited by D. A. Leeming et al., 732–35. New York / London: Springer, 2010.

Ybarrola, Steven. "An Anthropological Approach to Diaspora Missiology." (2011). http://www.ureachtoronto.com/sites/default/files/resources/An%20Anthropological%20Approach%20to%20Diaspora%20Missiology%20S11%20Final.pdf.

Yoder, John Howard. *The Politics of Jesus*. Grand Rapids, MI: W. B. Eerdmans, 1994.

———. "See how they go with their Face to the Sun." Opening address of colloquium on "Communities in Exile" convened by the Institute on Faith, Culture and the Arts, Loyola Marymount University, Los Angeles, CA, September 23, 1995. http://brandon.multics.org/library/John%20Howard%20Yoder/seehowgo.html.

Yun, Young Ho. "How does Immigrant Church see Immigrant Pastor's Return to Korean Church?" *Igoodnews* (May 2010). http://www.igoodnews.net/news/articleView.html?idxno=27924.

Zenner, Walter. "Middleman Minority Theories: A Critical Review." In *Sourcebook on the New Immigration*, edited by Roy S. Bryce-Laporte, 413–25. New Brunswick, NJ: Transaction, 1980.

———. *Minorities in the Middle: A Cross-Cultural Analysis*. Albany, NY: State University of New York Press, 1991.

Zerfass, Rolf. "Praktische Theologie als Handlungswissenschaft." In *Praktische Theologie heute*, edited by Ferdinand Klostermann et al., 164–77. München: Kaiser / Mainz: Grünewald, 1974.

Index

A
Abrams, Dominic, 282
Alfonso, Carolin, 214
Antioch church, 106-7
Acculturation, 63
Acts
  Diaspora and, 104-7, 228-29
  Holy Spirit, 129, 228-29
  Mission and, 105, 128
  Philip and, 7, 129, 171, 180, 182-83, 248, 252-53, 268
  Stephan and, 7, 180, 182-83, 252-53, 268
  Globalizing hermeneutics in, 194
African
  Civilization, 39
  Diaspora, 40, 138
  Migration, 3, 30
  Refugee in, 59
  Sub-Saharan, 52
  Symbols, 40
  To America, 15
Aggressive or aggression, 69, 285-86,
Aikins, Kingsley, 291
Alders, Charles, 85
Alienation, 80
Aliens, 131-32, 205
Anthropology
  Complementarity in, 58, 193
  Diaspora studies, 33-34
  Emic and *etic*, 193
  Interpretive, 186-87
  Symbolic, 186-87
Anthropological Studies of Religion, 76
Anthropologist, 172, 194

Anticolonial, 192-94
Anxiety, 64, 78-79, 138
Apologetic, 140, 146
Appadurai, Arjun, 151-52
Asbury theological seminary, 33
ASREC, 75
Assimilation metaphor, 60
Augustine, 140, 242

B
Bailey, Kenneth, 251
Banishment, 84-85
Barber, Daniel Colucciello, 131
Barclay, William, 109
Beatitudes, 146, 227
Berkhof, Louis, 136
Berger, Peter, 20, 156, 160-61
Bible
  Applications of, 81, 82, 173, 215, 218, 220, 254,
  Interpretations of, 173, 215, 254
  Interdisciplinary applications of, 218
  Interdisciplinary descriptions, 82
  Interdisciplinary interpretations of, 215-16, 220
  Interpreter and, 188, 220,
Biblical Theology, 99
Bloemraad, Irene, 282
Book of the revelation, 113-14
Borderless world, 1
Bosch, David, 4, 170-71, 197-98
British Irish Association of Mission Studies (BIAMS), 2, 51-53,
Braziel Jana Evans, 35

Brubaker, Rogers, 40
Bruce, F.F, 112
Brueggemann, Walter, 5, 132
Bswm, 65
Bulmer, Martin, 38
Bunyan, John, 6, 141–44, 213
Bureaucracy, 296

C
Calvin, John, 105, 136, 143, 170, 230
Captivity, 84, 89–94
Carson, Thomas L., 157
Carey, George, 272
Casanova, José, 20
Church
    Antioch, 106–7
    As the gathering of the scattered, 116–17
    Babylonian captivity of, 133
    Birth of, 104
    Communion sanctorum, 136
    Decline of, 229,
    Definition of, 226–29
    Diaspora and, 104–5
    Diaspora identity of, 138
    Globalizing theology and, 224–26
    Hispanic, 178–79
    Holy Spirit, 104–5
    Institutional, 181
    in a theology of the laity, 147
    on the brink of extinction, 272
    Reformation of, 183
    Revival of, 229–40
    transcendence of, 243, 272–73
Church planting indicator, 246
Christianity
    A new religion of, 159
    Diaspora, 106
    Essence of, 133
    essential doctrine of, 157
    Religion, secularity and, 131
    Secularism and, 241
    Western, 177
Christology, 125–26
Class, 64, 245
Clifford, James, 282
CLSC, 53–54
Cohen, Robin, 21, 61

Collective consciousness, 66, 74
Colonial or colonialism, 56, 58, 282
Colonizer/colonized, 65
Communication, 51, 172, 199, 208, 217–18, 220, 227
Compartmentalization and specialization, 177
Compassion, 11, 220, 269, 277
Conflict, 42, 73, 208, 286, 289
    Issues, 72–74
    Solving, 75
    Healing in the gospel, 278–79
    Yangbanization and *han*, 279
Connectivity, 153–54
Connection, 3, 280
Context Interpreting, 188, 209
Contextual
    Bible and, 188
    Christ and, 189
    Liberal mission, 168–69
    Methodology, 187–88
    Ministries, 255–56
    Text and, 186
Contextual theologizing
    Back to the text, 188
    centrality of the Cross and Resurrection of Christ, 189
    Definition of, 185–86
    For diaspora missiology 185–95
    Processes of, 206–24
    Role of the Holy Spirit in, 191
    Symbolic anthropology, 186
    Theologizing subject, 207–9
Contextualization
    A sprit of, 128
    Biblical, 8, 169, 256
    Centrality of the gospel in, 216–17
    Critical, 11, 150–53, 190–92
    In the New Testament, 188
    Goal of, 217
    Liberal mission and, 168
    Economics and, 186
    of the Holy Spirit, 191–92, 200, 222–23,
Cooper, Elizabeth Elliott, 121
Cosmopolitanism, 38, 42, 152, 222
Crowell, Steven, 79
Cross-cultural transplantation, 55

Covenant of God, 96
  Biblical doctrine of, 144
  Calling for, 100
  Of grace, 144
  Toward Pilgrim, 100
Cox, Harvey, 160
Crabb, Larry, 279–80
Cross-cultural, 2, 55, 289–91
Culture and cultural
  Flows, 152–53
  Difference, 60, 208
  Identities, 62–63, 213
  Interpretation of, 187
  psychology, 64–65
Cultural shock, 64, 275–76

D
De-colonialization, 35
Deportation, 91–94
De-Europeanizing, 57
Demographic shift, 1, 2
Demography, 1–2, 59
Deterritorialization, 22, 151–52, 177, 214
Dreher, Sabine, 71
Diaspora
  Anthropology and, 33–34
  As an experience of exile, 210
  As God's choice for salvation and mission, 115–16
  As new concept of mission, 178
  As the seed of God's kingdom, 120
  Biblical understanding of, 83–90
  church, 9–10,
  definition of, 40–43
  existentialism, 77
  Filipino diasopra, 2
  Identities, 210–211
  Jewish, 31–32
  Literature and, 38–40
  phenomenon of, 10, 20–21,
  philosophy, 77
  social science and, 35–37
  sociology of, 69–70
  theorizing, 31–59
  theological foundations, 124–50
Diakonia, 147–49
Diaspora evangelism, 284–88
  The seed of the kingdom and, 284–85
  Interdisciplinary approach toward aggressive Diaspora, 285–88
"Diaspora Mission Church," 9, 10–11, 180–83
Diaspora missiology and, 203–6
  Directions of the Current Church for, 240–258
  Healing empowerment of, 275–96
  Mission dei and, 177, 180
  Missional frameworks of, 225–74
  Purpose of, 248
  Ten core values of, 236–39
  Zerfass and, 203
Diaspora missiology, 85, 172, 176
Diaspora missiology, 1–3, 5, 11,
  Discoveries of, 49
  For unreached people, 244
  Globalization and, 172
  Methodology for, 172–73
  Mission and, 24
  Mission Dei, 171–72
Diaspora Politics, 37
Dichotomized, 177
Discrimination, 45, 121
Disjunctive flows, 151
Diversity, 219
Doctrine
  Of the Father, 124–25
  Of the Holy Spirit, 127–30
  Of man, 138, 141
  Of the Son, 125–27
  Of the trinity, 124–30
Double hermeneutical model, 6, 195–99
Dryness, William A., 216
Durkheim, Emile, 74
Dutton, Edward, 64

E
Economics, 15, 17–18, 219–20
Economic
  inequalities, 15
  opportunities, 16
  theory, 71
Elmer, Duane, 290–291
Empathetic, 276–77

Empowering, 275–97
Elliott, John H. 128
Eepiphanic experiences, 184
Epp- Weaver, Alain, 97, 132–33
Ethnic
   Bias, 121
   enclave, 61–62
   diversity, 17
   group, 17, 94
   hierarchies, 17
   relations, 45
Eternal home, 239
Eternal life, 240
Ethnicity, 69
Ethnocentrism, 199, 121, 291
Ethnoscapres, 152
EU
   As a new mission fields, 161
   Diaspora and, 27–28,
   Second chance, 29–30
   Populations in, 14
Evangelism, 1, 238, 284–88
Evangelization, 1, 216
   Diaspora, 284
   Globalization and, 24
   Muslim, 155–56
Exodus, 3, 86, 87–88, 101, 209, 241, 263
Exchange, 51, 89, 116, 153, 155, 186, 290
Exile, 5–6, 210
   Babylonian, 67
   Biblical theology of, 5
   Experience of, 134
   Theology of, 6, 130
   Paroikoi, 54
   Scattered, 111
Exile diaspora, 34
Exile experience, 5, 242
Exile theology, 130–32
   Applications of, 132
   Major theme of, 131
   Necessity of, 130
Existentialism, 71–81, 139
Existential problem, 139–40
Experience- near theologizing, 199

F
Faith on the Move, 1, 14, 178
Fanon, Frantz Omar, 65
Fee, Gordon D., 223
Feiertag, Thomas E., 155
Filipino, 45–46
Flemming, Dean, 188
Foreigner, 100–101, 112, 114
Fourth self, 186
Frankl, Viktor, 277–78
Funk, Nathan C. 281

G
Gathered and scattered, 136–37
Geertz, Clifford, 187
Ger, 99–10
Gemeinschaft, 155
Gender, 64, 69
Gesellschaft, 155
Ghetto, 32
Giddens, Anthony, 8, 197
Gill, Brad, 151
Glazer, Nathan, 60
GDN (Global Diaspora Network), 176
Global Christianity, 2, 9, 10, 57–59, 138, 178, 249
Global
   culture, 18–20, 150–53
   Diaspora, 3, 252–52, 291–97
   issues, 151, 155
   flows, 11,
   migration, 48
   ministries, 254–55
   network, 2, 288–90
   partners, 58
   problems, 71
   trends, 13–20, 50
Globalizing Hermeneutics
   Authority of the Bible, 195
   Of the Jerusalem council in Acts 15, 194–95
   Hermeneutical community, 195
Global South, 10, 29–30,
Global North, 29–30
Global theologizing, 8, 244
Global Diaspora Network(GDN), 176, 291–97

Globalization, 10, 13–18, 153, 206–13, 250
  Economics and, 17–18
  Characteristics of, 153–54
  Cosmopolitan and, 21
  Critics of, 18
  Culture and, 18
  Current missiology and, 150–53
  Neo-liberalism and, 70
  Of the frontiers, 151
  Process of, 70
  Theory, 50
Globalization, Spirituality, and Justice, 215
Global network builder, 288–89, 291–92
Glocalization or glocal, 154
Gospel
  Four Gospels, 102–4
  Gospel of Diaspora, 114–15
  In human contexts, 153
  Therapy and healing of, 159
  Preaching, 279
  Prosperity, 141
Groody, Daniel G, 2, 53–54, 153, 215
Guder, Darrell L, 167

H
Habermas, J., 161
Hall, Stuart, 63, 214
Han, 69
Hammar, Edward, 136
Hancile, Jehu, 1, 3, 11, 30, 56–58,
Hannerz, Ulf, 152
Hauerwas, Stanly, 5, 130–32, 205
Healing Diaspora, 6, 220, 236
  Emphatic understanding of suffering, 276–77
  Logotherapy's Search for "Meaning," 277–78
  Preaching the gospel, 279–80
Healing empowerment, 275–96
Heaven, 6, 54, 86, 102–3, 146, 239
Heavenly
  citizenship, 109
  country, 114
  life, 109, 112

Hegemony, 69
Heitink. Gerben, 196
Hellenistic Jews and the Hebraic Jews, 182
Heterogeneity, Diversity, and Hybridity, 213
Hiebert, Paul, 193
Hogg, Michael, 282
Holistic
  Dichotomized or, 177
  Gospel, 257
  ministry, 173, 257–60
  mission, 220–226
  Holistic Mission Occasional Paper no.33, 174, 220
Holy Spirit
  Guidance and empowering power of, 222
  Contextualization of, 127, 128,
  Missionary works of, 128
  One body of Christ and, 128
  Power of, 128, 223
  Sanctifying works of, 128
Holyoake, George, 159
Homogeneous, 152
Hoof, W. A. Visser't, 173
Horton, M., 146
Hospitality, 207
Host church, 10–11, 49
  Emphatic hospitality of, 207–9
  Hosted and, 208
  Participation of, 206
  Revival principle of, 209
Humanistic, 59
Hunsberger, George, 167
Hurt, 6, 285
Hybridity, 63, 177, 214
Hybridization, 18,

I
Identity
  confusion, 280
  cultural, 63
  diaspora, culture and, 38
  national, 63
  of diaspora, 281
  Transcendent, 282

324 Index

Identity transformation, 262–63
The importance of the Bible for, 263
In new context of diasopra, 263
Immanent, 113, 184
Immigration, 11, 69, 263
Inequality, 69
Incarnation, 125
Incarantional, 136, 220–222, 255–58
Indigenous, 49
Integration, 177
Interdisciplinary methodology, 173, 253
Interdisciplinary perspective, 188, 253
Interdisciplinary research, 172, 293–94
Interdisciplinary studies, 172–73, 254
   Anthropologists, 218
   Demography, 218
   Economics, 219
   For global ministries, 254–55
   Geographers, 219
   Historians, 219
   Lawmakers, 219
   Political scientists, 219
   Sociologists, 219
   Syncreticism and, 173
   Under the bible, 172–73
Interdisciplinary understanding of Diaspora
   Anthropology and, 60–63
   Diaspora and, 81
   Psychology and, 64–68
In the bible, 82
Israel, Nico, 282

J
James, Wiiliam, 76
Jenkins, Richard, 282
Jesus Christ,
   Blood of, 127, 136
   Crucifixion of, 126–27
Jewish
   Community, 32
   Diaspora, 31–32, 36
   Experience, 33
Jenkins, Philip, 10, 29–30, 177
Johnson, Todd, M, 18, 252, 254
Judgment of God, 5, 6, 85, 95, 115

Jung, Carl, 77
Justice, 5, 35, 220

K
Kanter, Moss, 20
Keller, Tim, 232
Kierkegaard, Soren, 77
Kim, Jung Ha, 259
Kim, S. Hun, 3, 211
Kingdom of God, 5, 59, 181, 226–27
Kingdom dream, 264
Kokot, Waltraud, 214
Korean-American, 74
Korean Diaspora church, 262–64, 269–71
Korean Diaspora and Christian Mission, 211
Korean-ness, 64
Korteweg, Anna, 282
Kottak, Conrad, 151
Kotz, David M, 70
Knott, Kim, 43
Kraemer, Hendrik, 147–49
Kuznetsov, Yevgeny, 292
Kuyper, A, 232

L
Lalaki, Despina, 37
Language, 65
Local, 141
Latino, 53–54, 177, 179
   population, 54
   protestants, 179
Lausanne
   Cape Town Lausanne(2010), 2, 47–51, 250
   Lausanne Committee for the World Evangelization(LCWE), 13, 15, 84, 174–75, 203, 221, 265
   Lausanne Diaspora Leadership Team(LDLT), 22, 265
   Lausanne Movement, 1–3, 10, 27, 31, 43–51, 85, 173–74, 203, 250
   Lausanne Occasional Paper No.55, 13, 43–45
   Manila Consultation, 46,
   Seoul Consultation, 46–47, 206
Laity, 147

The Theology of the Laity, 147–49
   Place and responsibility of, 148
Lay apostle, 284
Lay and clergy, 183
Lay missionary, 147
Lay theologian, 148
Logotheraphy, 277–78
Long, Lynellyn D., 265
Lord, Andy, 191
Lundy, David, 24
Luzbetak, Louis J. 186
Luther, M, 130–31, 133–34, 136, 143

M
Maharaj, Brij, 69
Mahalingam, Ramaswami, 65
Mandryk, Jason, 264
Market-dominant minorities, 73
Marginalized, 53
Marginalization, 51–52
Mannur, Anita, 35
Martinez, Juan Francisco, 179
Ma. Wonsuk, 211
McLoughlin, Sean, 43
McQuilkin, Robertson, 224
Method of Correlation, 187
Mead, Loren B. 136, 241
Melting pot, 44
Meta-culturalism, 193–94
Middleman Minority theory, 72
Migration, 1, 13–15
   Background, 70
   Causes of, 16,
   Christian, 22–23
   Diaspora and, 22–25
   International, 21
   Patterns of, 219
   Population, 23–24
   Southern, 56–59
   Speed of, 70
   Theory of, 15–18
Min, Pyong Gap, 259
Ministries
   Contextualized, 255–56
   Incarnational, 256–57
   Holistic, 220, 221, 257–58
Mission
   As care and counsel, 250
   As healing, 251
   Beyond the diasporas, 267–69
   Centrality of, 216
   Diaspora and, 101, 225–74
   Integral, 220
   Migration and, 2
   Paradigm, 4
   Strategies, 173
   Subject of, 177
   Through the diasporas 264–66
   To the diasporas, 258–63
   To Europe and North America, 30
   Transforming Mission 4, 170
Missional church, 166–69, 220–250
Missional theology, 138, 166–69
Mission dei, 4, 9–10, 166–71
   Church and, 169–71
   Concept of, 53
   Delegated to the church, 248
   Diaspora as, 247
   'missional church' and, 166–67, 169, 180–84
   redemptive work, 54
   diaspora mission church and, 247–48
Missiology
   Contemporary issues and, 153
   Current, 150–53
   Interdisciplinary and, 218–19
   Globalization and, 150–54
   Traditional, 24, 121, 151, 177
Missiological
   Missiological paradigm, 3, 205
   Missiological expectations, 4
   Missiogical issues, 4, 9, 11, 17, 150, 245
   Missiological problems, 150–72
Mobile faith, 2, 3, 57
Mohler, Albert, 161
Morris, Brian, 76
Moser, Paul K., 157
Moynihan, Patrick, 60
Mtonga, George N, 77
Multiculturalism, 42, 44, 173, 259, 275, 280, 282
Muslim
   EU and, 27–28, 164–65
   Future of the Global Muslim population, 163–65
   Number of, 30, 164–66

326 Index

Muslim *(continued)*
    USA and, 163–64
Mwihia, David, 138

N
Naish, Tim, 3, 101–2, 125
Nelson, Robert, 75
Neo-liberalism, 70–71
Neo-liberalism and Migration, 71
Neo-liberal capitalism, 70–72
Newbigin, Lessile, 10, 166–67, 190
New Calvinism, 230–232
New Catholicity, 50
New people next door, 2
New paradigm, 1, 50, 176–77
New theory, 202–10
Nichols, Aidan, 134
Nihilism, 79
Non-Western immigrants, 2, 58
    Communicate with northern, 58
    For the northern, 58
    Global partners, 58–59
    Ministries of, 58
Northern
    Christianity, 29–30
    Hemisphere, 10, 29, 179
    world, 10, 179
North American
    Church, 3
    migration, 25
    mission, 8
Nova effect, 183

O
Oberg, Karl, 64
OMF, 260–262
O'Leary, Zina, 172
O'Malley J. Steven, 24
Otto, Craig, 5, 169, 244, 249
Oxford, Ellen, 265
Oxford Centre for Mission Studies(OCMS), 173

P
Participation, 22, 138, 171, 194, 207, 214, 224
Partnership, 208, 269–71

Between diasopra and homeland, 271
Between host and hosted, 208
For the gospel, 49
In Jesus, as its center, 59
Paroikos or *parrokoi*, 7, 54, 101, 112
Patriarchs, 87
Paul and Diaspora, 108–9
Payne, J.D, 6, 25–26, 258, 265
Pentecostalized, 179
People on the move, 1, 13, 22, 24, 203
Pew Research Center, 1, 12, 14, 23, 25–28,
Phan, Peter, 6, 118, 247
Philosophy, 135, 220
Pieterse, Jan Nederveen, 18
Pilgrim, 6, 141–44, 213
Pilgrim's Progress, 144–46
Pilgrimage, 121–22, 211, 236–39, 296
Pluralism, 9, 156
    Globalization and, 156–57
    Relativism and, 157–59
    Secularism and, 159
    Strangers and, 113
Pneumatology, 127, 135
Politics of Jesus, 131
Post-colonial, 39, 42, 66, 69
Post-exile, 94
Post-reformation, 143
Post-secular, 20, 161
Praxis, 39, 201–6, 210
Priest, Robert, 199, 218
Practical theology
    Doing mission theology and, 195
    Double hermeneutical model, 196–99, 201–10
    theological investigations, 196
Prayer, 293
Promised land, 54
Psychology, 220, 286–89
Psychology of Attacks and Attackers, 69
PTSD, 67
Public theology, 157
Proselytizing, 159

R
Raitt, Thomas, M., 5, 130–31, 242

Race, 17, 64
Racist culture, 66
Reimer, David, 96, 119, 121, 211
Reformation, 133-35, 183, 206

Relativism, 12, 13, 64, 156-59, 192, 194, 203, 214, 271
   Case study on, 158
   Moral, 158
   The apex of, 157
   Pluralism and, 157-58
Religion
   Sociology and, 74-75
   Economics of, 75-76
   Culture and, 76
   Pluralism and, 156, 271
   Privatization of, 159
   Psychology and, 76-77
   Public, 20
   Resurgence of, 20
Religious
   Makeup of nations, 16
   Symbols, 37
   persecution, 15
Religious pluralism, 156-57
Repent or repentance, 227-28
Residential aliens, 33, 132-33
Revival or renewal, 209, 273-74
Robbins, Richard H, 71
Robertson, O. Palmer, 98
Robertson, Roland, 154

S
Sahoo, Ajaya Kumar, 69
Said, Abdul Aziz, 281
Salad bowl, 44
Safran, William, 36, 40, 276
Salvation, 5-6, 94
   Judgment and, 98-99
   Individual and spiritual, 171
   Missio dei, 181
   Mission and, 12, 115-16, 210
   Of the lost, 125
   Of the pilgrim, 236
   The power of God and, 217
Scattered, 3, 5, 7, 9, 51, 54, 83-123
   by God's judgment, 95-96, 98
   Church, 171

Concept of, 84
For mission, 96-97
Identity of, 117
Life, 6
people, 1
Two kinds of, scatteredness, 95-98
Scattered to Gather, 22, 50, 84, 259
Schreiter, Robert, J., 50-51
Seed, 101-2, 210, 252
   of kingdom, 210, 238, 284
   diaspora and, 101
Secularism, 9, 13, 17, 19-20, 134, 145, 160, 184
Secularization, 141, 145, 148-49
   Against secularization, 240-242,
   Church and, 241
Secularization debate, 160
Secularized church, 160, 183-84, 205, 240, 272-73
Secular
   Secular city, 160
   Secular man, 161
   Secular church, 160-61, 272-73
   Secular society, 183
Secular Age, 183
Senior, Donald, 54
Self-theologizing, 186
Sexuality, 64
Single individuals, 77
Situational analysis, 202-5
Siever, Larry J., 287
Smith-Christopher, Daniel L., 5, 121, 130
Social
   Bonds, 67
   Change, 75
   Life, 153
   networks, 249
   processes, 153-55
   theory, 197
social ethic, 158
social science, 35, 198
socio-economic, 69, 75
sociology, 69, 74-75
sojourners, 111-12
Solidarity, 18, 36, 52
Soloviev, Vladimir, 135
Sorrow, 220

Southern
  Age, 55
  Contextual theology, 58
  Hemisphere, 29, 178–79
  Migration, 56–57
Spencer, Stenphen, 51
Spykman, Gordon J., 139
Steger, Manfred, 153
Stewardship, 295
Stolorow, Robert D, 65
Stranger, 54, 99–101,
Stranger in our midst, 125
Strangers Next Door, 9, 25–27
Stress or Stressful, 67, 275–76, 279, 285
Stewardship, 295
Suffering, 6, 139, 276
  Diakonos, 147
  Trauma, 139
Symbols, 187
Syncretism, 22, 157–59, 197, 222, 233

T
Taylor, Charles, 184
Territorial or Deterritorialization, 177
Text and context, 173
Theology
  Between the global and local, 50
  Biblical, 130
  Christian, 130
  Contextual, 11
  Of people, 216
  Of the Laity, 147
  Prosperity, 9, 59
  Reformational, 139
Theologizing subject, 207–10
Theology of the laity, 147
  Calling for the reformation of the church and mission, 148
  Church and, 147
  Diakonoi, 147–48
  For mission, 147
Third World, 12, 23
Tillich, Paul, 76, 187, 242
Tira, Sadiri Joy, 1, 216, 264
Tölölyan, Khachig, 214
Tomlinson, John, 18
Tönnies, Ferdinand, 155

Torch Trinity Graduate School (TTGS), 2, 47
Tracy, David, 188
Transcendent
  Christian life, 113
  Church, 225–74
  Conversion, 11, 225–50
  Heaven through Jesus, 228
  Transformation, 206
Transnational
  Culture, 61
  studies, 35
Transnationalism, 62, 69–70
Transnational ties, 61–62, 280
Trauma, 68–69
  Collective, 65
  Emotional, 65
  Social, 213
  Suffering, 139
Triangular model, 167

U
United kingdom, 28, 89
Unreached people, 163–66, 246, 249–50
UNHCR, 15–16
UNESCO, 35
Urban Ethnicity, 61
Ury, William, 290
USA
  As new mission, 57, 161
  Christian migrations, 22–23
  Diaspora and, 25–27
  Faith on the Move in, 177
  Missiological role of, 9
  Populations in, 14
  Second chance and, 29–30

V
Van Engen, Charles, 171, 188
Van Gelder, Craig, 166–67
Vanhoozer, Kevin J., 222
Veith, Jene, 145
Vicedom, Georg F., 170
Violence, 68–69, 285–86
Violent behavior, 68–69
Volf, Miroslav, 19, 280, 282–83
Vos, Geerhardus, 98

W
Walls, Andrew, 2, 11, 55–56
Wan, Enoch, 3, 10, 84, 171, 176, 204
Weber, Max, 74, 296
Wenham, Gordon, 85
West
   As a new missionary frontier, 57
   East and, 134
Western
   hemisphere, 178–79
   non-western and, 56
   signification, 39
   world, 56
Willimon, William, 131–32
World Christianity, 271
World economy, 21`
World evangelization, 2, 9, 11, 24, 29, 248
World mission, 25–30

World refugees, 15–16, 265
World Refugee Day, 268
World religions, 241
World system, 150, 154
Worldviews, 4, 135
Woolnough, Brain, 175
Wright, Chris, 258
Wulff, David H., 77

Y
Yamamori, Testunao, 1, 50
Yangbanization, 69
Ybarrola Steven, 33
Yoder, John Howard, 5, 131
Yurdakul, Gokçe, 282

Z
Zerfass, Rolf, 199–206

www.ingramcontent.com/pod-product-compliance
Lightning Source LLC
Chambersburg PA
CBHW050616300426
44112CB00012B/1531